Julia Eckel, Bernd Leiendecker, Daniela Olek, Christine Piepiorka (eds.)
(Dis)Orienting Media and Narrative Mazes

Cultural and Media Studies

Julia Eckel, Bernd Leiendecker,
Daniela Olek, Christine Piepiorka (eds.)
(Dis)Orienting Media and Narrative Mazes

[transcript]

Published with kind support of the Ruhr-University Research School.

Bibliographic information published by the Deutsche Nationalbibliothek
The Deutsche Nationalbibliothek lists this publication in the Deutsche Nationalbibliografie; detailed bibliographic data are available in the Internet at http://dnb.d-nb.de

© 2013 transcript Verlag, Bielefeld

All rights reserved. No part of this book may be reprinted or reproduced or utilised in any form or by any electronic, mechanical, or other means, now known or hereafter invented, including photocopying and recording, or in any information storage or retrieval system, without permission in writing from the publisher.

Cover layout: Kordula Röckenhaus, Bielefeld
Cover illustration: Julia Eckel
Proofread by Julia Eckel, Bernd Leiendecker, Daniela Olek,
    Christine Piepiorka
Typeset by Julia Eckel
Printed and bound in Great Britain by Marston Book Services Ltd, Oxfordshire
ISBN 978-3-8376-2338-3

Table of Contents

Acknowledgements | 9

Introduction

(Dis)Orienting Media and Narrative Mazes
Julia Eckel/Bernd Leiendecker | 11

(DIS)ORIENTING MEDIA

Spatiality

The Medium is the Method
Locative Media for Digital Archives
Nanna Verhoeff | 21

The Booth as an "Other Space"
Medial Positionings
Rolf F. Nohr | 35

(Dis)Orienting Databases

Lost in Digitalisation?
Profiles as Means of Orientation
in Computer-based Media Cultures
Julius Othmer/Andreas Weich | 55

(Dis)Orienting Memory
Shoah Testimonies in the Virtual Archive
Alina Bothe | 73

Productive Aberrations

Go Play Outside!
Game Glitches
Martin Schlesinger | 93

Captivating Screens
On 'Manipulation Aesthetics' as Style and Topos
Benjamin Eugster | 111

Negotiating Boundaries

TV for the Post-TV Generation?
How Transmedia Television Series Yearn for
Another Type of Audience
Daniela Olek | 129

Re-orienting Romantic Comedy
Genre Negotiations in Richard Linklater's BEFORE SUNRISE
Katja Hettich | 145

NARRATIVE MAZES

Televisual (Dis)Orientation

Serial Orientations
Paratexts and Contemporary Complex Television
Jason Mittell | 165

You're Supposed to Be Confused!
(Dis)Orienting Narrative Mazes
in Televisual Complex Narrations
Christine Piepiorka | 183

Filmic Incoherences

Amazing Maze
On the Concept of Diegese, Possible Worlds,
and the Aesthetics of Illness
Nele Uhl | 205

Ants, Games, Brains
The Complexity of Reality in Darren Aronofsky's π
Kathrin Rothemund | 221

Narrative Re-orientation

Navigation in Complex Films
Real-life Embodied Experiences
Underlying Narrative Categorisation
Miklós Kiss | 237

Leaving the Narrative Maze
The Plot Twist as a Device of Re-orientation
Bernd Leiendecker | 257

Temporality

Twisted Times
Non-linearity and Temporal Disorientation
in Contemporary Cinema
Julia Eckel | 275

When the Past Lies Ahead and the Future Lags Behind
Backward Narration in Film, Television, and Literature
Matthias Brütsch | 293

APPENDIX

About the Authors | 314

Acknowledgements

While the publication of a book appears to be a straight road with a clear destination, there are many obstacles along the way that might have left us disoriented without the help of a lot of great people.

First of all we want to thank the Ruhr-University Research School, whose support enabled us to publish this book, and Ursula Justus in particular, who was there to assist us at any time. Then we would like to thank all our contributors, who wrote these inspiring papers and took part in every step of this publishing process. And, of course, we would like to thank the people at transcript, who agreed to work with us on the project and made our very tight schedule work.

Because of its origin—the idea for this book was developed in the context of a corresponding conference which took place at the Ruhr-University Bochum from November 10th to 11th 2011—we would like to express our gratitude to our sponsors for this event once more: the Ruhr-University Research School, the Rectorate of the Ruhr-University Bochum, the Faculty of Philology, the 'Gesellschaft der Freunde der RUB e.V.' and especially the Bochum Media Studies Department. We thank all department members for their support during every step of our project—in particular Eva Warth and Vinzenz Hediger for having answered all our many questions, for having advised and helped us since we approached them with our idea. Furthermore, we would like to thank Eva Warth for her kind and heartfelt opening speech at the conference.

Moreover, we thank all the conference speakers who regrettably could not be part of this book but enriched this past event; and we are indebted to our hard-working volunteers, whose contributions to the success of our conference have been invaluable: Maximilian Busch, Eleni Kolitsi, Alexander Pötters, Mareike Theile and Peter Vignold. We also would like to express our gratitude to all the panel chairs, who created a productive atmosphere for the presentations and navigated the engaging discussions afterwards, especially Jacqueline Eikelmann, Sophie Einwächter, Elke Rentemeister, and Christian Stewen.

Bochum, October 2012
Julia Eckel, Bernd Leiendecker, Daniela Olek, Christine Piepiorka

Introduction

(Dis)Orienting Media and Narrative Mazes

Julia Eckel/Bernd Leiendecker

Due to technical media, spatial orientation in our world appears to be easier than ever before: Navigation systems, mobile screens, digital maps, and augmented reality applications tell users where they are and where to go. But at the same time it seems that media technologies—with their abundance of information, references, and functions—complicate orientation. Hypertext and databases, worldwide interconnectedness, and diversity of programmes open up virtual spaces in which orientation is only possible with the help of media themselves (e.g. search engines, web profiles, electronic programme guides, etc.). Even many recent narrations provided within these media networks feature disorienting structures by transgressing norms of storytelling and borders of (inter)-mediality, thereby raising the question of how far media and (dis)orientation can be considered mutually dependent.

But how can these contemporary, medial challenges to our senses of (dis)orientation be assessed? How exactly do media technologies orient and disorient us? And can the labyrinths of digital mediascapes be put in relation to the narrative mazes of contemporary film and television productions? These are the questions this book will focus on.

According to its title, the volume is divided into two major parts, which are entitled *(Dis)Orienting Media* and *Narrative Mazes* and which focus, on the one hand, on (dis)orientation caused by media technologies and structures and, on the other hand, on (dis)orientation occurring within media narrations—with the awareness, of course, that one focus hardly ever excludes the other completely. Enclosed in these major chapters are additional smaller ones consisting of two articles each. These are dealing with one facet of the main topic and are dedicated to a specific medium or more general questions concerning any type of media. Thus, the articles are put in smaller dialogues, which deal with specific questions and objects, but nevertheless shed a light on the big question of (dis)orientation in and across media. *(Dis)Orienting Media* and *Narrative Mazes* therefore must be considered as two faces of the same coin.

(Dis)Orienting Media...

The ability to orient oneself is, of course, neither a new nor a particularly contemporary challenge. Quite the contrary, finding one's way in the environment (e.g. back to one's cave, village, city, etc.) has always been a crucial skill. Hence, it is worth pointing out that the term 'orientation' was established only during the 18th to 19th century (see e.g. Bogen 2010, 268f.; Oxford Dictionaries 2012): Based on the Latin term for East ('oriens') and the French verb 'orienter', it signified the practice of aligning something—in most cases a map—towards the East.

Particularly interesting about this fact in the context of this book is that 'orientation' as a word and a phenomenon thus seems to be fundamentally connected to media: The map as a visual medium is the origin of 'orientation', thereby raising the question of how the medium primarily affects and encourages the search for a definite position in space. Because even when an individual may find her[1] way through the world only by looking at the sun or the stars or the moss on the trunk of a tree, it is only the map (or another medium) that may—in its abstraction—illustrate what it means to orientate oneself. Only the medium allows for reducing the 'big picture' to a (shortened and conceptional) smaller one, thereby offering the view on a minimised space that is comprehensible and structured. By giving an overview the medium makes it possible to plan, to 'map out', a way beyond the own field of view. The map as a medium thus generates an intersubjective knowledge space that is characterised by a reduction of details and that at the same time enables its user to comprehend space or at least parts of it as a whole (may it be a city, a continent, the world, or the universe). An increase in individual mobility is the desired effect.

But do these features only apply to media that visualise/generate knowledge about space? To pursue the aforementioned assumptions a little further, it could be said that the medium as such may be defined by its ability to gather information, to reduce its complexity and to transmit it to its user. As Niklas Luhmann points out:

"Whatever we know about our society, or indeed about the world in which we live, we know through the mass media. This is true not only of our knowledge of society and history but also of our knowledge of nature. What we know about the stratosphere is the same as what Plato knows about Atlantis: we've heard tell of it." (Luhmann 2000, 1)

Therefore, the correlation of media and orientation seems to be a universal one: By reducing the complexity of the world, by generating and transferring know-

---

[1] | Male or female pronouns used in this book shall always include all sexes and genders, unless it is explicitly indicated otherwise.

ledge about what we call 'reality', media become a main vehicle of orientation. They expand not only the (spatial) viewing range, but the range of knowledge about where, when, what, and who we are.

However, the facilitated and enhanced movement through these (mediatised knowledge) spaces also carries the risk of getting lost—not only by using an incorrect map or by reading it the wrong way, but also by the sheer abundance and uncertainty of possible paths. To continue with Luhmann:

"On the other hand, we know so much about the mass media that we are not able to trust these sources. Our way of dealing with this is to suspect that there is manipulation at work, and yet no consequences of any import ensue because knowledge acquired from the mass media merges together as if of its own accord into a self-reinforcing structure. Even if all knowledge were to carry a warning that it was open to doubt, it would still have to be used as a foundation, as a starting point." (ibid.)

Thus, the reduction of complexity does not only lead to a better overview and to facilitated comprehension, but also to a multiplication of perspectives and 'truths', to decontextualisations and conversions. The increased mobility thereby causes a heightened risk of getting lost.

Orientation as well as disorientation therefore seem to be immanent in all processes of a (mediatised or general) appropriation of the world—because they allow the individual to easily overview and know more, but thus leave her confronted with more options of where to go or what to see or do next. This holds true not only for the original understanding of (dis)orientation, but even more for its current use as a synonym for all kinds of (mis)alignment or (de)localisation in time and space as well as factual or mental states of (un)certainty or confusion.

To condense and systematise these thoughts and observations, one could conceive two interdependent realms in which orientation and disorientation (as forms of directed or strayed action) may occur. The first one comprehends orientation in the *subjective realm of experience*—which means an individual, subject-centred orientation that enables oneself to navigate the actual world (with or without a map): for example, finding one's way from the kitchen to the bathroom or from the office to the bakery around the corner, or knowing left from right and up from down. These are mental processes that enable everyday orientation concerning space and time as well as persons, causalities, and actions.

Second, a *virtual realm of mediatised knowledge and content* is conceivable which complements and augments the real world's space-time. This realm with its abundance of information produces and establishes structures of orientation and disorientation by generating abstract and simplifying knowledge systems, which organise or disorganise real-world-related or fictional contents. These mediatised structures of (dis)orientation therefore may be described more systematically and intersubjectively, allowing for more general thoughts about the phenomenon itself.

As mentioned before, these two realms are not separable and have to be conceived as constantly interdependent—on the one hand, due to the media space of knowledge shaping and transforming the subjective realm of experience; on the other hand, due to subjective mechanisms of real-world orientation being used for exploring media.

Especially the developments in the field of digital and mobile media during the last years make this interdependency of realms interesting for a current closer examination, because like the (mainly religiously relevant) East has been replaced by the (mainly physically relevant) North Pole as a central point of alignment for maps and the world, nowadays new structures of alignment and (dis)orientation seem to arise: Navigation systems, for example, do not align the map towards a compass point anymore, but centre the individual and its destination as a new and variable pole; augmented reality applications hybridise 'real' space into a virtual space in 'real'-time; and media narrations embed subjective experiences of disorientation in their contents and forms.

It is, therefore, the interdependency and intersection of realms that this book focuses on. While the lastly named aspect (the implementation of mechanisms of (dis)orientation in audiovisual narrations) is discussed in the second part, the first part analyses structural (dis)orientations which result from the steady and current transformation of the realm of mediatised knowledge and its impact on subjective realms of experience.

In the initial section of the first part, this analysis is conducted by Nanna Verhoeff and Rolf F. Nohr, who both investigate the transformation and (re)structuring of *Spatiality* through media. While Nanna Verhoeff focuses on mobile screens and their visual intersections with 'real' space, Rolf F. Nohr examines heterotopian spatial extensions of media, which, as he shows with the example of the photo booth, generate deviant spatial structures and seem to lead us to what Foucault describes as "other spaces".

The second section is centred on the generation and structuring of knowledge through *(Dis)Orienting Databases*. Julius Othmer and Andreas Weich use web-profiles (on dating and shopping websites) as evidence for the (dis)orienting effects of databases. While their objects of study are, hence, utilised for a future-oriented search for the best product or the ideal partner, the database focused in Alina Bothe's article deals with preserving the past: From a historian's perspective, she analyses the *Visual History Archive* of the *Survivors of the Shoah Visual History Foundation* by describing its orienting and disorienting effects on the re-creation of history.

In the next section, the heading *Productive Aberrations* unites two articles that deal with transgressive practices in digital media environments. Martin

Schlesinger focuses on Glitch art, which uncovers dysfunctionalities of digital interfaces and programming structures and thus consciously and purposefully causes disorienting effects. Such disturbing qualities of media images and sounds are also the main focus of Benjamin Eugster's article, which assesses disturbed and disturbing images of contemporary advertising campaigns and mashup videos through the concept of 'Manipulation Aesthetics'.

Negotiating Boundaries is the topic of the concluding section of *(Dis)Orienting Media*. The contributions of Daniela Olek and Katja Hettich focus on the exploration and variable definition of orienting boundaries within media systems. While Olek describes the prevalent (dis)orientation in the face of serial universes that expand beyond the boundaries of the medium of television, Hettich concentrates on the ambivalent relationship between the extra-filmic orientation of genre boundaries and their disorienting transgression in Richard Linklater's BEFORE SUNRISE.

With this last exploration of the (dis)orienting genre system in film we transgress the border to the second section of this book, which addresses media that are dealing with (dis)orientation as a topic and/or feature it as a narrative structural mechanism.

...AND NARRATIVE MAZES

In parallel to the phenomena described in the first part of the book, media themselves tend to reflect their disorienting properties self-referentially by using them as an effect of entertainment. Many media scholars have noticed a recent increase in audiovisual narrations that purposefully confuse their audiences in a way that makes disorientation a main feature of the narration. Certainly, some kinds of disorienting narrations can be observed throughout the history of audiovisual narration. However, they seem to have migrated from an art house niche to the mainstream and new forms seem to have emerged, replacing or complementing the old ones.

Depending on the particular kind of disorientation and the focus of the analysis, numerous terms have been used to describe such narrations: "mindfuck" (e.g. Eig 2003), "mind-bender" (e.g. Johnson 2005), "narrative complexity" (e.g. Mittell 2006), "modular narratives" (Cameron 2008), "puzzle films" (e.g. Buckland 2009), and "mind-game films" (e.g. Elsaesser 2009) are more general categories, while terms like "forking-path narratives" (e.g. Bordwell 2002), "twist movies" (e.g. Lavik 2006), "transmedia storytelling" (Jenkins 2006), "unreliable narration" (e.g. Laass 2008), or "temporal non-linearity" (e.g. Eckel 2012) focus on particular groups of disorienting narrations.

While the large amount of terms might be rather disorienting in itself, each term has its own merits and flaws, so that we did not want to limit the contributors to just one term and thus one approach. Consequently, we chose the umbrella term of 'narrative mazes' without intending to add another fully defined term to the list. Instead, narrative mazes is best understood as a metaphor that encompasses all the aforementioned terms and highlights their disorienting potential. In the end, it all boils down to this: If the classical narration with its goal-oriented plots, clear causal connections, and its general drive to facilitate viewer comprehension can be understood as a straight corridor (Bordwell 1986, 18ff.), there are other narrations that are better described as mazes. Or, in Bordwell's words:

"In classical narration, style typically encourages the spectator to construct a coherent, consistent time and space of the fabula action. Many other narrational norms value *disorienting* the spectator (albeit for different purposes). Only classical narration favors a style which strives for utmost denotative clarity from moment to moment." (ibid., 26; emphasis added)

As indicated by the number of concepts united by the term, the nature of a narrative maze can be manifold, dependent on the kind of divergence from the classical norm. The audience may be confronted with the vast universe of a television serial and its official or unofficial extensions in other media. Another possibility is that the temporal order diverges from the classical, rather linear chronology of a narration, leading to numerous possible effects. In other variations of narrative mazes, viewers may have to discard a lot of what they thought they knew about the story of an audiovisual narration and replace it with new hypotheses. They even might come to the conclusion that it is impossible to construct a coherent story out of the plot information that has been offered. What all of these narrations have in common, however, is that they transform being disoriented into an incentive, being confused into a pleasure, and achieving re-orientation into the prevalent purpose.

The second part of this book focuses on these audiovisual narrative mazes, covering several of the most common variations. In the first section titled *Televisual (Dis)Orientation*, Jason Mittell and Christine Piepiorka both analyse the narrative structures of contemporary television serials as well as their expansion into a transmedial environment. While Mittell puts his focus on strategies of re-orientation through orienting paratexts often developed by fans in a kind of "forensic fandom", Piepiorka describes how the need for re-orientation is created in the core text of the serial in the first place.

Filmic Incoherences, the second section, unites articles by Nele Uhl and Kathrin Rothemund, who develop their ideas about (dis)orienting effects in film with a special focus on two particular examples. Uhl presents her thoughts about the concepts of *Diegese* and *possible worlds* and applies them on Jean-Claude Lauzon's LÉOLO, while Kathrin Rothemund uses the theories of Siegfried Kracauer in order to make sense of the filmic rendition of mental disorientation in Darren Aronofsky's π.

The third section, titled *Narrative Re-orientation*, features articles by Miklós Kiss and Bernd Leiendecker that are also concerned with filmic narrations. However, their main interest is in the relationship between disorientation and re-orientation. Kiss offers a reconceptualisation of the categorisation into simple and complex, puzzle and art narrations by adding the category of the *riddle plot*. Leiendecker analyses the phenomenon of plot twists in film as a standardised element of conscious re-orientation.

Mirroring the section on spatiality that opened the book, *Temporality*, the last section of this volume, is devoted to time as a dimension of orientation and disorientation. The focus of Julia Eckel's article is on an array of contemporary films that feature a-chronological plot structures and serve as a foundation to establish a categorisation of non-linear plot temporalities. One particular form of a-chronology—the backward narration—is the main subject of Matthias Brütsch's article, which describes this phenomenon by using examples from film, TV, and literature.

Attempting to cover the vast field opened up by the concepts of *(Dis)Orienting Media* and *Narrative Mazes* in one book at this point in time is, of course, an undertaking that would be certain to fail: The evolution of existing media of (dis)-orientation and the emergence of new ones have led to some noteworthy innovative forms for the time being, but they will, of course, continue to develop and change. Furthermore, it is rather unclear if the abundance of narrative mazes in the last two decades of audiovisual narration are just a fashion that will (or perhaps has already started to) fade, or if these storytelling innovations are here to stay. Thus, all this book can offer is kind of a map, focusing on some details and leaving out others, so that comprehension of these parts is possible. It can serve as a starting point for a journey into researching one of the manifold phenomena of (dis)orientation (be it in past, contemporary, or future mediascapes). Hopefully, it will leave its readers better oriented for the rest of their way.

Bibliography

Bordwell, David (1986): Classical Hollywood Cinema: Narrational Principles and Procedures. In: Rosen, Philip (ed.): *Narrative, Apparatus, Ideology: A Film Theory Reader*. New York: Columbia University Press, 17–34.

Bordwell, David (2002): Film Futures. In: *Substance*, Issue 97, Vol. 31, No. 1, 88–104.

Bogen, Steffen (2010): Orienting map. Two historical case studies. In: Design-2context (eds.): *Des-/Orientierung, Dis-/Orientation, Dés-/Orientation 2*. Baden: Lars Müller Publishers, 268–272.

Buckland, Warren (ed.) (2009): *Puzzle Films: Complex Storytelling in Contemporary Cinema*. Malden/Oxford/Chichester: Wiley-Blackwell.

Cameron, Allan (2008): *Modular Narratives in Contemporary Cinema*. Hampshire/New York: Palgrave Macmillan.

Eckel, Julia (2012): *Zeitenwende(n) des Films – Temporale Nonlinearität im zeitgenössischen Erzählkino*. Marburg: Schüren.

Eig, Jonathan (2003): A beautiful mind(fuck): Hollywood structures of identity. In: *Jumpcut: A Review of Contemporary Media*, Vol. 46. Web. Retrieved from: [www.ejumpcut.org/archive/jc46.2003/eig.mindfilms/index.html]; access: 2012/10/10.

Elsaesser, Thomas (2009): *The Mind-Game Film*. In: Buckland 2009, 13–41.

Jenkins, Henry (2006): *Convergence Culture: Where Old and New Media Collide*. New York/London: New York University Press.

Johnson, Steven (2005): *Everything Bad is Good for You*. New York: Penguin Group.

Laass, Eva (2008): *Broken Taboos, Subjective Truths: Forms and Functions of Unreliable Narration in Contemporary American Cinema*. Trier: Wissenschaftlicher Verlag Trier.

Lavik, Erlend (2006): Narrative Structure in The Sixth Sense: A New Twist in "Twist Movies"? In: *The Velvet Light Trap*, No. 58, 55–64.

Luhmann, Niklas (2000 [1996]): *The Reality of the Mass Media* (transl. by Kathleen Cross). Stanford (CA): Stanford University Press.

Mittell, Jason (2006): Narrative Complexity in Contemporary American Television. In: *The Velvet Light Trap*, No. 58, 29–40.

Web Sources

Oxford Dictionaries: *Orientation*. Web. Retrieved from: [http://oxforddictionaries.com/definition/english/orientation?q=orientation]; access: 2012/10/10.

(DIS)ORIENTING MEDIA

Spatiality

The Medium is the Method
Locative Media for Digital Archives

Nanna Verhoeff

With the canonical phrase "the medium is the message", Marshall McLuhan refers to the inherent self-reflexivity of media. Regardless of the content or message, the medium puts forward the specificity of its technology and the way that it "shapes and controls the scale and form of human association and action" (1964, 9). To take this to its extreme consequence, we can say the message and the medium that communicates it cannot be separated. Even more, regardless of what the content is, the message of media is reflexive of the way the medium presents this message.

Elsewhere, I have pointed out that self-reflexivity of media is particularly striking at moments of technological innovation and media change. Specifically, visual media technologies have been used to demonstrate the new way in which they construct space. From a historical perspective we can see how *machines of the visible*, to invoke Jean-Louis Comolli's phrase (1980), ranging from panoramic paintings, photography, stereoscopy, cinema, television, the digital screen, and more recently, the mobile screen, show related, yet also different ways in which spatial relations are created and visualised. In comparing these media technologies through the practices for which we use them, we can discern in what way mobility and principles of navigation as a mode of looking and experiencing the world, are central to our current visual culture.[1]

In the following I will argue that the mobile screen, in particular in the case of the application of augmented reality technology, demonstrates how navigation emphasises a particularly active position and agency of the viewing subject: the subject as co-creator. Navigation, I propose, is the *activity* as well as *outcome* of orientation technologies. It is both product and process—unlike more traditional forms of 'representation'. Moreover, disorientation, I would hold, is the

---

[1] | For a more extensive discussion of mobility, navigation, the screen and other interface technologies, see my book *Mobile Screens: The Visual Regime of Navigation* (2012).

ever-present other aspect of orientation. Like silence in sound, stillness in motion, and vision in touch.

This entails both *continuity* with older visual practices and a *shift* through new media technologies. A marked difference of this shift is the emphasis on the medium not as bearer of messages, but the medium as a tool. Taking the functionality of media technologies as central, I wish to take a closer look at the principle of design: What is the role of design within this visual culture of navigation, and how can we conceptualise design not as a fixed 'object', as a finished product, but as the parameters of *creative* and performative practices? From an analytical perspective, this necessitates a new understanding of our *object*. When the medium is the method, design rather than content deserves our analytical attention.

A Visual Regime of Navigation

I consider navigation as the guiding principle in how we interact with screens. Navigation is an active engagement, keeping an eye out for where to move or what to do next. It is an active mode of vision and it is, literally, creative in that in navigation, viewing and making images coincide. This is the central principle in the interaction with mobile touchscreens, enabling navigation on- as well as off-screen. We can also see this principle in the use of interactive screens in public spaces, where we walk by and where we can manipulate input on screen. These may seem new, innovative phenomena of our time. However, these practices are related to an older paradigm of mobility—a deeper cultural logic with historical roots long predating the technology of mobile and interactive screen devices.

The predominant role of visuality in today's culture is tightly bound up with the fundamental role of mobility in modern culture and society—geographical and physical by means of transportation technologies, as well as *visual* (or *virtual*) through media and communication technologies. Coming after a visual culture of *instant nostalgia*—the cinematic ambition of bringing back to life the (recent) past—and the tele-visual ambition of *liveness* by making the elsewhere present, mobile media (and augmented reality) signal a shift towards a logic of cartographic access: a logic of navigation, not as vicarious experience of mediated mobility, but an active play of (dis)orientation within a temporally layered spatial present. The temporal layers to space do not so much signify a simultaneous presence of distinct pasts, foregrounding the temporal layers of space as archive, as they point to the possibility of 'making present' by the logic of *accessibility* and *agency*. This, I contend, characterises the visual regime of navigation.[2]

---

[2] | About instant nostalgia and virtual travel in early cinema, see Verhoeff 2006.

One of the most striking aspects of our mobile screens today is the possibility for people *in transit*, while travelling, to co-create the spatial arrangement within which they operate. The coincidence of mobility and the creation of spatial representations are characteristic of the visual regime of navigation: That which is depicted on screen, such as maps, panoramic views, or layered images, emerges simultaneously with someone's interaction with the screens. This simultaneity makes movement itself a performative, creative act. Mobility transports the body, but affects (*makes*) the virtual realm of spatial representation. In other words, the navigational paradigm that we can discern in our visual culture entails a shift of focus from (fixed, 'authored') 'objects' to (dynamic and collaborative) processes.

A fascination with this principle of navigation we see in popular culture as well. For example, it resonates with the key assertion of the blockbuster movie INCEPTION (USA 2010, Christopher Nolan), in which the main characters develope the technology to infiltrate people's dreams and thereby manipulate their subconscious by planting ideas. As the lead character Cobb explains to his new recruit Ariadne "in dreams we perceive and create our world, *simultaneously*". The spatial architecture of dreams is such that one navigates while constructing the space along the way. Hence, experiencing (dream)space enables—and requires!—simultaneous creation and exploration.

In my work I have compared a variety of screen technologies synchronically as well as diachronically, as sites of virtual mobility and navigation. Screens ranging from panoramas, the cinematic screen, urban screens or media facades, to micro screens on our smartphones, tablets, or mobile navigation devices, to installations and interactive touchscreens, are the objects of comparison. In this analysis, I understand a *visual regime* as a set of conditions considered valid at a certain time, under which usages of things are taken for granted as normal and legitimate. Regimes are usually mentioned in political terms, but the term can also pertain to cultural practice. Martin Jay (1988), for example, uses the term to name certain *ways of seeing* at specific historical moments; he speaks of a "scopic regime". Linear perspective, once invented, produced a regime in this sense. Navigation, I contend, produces another. Let's now look at some core aspects of navigational participatory models for design: the *dispositif* of mobility, the principle of installation, and of layers.

DESIGN: MOBILITY, INSTALLATION, LAYERS

Visuality in today's culture is tightly connected to mobility—bodily, by means of vehicular transportation, and virtually by media technologies. The screen is the site *par excellence* for this virtual mobility. Significantly, mobility figures as a recurring trope of self-reflection throughout the history of screen media.

Travel—its speed and sensation—was a major preoccupation, for example, in early cinema around 1900, and is so again on today's digital screens. Perhaps it owes this prominent position to the fact that it offers a distinctively (post)-modern mode of experiencing the reconfigurations of time and space—one we associate with technology, progress, change, but also with ensuing forms of (dis)orientation.

The screen as site for visual representation is in its essence at once a spatial and a temporal domain. Screen-based mobility, as the experience of moving through space and time, is situated somewhere between state and event. It takes time and place. A helpful perspective on the intersection of space and time in mobility is provided by the concept of *dispositif*. While developed as a theoretical construct of the *cinematic apparatus*, this concept helps us to analyse the arrangement, or installation, within which screens operate. The term, derived from 1970s film theory (Baudry 1986), has emerged from a range of different congenial terms. Foucault (1980) defined the concept of *dispositif* as a heterogeneous ensemble of elements connected by *relations*, which has a dominant strategic function. An often-alleged key example is the Panopticon as a dispositif of surveillance. The concept *dispositif* is useful for understanding navigation, as it asks the question of relations and how these are arranged. This is particularly relevant for dynamic constellations of interactive and mobile screen technologies.

The first case study in my project dealing with the organisation of space and mobility within this arrangement was the highway panorama for which I collaborated with the Netherlands Institute for Spatial Research in a study to develop tools for the design of highway panoramas (Piek et. al. 2007). The construction, design, and preservation of highway panoramas put a set of related issues on the agenda concerning *mobility* and *perception*. In the example of the highway panorama we can consider the unique viewing position of the driver: the gaze from behind the protective glass of the windshield. I have proposed a cinematographic understanding of the panorama: The view is framed, and the screen and the windshield are similar to one another because they both provide access to the moving image. In the instance of the highway panorama, the sight as seen from behind the (moving) windshield, we are dealing with a similar situation to watching moving images: Although seated in a moving vehicle, in fact we sit immobile behind a window and we view a moving landscape.

Through this comparison, moving-images screens can be considered as *virtual* windows—a term coined by Anne Friedberg (2006)—providing a framed, visual access to moving images. This comparison is therefore bi-directional. The concern with the design of highway panoramas is only a recent example of a longer history of panoramic desires in our culture. This entails a desire for perceptual, not physical, immersion. It is built on the visual arrangement or *dispositif* of spectator, visual field (or view), and medium that organises this gaze.

Panoramic desire is about the desire to expand embodied vision, with a trade-off of needing a mode of transportation or medium to facilitate this, or in the case of circular panorama's, the always-partial vision of having to turn around in order to see. Panoramic desire brings forward a paradox: a paradox between control and freedom, immersion and wonderment, between transparent immediacy and hypermediacy—to put it in Bolter and Grusin's terms (1999).

The specificity of navigation is situated in the intersection of mobility, agency, and perception, and the experience thereof. These key aspects constitute a *dispositif* of *mobility*: a dynamic arrangement of the viewing subject within a spatial field of perception, including the vectorialisation of 'going somewhere', and the media and/or transportation technology that sets this arrangement in motion. This cinematographic, moving-image perspective on the design of public space brings up questions related to the relationship between design and perception, but also concerning aesthetic and cultural norms. A media-based approach to the contemporary concern for spatial design is culturally significant. And also theoretically, I contend. Media have become pre-eminently relevant benchmarks for mobility and visuality (for 'moving images'). A media-theoretical reflection as part of the way we think about spatial design can also help us understand how media work.

In relation to the design of highway as a space for visual, panoramic experience, Norman Klein's description of what he calls "scripted spaces" seems appropriate. In his words, scripted spaces are spaces that are:

> "[...] a walk-through or click-through environment (a mall, a church, a casino, a theme park, a computer game). They are designed to *emphasize* the viewer's journey – the space between – rather than the gimmicks on the wall. The audience walks *into* the story. What's more, this walk should respond to each viewer's whims, even though each step along the way is prescribed [...]. It is gentle repression posing as free will." (2004, 11; original emphasis)

This brief but evocative description puts forward a goal of spatial design: a scripting of experience, which, as Klein rightly remarks, is in part a control of (supposedly) individual experience: a paradoxical scripting of freedom. Moreover, as he continues, with the notion of scripted spaces, he means "primarily a mode of perception, a way of seeing" (ibid.).

I find the equation between a scripted space, or to extend this, space as a machine of vision, and (resulting) vision itself slightly problematic. It conflates control and experience, as if experience could be fully controlled. Instead, within navigation, the subject has, perhaps paradoxically, a limited control of perception within the parameters of the route. But I do find the close connection between the (pre)structuring of space and the resulting experience of space helpful in understanding how experiences can be, at least partially, 'tainted' by design.

To remain in visual terms, this emphasis on the inherent relationship between design and perception makes it possible to understand culture at work beyond individual experience alone. Because of the complex relationship with perception and the fact that such design is not neutral, it is important to consider the underlying motivations and ambitions of design.

Moreover, as I pointed out, panoramic desire itself brings forward a cultural paradox: a paradox between freedom and control and between spectacle and immersion; or, in other words, between agency and design. This raises the question in what way 'freedom' can be included within design, and how navigation can work as a design principle. When we consider the spatial arrangements in terms of freedom and restrictions that are designed, arranged, scripted, we can consider the spatial *dispositif* as a form of *installation*: the act of putting in place and designing experience. Here we see the intersection of cinema, theatre, and architecture or spatial design at work.

When we zoom in and take a closer look at interactive, augmented reality applications for mobile screens we can see how a principle of layers is at work in the spatial logic put forward by the apparatus. Augmented reality browsing makes use of a combination of built-in features of mobile devices: GPS sensor to locate the position, camera feed to display the surrounding environment, and an internet connectivity to import geotagged content from an online database. Web-based mobile websites as well as native apps for these devices have opened up a wide range of interactive navigation, touring, and mapping practices.

Again, the basic principle of this screen-based navigation is that we see how we move—while how we move enables this vision. As such, in navigation both space and time unfold in practice. It is a process of simultaneous image capture and experience. It establishes a mutually constitutive relationship between seeing and moving—between experience and activity—the fundamental principle in real-time, digital navigation. Producing images while viewing them, the user-navigator engages physically with the screen in a temporally dynamic and spatially layered process.

ARCHIVAL ACCESS

Recently cultural archives and museums are exploring the possibilities of locative media and mobile platforms and offer content from their collections in geo-tours or augmented reality applications. The Museum of London launched the *Museum of London: StreetMuseum app* for iPhone. One Dutch case is *Erfgoed in Beeld* [imaging heritage], a project that has developed an iPhone app for accessing information about war monuments in the Netherlands. The Netherlands Institute for Architecture has also launched *UAR*, the Urban Augmented Reality application, for location-based information about, and visualisation of, architectural design. The Stedelijk Museum in Amsterdam has invested in *ARtours*, a project which does not only offer access to their collection outside of their building, but also aims to develop contributions to their collection in the form of digital art for augmented reality platforms.

Besides these institutional archives and museums that experiment with innovative interfaces to their collections, we can also think of more personal (bottom-up) or collaborative online collections, with travel itineraries, photos and personal annotations, and applications to share this material. Digital archives—whether collective or institutional—need interfaces for access as well as participation. Locative media *projects*, unlike (museum) *exhibitions* or (film) *programmes* as more traditional models for access and exhibition, are mainly individually organised and designed for interaction and participation. The new cultural format of locative, interactive projects integrates aspects of programming such as selecting, shaping and arranging content (the digital collection) for presentation and design. At the same time, the incipient status and the great diversity, as well as rapid changes in technology, also make these new interfaces to our digital collections relatively unstable. This raises questions about not so much the specificity of the digital artefact, but rather of the media-project as 'a tool to think with' as our new object of analysis. For this, it is important to understand the underlying logic, the specificity of their status as *project* rather than *object*, and their principles of design.

Amidst the fast changing gadgets, platforms, and applications for mobility and navigation, we can discern a new archival logic, which is location-based and interactive—a logic of layers. In these projects, interfaces are made mobile, so that collections of objects that are de-contextualised within these collections become re-attached to places and are re-contextualised. We can understand this logic in terms of indexicality. This semiotic concept as defined by Charles Sanders Peirce refers to the intersection of time, place, and subject in their relative *relationality*. This, I think, offers a theoretical grasp on the structural aspects of navigation, particularly helpful for understanding the layering of space and time on our mobile screens.

In a special issue on indexicality and the moving image, film theorist Mary Ann Doane comes up with the obvious, yet strangely overlooked distinction between the index that comes to us from the *past*—a trace of things long gone (the 'footprint in the sand'); and the index in the *present*—the pointing of a finger. Doane brings together the two very different characteristics of the index that we can discern in Peirce's writing: the temporality and directionality of the index. In his own words:

"[T]he sign signifies its object solely by virtue of being really connected with it. Of this nature are all natural signs and physical symptoms. I call such a sign an *index*, a pointing finger being the type of the class. The index asserts nothing; it only says

'There!' It takes hold of our eyes, as it were, and forcibly directs them to a particular object, and there it stops. Demonstrative and relative pronouns are nearly pure indices, because they denote things without describing them [...]." (Peirce 1885, 181; original emphasis)

In linguistic terms the index in the present is called *deixis*. Deixis refers to the here-and-now, the 'situation' which positions a subject, or deictic centre. In visual terms we may call this point-of-view. What I call 'there', 'then' and 'now' is relative to my position in time and space. I propose to add to these two temporalities of past and present a third kind that is brought about by navigation. With its key features of possibility and future-orientation, we can speak of a *destination index*.[3]

The mobile and hybrid interface of the mobile screen of smartphones and tablets allows for a connection between these layers: the here-and-now in the present, its traces in the past, and the future toward which the subject moves—a connection, which evolves in navigation. As such, navigation involves a layered temporality, establishing the subject as the mobile, deictic centre. The interface serves to make this spatio-temporal logic operable.

This interfacing takes place within a mobile *dispositif*, or screening situation that encompasses both the perceptual positioning of the (mobile) user, and the physical (interactive) interfacing with the screen. This screening arrangement-in-motion, taking place within public space and making connections with this space, establishes a mobile sphere: a private/public space that is marked by (individual) mobility and (networked) connectivity, and which is constructed within the (mobile) arrangement of user, location, and device. Given the use of the mobile screen for navigation both with and on the (touch) screen, the mobility of the device makes it both a haptic and a visceral interface: The entire body of the user is incorporated in mobility and space-making. This puts the user at the centre of a deictic network.

As such, the mobile screen is in essence a cartographic interface for the simultaneous navigation of both on-screen and off-screen space. In a marked difference to the cinematic and televisual screen, the mobile screen enables a navigation of both the apparatus itself, and the physical space surrounding its user, thereby layering the dispositif. It encapsulates the user and the apparatus within a mobile *dispositif* of navigation. Hence, it positions the user within a mobile sphere implying an *ambulant locatedness* and, thereby, flexible site-specificity. The layered constellation of the interface is the condition of possibility for

---

3 | For a more extensive discussion of Peirce and indexicality, see my contribution in *Studying Mobile Media: Cultural Technologies, Mobile Communication, and the iPhone* (Hjorth/Burgess/Richardson 2012).

navigation and the access of the archive of urban space. It is here that navigation becomes the method.

Interface

Different from earlier screen-based interfaces, the mobile interface itself is layered. While intricately connected and hard to separate and isolate, conceptually there are three (non-hierarchical) levels, all essential for navigation:

First, navigation comprises the *internal interfacing* of applications: the back-end operating system and software, and consequently, the processing of data. The Google-maps API, for example, is suitable for mapping applications, because it provides tools for web-application hybrids, or mashups. These allow the integration of data from different sources within, in this case, the mapping environment of Google Maps.

The second layer of the interface concerns the spatial *positioning* and *connectivity* of the apparatus in relation to physical as well as data space: the interface of the internal instruments of the smartphone that connect it to external space. This level of the interface communicates between the device and its surrounding 'reality'. It includes what is called an *inertial* navigation system to calculate position and orientation, which is necessary, for example, for augmented reality applications as interface for location-based data, or ambient intelligence. Moreover, internet connectivity also positions the device via wireless connection. The second layer of the interface, then, concerns connecting and positioning the interface whether based on inertial, absolute, camera-based, or wireless technologies.

This positioning is communicated to the user who may see the on-screen image tilt, or who may find a representation of her position and movement signified by an 'arrow' in the on-screen maps, and then may read this orientation accordingly and act or move. This is all taking place on a third level of the interface of *user interaction*, enabling the communication between the user and the internal operation of the device (first level) as it is connected to the space surrounding it (second level). Significant for touchscreens is the fact that at the level of user interaction they are an instrument for both input and for output. This is the level of access to, manipulation of, and experience of data; the action seems to literally take place on the screen—yet, paradoxically the screen seems also more transparent, with its instantaneous manipulability and connectivity with space and by touch.

The way that these levels work together is the condition of possibility for navigation. As a tool set for navigation, the interface enables the specific negotiation between orientation and disorientation that is characteristic of a dialogic engagement by the subject with technology and space, simultaneously. The using of the interface as such is, in essence, a method: the act of creating, by doing, by reading. The intimacy between user, apparatus, and the output or message of the machine is inherent in interactive interfaces. In the case of mobile cartographic interfaces, the reading of space as procedural and creative act is the essence of this output.

Cartographic Index

The interplay of deictic directionality and the meaning of the trace are very clear in the case of digital navigation and can be clarified through the principle of *geotagging*—perhaps the key principle of the cartographic turn in digital interfaces for navigation and of what we can call the *cartographic-archival complex* of locative media. The attachment of information to objects and locations, and vice versa, based on global positioning (GPS) makes a whole range of uses possible: from adding locations to photographs, to providing on-site information and adding hyperlinks to maps. Geo-coordinates make it possible to annotate location-specific information to objects, or to connect archives with a vast information database to particular locations.

On mobile screens, tags can activate different spatial and temporal layers. Dots on the screen/map unfold as spatio-temporal hyperlinks. The city becomes a navigable and clickable screenspace, a terrain of pop-ups that are triggered by real-life avatars in the physical world whose movements are traced on-screen by GPS. Two-dimensional maps are a flat and still representation of space within a fixed frame, based on a fixed scale, with an abstract perspective. The digital map is dynamic, layered, expandable, mutable, and with flexible points of view. Geotags bring together all levels of the hybrid interface of smartphones. By combining and locating data, geotags are visible mainly through their effects in screen navigation, activating content by physical movement in the world.

Geotagging re-activates the indexical principle of the trace—once lost in the transition from analogue to digital photography—in the shift to 'destination'. Geotagging photographs, for example, entails adding GPS coordinates—including a time-stamp—of the position the picture was taken from to a data file in which the digital image is stored. By using this data for navigation—as 'destination'—it allows for a mnemonic mobility: the tracing of digital footprints into the future.

In their capacity to create locative and semiotic connections, tagging entails a potential for participatory engagement. People can make their own personal archives, use them for exchange, or participate in creating collective archives. Tagged "mobile mementos" (de Vries 2009) make collective image gathering possible, based on the collection, connection, or contribution of information derived from large, social databases. This is where the trace (of the past) joins the *deixis* (in the present), but also pointing to a future.

Navigation as orientation entails constantly registering presence (where am I?). But rather than focusing on the trace of the past, navigation is geared towards deciding where to go next. For this, the navigator decodes the (imaginary) phrase "you are here" (signified by an arrow or another symbol) on the screen/map, into "I am here". The map is only usable once the subject knows where the I exactly is positioned. The act of establishing a deictic centre lies at the heart of navigation. I contend that performativity—in this context, but perhaps more generally speaking as well—requires an activation of *deixis*: positioning a deictic centre within a visual, spatial field.

Interactive navigation with the smartphone visualises this situation in two ways. The screen visualises the user's position as focaliser of the map. It also reflects back what the user does, what itinerary the user creates and simultaneously travels. In short, what space she makes. Hence, in navigation destination (where will I go?) becomes the new centre of indexicality. Space is constructed in this indexical reading of space where these three temporalities merge.

Augmented reality applications for smartphones exemplify the way in which the hybrid, layered interface of the device can be used to visualise and access geo-specific content. AR browsers such as *Layar, Wikitude, Junaio*, or *Acrossair* are rapidly expanding the possibilities of (consumer) augmented reality. AR browsing entails a new way of engaging with screenspace by effacing the map representation and using direct camera feed with a superimposed layer of data. These browsers make it possible to browse for data directly within 'reality' as it is represented on the screen. The camera on the device registers (rather than 'captures', or 'imprints' as a trace) physical objects on location, and transmits these images in real time on the screen, where the image is combined with different layers of data in image or text. Information is, thus, superimposed on a real-time image on screen.

To go back to the earlier mentioned *UAR* (Urban Augmented Reality) app of the Netherlands Architecture Institute (NAi): It makes use of the *Layar*-infrastructure for an augmented reality browser, which is connected to their digitised archive. It shows 3D visualisations of buildings on location that were either once there in the past, information about current buildings, visualisations of plans for the near future, or designs were made but were never actually built at all. In the hybrid screenspace that this tour constructs by layering information on the live camera feed, the present, past, future and even the past future, indeed, can coincide.

I have pointed out how digital navigation can be understood as a cultural trope which makes our sense of presence centrally deictic, determining one's current position, with a forward-slanted orientation towards possible destinations. This trope builds on the logic of layers, breaking with the regime of fixed

Figure 1: AR view of the future: the IDMC building in The Hague, the Netherlands.

framing in representation. Navigation provides a temporal texture to space—a fourth dimension, if you will. It has the potential to transpose the archive to a live stream of deictic experience—an experience of an intersection of past, present, and future.

Studying Design

The speed of technological innovation in mobile media devices in the past years presents a dilemma for cultural institutions in terms of the choices to be made regarding platforms and interaction design that provide sustainable access to digital archives. For designers this requires negotiating between innovative and sustainable ambitions, scalability and cross-platform transferability, usability and complexity. Moreover, creative ambitions of designers, technological expertise, and archival ambitions are not always compatible. This entails a translation from ideals concerning access and participation, to visual imagination, to programming language, and a balance of institutional, creative, and technological forces in the design process.

At the moment of writing it seems to be timely to develop a cultural-analytical and critical approach to the study of design of locative media projects—of design both as structure and as (creative) process. A cultural shift from valuing fixed and isolated objects towards developing design for engagement with, and re-contextualising of these objects though the use of interactive media technologies, predicates the need for the development of concepts for analysing media projects as a new type of dynamic cultural object. The medium as a tool to think *with* is something to also think *about*.

A focus on design as collaborative process, for example, would analyse how different perspectives and motivations of different 'players' (i.e. archivists and designers—and, indeed, users) work together. Moreover, the analysis of media projects has to take into account the way these are built on cross-media concepts, by for example discerning focus areas of storytelling or meaning-making, usability, and participatory co-creation, that are embedded in historical traditions. A media-archeological approach to locative media as new cultural form for archival practices can inform our perspective on the entanglements of culture and technology, of historical tropes and innovation, and of creativity and usability.

Based on a cultural logic of navigation, characterised by a cartographic-archival complex, locative media such as augmented reality for mobile screens, perhaps, engage publics in a different way—yet, for this logic new skills are required. The medium is, in that sense, not self-reflexive only, since it also becomes a tool for the serious play of doing and making. The medium is not just a tool for making visible—for visualisation of data—but it is perhaps more about the desire to make visible. This is where the medium becomes the method.

Any cultural form or visual regime proposes, selects, and 'naturalises' that which is utterly historical and cultural. A critical question then is—or in fact, remains: Within the visual regime of navigation, what is made invisible? What remains inaccessible? Navigation as a design principle for a more active and creative engagement of the subject, paradoxically, makes clear (is transparent—to use a visual metaphor), perhaps more than ever before, that any visual form is as much about invisibility, inasmuch as orientation is about disorientation.

Bibliography

Bolter, Jay David/Grusin, Richard (1999): *Remediation: Understanding New Media*. Cambridge: MIT Press.

Baudry, Jean-Louis (1986): Ideological Effects of the Basic Cinematographic Apparatus and The Apparatus: Metapsychological Approaches to the Impression of Reality in the Cinema. In: Rosen, Philip (ed.): *Narrative, Apparatus, Ideology*. New York: Columbia University Press, 286–318.

Comolli, Jean Louis (1980): Machines of the Visible. In: De Lauretis, Teresa/Health, Steven (eds.): *The Cinematic Apparatus*. New York: St. Martin Press, 121–142.

Doane, Mary Ann (2007): Indexicality: Trace and Sign: Introduction. In: *Differences*, Vol. 18, No. 1, 1–6.

Foucault, Michel (1980): *Power/Knowledge. Selected Interviews and Other Writings 1972–1977* (ed. by Colin Gordon). New York: Pantheon Books.
Friedberg, Anne (2006): *The Virtual Window: From Alberti to Microsoft*. Cambridge: MIT Press.
Jay, Martin (1988): Scopic Regimes of Modernity. In: Foster, Hal (ed.): *Vision and Visuality*. Seattle: Bay Press, 3–23.
Klein, Norman (2004): *The Vatican to Vegas: A History of Special Effects*. New York: The New Press.
McLuhan, Marshall (1964): *Understanding Media. The Extension of Men*. London/New York: Routledge.
Peirce, Charles Sanders (1993 [1885]): On The Algebra of Logic: A Contribution to the Philosophy of Notation. In: *The American Journal of Mathematics* 7, 1885: 180–202. Reprinted in: *The Writings of Charles S. Peirce. Vol. 5.* Compiled by the Editors of the Peirce Edition Project. Bloomington: Indiana University Press, 1993: 162–190.
Piek, Maarten et al. (2007): *Snelwegpanorama's in Nederland*. Rotterdam: NAi Publishers.
Verhoeff, Nanna (2012a): *Mobile Screens: The Visual Regime of Navigation. (MediaMatters)*. Amsterdam: Amsterdam University Press.
Verhoeff, Nanna (2012b): A Logic of Layers: Indexicality of iPhone Navigation in Augmented Reality. In: Hjorth, Larissa/Burgess, Jean/Richardson, Ingrid (eds.): *Studying Mobile Media: Cultural Technologies, Mobile Communication, and the iPhone*. London/New York: Routledge, 118-132.
Verhoeff, Nanna (2006) *The West in Early Cinema: After the Beginning*. (Film Culture in Transition). Amsterdam: Amsterdam University Press.
Vries, Imar de (2009) *Mobile Mementos: Expanded Archives, Fragmented Access*. Paper delivered at MiT6 (MIT, Cambridge, MA).

Films

INCEPTION (USA 2010, Christopher Nolan)

Image Sources

Figure 1: Image by Netherlands Architecture Institute (NAi), 2011.

The Booth as an "Other Space"
Medial Positionings

ROLF F. NOHR

The question about orientation and disorientation raises the question of the order of space. The question about the order—and therefore also about the structures and institutions that evoke this order—is also a question about the conceptualisation of the 'public'. No matter what the detailed answer to such a fundamental question might be, two premises seem to be given. First, that the question about the order of space as a public sphere will always aim at assuming heterogeneous structures and arrangements. Second, that media-evoked subject-effects will play a crucial role within a culture that is as mediatised as ours.

If we go searching for the structures that are involved in producing orientation and disorientation in public topographies, we will find—that is my thesis—some remarkable architectures with a specific inherent law at certain places; architectures that I will introduce and discuss as 'cabins'. These cabins are, on the one hand, specifically connected to mediality and are, on the other hand, characterised by an essentially 'heterotopic nature'. This idea of the cabin—not in terms of a generalising approach but rather in terms of analysing a specific domain of phenomena—appears to be reasonable in order to work on the question of order and (dis)orientation. The (media-using) subject shall preferentially be set in the centre of my considerations. In anticipation of my argumentation, I want to put in front that my idea is to conceptualise specific spatial arrangements that unfold temporarily and 'invisibly' around the media-using subject as 'ad-hoc-cabins'. They can make—in a punctual way, of short duration, and far from being stable—heterotopic spatial arrangements emerge that are crucial for the understanding of certain forms of media use.

The photo booth is supposed to be the central example (and maybe even the primal scene) for such a cabin. A photo booth constitutes a remarkable topology within a public space. First, because it belongs to the technical-medial arrangements that have a place, that are spatially stable and immutably locatable. At first glance, those seem to be vanishing characteristics when we consider the multitude of current mobile, hybrid, and linked media devices. Furthermore, in contrast to the cinema or the theatre the photo booth is also a site for production and no site for staging. But first and foremost, the photo booth is a cabin, a spatial situation that isolates the subject and that allows to step out of a public topography. It walls off—but it does not completely seal off the outside space: The legs of the one that is photographed remain visible; the 'products' of the photo booths are handed out within the transitory spaces of the train station, the airport, or the registration office. Hence, a reading is at hand that understands the passport photomat cabin as an "other space".

Heterotopia

Analysing cabins as "other spaces", as heterotopias, initially refers to Michel Foucault's concept of heterotopia. *Of Other Spaces* is the title of a lecture by Foucault from 1967 in which he elaborates the concept of heterotopia: *Des Espaces Autres*.[1] In reference to Georges Bataille's *Heterology* (1975 [1930])[2] Foucault's concept is designed as a topography of the modern age: Social life does not organise itself within an empty space but within a heterogeneous, filled and structured space. However, there are islands that abscond from the regulation and that stand in opposition to the arrangements of this space. On the one hand, these are the utopias: unreal 'spaces'. On the other hand, these are the heterotopias that are absolutely different from all the sites that they reflect and speak about. This differentiation can be clarified pointedly by the example of the mirror: The mirror is a utopia as it shows the beholder within a space that does not exist and in which he or she is not; and it is a heterotopia as it shows the beholder him- or herself, his or her image whose reflection refers to him- or herself. It connects the recipient immediately with the space he or she takes (Foucault 1991, 39).

---

1 | Foucault's conception of the idea of the heterotopia (and its reception) is rather an 'evolutionary process': Foucault introduced the concept of heterotopia in 1966 as an opposing concept to the utopia within *The Order of Things*. In 1967, he unfolded it in a lecture on architecture (*L'Espace Autre*)—both explanations remained poorly received and commented at first. It was not until the posthumous publication in 1986/1987 as *Des Epaces Autres. Hétérotopies* (amongst others) in the broadly discussed *Aisthesis*-anthology (Barck et al. 1991) that a broad public perception and adoption of the concept took place. As the heterotopias are first and foremost being read in the context of the volumes 2 and 3 of the *History of Sexuality* at this time, the heterotopology was primarily established in the field of social sciences and in close relation to the concepts of biopolitics and gendered spaces in the first place (Chlada 2005, 17ff.).

The starting point of Foucault's argumentation is the observation that heterotopias are 'trans-historical'. Heterotopias exist in all cultures and at all times—however, they are specifically being established, transformed or abandoned due to the given historic and societal context. First (premodern) heterotopias are mostly "crisis heterotopias"—sacred places for people that are in a state of 'crisis' in relation to the society (tower of the cloister, colleges, cabins for menstruating and bearing children, honeymoon suites) (ibid., 40). But Foucault sees the modern age rather characterised by heterotopias of deviation: In these places individuals are housed that are deviant to the norm (retirement homes, the psychiatry, prisons) (ibid., 40f.). However, both forms of heterotopia are linked to a similar function in terms of time (heterochrony)—they take their effect only if the people transgress the usual time and if they enter an order of an "endlessly accumulated time" (ibid., 43).[3] Furthermore, heterotopias always call for a system of opening and closure; they have to be made isolatable and pervadable at the same time. One is either forced to enter (prison, casern) or one has to clean and purify oneself in order to be allowed to enter (sauna, hammam) (ibid., 44).

That all this appears to be an architectural-topographical definition until now may not diminish the fact that the heterotopia is by no means 'only' a topographical constellation. It is rather essentially connected to discourse—which is already indicated by the adjacency of the heterotopia to the utopia. According to Foucault, the heterotopia is characterised by a 'different thinking', by a disintegration of the unambiguous referential symbolic system:

"*Utopias* afford consolation; although they have no real locality there is nevertheless a fantastic, untroubled region in which they are able to unfold; they open up cities with vast avenues, superbly planted gardens, countries where life is easy, even though the road to them is chimerical. *Heterotopias* are distributing, probably because they secretly undermine language, because they shatter or tangle common names, because they destroy 'syntax' in advance, and not only the syntax which causes words and things (next to and also opposite one another) to 'hold together'." (Foucault 2004, XIX)

---

2 | Bataille's *Heterology* is conceptualised—as modern critique of the Enlightenment—as a theory of the 'other'. It deals with the scum of society, the ostracised part, the mad people, the laughter, the erotic, the violence.

3 | Such a time-accumulating heterotopia is opposed by a heterotopia of an 'ephemeral inherent time' that is evoked by the festival or the vacation village (Foucault 1991, 44).

Mediality

Now, it is most interesting to take a perspective that connects the concept of heterotopia with media and mediality. If we refer to Foucault's concept again, the heterotopias consist of a polar dichotomy: Heterotopias are differentiated as heterotopias of illusion and compensation (Foucault 1991, 45). The heterotopia of illusion denunciates the illusion of a normal space by exposing its artificiality (brothel, gay sauna), whereas the heterotopia of compensation generates a perfect order in order to establish an antipole to the disordered reality of the normal space (colonies, protected communities, Disneyland). Particularly, this distinction allows a gaze on media and medial systems that helps to clarify how heterotopias can be applied for (technical) media. Foucault himself, for example, subsumes the cinema as an architectural and topographical arrangement that can count as a heterotopia of compensation due to its mode of the experience of immediacy. It is interesting that he accounts for the heterotopic function of the cinema particularly due to the 'evocation' of a heterotopic space within a non-heterotopic arrangement. A heterotopia is capable of integrating multiple spaces and positions in one place: "[...] thus it is that the cinema is a very odd rectangular room, at the end of which, on a two-dimensional screen, one sees the projection of a three-dimensional space" (Foucault 1991, 42). Wunderlich (1999) or Poster (1990), for example, characterise the net-architecture and first and foremost the ordering structures of the internet in a similar way. Within information architectures that are disspatialised and latently disembodied and being conceptualised as virtual, power becomes invisible and affects the subject in a rather interpellating and adapting way. Also in this case, that is the thesis formulated on various occasions, a heterotopic order emerges as a function of illusion or compensation in terms of an 'other symbolic order'.

At this point of my argumentation, I do not want to swing into the discussion of the organisational space of the symbolic within digital networks (although my argument will go for a form of dematerialisation, too). I will rather continue to elaborate on the factual and architectural form of the medial and its development within such heterotopias of illusion and compensation. In the first instance, I am interested in concretely built architectures within the public space that stand out due to their close connection to media.

Cabins

Before we can define the heterotopic function of the (medial) cabins in a more detailed way, we have to elaborate on the arrangement within the cabin-situation itself. What are cabins—where do we find them? In the broadest sense, the term 'cabin'[4] signifies an enclosed, marked-off room and suggests (in contrast to the container, for example) a latent spatial stability. I do not want to elaborate a consistent definition of the cabin here—I rather want to follow three (more or less) obvious 'traces' that might show how the cabin, focused on the thesis of the cabin-heterotopia, can be outlined.

In terms of an architecture—this would be the first trace—the cabin refers to the partition and the sealing-off from the outside space but also (latently) to the individual separation, the return of the subject, partly also to the concepts of intimacy, the arcanum, the unspeakable, the secret. From a certain perspective, cabin spaces are spaces of the subject (shower cubicle, toilet, changing room). They are spaces of a specific arrangement and therefore latently distinguish themselves from the space outside and evoke certain subject-effects during their usage (withdrawal, security, safety, uncertainty, etc.). Usually, there are clear rules of opening and closure, of entering and leaving and therefore also adequate functional architectures (doors, bars, locks). However, cabins are also (more or less) political places as they invite the subject to compensate, to be dissident and emancipative. They open up domains of action that exceed the (repressive) practices of power (although they are open for forms of governmental regimes). In this discursive contour, the 'secret cabinet', the gay sauna, the shower, or the (Japanese) love hotel, for example, are obviously related to the concept of heterotopia in its different arrangements. Nevertheless, cabins also belong to the repertoire of the establishment of spaces within spaces (e.g. dais). They are sometimes transitory spaces, an 'interspace' as well (e.g. winter garden). The cabin—we could say simplistically—is demarcating itself from the space outside and declines itself by the presence of its demarcation.

A second trace to an understanding of the cabin is transportation (box, container)[5] and technical travelling. The cabin in aeroplanes, ships or the driving cab, elevators and aerial tramway are functional arrangements for transport. In terms of the dromologic "rushing standstill" (Virilio 1998) they function within the mode of (modern) acceleration—at the same time, though, they are immobilisations within the movement. They are demarcations from the outside space that are supporting the elimination of the interspace during the movement from A to B. In the remainder of this article, this trace of the cabin is not supposed to be considered in terms of its mode of transport or as a carrier. It is rather supposed to be thought of in terms of its static function of demarcation

---

4 | Derived from the French word *cabine*, from Old French *cabane*; Middle English *cabane*, roman. *capanna* (all: tent, cottage).

5 | Due to the limited space of this article, I cannot elaborate further on the specific productivity of the concept/metaphor of the container and its mode of demarcation, enclosure, and transport (e.g. in terms of the philosophy of space or media studies); see exemplarily Alexander Klose (2009) for this subject-matter.

from the outside space and thus the immobilisation within dynamic spatial arrangements.

It is just as important to understand the cabin—as a third trace—in terms of a 'political space', as a discoursively superimposed, 'charged' place. The cabin marks the two extremes of the political subject: Inside the polling booth the subject is (ideally) by itself and free in its decisions. If one dis-idealises this utopian idea of this secret (and therefore free from domination and influence) place, the polling booth can be conceptualised as a governmental space. This concept is opposed by the confessional booth as a place of (classical) application of power and a repressive subject-politics. Within the confessional booth the subject is interpellated, declined and ruled by the pastoral power and the compulsion to confess. This ensemble of 'political cabins' is consequently extended by the prison cell: The subject either becomes excluded and separated or is led to self-governance (in terms of panopticism (Foucault 1994)).

If we bring those traces together, a picture of the cabin emerges that shows a basically architectural arrangement that has a specific relation to the mode of transportation and guarantees a mode of immobilising the subject within the mode of velocity and travelling through space, respectively. Furthermore, the cabin is also a place of specific constellations of power. Within the cabin, the "care of the self"[6], the pastoral power, panopticism and repression culminate. Cabins are a constructed and static space that demarcates itself from the space outside and in which specific discourses of power unfold[7]—hence, it seems reasonable to discuss them under the premise of the heterotopic.

Foucault's spatial concept of the heterotopia can also be seen as an argumentation against the "orthotopographical thinking", a thinking that allots each 'thing' its distinct place (see e.g. Lax 1998). In an incisive way, one could also understand the concept of the heterotopia that negotiates the border between subject and the outside world and that therefore also operates in the context of a negotiation between orientation and disorientation. The cabin is a heterotopic formation that has to be seen as a subject-practice that is political and constitutive for the subject. It functions in the mode of assigning 'place'[8] and hence

---

6 | *The Care of the Self* is the title of the third part of Foucault's History of Sexuality (originally: *Le souci de soi*, 1984).

7 | We could also add the transitoric, the arcane and not least biopolitics.

8 | "The place contains the own, unmistakable, incomparable, in contrast to spaces, places are not comparable; reproducible as they are not quantifiable. Furthermore, the concept aims rather at the 'content' and to a lesser extent at the 'voluminous extension'" (Brauns 1992, 163; transl. R.F.N.; original citation: "[Im Ort] ist das Eigene, Unverwechselbare, Nichtvergleichbare aufgehoben, anders als Räume sind Orte nicht vergleichbar; reproduzierbar, weil nicht quantifizierbar. Außerdem zielt der Begriff stärker auf den ‚Inhalt' und weniger auf die ‚Ausdehnung'").

relates and in a certain way also separates the subject, practices, and space in a specific way.

From this perspective—also in reference to mediality—it is not that hard to find cabins that are formed by discourses and technologies: The projection cabin in the movie theatre, the phone booth, and also adult video arcades would obviously have to be integrated into this cabin-discourse. Using the example of the photo booth, I want to explain how this could be discussed reasonably.

Fotofix

In the following, I want to outline a media-theoretical utilisation of this concept of the cabin as a heterotopia in reference to the photo booth. In a first step, I want to describe what it is about when we take a look at a *Fotofix*-machine (and apart from that I want to introduce the German brand name). Let us start with the mere architecture of the cabin: The Fotofix[9] is certainly outstanding due to the very fact that it is one of the rare (contemporary) media-technical arrangements that have a place. It is a cabin, but only to the extent to which it is characterised by a spatial enclosure and demarcation from the outside space. However, the closure is only latent—no door closes the Fotofix cabin, but merely a curtain (if anything at all) that still allows a gaze on the legs.

However, it is not just the architecture of the cabin but first and foremost its usage and its construction of meaning as a topographical setting that characterises the Fotofix cabin. This cabin can almost exclusively be found in public space. It is most likely to find them in transitory places in the public, in the context of travelling and passing through: train stations, airports, shopping malls. We also find them (and this is an intersection to the transitory) in places in which a souvenir picture, a gesture of 'archiving' is used to be made. This refers to public spaces that are characterised by (temporary) parting or an outstanding experience (e.g. train stations and amusement parks). And photo booths are traditionally (and not least) installed in places that are dedicated for legitimation: passport offices, registration offices, etc.

When we take a closer look at the places and instances, we can already gain some insight into the inherent discursive practices of the Fotofix. The photo booth as an image producing technology focuses on the face. The Fotofix forms the subject in terms of its faciality—not by the mere imaging but also by its whole architecture. In its entire design and its historic genesis, the arrangement of the Fotofix aims at the production of serial portraits. In this process, only two forms can be produced (in terms of a heuristic distinction): the 'serious' portrait

---

[9] | I will use the term 'Fotofix' (and later on 'Polaroid') not as a brand name but as a medial object that is characterised by a specific use and materiality.

that is more likely to follow the legitimatory than the aesthetic discourse and, on the other hand, the 'funny picture' (the grimace, alone or in pairs; mostly used as a souvenir picture); a game of appropriation that seems to elude the legitimatory aspect.

Thus, a passport photomat can be conceptualised as a medial discursive constellation that produces a self-portrait in an ambivalent gesture between intimacy and automation. On the one hand, it is informed by a specific symbolic order. On the other hand, though, it also invites to step out of this order by the momentum of intimacy that is 'induced by the cabin'. In order to approach this ambivalence it seems reasonable to distinguish different genealogical and archeological axes that inform the Fotofix. In the following, a couple of these axes (mainly of an archeological and historical kind) that outline the discursive constellation Fotofix shall be sketched in some reductive suggestions.

The Fotofix is obviously a media technology. Hence, it is reasonable to mention the axis of the history of technology.[10] The innovation-history of the photo booth is closely related to the beginning of photography itself (Nohr 2004)[11]—for example the 'Bosco-Photography-Technique'[12] (patented in 1894 by Conrad Beritt), which is typical for a great number of these early patents and techniques. These early machines are stand-alone arrangements that consist of a photography column and a chair for 'poseying the subject' (see fig. 1a). However, almost all of these early techniques are just 'semi-automatic' techniques that require a 'machinist' that takes care of the coin-automatism, carries out the regulation of chemistry, explains the function of the machine to the customer, or just takes reorders (Behme 1996, note 1).

These early Fotofix machines are mostly based on ferrotype: The Bosco-technique (see fig. 1b) has already integrated the liquids for the developing process into the margins of a paper-sheath that serves as a decorative frame for the picture at the same time—an anticipation of the Polaroid-technique. Due to the reduction of exposure time and a better functionality of the machines, the

---

10 | Such a technology-historical axis that uses the history of innovation and patent-discourses tends, of course, towards a homogenisation and linearisation of its 'objects'—a threat that I hope to avoid by using a generally discourse-theoretical approach. In the description of the technology-historical data I basically refer to the works of Maas/Maas (1981), Boyle/Duchin (1987), Behme (1996), and Pellicier (2011).

11 | In terms of the history of patents, a 'due date' of the Fotofix can be defined. On September 17, 1889, the Frenchman Ernest Enjalbert applies for a patent for an 'Apparatus for automatic production of photographs to operate by inserting a coin' (transl. R.F.N.; original title: "Durch Einwerfen einer Münze zu bethätigender Apparat zur selbstständigen Herstellung von Photografien").

12 | Transl. R.F.N.; original term: "Bosco-Photografie-Verfahren".

establishment of the self-photography begins until the mid to late 1920s (at this time even in the form of cabins).

The positioning of these early machines opens up a second axis of the archeological classification. The early self-photographers are mainly integrated into the amusement and fairground cultures by the place they were installed. Therefore, the medial form of self-photography is closely related to the cinema at this stage of its development: Many of the pre-cinematographic technologies, like the zoetrope or the bioscope, but also the early cinema itself were initially located within the fairground and amusement culture, for example in the nickelodeons (McCauley 1985, 23). Today, the Japanese *purinto kurabu* (or: *purikura*) are the quintessence of such an axis: small sticky portraits that can be produced in public purikura cabins that combine the portrait with a multitude of different ornamental and comic-like predefined visual elements. Particularly, this example leads to yet another axis—the automaton culture.

The early self-photography-automatons are vending machines. They occur around 1883 with the invention of the coin-based vending machine of Percival Everett (Boyle/Duchin 1987). This shows a connection of the Fotofix with spaces and public spheres of consumption, commodification, and production. Early photo booth machines are positioned in the big stores and shopping arcades that have been characterised exemplarily by Walter Benjamin's Arcades Project (*Passagen-Werk*, 1983); transitory urban spaces of dandering, consuming, and the commodity fetishism. Hence, the Fotofix does not only join the discourse of urbanity but also the discourse of industrialisation.

But most of all the Polaroid technique has to be seen as the significant axis for an understanding of the Fotofix. In my opinion, this constitutes the most important and the most productive connection. In the years 1947/1948 Polaroid introduces the Land Modell 95 (Gethman 2005). By this, a form of amateur

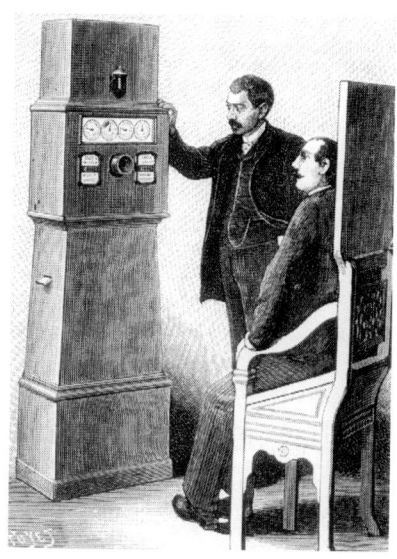

Figure 1a + 1b: Self-photographer by Ernest Enjalbert (1889) and 'Bosco-Card' made by the technique of Conrad Beritt (1894).

photography comes into being that can be characterised by its great experience of immediacy. At the same time, the Polaroid seems to fulfill the Benjaminian dictum of the mechanical reproduction and the affront towards the auratic function of the original most consequently—remarkably by using a technology that pretends to produce nothing but originals. Two points are important here: the immediacy of the Polaroid and the specific use of the "gesture of Polaroid".[13] On the one hand, a 'dissidence' of the technology remains recognisable in the 'Polasnapshot'. Particularly the 'mechanical' form of making pictures, the needed power to 'pull the trigger', the buzz of the picture sliding out, the latent 'plastic chunkiness' of the apparatus expose the technology at the same time. The Polaroid is always noticeable in its use and its specific materiality. It presents media technology as a technique that displays itself permanently. On the other hand, Polaroid also demands a photographic practice in its usage that tends to make itself invisible as an apparatus and organisation of reality. This can be seen especially in the almost simultaneous production and reception of a technical image. The Polaroid seems to be made for the moment and the gesture; not so much for archiving and representation.[14] The Polaroid is closely connected to a form of usage; a specific quality of gesture within photographing. Thus, the Polaroid as another axis introduces an ambivalence of the simultaneous presence and absence of the apparatus, a specific materiality of the produced image, a specific form of usage during the reception, and most importantly: a certain form of immediacy in the practice of representation.[15]

Therefore, the Fotofix-dispositif can also be explained based on the axis of the portrait.[16] It is one possible explanation for the cultural establishment of the Fotofix as a portrait-machine. At a certain point in history the social history of the technical portrait and the technical history of the self-photography intersect. In the course of the 'discovery' of privacy and citizenship at the beginning

---

13 | See Nohr/Kröncke 2005 for this subject-matter.

14 | All forms of 'fast documentary'—like the Polaroid—are connoted with rather 'specialised' fields of duty and forms of action.

15 | At this point, we have to qualify that the axis of Polaroid can only be interpreted in a historical perspective: In Central Europe we do not have 'wet' (thus Polaroid-based) photo automata anymore but actually only cabins with digital printing techniques. The mirror inside the cabin has been replaced by a monitor. Hence, the cameraphone or the digital snapshot photography would be the appropriate discursive framing. However, the thesis here is that the Fotofix cabin can rather be approached (mediatheoretically) with the discourse-pattern of Polaroid than with the concepts of digital photography—e.g. that the digital snapshot photography would have to be outlined in a different way in terms of technology but could strictly be understood in terms of the Polaroid gesture when it comes to usage.

16 | See Nohr 2004 for more details.

of the modern age, the action of producing portraits generally gains in (new) importance (see Freund 1979). A transformation of perception and consciousness, along with the economic rise of the middle class in the 18th century, cause a practice of private possession of photographs in a double-motif between the private and the public. This doubling manifests itself in the non-public portrait in an album or a wallet, in the public portrait on a business card, or in the family portrait that is presented in the living room. The (technical) testimony of the bourgeois-individual existence within the portrait gains massively in importance with the development of the civil society. The photograph from the studio and later on the photomaton portrait is preferentially cheap and therefore no longer elitist.

Besides, the turn towards the identifying and classifying aspect of photography is yet another aspect in terms of the photographic portrait and the 'gentrification' of the portrait and the automatic portrayal. The axis of photographic identification is closely linked to the axis of portrait (Meyer 2008, 106). Within the discourses of criminology, human sciences, and medicine, the face serves as a means for attribution of normality and deviance and therefore also for the definition of individuality and identity. Photographic techniques of classification are not only used for a typology of moods but also for establishing a paradigm of the visibility of the delinquent existence (as it has been worked on by Cesare Lombroso or Alphonse Bertillon) (ibid., 106f.).[17] This is closely connected to strategies for making the face readable for social control and self-control: Reading a face also means to classify it (intelligibly). Hence, this (rather repressive) discourse on legitimation parallels a culture of appropriation to a certain degree. As I suggested, the culture of remembrance of the Fotofix portrait and the Polaroid is also a culture of a subjective self-assurance in the light of a dominant symbolic practice.

The axes I have traced here sketchily are of course not elaborated in the necessary depth and can only hint at the things that would have to be examined. Neither can we assume that all of the discursive constellations that influence the Fotofix have been identified by this. At this point, I only want to indicate how the space of the Fotofix cabin is formed by the most diverse practices, politics, and discursive constellations. Apart from the technology and the architecture that constitute this specific medial constellation, we have to consider particularly levels of experience and forms of usage (amusement culture), economic constellations (automaton culture), medial impressions of immediacy (Polaroid), technologies of the self (portraits) or politics (legitimation) here.

---

17 | See the article by Othmer/Weich in this book.

Fotofix as Heterotopia

But why can we conceptualise the ensemble of the Fotofix as a heterotopia? Heterotopias, that is what we have elaborated above, always require a system of opening and closure; they have to be made isolable and permeable at the same time. Entering the heterotopia is connected to a symbolic action of cleaning or self-conquest. According to my thesis, the heterotopic manifests itself in the semi-closed form of the cabin (without a door but with a curtain), the ambivalence of encapsulation and transparency, a space of entering and leaving. It can most likely be compared to the confessional booth: Inside the Fotofix cabin, too, the discursive power effects of the compulsion to confess and the self-governance apply. However, the Fotofix cabin is a remarkable topography that can be entered and that subjects the visitor to a spatial modification. And just in terms of these specifications it can be conceptualised as an "other space" in terms of Foucault, as a heterotopia and not least as a medial setting in space.

Heterotopias, that is the second crucial definition, do have a function in respect to the outside space. They are mere spaces for escape and no mere topographies for stepping out of the spatial societal order of knowledge. The heterotopia Fotofix does not only unfold an "other space" but also an 'other order'—an order that is allowed to exist within the order of a society (just like any heterotopia) as long as it does not threaten it substantially. It culminates in the ambivalent outline of the generated images that has already been mentioned. In terms of the photo booth we have to consider the mirror inside the cabin in particular. Current machines position the subject in front of a mirror. This arrangement makes the situation inside the cabin so special: The Fotofix interpellates the subject. The machine summons the subject to stylise itself previously to the image-producing moment and to perform a gesture of self-screening: Which representation of myself would I like to match? This arrangement of the mirror leads to another ambivalence in the use of a media technology. The gaze into the mirror reveals the technique of self-portrayal as a technical procedure as it seems to anticipate the result and to request a self-adaption and a self-stylisation. On the other hand, the mirror veils and naturalises the media technology—the apparatus becomes invisible and transparent.

The counter-part within the Fotofix is not the apparatus itself but the mirror: The technical objective lens, which is put in between the photographer and the subject in the usual photographic situation, is being replaced by the anticipated result of the photographic process, the image as a reflection of the subject and as the naturalisation of the technical system of photography. The mirror—as we have already discussed above—is a hybrid experience of utopia and heterotopia.[18] It shows the beholder within a room that does not exist and in which he or she is not; and it is a heterotopia as it shows the beholder himself, his or her representation, his or her reflection to him- or herself. It immediately connects the recipient with the space he or she takes. The Fotofix seems to make its technical part invisible and at the same time exposes it by its dominant architecture and its 'mechanical' qualities as a technology. The essential structural characteristic of photography, and thus the objective lens of the apparatus that constitutes the actual counterpart, become invisible. Hence, the power of the technological apparatus that organises and disciplines the self becomes invisible due to the gaze in the mirror. However, the product of the Fotofix as a heterotopic dispositif is not a mere reflection but a passport photo, a self-portrait or a funny souvenir picture. Hence, the discursive formation of the Fotofix produces self-images in a quite ambivalent way. They oscillate exactly between the poles of a self-disciplinary symbolic order and an appropriating and dissident practice as Foucault described it.

Thus, several dimensions of the heterotopia introduced above that we find inside the 'media cabin' also speak in favour of the concept of the heterotopia in reference to the cabin (apart from the constellation of reflection and invisibility in terms of the mirror). Cabins like the Fotofix constitute (just like the movie theatre and its screen) several spaces in one place: within the transitory place a place of self-reflection, of technologies of the self or the pastoral power; within the legitimatory place a space of dissidence. At the same time, the cabins produce a special time, a heterochroneous time of staying or leaving, of remembrance within the endlessly stretched time of the festival. The cabin of the Fotofix is a heterotopia of compensation, the promise of a regulated, isolated and well-organised space within the 'outside space'; in an 'extreme case' even a heterotopia of crisis—a refuge for separation within the filled and 'charged' outside space.

MEDIAL CABIN-HETEROTOPIAS

What I elaborated with respect to the Fotofix cabin outlines—that is my thesis—a kind of ideal primal scene of a medial cabin-heterotopia that we can trace a little further. I want to suggest that we can retrieve the arrangement of the Fotofix cabin in different variations. However, the fundamental difference is that we do not have to focus anymore on the architectural enclosure that is factually built. We rather have to assume the construction of this enclosure to be 'virtual',

---

18 | Of course, the mirror is one of the key elements for the understanding of the photo booth dispositif. For a reading of the mirror as a (e.g.) more narcissistic element and constitution of a photographic 'off', see Meyer (2008).

invisible and we have to conceptualise it as a form of action and social gesture within space.

Furthermore, let us take a look at a rather obvious 'intermediate form': the telephone booth. In media history it initially appears as a visible cabin: a clear partition to the outside space that is (just like the Fotofix) not absolute but—by its glass construction—latent. Like the Fotofix, the telephone booth also produces a specific 'other' order. Talking to someone in a telephone booth means separating oneself from the outside space (that is also a transitory and public space in most cases) and to enter a specifically 'peculiar' order. The medial scene is informed by the specific order of the telephone call: the dialogue that is in line with the social act of communication but always has to cope with the physical absence and the uncertainty concerning the situation the counterpart is in. However, driven by the establishment of mobile phones the telephone booth has become rather obsolete. Nowadays, public telephones do not occur as a cabin architecture but as open stand-alone devices—and therefore in line with the order that has been established by mobile phones. One could postulate that telephoning in public space today means to reproduce the ad-hoc constitution of a cell or cabin without the architectural component but with the same effect. For the telephoner making a phone call in public space means to enter such a cabin.[19] The order of the telephone call is additionally informed by the uncertainty in which situation the dialogue partner is in at the given moment. The semi-openness of the arrangement is mostly implemented by the fact that the listeners become more or less inevitably integrated into the heterotopic space of the ad-hoc cabin and get an 'insight'. At the same time the dialogue partners move deeper and deeper back into the 'constructed' cabin; they compensate the normal space in favour of an ad-hoc space.

The cabin architecture is gone. But the symbolic part of the heterotopia is preserved and transforms itself continuously. The specific discursive order that is capable of transforming media-cabins into heterotopias outlasts, even if the (material, architectural) cabin disappears. Such an argument is—though still sketchy—compatible to a couple of other thoughts and concepts. Hence, the constitution of ad-hoc cabins as a social and/or subjective gesture could be related to considerations about portable media (Thiele/Stingelin 2010); this would be a variation to describe scenes within the portable media culture in which portability and mobility are linked to the constitution of selective and temporal qualities of stable places. Particularly, from the perspective of heterotopia-analysis we would have to ask then to which extent especially the mobilisation of media leads to transformations concerning the potential production of

---

19 | The gesture of telephoning within a car may count as an interesting hybrid—in this case we can find some of the well-known components: immutable movement, cabin architecture, separation from the outside space, and the remaining visibility.

meaning and the social organisation of media usage and media action.[20] In a similar way, we could also consult some positions of postmodern aesthetics again—to a lesser extent in terms of the postmodern age but rather in terms of thinking about radically transformed subject positions (that got their crucial 'drive' in the 1980s). Shihei Hosokawa (1991) for example postulated the so-called "Walkman-effect" in 1984. According to his considerations, listening to music with a Walkman establishes a kind of theatre of the urban space. Hosokawa conceptualises the movement within the real space and the simultaneous exposure to an auditive 'other' as a gesture of a "covert theatre". The one who listens to the Walkman listens to a secret. The walk through the city turns the reception of this secret into a performative speech act. It is obvious that listening to music in a public space can be understood as an ad-hoc cabin in similar ways, as a heterotopic situation of separation from the normal space.[21]

"[The activity of listening to music with a Walkman] constitutes an autonomous 'space' between the Walkman-listener and his or her environment. By this, the act of hearing is alienated from the listener and his or her environment—hence, it is not about confirming what is already known. The result is a mobility of the self [...]. So, the Walkman-listener opens up a refuge by a self-isolation or a narcissistic regression that is structured in an autonomous and pluralistic way." (ibid. 1991, 243; transl. R.F.N.)[22]

At this point, also the ambivalence of the cabin in the area of conflict between 'privatised mobility' and 'mobile privatisation' comes up quite radically. Especially due to its contrariness they constitute the framing for the 'immutable movement' and the 'public privacy' of the cabin-heterotopias (see Thiele/Stingelin 2010, 11).

Thus, no matter whether we talk about passport photomats, video game arcade cabins, telephone cells, MP3 players, or mobile phones and portable DVD

---

20 | One could mainly agree with the aspects in the project 'Portable Media' that focus on portability, mobility, and subjectivity of media; but in detail we would have to broaden the perspective from the 'writing scenes' of media to the 'reading scenes' (Thiele/Stingelin 2010).

21 | Current smartphones offer the fancy variation to integrate telephoning, reception of films, and music in just one 'cabin' on an analytical level.

22 | Original citation: "[...] konstituiert einen autonomen ‚Raum' zwischen dem Walkman-Hörer und seiner Umgebung. Dadurch entfremdet sich die Hörtätigkeit vom Hörer und seiner Umgebung – es geht also nicht darum, schon Bekanntes bestätigt zu finden. Das Resultat ist eine Mobilität des Selbst [...] Der Walkman-Hörer erschließt sich dadurch eine autonome pluralistisch strukturierte Zuflucht in der Selbstisolierung oder in einer narzißtischen Regression" (Hosokawa 1991, 243).

players that are used in pedestrian areas, airports, train stations and trains, buses, and aeroplanes—it seems comprehensible that all these technologies and spaces are pervaded by acts of media usage that do not evolve from the technology but from the specific arrangement and the specific subject positions that unfold around these technologies. Everywhere 'social cabins' come into being as heterotopias in consequence of media actions. And therefore—that is my last thesis—the outside space that is already heterogeneous itself 'breaks' and 'folds' itself on and on: The disorientation increases.[23]

Hence, it is not the technology that 'forms' the subjects attached to it. Rather the subjects 'reconfigure' the techniques and technologies by actions and usage and surround themselves and their media by cabin walls. Even though we can hardly conceptualise the cabins that become evoked in this way as architectures, it is reasonable to understand the resulting arrangements as heterotopic.

(Dis)Orientation

However, it is important for such a conceptualisation to emphasise a crucial quality of these cabins. In contrast to the 'classic' Foucauldian heterotopia, the social cabins seem to be specified for the separated and isolated (or rather self-isolating) subject. While the heterotopia can also be a place of community according to Foucault, the medial cabin-heterotopia—beginning with cinema—seems to be characterised as a subject-effect.[24] However, the medial scene always includes the constitution of a counterpart and of an intersection; but by its very nature, the social cabin consists of a subject that is connected to media (and mostly also to networks). When we want to reason about heterotopias in terms of orientation, we have to do it under the premise to understand such cabins as architectures of the subject; architectures that relate subjects to themselves and put them into a specific relation to the outside space within the "room of sites"[25] of the modern age (Foucault 1991, 34; transl. R.F.N.). This relation evolves from a transgressive and segregative dynamic. It situates the subjects (and their media) in a 'quivering' simultaneity, in an overlapping and separation, in participation and isolation—hence: (dis)orientation. The concept of the

---

23 | In this case, we are willing to assume that an increasingly heterogeneous space can be described in the mode of an also increasing disorientation.
24 | At this point, it would be reasonable to relate this argument to the constitution of an ideal or transcendental subject in the cinema, as the apparatus debate suggests it. Due to the limited space of this article, this argument and further quite obvious relations concerning the invisibilisation of technical apparatuses have to be left out here.
25 | Original citation: "relations d'emplacement" (Foucault 1991, 34).

Walkman-effect, the transformation of perception. and the latent dropping out of a homogeneous space sharpen this quite well.

Heterotopias and subject-cabins are parts of a 'new' geography. A geography that could also be called "Foucault's Geography" (Philo 1992). In this concept subjects, power, and order are conceptualised as spatial functions: The panopticon, the techniques of inclusion in the clinic and the madhouse, the confessional booth, and also the heterotopias are topological structures. The consideration of the body as a place in which discourses of power are being negotiated makes the spatial dimension of the analysis of power quite clear, as well: The body is a pointed projection of the self and the subject and it is material, spatially consistent and located.

Cabin-heterotopias—no matter if they are generated in a 'factual-architectural' or 'subjective-social' way—are constellations of the production and disintegration of order and arrangement. Most diverse axes and constellations intersect in it that are partly utopistic-emancipatory (within the possibilities of discourse) but also informed by effects of power and ideology. The concept of heterotopia—that has to be clear—is no fantasy of salvation. The concept of heterotopia describes a space within a space, an 'other discoursive constellation' within the constellation of discourses. Cabins, heterotopias, Fotofix machines are spaces that are by no means free of power structures and no unregulated statements. But they are also comments on the regulation of the statements, on the order of space. The social cabins are compensative and illusionary, they order and segregate, they are political constellations and subject-practices—and they establish a border between themselves and the outside space. Entering them means to perform a ritual act.

Bibliography

Barck, Karlheinz et. al. (eds.) (1991): *Aisthesis. Wahrnehmung heute oder Perspektiven einer anderen Ästhetik.* Leipzig: Reclam.

Bataille, Georges (1975 [1933]): *Das theoretische Werk I: Die Aufhebung der Ökonomie (Der Begriff der Verausgabung – Der verfemte Teil – Kommunismus und Stalinismus.* München: Rogner & Bernhard.

Behme, Rolf (1996): *Fotofix. Es blitzt viermal.* Düsseldorf: Parerga.

Benjamin, Walter (1983 [1928–1929, 1934–1940]): *Das Passagen-Werk.* Frankfurt a. M.: Suhrkamp.

Boyle, Bern/Duchin, Linda (1987): *Photomaton: a contemporary survey of photobooth art.* Exhibition catalogue; Pyramid Arts Center, Rochester N.Y. New York: Artistic Press.

Brauns, Jörg (1992): Heterotopien. In: *Wissenschaftliche Zeitschrift der Hochschule für Architektur und Bauwesen Weimar* (3/4), 163–169.

Chlada, Marvin (2005): *Heterotopie und Erfahrung. Abriss der Heterotopologie nach Michel Foucault.* Aschaffenburg: Alibri.
Foucault, Michel (1994 [1976]): *Überwachen und Strafen. Die Geburt des Gefängnisses.* Frankfurt a. M.: Suhrkamp.
Foucault, Michel (1991 [1967]): Andere Räume. In: Barck et. al. 1991, 34–46. (for English version see: [http://foucault.info/documents/heteroTopia/foucault.heteroTopia.en.html]; access: 2012/10/10).
Foucault, Michel (1985): Hermeneutik des Subjekts. Vorlesung am Collège de France (1982). In: Foucault, Michel (1985): *Freiheit und Selbstsorge. Interview 1984 und Vorlesung 1982.* Frankfurt a. M.: Materialis.
Foucault, Michel (2004 [1966]): *The Order of Things.* New York: Routledge.
Freund, Gisèle (1979): *Fotografie und Gesellschaft.* Reinbek (Hamburg): Rowohlt.
Gethmann, Daniel (2005): Das Prinzip Polaroid. In: Kröncke/Nohr/Lauterbach 2005, 44–65.
Hosokawa, Shuhei (1991 [1984]): Der Walkman-Effekt. In: Barck et. al. 1991, 229–251.
Klose, Alexander (2009): *Das Container-Prinzip: Wie eine Box unser Denken verändert.* Hamburg: Mare.
Kröncke, Meike/Nohr, Rolf F./Lauterbach, Barbara (eds.) (2005): *Polaroid als Geste. Über die Gebrauchsweisen einer fotografischen Praxis.* Ostfildern: Hatje-Cantz.
Kröncke, Meike/Nohr, Rolf F. (2005): Polaroids und die Ungewissheit des Augenblicks. In: Kröncke/Nohr/Lauterbach 2005, 6–19
Lax, Sigurd F. (1998): ‚Heterotopie' aus Sicht der Biologie und Humanmedizin. In: Knaller-Vlay, Bernd/Ritter, Roland (eds.): *Other Spaces: The Affair of the Heterotopia.* Graz: Haus der Architektur (HDA Dokumente zur Architektur, 10), 114–123.
Maas, Ellen/Maas Klaus (1981): Das Photomaton – Eine alte Idee wird vermarktet. In: Starl, Timm (ed.): *Fotogeschichte. Beiträge zur Geschichte und Ästhetik der Fotografie*, Vol. 1, Issue 1, Frankfurt a. M.
McCauley, Elizabeth Anne (1985): *A.A.E. Disdéri and the Carte De Visite Portrait Photograph.* New Haven/London: Yale University Press
Meyer, Roland (2008): Aufnahmebedingungen. Versuchsanordnung Fotoautomat. In: Hinterwaldner, Inge/Juwig, Carsten/Klemm, Tanja/Meyer, Roland (eds.): *Topologien der Bilder.* Paderborn: Fink, 99–116.
Nohr, Rolf F. (2004): A Dime – A Minute – A Picture. Polaroid & Fotofix. In: Löffler, Petra/Scholz, Leander (eds.): *Das Gesicht ist eine starke Organisation.* Köln: DuMont, 160–180.
Pellicer, Raynal (2011): *Photomaton.* Paris: Éditions de la Martinière.
Philo, Chris (1992): Foucault´s Geography. In: *Enviroment and Planning D: Society and Space*, Vol. 10, 137–161.

Poster, Mark (1990): *The Mode of Information: Poststructuralism and Social Context*. Chicago: University of Chicago Press.

Thiele, Matthias/Stingelin, Martin (2010): Portable Media. Von der Schreibszene zur mobilen Aufzeichnungsszene. In: Thiele, Matthias/Stingelin, Martin (eds.): *Portable Media. Schreibszenen in Bewegung zwischen Peripatetik und Mobiltelefon*. München: Fink, 7–28.

Virilio, Paul (1998): *Rasender Stillstand*. Frankfurt a. M.: Fischer.

Wunderlich, Stefan (1999): Vom digitalen Panopticum zur elektrischen Heterotopie. Foucaultsche Topographien der Macht. In: Maresch, Rudolf/Werber, Niels (eds.): *Kommunikation, Medien, Macht*. Frankfurt a. M.: Suhrkamp, 342–367.

Image Sources

Figure 1a: Pellicer 2011, 16; © Collection Raynal Pellicer (Revue La Nature).
Figure 1b: Pellicer 2011, 17; © Münchner Stadtmuseum.

(Dis)Orienting Databases

Lost in Digitalisation?
Profiles as Means of Orientation in Computer-based Media Cultures

JULIUS OTHMER/ANDREAS WEICH

Any medium develops its own specific set of means of orientation. This set can facilitate orientation in terms of sorting formats and content and of structuring time, space and knowledge, for example. But these means are not necessarily invented by the given medium itself but adopted and remediated (Bolter/Grusin 2000) according to its needs and conditions. TV, for example, borrowed the programme structure from the theatre, reconfigured it on an everyday level, and finally challenged it by the concept of the flow as Raymond Williams (1990, 178ff.) describes it. Computer games took maps from print media, made them interactive (Sandkühler 2012), and the early WWW obviously reproduced the books' or catalogues logic of pages and tables of contents and transformed it into databases. Now, and that is the initial observation for this paper, recent developments of the internet have (re)established the concept of profiles as a means of orientation. On the following pages, we are going to work on the circumstances that lead to this and ask the question from which domains the concept of profiles has been adapted and what this might tell about current media culture.

DIGITAL DISORIENTATION

In a first step, we have to point out some basic assumptions about the relation of (dis)orientation and computer based media. Orientation is always a way of positioning oneself and others within a certain space in order to be able to navigate through it. Thus, we have to produce a certain knowledge about this given space, as well as a knowledge about ourselves and other objects that are compatible to it. In digital media, this space is quite abstract and not intuitively understandable or similar to already established spaces and the knowledge about them. It is made of memory structures, algorithms, protocols, and bits that we

Figure 1: The OSI-model.

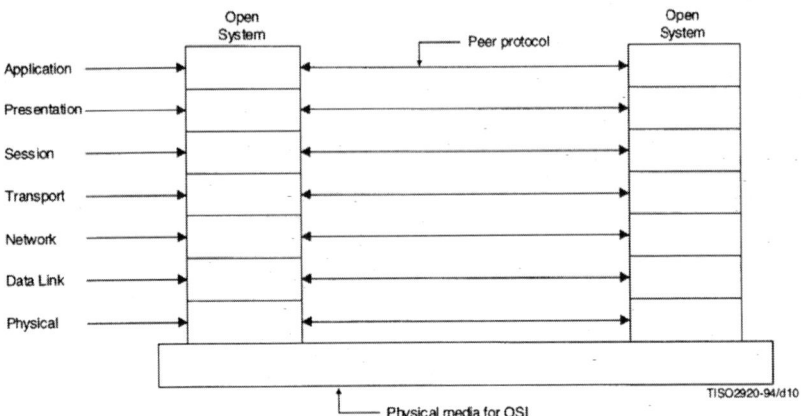

cannot relate to at all—we are disoriented. We have to produce a certain kind of knowledge to make this space accessible. A prominent example for a concept to achieve this is the OSI model (see fig. 1).

As we can see, the layers one to five consist of rather abstract technical information, such as bit-streams, protocols, and codes. The two upper levels (presentation and application) are needed to translate this information into some kind of knowledge that the user can understand in order to deal with this qualitative disorientation. This is the very place where the means of orientation that are specifically needed for computer based media come into play. They have to be compatible to the underlying technology that works with distinct bits of information and at the same time compatible to existing forms of perception and meaningful representation.

Apart from this qualitative disorientation, an additional and merely quantitative factor for disorientation on the internet is the overwhelming mass of potential information, content, and actors: Most queries in *Google* provide billions of results, *Facebook* has hundreds of millions of users and *Amazon* offers an unclear mass of products. This means that even if the abstract information is presented in a way we could call 'knowledge', we need to find a way of organising it and of putting ourselves and others in relation to it. So, within these huge computer based spaces of knowledge we can assume three basic (and heuristic) necessities for accomplishing the user's orientation:

1. The user and relevant objects have to be modeled and 'translated' into a type of knowledge that is compatible to the computer technology.
2. The huge amount of data has to be transformed into manageable structures.
3. The user and relevant objects have to be locatable within these structures.

The thesis of this article is that the concept of profiles is most capable of providing these functions and further on that this is the reason why it is so omnipresent today.

Functions of Profiles Concerning Orientation in Computer-based Media

In the remainder of this article, we conceptualise profiles as a specific form of knowledge to represent a certain object or a group of objects. Profiles are based on the idea that a formalised set of distinct features is able to represent and characterise nearly any kind of facts and things from the 'real world': material items, persons, institutions, etc. In this way, it can represent singular entities (like a certain person, e.g. 'John Q. Public') or larger groups of entities that share certain features (like white, middle class, male). Both levels are often interconnected, as the group profiles may be derived from the evaluation of a mass of individual profiles and the individual profiles may be constituted of the information to which different group profiles the person or the object belongs.

As profiles consist of a set of distinct features, they are per se formatted for being implemented and processed within computer based databases. At the same time, they are a historically developed medium for representing both objects and human beings. Therefore, they provide the means for the first requirement of facilitating orientation in computer based media: translating objects and users into a type of knowledge that is compatible to computer technology. The second requirement is to provide a way of establishing structures for organising this knowledge. Profiles do this in two kinds of ways.

First, by the distinct categories they are made of. If a profile is constituted by the items 'sex', 'income' and 'color of skin', for example, a specific (and in this case also very debatable) organisation of knowledge is being provided. Therefore, we can question any profile in terms of discursive inscriptions and power relations.

Second, an organising structure can be derived from the values that are being put into the given categories. The formalised structure allows to compare, evaluate, interpret, and relate values of different categories or identical categories in different individual profiles in order to produce clusters or rankings. As Mireille Hildebrandt (2008) points out, using data mining technologies can also produce new group profiles based on the combination of categories and values that appear to be significant:

"Once the process of data mining establishes the correlations two interrelated things happen: (1) a certain category is constituted (2) as having certain attributes. The category is usually called a group and the set of attributes is called the group's profile." (ibid., 20)

In both cases, the user subject and the objects he or she has to deal with can be located in the given structure of knowledge. Hence, also the third and last requirement for orientation within computer based media can be accomplished via profiles. So, we can heuristically summarise the *three basic functions of profiles* in terms of orientation like this:

1. Translating users and objects into formalised knowledge that is compatible to computer technology
2. Establishing a structure for organising knowledge by
   a. the categories that constitute the profiles
   b. the values within these categories that generate the basis for clustering, ranking and group profiles
3. Locating and navigating (that means orienting) users and objects within these structures of knowledge

But how is this abstract constellation implemented in everyday media products and practices?

EXEMPLARY CASE STUDIES: *AMAZON* AND *PARSHIP*

As mentioned above, *Amazon* distributes the largest number of various products to a range of customers that is highly heterogeneous. Hence, profiles are used to organise searching and recommendation systems for providing orientation on two levels. First, products have to have a distinct profile. They have a name, a description, a price, tags and up to five stars based on the user reviews, and are sorted into various categories.

Second, it is also necessary to profile the customers in order to implement a functional customer relationship management (CRM). By recording the history of purchases, the terms a customer has been using in queries, the duration of viewing a certain product page, the stars he or she gave a certain product, and the paths he or she used browsing the products, *Amazon* builds a comprehensive profile of each customer via the account and/or cookies. Thus, *Amazon* translates both products and customers into the formalised form of profiles and therefore makes them compatible to the computer technology (the first basic function). Through the selected categories, *Amazon* also provides a certain structure that organises the knowledge and makes the objects (products and customers) relatable and comparable to each other (this can be seen as basic function 2a).

Figure 2a + 2b: Recommendations in Amazon.

 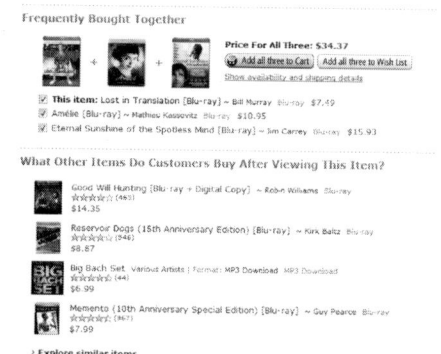

The profiles on the two levels are complementary and influence one another: The product is characterised by the profiles of the customers who search for it or buy it and by the profiles of the products these customers had a look at before and after that. The customer, on the other hand, is profiled by the products he or she searches for, buys and/or reviews or puts in his or her lists. Furthermore, profiles produce specific relations, clusters, and rankings on a more abstract level (basic function 2b). Based on this, products can be ranked by review ratings, popularity (which means sales), price or date of appearance, or browsed by categories such as books, blu rays etc. and genres like action, romantic comedy, and so on. The customer can now browse through the immense product range by using these structures and anchors for orientation that are based on profiles (function 3). But the central feature of *Amazon* that makes these structures operational and profitable is the recommendation system. Amongst other concepts it uses item-to-item collaborative filtering that "matches each of the user's purchased and rated items to similar items, then combines those similar items into a recommendation list" (Linden/Smith/York 2003, 78). When browsing the *Amazon* website, the user can orientate him- or herself with the help of those recommendations (fig. 2a + 2b). The profiles are not necessarily obvious, visible and explicit, but in any case they do facilitate orientation.

Parship, on the other hand, processes a vast amount of profiling practices explicitly at its very surface. There are several other online dating websites such as *eharmony.com*, *match.com*, or *zoosk*. They mainly function in similar ways. We will have a closer look at *Parship*, as it is the biggest German online dating website and available in 13 other European countries such as the UK and France. It went online in 2001 and it is estimated that there are about 10 million registered users (according to *wikipedia.org*).

In online dating, we are confronted with disorientation in a fundamental and very personalised way: How can I find the one that is waiting for me

Figure 3a +3b: A question from the personality test and a profile form in Parship.

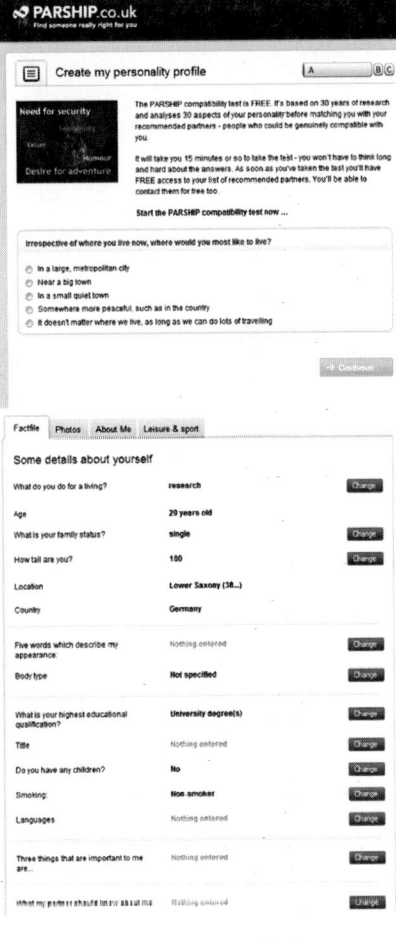

amongst 10 million users? And how will I be found? Thus, the three requirements to face disorientation in computer based media apply here as well: The users have to be translated into knowledge that is compatible to the database structure, there has to be a structure for organising this knowledge and there have to be mechanisms for locating each element within this structure. *Parship* implements these requirements mainly by two technologies: the profile and the matching algorithm.

So, how is the profile constructed? As Stefan Böhme (2012) already described, you have to do a multiple choice psycho test in the first instance. It is stressed on the website that it is a "scientific" personality and compatibility test (*parship.com*). It first tries to figure out your desires and imaginations of how life and a relationship should be according to you. There are questions about the place you would like to live (in) and about activities, ideologies, qualities, and behaviours in special situations of you or your imagined ideal partner (fig. 3a).

The second category of the test is about valuating different rather abstract figures or patterns. The test suggests that your intuitive choice helps to sharpen your personal profile. Do you like symmetry and centric arrangements or more dynamic and fuzzy ones? The third category lets you interpret and also valuate more concrete pictures or situations, for instance slipping on a banana skin.

After having answered these questions, you have to enter some hard facts concerning yourself (fig. 3b). Apart from numeric or categorical information such as age or body type you can also enter free texts describing your leisure activities for example. In this whole procedure you "split your life into categories, grade and order them and put your personality into lots of little boxes, namely the Parship database", as Stefan Böhme (ibid.) points out. Thus, your personality gets restructured according to the conditions of a profile (basic function 1), which allows *Parship* to implement the necessary searching and browsing tools, as well as the matching algorithm. The different categories of the profile generate a structure (function 2a) in which every single profile can be located (function 3). Hence, you can do queries with certain search-terms or just browse through the profiles based on the categories. But as there are so many potential partners available in *Parship*, the disorientation is at first multiplied. Usually, the search results in hundreds to thousands of potential partners. But as *Parship* promises, you will find "not just anyone, but the ONE".

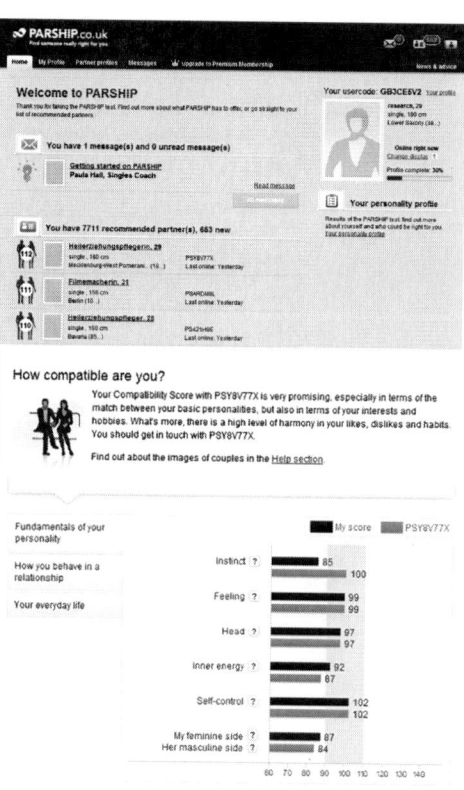

Figure 4a + 4b: Compatibility of profiles in Parship.

Parship therefore calculates with its (secret and also very scientific) matching algorithm which of the other members' profiles does fit yours to what degree. This culminates in a single value: the "compatibility level" that is used to rank promising partners (fig. 4a).

This compatibility score can be broken down to several smaller categories that are based on the profiles and visualised in statistical aesthetics (fig. 4b). Thus, the matching algorithm is a kind of filter that aims at locating and relating (function 3) the users within the knowledge-structure that is generated from the mass of information within the millions of profiles (function 2b).[1]

---

1 | In addition to the statistical diagrams, the potential of the profile combination is represented by an iconic image showing a couple in a spatial arrangement that gets closer, the higher the value is. By this rudimental narrative, representing a meeting scenery, an iconic reference to the ideas of romantic love is established. This kind of a clumsy try already shows that transforming the cultural concept of love by concepts

A Short History of Profiles as Formalised Knowledge

Although it seems pretty normal, even 'natural' to organise knowledge about things, ourselves, and others in this way, profiles, as we understand them today, have a certain history.

However, the most important quality of current profiles for translating persons and objects into computer-based media and thus for facilitating orientation is formalisation. It makes the translation storable and processable for computers. But when we take a look at the history and etymology of the word 'profile', formalisation does not play a role at all in the original context: "mid 17th century: from obsolete Italian *profilo*, from the verb *profilare*, from *pro-* 'forth' + *filare* 'to spin', formerly 'draw a line' (from Latin *filare*, from *filum* 'thread')" (*oxforddictionaries.com*). This kind of outlining was initially done in textile manufacturing but then found its way to other domains as the reductionist reproduction of an object from side-view (fig. 5a). In the 17th century the term was established in the domain of (mainly European) fortification architecture. In this discourse, it was transformed by the traditions of technical drawing and therefore by the ideas of measurement and formalisation. It took nearly 150 years until this concept of a profile was adapted by the physiognomic Johann Caspar Lavater (1968 [1776]) for formalising human beings by measuring their silhouettes (fig. 5b).[2]

Figure 5a + 5b: Adam Freitag's profile of a rampart (1631) and Lavater's silhouettes (1776).

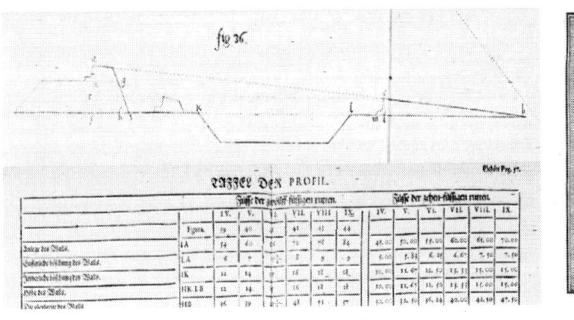

of risk management based on database structures and algorithms does not go without friction. See also Dombrowski 2011.

2 | The measurement of human bodies has a much older tradition, of course. Albrecht Dürer, for example, already measured humans for aesthetical reasons in the 15th century (see exemplarily Drach 2012 for this subject-matter; especially 39ff.). The shift that Lavater stands for is the one from aesthetics to an operational knowledge about character traits.

In reference to Michel Foucault's theory of discourse, this formalisation of human beings, their translation into a set of distinct items and values can be conceptualised as the emergence of a new object of knowledge (Foucault 2006 [1969], 44ff.). In our perspective, this is a very important epistemological shift without which the idea of profiles probably would not have made it into computer-based media. But before this, the concept of profiling was used and elaborated in different domains during the 19th and 20th century. The function was almost always a twofold one: On the one hand, personal profiles were used to identify one specific individual; on the other hand, group profiles were used to create categories the personal profiles could be sorted into (see e.g. Hildebrandt 2008, 20ff.; Ewen/Ewen 2009 [2006], 285ff). In the 19th century, for example, the Bertillonage was used to measure the body of criminals in order to identify and to recognise them in the case of being a repeat offender (Ewen/Ewen 2009 [2006], 299ff.). Each delinquent person was photographed *en profil* and *en face* and his or her limbs and body parts were measured and listed in a standardised form (fig. 6).

At the same time, categories were made out of these measurements and used to 'locate' the individuals within a lager system of classification. The formalised and standardised structure of the profiles made it possible to relate each profile to all the others and also to relate the single items to one another. By using the

Figure 6: Bertillonage of Sir Francis Galton.

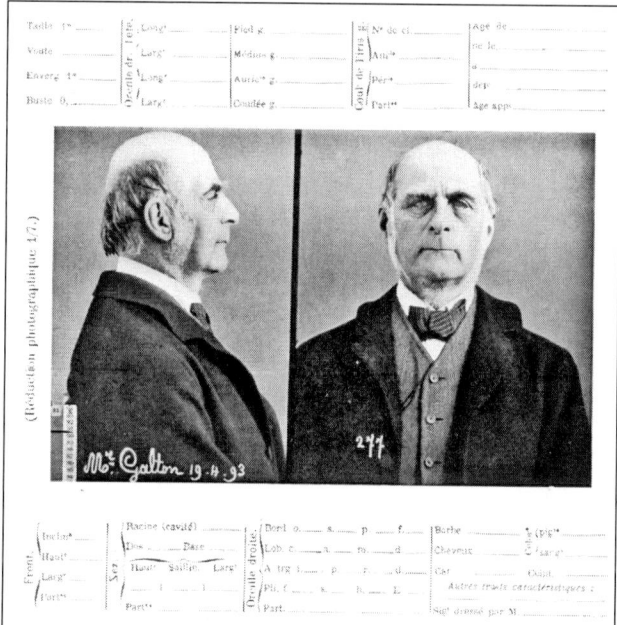

Figure 7a + 7b: Census form from 1890 and Hollerith punched card.

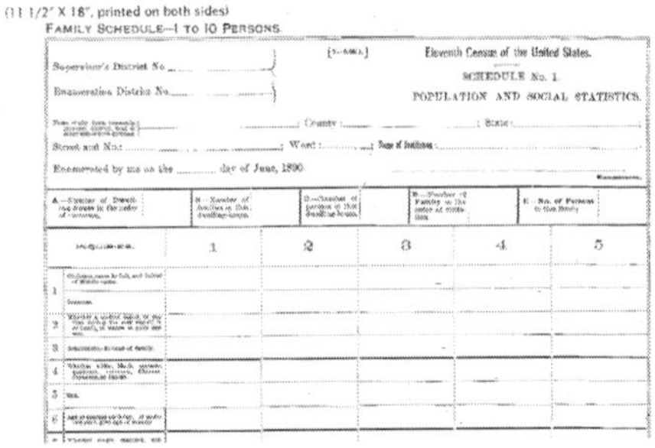

(11 1/2" X 18", printed on both sides)

FAMILY SCHEDULE—1 TO 10 PERSONS

Eleventh Census of the United States.

SCHEDULE No. 1.

POPULATION AND SOCIAL STATISTICS.

Supervisor's District No. ______

Enumeration District No. ______

County: ______ ; State: ______

Street and No.: ______ ; Ward: ______

Enumerated by me on the ______ day of June, 1890.

	1	2	3	4	5
1					
2					
3					
4					
5					
6					

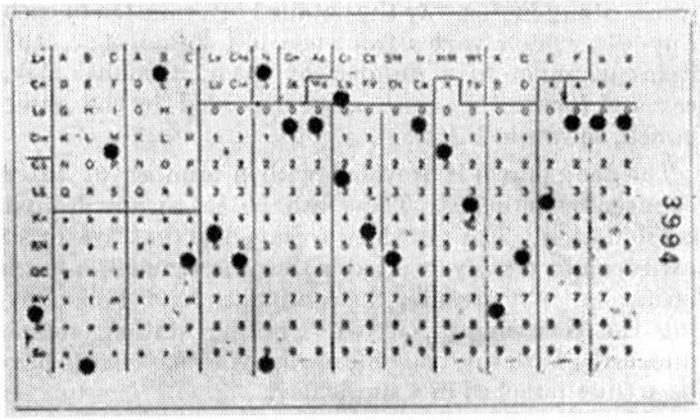

means of upcoming statistics, numerical evaluations of a multitude of profiles could be made for diagnostic and even prognostic purposes. In this process, certain values were used to construct different classes that were denoted with clear meanings and juristic and moral judgments. Caesare Lombroso, for instance, established categories like 'murderer' or 'homicide' on the basis of skull measurements (see e.g. Lombroso 1894 [1886], 138ff.). Another field in which the logic of profiles was (and even still is) used are anthropometric and psychometric testing practices. In the middle of the 19th century, Alfred Binet was one of the first to develop a test for measuring intelligence. In his tests he used a set of thirty standardised tasks to measure each individual and constructed classes out of all these formalised and comparable results (Funke 2006). In the late 19th century Francis Galton was one of the most prominent persons who started measuring people in terms of intelligence and other abilities at a large scale. For this, he also used standardised forms with distinct features to represent a person's qualities. This was the very informational infrastructure that provided the means for the terrible eugenics that cost so many lives of people that were 'sorted out' (Ewen/Ewen 2009 [2006], 336ff.).

One of the first and largest projects in this domain were the Army Mental Tests (see Yoakum/Yerkes 1920) in the first decades of the 20th century. Those were evaluations of the intellectual capabilities of US-Army recruits and soldiers. Various test forms had to be filled out and the results were then recorded in a personal file for each individual soldier. In this case, too, those individual profiles were used to do larger scale evaluations and to construct classes on this basis, in which the individuals could be located and sorted into. It is obvious that all these standardised information demanded a huge amount of administrative work. Each profile had to be stored, retrieved, and read out. A project which had to deal with quite similar problems was the American Census. It required standardised individual forms with items like name, sex, address etc. from hundreds of thousands of citizens that had to be administrated (fig. 7a). A revolutionary tool for handling this huge amount of profiles and data was Hollerith's punched card and tabulating machine that was first used in the American Census of 1880 (Beniger 1986, 411ff.) (fig. 7b).

They were able to make the formalised information readable for machines thereby making the evaluation much faster and more precise. These electro-mechanical machines were adopted in many other countries and domains (ibid., 416ff.) and can be seen as one of the milestones on the way to current database technologies. The crucial point for our argument is that the formalisation as a fundamental quality of profiles was highly compatible with this kind of technology. As each distinct item could be represented as a certain hole in a punched card, profiles could be stored and processed by machines now. Thus, the formalisation of profiles and the early computer technologies and databases constitute a functional combination that facilitated administrative orientation in a situation of information overflows and complex problems in management and controlling (see Gugerli 2007, Burkhardt 2012). It provided both a formal representation of objects (profile) that had been established during the former decades and centuries and a way of processing it automatically. Hence, we can say that the constellation of profiles and computer technology is no coincidence but a reaction to a certain urgency for orientation. Nevertheless, there is no unidirectional relation between both levels: A mass of profiles produces the need for administrative automation and simultaneously makes this automation possible in the first place.

Objects of Knowledge and the Matter of Genealogy

After this sketchy description of the genealogy of profiles, two short illustrative examples and some theses on the connection between profiles, computer based media, and (dis)orientation, we would like to go for a critical interpretation of these findings.

In all media, the concept of the profile is no 'innocent' and neutral carrier of information, but it informs and even constitutes all that is represented within its structure in a certain way. As Sybille Krämer points out: "Media do not simply carry messages but unfold an influential force that forms our modes of thinking, perceiving, remembering, and communicating" (Krämer 2008, 14; transl. A.W.).[3] In the case of the profile, this influence becomes manifest in the way it translates every object it represents into a formalised kind of knowledge. It conceptualises any 'content' as a set of distinct features—no matter if it is a human being or a fortification. In this perspective, the concept of the profile does

---

3 | Original citation: "Medien übertragen nicht einfach Botschaften, sondern entfalten eine Wirkkraft, welche die Modalitäten unseres Denkens, Wahrnehmens, Erinnerns und Kommunizierens prägt" (Krämer 1998, 14).

not only represent but also inform and constitute objects and subjects according to its specific conditions. In the light of discourse theory, we saw that this concept has a certain history and genealogy. As mentioned above, a crucial development in respect to today's computer based profiles was the establishing of the measurement of human beings as an object of knowledge on a discoursive level (as exemplarily shown in reference to Lavater's silhouettes). As Michel Foucault points out in *The Order of Things*, the human being becomes an epistemological double that knows and is known at the same time (Foucault 1974 [1966]; especially 367ff.). Thus, the concept of profiling is linked to the rise of what Foucault calls the "human sciences" (ibid., 413ff.). Hence, the profile in terms of formalised knowledge about human beings has been used in many of those emerging disciplines. As we saw above, it was implemented in early biometrics (e.g. Bertillonage, Galton, Lombroso), psychometrics (e.g. Army Mental Tests, IQ-Testing), and also administration and bureaucracy (e.g. Census, Taxes). Thus, we can say that based on Jürgen Link's theory of discourse the profile can be seen as an object of knowledge that was established in special-discourses. Those are discourses "that tend to a maximum of immanent consistency and to a corresponding closure against 'external' discourse-material based on the division of labor. The typical example are scientific discourses" (Link 1997, 50; transl. A.W.).[4] Furthermore, they try to eliminate polysemy and connotation (ibid.). This is also what profiles do in these contexts: They clearly denote a certain character(istic) or personality in form of a defined set of distinct items. These basic assumptions and specific types of knowledge that stem from the special-discourses are therefore inscribed into the concept of profiles itself. At the same time, it can be seen as a mediating concept that connects these different special-discourses with one another by being applicable in all of them. Although the discoursive practices and formations differ in all the mentioned disciplines, the idea of the profile can be applied in all of them with minor adjustments. Accordingly, it could be understood in terms of what Link conceptualises an inter-special-discoursive object of knowledge: "One can describe special-discoursive (denotative) discourse-elements that, though, can be applied within multiple special-discourses (like mathematical, but also experimental and/or technical instruments) as *inter-special-discoursive*" (ibid.; transl. A.W.).[5]

---

4 | Original citation: "[...]die zu einem Maximum an immanenter Konsistenz und zu entsprechender Abschließung gegen arbeitsteilig externes Diskursmaterial tendieren. Das typische Beispiel sind die wissenschaftlichen Diskurse" (Link 1997, 50).

5 | Original citation: "Als interspezialdiskursiv seien drittens spezialdiskursive (denotative) Diskurselemente bezeichnet, die aber dennoch (wie mathematische, aber auch experimentelle bzw. technische Instrumentarien) in mehreren Spezialdiskursen eingesetzt werden können" (ibid.).

What is most interesting in terms of our argument is the fact that the concept of the profile is established today within a multitude of everyday-discourses like shopping, dating, social networking or information retrieval. Hence, in Link's terms, the profile constitutes an "operative interconnection" with the common sense or the *"elementary discourse"* (ibid., 51; transl. A.W.).[6] Thus, when we take a look at today's popular profiles as in *Amazon, Parship* and also *Facebook, Google, Apple iTunes,* or even computer games, we can assume that they transport what Rolf F. Nohr described as "implicit knowledge" in respect to computer games (Nohr 2008, 1). That means that when we translate ourselves into profiles, we reproduce and internalise this implicit (and special-discursive) knowledge that is inherent in the concept itself, the fundamental assumptions it is based on, the modes of representation, articulation and constitution, and the meanings that are connected with it. As Siegfried Jäger points out we do adjust ourselves to this knowledge structures and partly even to the practices that are connected with it:

"Within the discourses there are so called application concepts for the formation/constitution of the subjects and their consciousness, and therefore also for their actions and doings." (Jäger 2004, 22; transl. A.W.)[7]

In reference to the genealogy of profiling sketched above, these concepts are heavily informed by things like scientific measurement and the idea of classifying. Thus, when the subject constitutes itself within a profile on the basis of this knowledge this might also impact its self-understanding, its actions and doings. This is even more likely as profiles have often been closely (sometimes inevitably) connected to the idea of an operational knowledge that leads to certain actions. They have been a foundation and also a legitimation for certain actions in various domains: arresting and punishing a criminal, being hired or fired in the army, special control in terms of tax return, or just buying things or dating people. Against this backdrop, one of the most crucial aspects is the transformation of profiling into an everyday practice. In criminology, the object of profiling was the delinquent, a person that was to be marked as abnormal, dangerous and in a way extraordinary. It was a mere object, that was analysed and judged by powerful institutions and according to powerful discourses that lead to consequences like therapy, punishment and/or exclusion. Whereas in former days profiles used to be created only of a minority of people, the vast majority of the western world has a variety of profiles today. Thus, the objects of profiling become more and more trivial and normal. One reason, and that is

---

6 | Original citation: "Operative Kopplung"; "Elementardiskurs" (ibid., 51).

7 | Original citation: "In den Diskursen liegen sog. Applikationsvorgaben für die Formierung/Konstituierung der Subjekte und von deren Bewusstsein und damit auch für ihre Tätigkeiten und ihr Handeln vor" (Jäger 2004, 22).

the thesis of this paper, is that the disorientation emerged from computer based media produced an urgency for the use of profiles. And as more and more of our everyday life is based on or at least influenced by computer based media, more and more profiles are being generated and applied. But we have to ask ourselves to which extent the application concepts and the forms of subjectivity this development provokes are desirable in so many fields of everyday life.

THE NEED FOR ORIENTATION VS. THE AFTERMATH OF PROFILES

Let us go back to the beginning of our considerations in order to summarise and to draw some conclusions. We stated that computer based media produce a quantitative and a qualitative disorientation. Profiles, that was our thesis, are capable of providing a translation into a kind of knowledge that is compatible with both the technological infrastructure and already established modes of representation. Hence, they can be seen as a remediation of a structure that had originally been established in special discourses like physiognomy, criminology, or psychometrics. In reference to Link, we conceptualised it as an inter-special-discursive object that recently established an operational interconnection with the elementary discourse within the computer based media culture. By transferring Nohr's theses of implicit knowledge within computer games into this larger domain, we can argue that popular profiles reproduce and mediate knowledge from special-discourses in everyday practices in the context of applications like *Amazon* or *Parship*. As media is never a neutral carrier of information but a means of constituting reality, we can assume that on a qualitative level profiles transform the existing domains we use them in according to their conditions. They provide new application concepts that might not be compatible to the established ones. They formalise and objectify the concept of the customer in Amazon, and the concept of the friend in *Facebook* or the searcher in *Google*. But the frictions become most evident when they question most personal and intimate concepts as romantic love in online dating like *Parship*, for example. As Julia Dombrowski pointed out in reference to profiles in online dating:

"The categories are a problematic fact for many online daters: The website members have doubts about the practice of categorisation on the one hand as they understand it as too much simplifying or ethically questionable. [...] On the other hand, some online daters have the opinion that they have certain ideas about a future partner that can be expressed in categories." (Dombrowski 2011, 102; transl. A.W.)[8]

---

8 | Original citation: "Die Kategorien stellen für viele Online-Dater einen problematischen Sachverhalt dar: Die Börsenmitglieder zweifeln auf der einen Seite an der Praxis des Kategorisierens, weil sie sie als zu stark vereinfachend oder ethisch be-

This shows both a certain discomfort about this transformation that comes along with the use of profiles and the increasing (maybe unavoidable) acceptance of it. In respect to our thesis, we could argue that the transformation itself is quite inevitable due to the need for orientation by profiles and that (in terms of Jäger) the application concept simply changes the constitution and the quality of the subject(s) of love.

On a quantitative level, we even have to face another problem. Within the logic of profiling, it is clear that the more detailed a profile is the better it facilitates orientation. If *Amazon* collects more and more information in more and more categories, that is our assumption, it can give more fitting recommendations and therefore also a better orientation. It could do even better, if it could combine its own customer profiles with those that a person created on different platforms like *Facebook*, *Google*, or *iTunes*. Of course, it is obvious that this is an open-end process that will never achieve the perfect profile. A profile is always a formalised reduction of a real-world object or subject, but it promises to enhance the benefit in terms of orientation. Hence, the improvement of orientation by using a more and more detailed profile is a promise that can never be fulfilled or accomplished.

Therefore, we have to ask ourselves in which domains and to what extent this development is desirable. This is a question of individual media usage as well as a question of discoursive negotiation at a larger scale. A debate that takes the considerations of this paper into account would probably lead to a more fundamental and thus more comprehensive discussion than the ones on privacy and surveillance that are being reproduced during the last decades.

Bibliography

Beniger, James R. (1986): *The Control Revolution. Technological and Economic Origins of the Information Society*. Cambridge/London: Harvard Univerity Press.
Böhme, Stefan (2012): Playing with Numbers: Games as Training in Numerical Practices. In: Ouellette, Marc A./Thompson, Jason C. (eds.): *The Game Culture Reader*. Newcastle: Cambrigde Scholars Press.
Böhme, Stefan/Nohr, Rolf F./Wiemer, Serjoscha (eds.) (2012): *Sortieren, Sammeln, Suchen, Spielen: Die Datenbank als mediale Praxis*. Münster: LIT-Verlag (Medien'Welten Vol. 18).
Bolter, Jay David/Grusin, Richard (2000): *Remediation: Understanding New Media*. Cambirdge (MA)/London: MIT Press.

---

denklich verstehen. [...] Andererseits sind manche Online-Dater der Ansicht, dass sie bestimmte Vorstellungen über einen zukünftigen Partner haben, die sich in Kategorien ausdrücken lassen" (Dombrowski 2011, 102).

Burkhardt, Markus (2012): Informationspotentiale: Vom Kommunizieren mit digitalen Datenbanken. In: Böhme/Nohr/Wiemer 2012, 55–74.

Dombrowski, Julia (2011): *Die Suche nach der Liebe im Netz: Eine Ethnographie des Online-Datings.* Bielefeld: transcript.

Drach, Ekkehard (2012): *Architektur und Geometrie: Zur Historizität formaler Ordnungssysteme.* Bielefeld: transcript.

Ewen, Elizabeth/Ewen, Stuart (2009 [2006]): *Typen und Stereotype: Die Geschichte des Vorurteils.* Berlin: Parthas Verlag.

Foucault, Michel (1974 [1966]): *Die Ordnung der Dinge: Eine Archäologie der Humanwissenschaften.* Frankfurt a. M.: Suhrkamp.

Foucault, Michel (2006 [1969]): *Archaeology of Knowledge.* London/New York: Routlegde.

Freitag, Adam (1631): *Architectura militaris nova et actua, oder Newe vermehrte Fortification.* Leyden: Elzeviers.

Funke, Joachim (2006): Alfred Binet (1857–1911) und der erste Intelligenztest der Welt. In: Lamberti, Georg (ed.): *Intelligenz auf dem Prüfstand: 100 Jahre Psychometrie.* Göttingen: Vandenhoeck und Ruprecht, 41–57.

Gugerli, David (2007): Die Welt als Datenbank: Zur Relation von Softwareentwicklung, Abfragetechnik und Deutungsautonomie. In: *Nach Feierabend: Zürcher Jahrbuch für Wissensgeschichte 3.* Zürich: Diaphanes, 11–36.

Hildebrandt, Mireille (2008): Defining Profiling: A New Type of Knowledge? In: Hildebrandt, Mireille/Gutwirth, Serge (eds.): *Profiling the European Citizen: Cross-Disciplinary Perspectives.* New York: Springer Verlag, 17–29.

Jäger, Siegfried (2004): *Kritische Diskursanalyse. Eine Einführung.* Münster: Edition Diss.

Krämer, Sybille (1998): *Medium, Computer, Realität: Wirklichkeitsvorstellungen und neue Medien.* Frankfurt a. M.: Suhrkamp.

Lavater, Johann Caspar (1968 [1776]): *Physiognomische Fragmente, zur Beförderung der Menschenkenntnis und Menschenliebe. Band 2.* Zürich: Orell Füssli Verlag.

Linden, Greg/Smith, Brent/York, Jeremy (2003): Amazon.com Recommendations: Item-to-Item Collaborative Filtering. In: *IEEE Internet Computing* Vol. 7/No. 1, 76–80.

Link, Jürgen (1997): *Versuch über den Normalismus: Wie Normalität produziert wird.* Opladen: Westdeutscher Verlag.

Lombroso, Cesare (1894 [1886]): *Der Verbrecher in anthropologischer, aerztlicher und juristischer Beziehung. Band 1.* Hamburg: Richter.

Nohr, Rolf F. (2008): Implizites Wissen. Vortrag im Rahmen der Jahrestagung der Gesellschaft für Medienwissenschaft "Was wissen Medien?" 2.–4. Oktober 2008, Institut für Medienwissenschaft, Ruhr-Universität Bochum. Web. Retrieved from: [http://www.gfmedienwissenschaft.de/gfm/webcontent/files/2008-abstracts/Panel_LudischesWissenGfM2008.pdf]; access: 2012/10/10.

Pearson, Karl (1924): *The Life, Letters, and Labors of Francis Galton*, Vol. 2 (Researches of Middle Life). Cambridge: Cambridge University Press. Web source: [http://galton.org/pearson/index.html]; access: 2012/10/10.
Sandkühler, Gunnar (2012): Die Datenbank als Karte: Zur Verwendung von Geo-Informationssystemen im Computerspiel. In: Böhme/Nohr/Wiemer 2012, 233–252.
Williams, Raymond (1990 [1974]): *Television: Technology and Cultural Form*. London: Routledge.
Yerkes, Robert Mearns/Yoakum, Clarence Stone (eds.) (1920): *Army Mental Tests*. New York: Holt.

Web Sources

Oxford Dictionaries: *Profile*. Web. Retrieved from: [http://oxforddictionaries.com/definition/profile?q=profile.com]; access: 2012/10/10.
Wikipedia: *Parship*. Web. Retrieved from: [http://de.wikipedia.org/wiki/Parship]; access: 2012/10/10.
Parship: *Über Parship*. Web. Retrieved from: [http://www.parship.de/ueber-parship.htm]; access: 2012/10/10.

Image Sources

Figure 1: Table taken from: ISO/EIC 7498-1 (1996 [1994]): *Information technology—Open Systems Interconnection—Basic Reference Model: The Basic Model*, 29 (Table 12 – Communication involving relay open systems). Web source: [http://standards.iso.org/ittf/PubliclyAvailableStandards/s020269_ISO_IEC_7498-1_1994(E).zip]; access: 2012/10/10.
Figure 2a + 2b: Screenshots from http://www.amazon.com; access: 2012/05/15.
Figure 3a + 3b: Screenshots from http://www.parship.co.uk; access: 2011/06/09.
Figure 4a + 4b: Screenshots from http://www.parship.co.uk; access: 2011/06/09.
Figure 5a: Freitag 1631, 31f./40f.
Figure 5b: Lavater 1776, 99.
Figure 6: Pearson 1924, between 382 and 383 (Ch. 13, plate LII). Retrieved from: [http://galton.org/pearson/vol2/new/ch13.pdf]; access: 2012/10/10.
Figure 7a: Detail taken from: U.S. Census Bureau (2002): *Measuring America. The Decennial Censuses From 1790 to 2000*, 22. Web source: [https://www.census.gov/prod/2002pubs/pol02marv.pdf]; access: 2012/10/10.
Figure 7b: Retrieved from [http://historio.researchlabs.ibm.com/system/attachments/18/original/open-uri20110930-5481-r7dm7n?1317414372]; access: 2012/10/10.

(Dis)Orienting Memory
Shoah Testimonies in the Virtual Archive

ALINA BOTHE

SHOAH TESTIMONIES AS (DIS)ORIENTED MEMORIES

Shoah memories are fragmented; they are non-linear narrations. Shoah memories are those of survivors who tell their personal traumatic stories about unsayable events. These memories fail language and language fails them. To listen, watch, or read a survivor's account of what happened can be a very emotional and disturbing experience. To be confronted with a survivor's testimony can be an experience that is orienting and disorienting at the same time. Orienting in an ethical way, "never again" as a premise, gets a face, a personal story. On the one hand, perceiving a survivor's testimony and taking responsibility for it is a political and ethical act through which recipients can gain a feeling of orientation. On the other hand, the history of the Shoah itself as the most senseless and brutal event in the history of mankind, the industrialised mass murder of six million human beings, is disorienting in itself. The memories of those who survived are incomplete, often there are gaps and blanks in the testimony when a survivor cannot remember or speak. Thus, perceiving a testimony as a narration leaves the recipient with a lot of questions, moments that were ungraspable or incomprehensible. Mentioned names and places that can no longer be found on any map. This is one way in which Shoah testimonies are disorienting. The other is their traumatic quality. According to Jörn Rüsen, "trauma destroys contingency" and therefore meaning in a narration (Rüsen 2001, 148). As Primo Levi wrote, there is neither a why nor an explanation to why the Shoah happened (Levi 2007, 31). Senselessness is part of meaning here. The absolute senselessness of the Shoah is disorienting as well.

Shoah testimonies can be found in a variety of media: written, oral, audiovisual, digital, and virtual testimonies can be distinguished (Bothe 2012a). This typology can of course be further differentiated. In this article virtual testimonies, which appeared for the first time about ten years ago, will be discussed. In the 1990s, the USC Shoah Foundation, founded by Steven Spielberg after completing SCHINDLER'S LIST (USA 1993), collected nearly 52,000 interviews with different groups of people involved in the Shoah or its aftermath, e.g. Jewish survivors, surviving Roma and Sinti, homosexuals, liberators, aid givers, people who took part in war crimes trials and so on. The vast majority of more than 48,000 of these interviews were conducted with Jewish survivors, who gave their testimony of the Shoah. Initially these interviews were taped in VHS format, afterwards they were digitised and catalogued in the virtual archive. In this process of mediation, *audiovisual testimonies* first became *digital testimonies* and then *virtual testimonies*. The term 'digital testimony' therefore describes mainly the technical aspects, while virtual testimony hints at a new quality of perceiving testimonies in the virtual sphere. So even though testimonies were first digitised and then transformed into virtual ones, they inherit both mediatic qualities at the same time. They are digital testimonies intended to be perceived as virtual testimonies.

The Shoah Foundation established the Visual History Archive (VHA) to store and share all these testimonies. When discussing (dis)orienting memories of the Shoah in terms of the Visual History Archive and virtual testimonies, we should consider two levels on which orientation and disorientation take place: firstly, the level of the testimonies themselves because of their ethical meaning and traumatic content and secondly, the level of the archive itself, because of its structure and possibilities. In this article I will take a look at both levels.

Based on its technicity and sheer quantity, the USC's VHA is paradigmatic for digital or virtual archives of the Shoah. This examination will be based on Homi Bhabha's concept of the 'space in-between' relating it to memory. In this way the article will show the VHA's orienting and disorienting aspects of memory and commemoration in their ambivalences. Linearity and fragmentarity will be discussed as corresponding poles to orientation and disorientation. Both poles will be reflected and related to the archive as well as to the mediatic specificity of the testimonies.

In a first step, the VHA will be introduced and the importance of testimonies for Shoah memory will be demonstrated. In the next step, the archive will be conceptualised as a virtual 'space in-between' of memory. Therefore it is necessary to discuss the theory of the 'space in-between' or 'third space' as well as the meaning of virtuality. To be able to describe and analyse the orienting and disorienting qualities of the VHA more deeply, the term ‚secondary dialogue' will be introduced as the mode of perceiving the virtual testimonies and as the central practice of commemoration in the virtual archive. After this framework has been developed theoretically and practically, the article will focus on orienting and disorienting parameters of memory in the archive.

THE VISUAL HISTORY ARCHIVE: A FEW REMARKS

After shooting and screening SCHINDLER'S LIST, Steven Spielberg and the Survivors of the Shoah Visual History Foundation, or Shoah Foundation for short, launched an enormous campaign. All over the world, they searched for survivors who were willing to give their testimonies. At the same time, they employed and trained volunteer interviewers. Interviewees and interviewers usually met at the house of the interviewee. A videographer accompanied the interviewer and taped the entire testimony, which was conducted loosely following a questionnaire developed by the Shoah Foundation. They talked to tens of thousands of survivors, and the project grew into the biggest oral and visual history collection to date. The Shoah Foundation owns the legal rights to all testimonies they collected and the survivors signed an agreement that allows the Shoah Foundation to use the testimonies in any way they deem fit.

"Consistent with these purposes, we may use the interview edited or unedited, by itself or combined with other interviews or with other materials, in any medium including literary, print, audio, audio-visual, computer-based or any other medium now known or created in the future." (USC Shoah Foundation 2007, 1)

The testimonies were given in 56 countries and in more than 30 languages. More than 19,000 interviews were taped in the US, more than 8,000 in Israel and 3,000 in the Ukraine. English is the main language of the archive: More than 25,000 testimonies are in English, 7,000 in Russian and 6,000 in Ivrit, modern Hebrew. The length of the interviews varies between 40 minutes and more than 17 hours, an average testimony lasts about two to three hours.

The entire set of testimonies is available only in a very few locations. Some thirty US-American universities and a handful of European institutions have full access. The Free University of Berlin was the first European institution to gain full access in 2006 and since then has been using the VHA for research and education.

In addition to the licensed VHA, the Shoah Foundation and the Dornsife Visual History Institute have developed further forms of usage of the testimonies. These include online exhibitions, educational curricula, the Foundation's own *YouTube* Channel, the educational platform *iWitness*, and the *Visual History Archive online*. On *YouTube*, *iWitness*, and the *Visual History Archive online*, users are able to access complete testimonies. Roughly 1,000 interviews out of the 52,000 conducted by the Shoah Foundation are available online. The other testimonies are only viewable at institutions which provide full access to the Visual History Archive.

It was on *YouTube* that users were first able to watch about 100 of the Foundation's testimonies online. But in the course of the past two years, a fundamental change took place: Until that time a mere 0.2 per cent of all testimonies had been available, which means that the number has increased tenfold. Judging from this trend on this development, one can assume that more and more testimonies will be available online.

The *VHA online* was launched in 2012. In essence, it is the search 'mask of the VHA, which is extremely complex and can simultaneously orientate and disorientate, as will be shown further on. Initially, the search mask was only accessible at places with full access to the VHA. Now it is possible for everyone (after registration) to search the sources of the *VHA online* and to watch about 1,000 of the interviews of the Shoah Foundation in full length. For the most part, these are testimonies given in English. For the rest, the keyword segmentation (as completed to date), biographical information, and, for some, a slide show is researchable. Segmentation means that for sequences of approximately one minute the content of the testimony is summarised in keywords. To give an example: In sequences 3 to 6 of his testimony, Abraham Brumberg (whose interview will be described in more detail below) speaks about his father's work and commitment to the Bund, the socialist or social democratic Jewish party of Eastern Europe[1], his anti-Zionist father's flight to Palestine, supported by the German Social Democrats, him being prosecuted in Poland as a socialist, his mother's migration to Palestine, himself being born in Palestine, and his parents' remigration to Poland, where they took up positions at the Medem-Sanatorium in Międzeszyn (Brumberg 1997) (see fig. 1). This short overview of a personal life story and the interconnected Eastern European, Western European, and Middle Eastern history of the 1920s and early 1930s can be quite disorienting without profound knowledge of these histories in themselves. The segmentation in the archive reveals, in keywords, just a glimpse of what Abraham Brumberg talks about in this four minutes from segment 3 to segment 6: "family histories", "Jozef Brumberg – fathers, biological" and "Lola Brumberg – mothers" are the recorded keywords (Brumberg 1997). Further information about the interview can be found in the biographical profile: It consists of a written questionnaire that interviewer and interviewee filled in while preparing the interview. It contains basic biographical data, date of birth, city and country of birth, questions about types of experiences during the Shoah (e.g. concentration camps, ghettos, flight from German occupied territories, or participation in the resistance), data about the interview, its archival code, its length, language, and

---

1 | The Bund, 'der yidishe arbeterbund in poyln un lite', was a socialist or social democratic Jewish party in Eastern Europe. It was founded 1897 and dissolved after the Shoah in 1949. Opposing Zionism, the Bund argued for its concept of 'doikeyt', which is yiddish for "being here", for "staying and living in Eastern Europe" (for further reading about the Bund, see Pickhan 2001, Blatman 2010, or the website *www.bundism.net)*.

Figure 1: Screenshot from the interview with Abraham Brumberg in the VHA online.

location. Another part of the deictic information contains the indexing terms in a testimony: a wide range of terms, based on an enormous thesaurus, which includes, for example, terms like 'Jewish identity', 'loved ones' deaths', or 'Warsaw'. The terms are linked to (almost) exact sequences in the testimony, during which the survivor talks about these topics. Abraham Brumberg, for example, talks about Warsaw in different passages of the interview, in segments 7, 39, 53, 76, 78, and 179. Further on, a list of names Brumberg introduces to the archive's user and their relation to himself (e.g. that Jozef Brumberg is his father or Marek Edelman is a friend of his) is available. The slide show presents a still of the interviewee and images, mostly photographs, pre- and post-Shoah, which the interviewee mentions during the interview. The biographical profile is available for review with all testimonies; for all other deictic information archival itemisation is necessary. This process is currently being undertaken.

The appearance of the new resource *VHA online* is identical to the original full VHA interface. The aesthetics of the archive make it appear calm, dignified, and reliable. Grey and white are the dominant colours. When the user exits the search mask and visits a testimony, the player is positioned in the centre of the screen and appears easy to operate. Surrounding the player, the deictic signs mentioned above are neatly arranged. Visually, the archive is very orienting for users.

A more general review of the archive and a description of its very complex indexing and cataloguing structure, which provides many new research options, will follow an analysis of the orienting and disorienting factors.

The VHA as a Virtual 'Space In-between'

While working with the VHA, it is worth noting that many users establish a distinct relationship with the survivors, they 'meet in there'. This phenomenon has been called a "virtual encounter"[2] by Aleida Assmann and Juliane Brauer (2011; transl. A.B.) and has been observed in different settings (Brauer/Wein 2010; Bothe/Lücke 2013). For a more precise analysis of the virtual encounter, this article conceptualises the VHA as a virtual 'space in-between', within which a secondary or 'as-if' dialogue between survivors and archive users emerges. This new kind of encounter is bound to the medium through which memory is transmitted. Shoah memory has always been connected to the medium through which it was transported, as James Young observed: "None of us coming to the Holocaust afterwards can know these events outside the ways they are passed down to us" (Young 1988, vii). Young noted that the knowledge about history as well as the remembrance of the Shoah is handed on or passed down in various ways. These ways have always been different and they have changed during the past decades, including books, memorials, exhibitions, and oral testimonies as well as films and even computer games. Digital media, whether the web or the virtual archive of the USC Shoah Foundation Institute, is now the strongest and fastest growing path along which the memory of Shoah survivors is passed down to us. It is based on the special source of testimonies about which an enormous amount of literature has been compiled to date (see Young 1988; LaCapra 1994; Hartman 1994; Baer 2000). Their essence can be represented as follows: A testimony, especially one of a survivor of the Shoah, is a narration in which an individual personally guarantees the truth of what he or she is telling. The survivor testifies traumatic experiences he or she has undergone, heard and seen in the past, and transmits these. A testimony can only become a testimony if at least one other person has read, listened, watched, or perceived what is remembered (Baer 2000, 16). Even during the destruction, during the Shoah, Jewish victims tried to give or leave their testimony of what happened, sometimes buried in the ground like the well-known Warsaw Ringelblum-Archive. Immediately after the Shoah, memories were written, oral accounts were given in front of historical commissions, and the first audio interviews with survivors were conducted by David Boder. In the 1970s, a new form of testimony was established: the video testimony. The team of the Fortunoff Archive at Yale Univer-

---

2 | Original citation: "virtuelle Begegnung" (Assmann/Brauer 2011, 97).

sity started taping survivors telling their story, until in the mid-1990s the USC Shoah Foundation undertook its global campaign for collecting videographed testimonies (for further information about the medial transformations of the virtual testimony, see Bothe 2012a).

Each medium shapes the way the content is perceived (McLuhan 2001; Krämer 1998 and 2007). Philosopher Sibylle Krämer uses the category of 'trace' to describe the connection between media and message: "The medium is not only the message, rather the trace of the medium is preserved with the message" (Krämer 1998, 81; transl. A.B.).[3] Thus it will be necessary to reflect on the 'trace' of the virtual sphere on Shoah testimonies, but first I will introduce the concept of the 'space in-between' or 'third space'.

Since the 1990s, researchers have been publishing works about the concept of the 'space in-between' or 'third space'. In the debates of the cultural and spatial 'turns', this concept is most often connected with Homi K. Bhabha (2007 [1994]) and Edward Soja (1996), but Hannah Arendt for example had already described the 'space in-between' as a space of intersubjective and intersocietal negotiations in *The Human Condition* (Arendt 2010 [1967], 222ff.). The more spatial interpretation of the 'third space', as articulated by Soja, is based on Michel Foucault's and Henri Lefebvre's works about heterotopia and the production of space.[4] In the current debates, the 'space in-between' was developed in Literary Studies in response to the postcolonial turn. Its aim is to establish the opening of binary dichotomies. 'Spaces in-between' are places of negotiation, where thinking of and experiencing something more, different, or new is possible.

"These ‚in-between' spaces provide the terrain for elaborating strategies of selfhood – singular or communal – that initiate new signs of identity, and innovative sites of collaboration, and contestation, in the act of defining the idea of society itself." (Bhabha 2010)

Therefore, it is a space of contact, communication, interaction, and agency. Bhabha points out that the 'space in-between' is "neither the one nor the other" (Bhabha 2007, 37) "but something else besides" (ibid., 41). For Edward Soja, the 'space in-between' enables one to take position of *"toujours l'Autre"* (Soja 2009, 52; original emphasis)

Additionally, the 'space in-between' is the place where individuals negotiate meaning, "we should remember that it is the ‚inter' [...] that carries the burden of meaning of culture" (Bhabha 2007, 56). By calling the 'space in-between' the

---

3 | Original citation: "Das Medium ist nicht einfach die Botschaft; vielmehr bewahrt sich an der Botschaft die Spur des Mediums" (Krämer 1998, 81).
4 | See as well Rolf F. Nohr's article in this book.

"living flux of meaning" (Bhabha 2009, x), Bhabha highlights that the production of meaning in the space in-between is unstable and in permanent processing.

The postcolonial migrant was originally the main character in Bhabha's 'spaces in-between', the exiled, the other, whose experience of liminality is not only a question of transference but of translation. This has been further developed by Bhabha. Following Emmanuel Levinas, he declares the witness to be the main agent of the third space: "[T]he third space as an interstitial moment in-between, [...] must now be understood as the site of the witness" (Bhabha 2010). In relation to Levinas, Bhabha's conclusion "the third then is the space of the witness" (ibid.) opens up the 'space-in-between' as the space where, according to James Young, the knowledge and memory of the Shoah is passed down to us.

Virtuality has been discussed from various points of view in the past years, but always in close relation to reality, even though both concepts have become more permeable. On the one hand, virtuality is defined as the entire process of shifting elements of everyday life, as well as research into the web, so that nearly everything gains a virtual sibling. On the other hand, a loss of substance is discussed: How real is a scanned document in an online archive compared to the original paper document in a physical archive? Is it the same, something different or new? A similar discussion centres on social media: Is a friendship maintained through social networks the same as an 'offline' friendship? The third aspect of the discussion is virtual reality. In this article, I consider virtuality as a new sphere, something new in the cultural realm, something that is just evolving, and can be understood as a challenging new layer to reality, or as its supplement. It is based on digitality, the translation of all information into a binary system using the digits of 0 and 1. Digitality enables a transmedial environment.

Virtuality is best described in terms of the following three aspects: intense immersion, interactivity, and immediacy. Intense immersion into the virtual sphere as an everyday experience is depicted by Nicholas Carr in *The Shallows*: "When we are online, we're often oblivious to everything else going on around us. The real world recedes as we process the flood of symbols and stimuli coming through our devices" (Carr 2011, 114). From the perspective of digital aesthetics Jay Bolter and Richard Grusin defined immersion in *Remediation* as: "A style of visual representation whose goal it is to make the viewer forget the presence of the medium and believe that he is in the presence of the objects of representation" (Bolter/Grusin 2000, 272). Interactivity as the second fundamental aspect of the virtual sphere highlights the fact that the virtual medium is not a classical one-way medium (like television, radio, books, or newspapers), but a two-way medium. Users do not only consume but are able to produce content themselves, e.g. by blogging, building websites, or interacting with other users on internet platforms. Moreover, they are not only interacting with other users but also with the technologies underlying the media. The third aspect of immediacy refers to the idiomatic reduction of time and space and can be described also as tele-presence or up-to-dateness. Technical progress intensifies immediacy. These three aspects are of course interwoven.

The virtual archive is first of all a space—the space of the archive. But it is an unstable space. There is only limited access to the archive, as it exists only as a database and on a screen. Thus, it is only virtually possible to enter the space of the archive; no real door is opened, no building entered. Even though the virtual archive-space cannot be entered physically, it is perceivable in reality and thus not unreal. To use Bhabha's (2007, 28) words, it is "neither the one, nor the other", neither real nor unreal, but enables "something else besides". Further on, as a 'space in-between' it is the space of the witness. This is obvious in the case of the VHA. Its users are intensely immersed in the testimonies, based on their content as well as their mediality. They interact with the archive as they search and browse it and take in the deictic information which is offered alongside each testimony. Immediacy has two levels: Firstly, on a technical level, it describes how fast testimonies are available and if they are perceivable without interruption. Secondly, immediacy refers to how testimonies given in the 1990s are transported in time and are perceived by users as contemporary.

In this virtual 'space in-between' the virtual encounter takes place. But how can it be described in more detail?

In the virtual encounter, the act of giving testimony is taken out of the original situation and is—in a certain way—performed again. The performative act of giving testimony took place when the testimonies were originally given and recorded. As Ulrich Baer pointed out, in order to become a testimony it is necessary that one person gives the testimony and at least one other person perceives it. This is the performative act repeated in the virtual archive. We can call this a secondary dialogue or as-if dialogue, as mentioned above. The survivor gives his or her testimony again in the virtual 'space in-between' and a user perceives it. This is made possible by the 'space in-between' which enables new forms of speech-acts, interactions, and, last but not least, communicating agents. Of course, there are natural limitations to virtual encounters: Archive users cannot directly respond to the speech-act of the survivors, but still there seems to be a close relationship. In view of this theoretical framework, questions of orientation and disorientation in a digital archive of Shoah testimonies become even more relevant.

ORIENTING AND DISORIENTING FACTORS OF MEMORY

In the following paragraphs I will be discussing some orienting and disorienting factors of memory in the VHA. This discussion will take place within the tension that emerges between linearity and fragmentation and with special attention to the secondary dialogue. It should be noted that orientation and disorientation tend to be quite ambiguous: Factors that seem orienting from one perspective might be disorienting from a different point of view.

Firstly, the search mask and its options will be discussed. Secondly, I will focus on three orienting and linearising elements. Afterwards, three disorienting factors of the archive will be presented.

Analysing the search mask as a tool to navigate through the archive, I will discuss ambigious tendencies. The archive offers four different search modes. The first one is the *Quick Search*, which is a free search through all the testimonies. The second is the *People Search*, which applies if the name of a survivor is known or which screens all testimonies in which a person is mentioned. The third search is the *Biographical Search by Experience Group*, which, for instance, allows the user to find all testimonies given by female survivors born in Vilna, Lithuania (former Poland), who relocated to the United States, gave their testimony in English, and were members of the Jewish resistance or the Polish or Lithuanian Partisans under the direction of Moscow (in this case, ten matching testimonies can be found). The fourth is the *Keyword Search*, which enables users to search with keywords included in the archive's thesaurus. The *Quick Search* and the *Biographical Search* results are full-length testimonies, the other searches call up segments.

The search mask can be used as a tool for gaining statistical information in the attempt to find orientation through the archive. Whether it is really helpful depends on one's expectations and search results. This will be demonstrated by the following example: A question about the strikingly asymmetrical gender distribution of Yiddish interviews led to hours of statistical research through the search mask. In general, 53.2 percent of those who gave their testimonies were women, 46.8 percent were men. This is different from the Yiddish-speaking testimonies, within the total number of 554 testimonies, 326 interviewees were male (58.2 percent) and 228 female (41.8 percent). In an attempt to account for this discrepancy, further statistical inquiry was undertaken. Is it possible to find an explanation by looking at the different countries where Yiddish testimonies have been recorded? This approach results in a range of insights (see fig. 2). Yiddish was once the vernacular of Jewish Eastern Europe, but almost none of the Yiddish interviews have been conducted in Eastern European countries. The majority took place in Canada, Israel, and the United States. In Israel, more interviews were held with female survivors, in Canada and the US male survivors were clearly the majority. Furthermore, it is noticeable that a relatively large number of Yiddish interviews (in relation to all interviews conducted in one country) was recorded in Belgium and Lithuania. In Lithuania 62 percent of the interviewees were female, in Belgium nearly three quarters were male. The percentage difference of male and female Yiddish-speaking interviewees in different countries in relation to the average gender distribution across all

Figure 2: Yiddish interviews in the VHA, diverse aspects.

Country of the interview	Interviews					Yiddish Interviews					
	total amount	with women		with men		total number in the country	in relation to the total of interviews in the country	with women		with men	
		total	%	total	%		%	total	%	total	%
Mexico	111	55	49,5	56	50,5	1	0,9	1	100	0	0
Russia	635	275	43,3	360	56,7	1	0,2	0	0	1	100
Poland	745	377	50,6	368	49,4	2	0,3	1	50	1	50
Brazil	562	271	48,2	291	51,8	2	0,4	0	0	2	100
Sweden	321	216	67,3	105	32,7	4	1,2	0	0	4	100
Ukraine	2846	1622	57,0	1224	43,0	5	0,2	2	40	3	60
France	1618	776	48,0	842	52,0	6	0,4	0	0	6	100
Germany	569	247	43,4	322	56,6	9	1,6	3	33,3	6	66,7
Argentina	723	393	54,4	330	45,6	12	1,7	5	41,7	7	48,3
Australia	2450	1322	54,0	1128	46,0	18	0,7	7	38,9	11	61,1
Lithuania	128	79	61,7	49	38,3	24	18,75	15	62,5	9	37,5
Belgium	196	79	40,3	117	59,7	27	13,8	7	25,9	20	74,1
Canada	2775	1339	48,3	1436	51,7	100	3,6	45	45	55	55
Israel	8427	4500	53,4	3926	46,6	117	1,4	64	54,7	53	45,2
U.S.	19263	10176	52,8	9078	47,2	226	1,8	78	34,5	148	65,5

interviews conducted in these countries does not explain the observed gender gap stated above. But it allows an insight into other, unexpected questions and raises new ones, for example about the significant gender gap in all interviews conducted in Sweden, where more than two thirds of the interviewees were female. In examining the gender distribution of Yiddish-speaking survivors based on the search marker 'country of birth', it emerges that nearly 40 percent of all interviews have been conducted with survivors born in Russia. 68 percent of Russian-born interviewees were male and nearly half of them gave their testimony in the US. However, more than one hundred Yiddish testimonies were conducted with Polish-born survivors, and 75 with survivors born in Austria-Hungary. Interviews with Polish-born survivors were distributed nearly balanced, with 46 percent with women and 54 with men. This differs from interviewees born in Austria-Hungary, of whom more than 70 percent were male. These further statistical investigations are linked to questions that must be asked about the course of the Shoah in different countries, where differences in the possibilities of survival between the genders can be stated. Again, taken by itself, this does not provide a sufficient explanation, but offers a possible lead. Looking at the diverse religious affiliations of the interviewees pre-war and post-war was not conclusive either. Ultimately this exercise provided a few hints that might be part of an explanation of the gender gap but it led also to interesting results and new questions that require further research. In short, it was orienting in providing some numerical data, but disorienting in that it hinted at many additional aspects worth taking into consideration at the same time.

The archive offers orientation in a variety of ways. The first aspect has proven effective when the testimonies were given with the questionnaire as the basis of the interviews. Even prior to that, most interviewers had conducted pre-interview talks with the survivors to prepare the testimony. The questionnaire's task was to structure the narrative of the survivor. It consists of questions about pre-war and post-war life, about the family of the survivor, camps and ghettos he or she might have been interned in, and so on. Survivors were expected to first talk about their pre-war life, then about persecution and survival, next about the life they rebuilt after liberation, and then to conclude with a message for the future. This is the ideally intended structure by the Shoah Foundation. Other witness history projects, like the aforementioned Fortunoff Archive in Yale, completely abandoned such a questionnaire and let the survivors tell their story using their own structure, time, and language. Without judging either concept, the differences have to be taken into consideration: The VHA testimonies deviate very much from their intended structure, which is not surprising with 48,000 interviews conducted by voluntary interviewers. It happens because survivors follow their own narration or because the dialogic interaction between interviewee and interviewer does not allow them to follow the questionnaire. Nevertheless, especially when perceiving more than one testimony, the questionnaire has an orienting quality. It constitutes a linearised traumatic, fragmented narration, but at the same time, it could be disorienting that many survivors tell their stories following the same pattern and not their own narrative structure. Sometimes, when interviewers stuck too closely to the questionnaire, the testimony, even if it did not fail completely, was not as successful as it might have been otherwise (as to the perception of interviewers see Bothe 2012b, 7). There are also examples where interviewer and interviewee jointly deviated from the strict script of the interview questionnaire, which is not disorienting but allows further insight. Normally, the testimonies were conducted at the home of the survivor. In his aforementioned testimony, Abraham Brumberg and his interviewer deviated from this procedure and conducted parts of the interview at the original site of the Medem Sanatorium outside Warsaw, where Brumberg spent parts of his childhood after his parents' remigration to Poland.

The second orienting aspect is the segmentation. As already described, this is part of the digitalisation and archival itemisation of the source collection. Currently, mainly the English, Spanish, and German testimonies have been thoroughly indexed. The segmentation functions as the secondary literature of the testimonies. It is possible to read it before, while, or after witnessing a testimony. This secondary literature is orienting both during critical perceiving and in researching the testimonies. Nevertheless, as this itemisation has been done by a standard procedure but manually, there are debatable interpretations and sometimes mistakes can be found in the secondary literature. To give an example: In reviewing Abraham Brumberg's testimony, the index as well as the segments list state that in segment 10 he is refering to the Bund, but in fact he is giving insights into the history of the Bund in segment 3 to 6 where he talks about his father's commitment to and activism for the Bund. Arguably, he is speaking more precisely about the Bund in segment 10 and following, but in viewing segment 10, an attentive user may recognise that he or she has already seen a reference to this topic.

The third orienting factor to be discussed can be labelled as 'deictic signs'. The process of itemisation did add further information to the testimonies, which may be difficult to comprehend by only listening to and watching the testimony itself. This pertains especially to names of persons and places. Names mentioned by the survivor in the testimony are often very difficult to understand. When the survivor does not spell out a name, it is sometimes impossible to be sure about its written form. Many survivors came from Eastern Europe. This is compounded by the fact that many first names are no longer used and that they were frequently written in different alphabets. A person's name, due to his or her personal migration history and the territorial political changes in Eastern Europe after World War One and later on, might be written in Latin, with some Polish letters, in Yiddish, the religious name in Hebrew (different from Yiddish), and in Russian. The deictic signs that encompass often more than one name and spelling for a person enhance orientation significantly. Moreover, nicknames like Abrasha for Abraham or *noms de guerre* are indexed. Thus, when looking for Antek through the *People Search*, one can find all testimonies in which Icchak Cukierman, Zionist commander of the Warsaw Ghetto Uprising, whose *nom de guerre* was Antek, is mentioned. This is definitely orienting. The same applies to places, which had many different names in different languages in Eastern Europe before 1945. For example, the capital of Lithuania was known as Wilna, Vilnius, Vilne and more emotionally yerushaliam de lite (Yerusalem of Lithuania). Of course, for small villages, this problem is even more relevant. Thus, the deictic signs initially allow users to understand some segments of the testimonies.

But what about the factors that hinder orientation in the archive? The first disorienting aspect is the thesaurus, already mentioned when the *Keyword Search* was explained. It contains the keywords that the USC Shoah Foundation used and still uses when segmenting and indexing the testimonies, and it also contains the definitions used by the Shoah Foundation for each keyword.[5] When a keyword is used in the segments, the definition appears as soon as the cursor is moved over the keyword in the secondary literature. Sometimes it includes, as shown with the definition for the Bund, quite a lot of information, too much to read while carefully witnessing a testimony. Although this is not disorienting in itself, it is, however, irritating that some keywords are missing altogether. One example will illustrate this: The aforementioned Medem Sanatorium was an important institution in pre-war Poland, where thousands of children from the Jewish working class spent months recovering from poverty and illness (Pickhan 2010). Abraham Brumberg describes it in detail in his testimony, which was even taped at the original site. But the Medem Sanatorium is not included in the keyword list of the VHA. Thus, missing keywords that cannot be searched as they are not included in the thesaurus are disorienting.

The second disorienting factor can be termed 'multiperspective memories'. When a keyword combination has been entered into the thesaurus, all segments matching these keywords are shown and can be viewed sequentially. For the keywords 'Warsaw Ghetto Uprising', segments from more than 500 testimonies can be found. In all these segments, testimony to the most famous act of Jewish resistance against the destruction is given. Naturally, what is remembered may vary from person to person. One person was close to the inner circle of the Jewish Fighting Organisation, another threw Molotov-Cocktails at the Germans. Perceiving all these testimonies about the Warsaw Ghetto Uprising makes it possible to develop a multiperspective narrative that incorporates different angles and viewpoints. Memories of one event multiply and become fragmented at the same instance; linearity is broken up. Some memories are even contradictory. When disorientation is thought of as being connected to fragmentation, multiperspective memories can be disorienting in a very productive way.

The third disorienting aspect can be called 'switching'. It describes what happens when a testimony is not perceived in its entirety but only in segments.

---

5 | See for example the keyword definition for the Bund which is—as many definitions—of very high quality: "The Algemeyner Yidisher Arbeter Bund (Lite, Polyn un Rusland) (General Jewish Workers' Union of Lithuania, Poland and Russia), or Bund, is a Jewish political party and social organization that stresses Yiddish culture, non-Zionist Jewish autonomy, and socialism. The Bund was founded in Russia in October 1897 at a secret meeting in Vilna. In 1914, an independent Bundist political party was established in Poland. The Polish Bund existed until 1948, when it was forced to disband by the communist powers. During World War II, the Bund was involved in numerous resistance activities. In the 1930s the Bund movement spread to the United States, where a World Coordinating Committee of Bundist and Affiliated Socialist Jewish Organizations were established in New York. This organization is affiliated with various Bundist movements around the world"(USC Shoah Foundation, Thesaurus).

This can take place when searching for keywords and viewing the more than 500 testimonies in which the Warsaw Ghetto Uprising is a topic. It can also be done in one testimony, when the index is used to locate only certain segments contained in it. It is not possible to witness all 500 testimonies when researching aspects of the Uprising, so switching is a necessary technique. But the question must be asked whether this is an appropriate way of dealing with personal, very private memories at all. By the act of switching, segments are decontextualised and testimonies are perceived in fragments. Switching can be an obstacle for the users' experience of immersing themselves in the secondary dialogue because the segments are too short to really involve the listener in the testimony. The secondary dialogue, like every other dialogue, can only take place, when the recipient is ready to listen. Thus, decontextualisation and uncritical perceiving are the disorienting results of switching.

Summary

More than 48,000 Shoah testimonies are stored in the VHA. This sheer mass is disorienting. How can one find anything in there? The interview with Abraham Brumberg was found by pure chance while looking for something completely different. Coincidence is an important marker of orientation in the VHA, the result can be both orienting and disorienting at the same time.

This article discussed orienting and disorienting factors of Shoah memories based on the VHA. It was the aim of this article to conceptualise the VHA as a virtual 'space in-between' and to show its importance by analysing the media-induced secondary dialogue into which users can be immersed in virtual encounters with survivors. Hopefully, the text drew attention to the argument that orienting and disorienting aspects can be very ambivalent, first on the level of assignment and second on the level of the effect.

Just as orientation is not only understood as a necessarily positive phenomenon, disorientation is not necessarily presented negatively. Linearising a Shoah testimony can also mean reducing the individualistic aspect of the narrative. Fragmentarisation, on the other hand, complies with the internal structure of traumatic memories and creates new insights.

Through its database and search mask, the Shoah Foundation tries to help users navigate and orientate themselves in the VHA. As the analysis above is intended to show, these tools have orienting and disorienting qualities. Thus, the search options allow users to find testimonies about one topic, but they also compel them to perceive these testimonies in segmented form, so that the secondary dialogue is disrupted.

Shoah memories are generally both, orienting and disorienting. The same applies to any attempt to make them accessible. Thus, this analysis is not intended as a judgement but as a reflection of the implications and consequences of (dis)orienting factors in virtual Shoah testimonies.

Bibliography

Arendt, Hannah (2010 [1967]): *Vita activa oder Vom tätigen Leben*. München: Piper.

Assmann, Aleida/Brauer, Juliane (2011): Bilder, Gefühle, Erwartungen. Über die emotionale Dimension von Gedenkstätten und den Umgang von Jugendlichen mit dem Holocaust. In: *Geschichte und Gesellschaft*, Vol. 37, No. 1, 72–103.

Baer, Ulrich (2000): Einleitung. In: Baer, Ulrich (ed.): *"Niemand zeugt für den Zeugen". Erinnerungskultur und historische Verantwortung nach der Shoah*. Frankfurt a. M.: Suhrkamp, 7–34.

Bhabha, Homi K. (2007): *The Location of Culture*. Reprinted. London: Routledge.

Bhabha, Homi K. (2009): Preface. In the Cave of Making: Thoughts on Third Space. In: Ikas, Karin Rosa/Wagner, Gerhard (eds.): *Communicating in the Third Space*. New York: Routledge, ix–xiv.

Bhabha, Homi K. (2010): *Our Neighbors, Ourselves: Contemporary Reflections on Survival*, Hegel-Lecture des Dahlem Humanities Centers der Freien Universität Berlin, 28.01.2010. Web. Retrieved from: [http://www.fu-berlin.de/sites/dhc/yAudiothek/Homi_Bhabha/audio_Homi_Bhabha/index.html]; access: 2012/10/10.

Blatman, Daniel (2010): Bund. *YIVO Encyclopedia of Jews in Eastern Europe*. Web. Retrieved from: [http://www.yivoencyclopedia.org/article.aspx/Bund]; access: 2012/10/10.

Bolter, Jay David/Grusin, Richard (2000): *Remediation. Understanding New Media*. Cambridge/London: MIT Press.

Bothe, Alina (2012a): Das digitale Zeugnis: Erinnerung an die Shoah in den digitalen Medien. In: Nünning, Ansgar et al. (eds.): *Narrative Genres im Internet: Theoretische Bezugsrahmen, Mediengattungstypologie und Funktionen*. Trier: Wissenschaftlicher Verlag Trier, 241–259.

Bothe, Alina (2012b): Im Zwischen der Erinnerung. Virtuelle Zeugnisse der Shoah in: *kunsttexte.de*, 1/2012. Web. Retrieved from: [http://edoc.hu-berlin.de/kunsttexte/2012-1/bothe-alina-6/PDF/bothe.pdf]; access: 2012/10/10.

Bothe, Alina/Lücke, Martin (2013/forthcoming): Im Dialog mit den Opfern: Shoah und Historisches Lernen mit virtuellen Zeugnissen. In: Gautschi, Peter/Zülsdorf-Kersting, Meik (eds.): *Die Shoa in Schule und Öffentlichkeit*.

Brauer, Juliane/Wein, Dorothee (2010): Historisches Lernen mit lebensgeschichtlichen Videointerviews. Beobachtungen aus der schulischen Praxis mit dem Visual History Archive. In: Stiftung Topografie des Terrors (ed.): *Gedenkstättenrundbrief* 153, 9–22. Web. Retrieved from: [http://www.gedenkstaettenforum.de/nc/gedenkstaetten-rundbrief/rundbrief/news/historisches_lernen_mit_lebensgeschichtlichen_videointerviews_beobach tungen_aus_der_schulischen_pr/]; access: 2012/10/10.

Brumberg, Abraham (1997): *Interview 43810, Visual History Archive. USC Shoah Foundation Institute* [1997]. Web. Retrieved from [http://vhaonline.usc.edu/]; access: 2012/10/10.

Carr, Nicholas (2010): *The Shallows. What the Internet is Doing to Our Brains.* New York/London: Norton.

Hartman, Geoffrey H. (ed.) (1994): *Holocaust Remembrance. The Shapes of Memory.* Oxford: Blackwell.

Krämer, Sybille (1998): Das Medium als Spur und Apparat. In: Krämer, Sybille (ed.): *Medien, Computer, Realität. Wirklichkeitsvorstellungen und Neue Medien.* Frankfurt a. M.: Suhrkamp, 73–94.

Krämer, Sybille (2007): Was also ist eine Spur? Und worin besteht ihre epistemologische Rolle? Eine Bestandsaufnahme. In: Krämer, Sybille/Kogge, Werner/Grube, Gernot (eds.): *Spur. Spuren lesen als Orientierungstechnik und Wissenskunst.* Frankfurt a. M.: Suhrkamp, 11–36.

LaCapra, Dominick (1994): *Representing the Holocaust. History, Theory, Trauma.* Ithaca/London: Cornell University Press.

Levi, Primo (2007): *Ist das ein Mensch? Ein autobiographischer Bericht.* München: dtv.

McLuhan, Marshall (2001): *Das Medium ist die Botschaft. ‚The Media is the Message'* (ed. and transl. by Baltes, Martin et al.). Dresden: Philo Fine Arts Verlag der Kunst (Fundus-Bücher, 154).

Pickhan, Gertrud (2001): *Gegen den Strom. Der Allgemeine Jüdische Arbeiterbund "Bund" in Polen 1918–1939.* Stuttgart/München: Deutsche Verlags-Anstalt.

Pickhan, Gertrud (2010): *Medem Sanatorium. YIVO Encyclopedia of Jews in Eastern Europe.* Web. Retrieved from: [http://www.yivoencyclopedia.org/article.aspx/Medem_Sanatorium]; access: 2012/10/10.

Rüsen, Jörn (2001): *Zerbrechende Zeit. Über den Sinn der Geschichte.* Köln: Böhlau.

Soja, Edward W. (1996): *Thirdspace. Journeys to Los Angeles and Other Real-and-Imagined Places.* Cambridge: Blackwell.

Soja, Edward W. (2009): Thirdspace: Toward a New Consciousness of Space and Spatiality. In: Ikas, Karin Rosa/Wagner, Gerhard (eds.): *Communicating in the Third Space.* New York: Routledge, 49–61.

USC Shoah Foundation Institute for Visual History and Education (2007): *Interviewee Release Agreement.* Web. Retrieved from: [http://www.vha.fu-berlin.de/media/pdf/vha_release_agreement.pdf]; access: 2012/10/10.

Young, James Edward (1988): *Writing and Rewriting the Holocaust. Narrative and the Consequences of Interpretation.* Bloomington: Indiana University Press.

Web Sources

Dornsife Visual History Institue. Web. Retrieved from: [http://dornsife.usc.edu/dornsife]; access: 2012/10/10.
Fortunoff Archive. Web. Retrieved from: [http://www.library.yale.edu/testimonies/]; access: 2012/10/10.
IWitness. Web. Retrieved from: [http://iwitness.usc.edu/SFI/]; access: 2012/10/10.
Visual History Archive at Freie Universität Berlin. Web. Retrieved from: [http://www.vha.fu-berlin.de/en/index.html] (English version) and [http://www.vha.fu-berlin.de/] (German Version); access: 2012/10/10.
Shoah Foundation YouTube Channel. Web. Retrieved from: [http://www.youtube.com/user/USCShoahFoundation]; access: 2012/10/10.
Visual History Archive Online. Web. Retrieved from: [http://vhaonline.usc.edu/login.aspx]; access: 2012/10/10.
Voices of the Holocaust (Boder-Archive). Web. Retrieved from: [http://voices.iit.edu/]; access: 2012/10/10.

Films

SCHINDLER'S LIST (USA 1993, Steven Spielberg)

Image Sources

Figure 1: USC Shoah Foundation. Screenshot from the interview with Abraham Brumberg in the VHA online. Retrieved from: [http://vhaonline.usc.edu/viewingPage.aspx?testimonyID=47208&returnIndex=0]; access: 2012/10/10.
Figure 2: Table by Alina Bothe.

Productive Aberrations

Go Play Outside!
Game Glitches

MARTIN SCHLESINGER

> "Flow cannot be understood without interruption or function without glitching. This is why glitch studies is necessary."
> Rosa Menkman – *Glitch Studies Manifesto*

GLITCH HAPPENS

Glitch[1]. Where the term originates from is uncertain. The dictionaries, which are trying to prove it etymologically, agree in that point. While it probably derives from the German word 'glitschen' and the Jewish word 'gletshn' (to slide or skid), *The Oxford Dictionary of Slang*, for example, dates the oldest evidence for its appearance on the year 1962 and describes glitch as "a sudden brief irregularity or malfunction of equipment, etc., originally especially in a spacecraft" (Ayto 1998, 418).

It is for sure that, besides astronautics, in the last decades glitches have been observed and described in different contexts and as phenomena of different visual and audible forms and formats. In one of her definitions Rosa Menkman notes: "Defining what a glitch is, if possible is even harder than defining noise. [...] It seems that over the past few years the word glitch has been demoted into a figure of speech, a metaphor for all kinds of accidents involving anything erroneous" (Menkman 2009).

In recent years some books and dissertations (e.g. Moradi 2004) discussed glitches of different media, and especially on the internet new websites presented theoretical, but above all practical work and diverse definitions. Right on the cover of his book *Glitch. The hidden impact of faulty software* (2011) Jeff Papows

---

1 | This article revisits and expands ideas that I have already discussed in the conference catalogue *Avanca | Cinema 2011*. Coordinated by Costa Valente, António/Capucho, Rita; Edições Cine-Clube de Avanca, 630-639.

promises the reader that he will learn how software glitches cause devastating economic and human losses and how these can be controlled and eliminated. Even Eric Lundquist, the book's foreword author, cherishes the hope for prevention and improvement in the software of the IT industry, of communication networks, of financial and governmental systems, since he argues that glitches are fatal: "Glitch might be too kind a word for too big a problem. In the technology industry, a glitch can be a simple, short, unnoticed interruption in a network connection or a file that gets saved in the wrong place. However, a glitch can also be as serious as life and death" (Papows 2011, vi).

Artists whose works live from the analysis of the aesthetics of breaks have to deal with less life-threatening problems. In 2008/2009 a few music videos came out, such as Chairlift's EVIDENT UTENSIL (Data Mosher 2009) and Kanye West's WELCOME TO HEARTBREAK (Nabil Elderkin 2009), in which glitches became an aesthetic principle. And also some video tutorials like HOW TO DATAMOSH (Data Mosher 2009) presented compression artifacts as reproducible effects. In the discussions about video works by David O'Reilly[2] people argued more about the extent to which in certain random or reproducible noise we actually do have to deal with glitches or can only speak of predictable filters. With the popularisation of certain artifacts at the same time artists such as O'Reilly distanced themselves from the simple reproduction of glitch methods, filters and design:

"My goal aesthetically has always been the more broader aim of simply not hiding the artefacts of software, the same way Bacon didn't hide paint strokes, that includes compression but about 1000 other things. It's not a big deal that it's now mainstream." (O'Reilly 2009)

Also in music controllable glitches made sure that a new aesthetic became heard and seen and could develop its own forms. In his book *Cracked media: The sound of malfunction* Caleb Kelly claims: "[T]he practice identified as 'glitch', which became popular in the late twentieth century, was a key marker in the development of digital arts practices" (Kelly 2009, 7).[3]

Whether dangerous or just art, at first sight and independently from specific media a glitch can be described as an interruption that produces visual or sonic effects. On the one hand, they can occur suddenly and unintentionally, but on the other hand, media can be manipulated and stimulated deliberately by terrorists (see Papows 2011, 39) or by artistic strategies in order to produce glitches. Therefore it seems that among the authors and artists who deal with glitches two directions exist: on the one hand, those who understand a glitch

---

2 | In 2009 David O'Reilly won the Golden Bear for best short film at the Berlinale with PLEASE SAY SOMETHING (2008).

3 | See also Cascone 2000.

as an anomaly within a shape or media that can be tracked down, understood, programmed and eliminated, so that e.g. a software finally works correctly or a video effect can be repeated; and on the other hand, those who understand a glitch as an interruption that opposes controllability. In the second case it must be clearly distinguished from a mere bug and described as an interference that cannot simply be manipulated or explained as an improvable error of a software. According to this, the real glitches that arise in a medium or in the interaction of media are not considered as purely aesthetic, but as transitory events that make a real difference. And so Rosa Menkman (2009) also distinguishes between "glitch art that emphasizes the processuality and glitch art that finds a point of gravitation in outcome or design".

Even though Rosa Menkman does not talk about games, I will firstly refer to her definition of the notion of glitch, before I consider that particular medium: the game glitches in computer and video games and, more accurately, its documentations. Especially in her *Glitch Studies Manifesto* (2009/2010/2011), Menkman presents a framework for further analyses and explicitly calls for glitch studies: "Study what is outside of knowledge, start with glitch studies. Glitch theory is what you can just get away with!" (Menkman 2009/10, 11). Such an "outside of knowledge" also plays an important role in the research on game glitches and the 'dark side' of games.

GLITCH STUDIES MANIFESTO

The Dutch artist and theorist Rosa Menkman is probably one of those who devoted themselves most intensely to the glitch, whereby the production of glitches in and between theory and practice is part of her conceptual programme. Referring to thinkers such as Michel Foucault she inscribes the glitch in a wider media theory and a history of dysfunction, and above all of the technical visual noise under digital conditions; in a theory that also without using the term glitch understands the noise of representation as part of the history of the technical and digital pictures and that detects errors and failures not as purely aesthetic phenomena, but as epistemologically important visualisations of the functioning of an image-generating medium. In doing so Menkman claims that glitches show gaps in knowledge that are beyond the purely theoretical description and always need to be explored in practical experiments. Here we won't further pursue this comprehensive history of the visual noise, such as in photography (see e.g. Geimer 2010), but it should resonate in the background when we study glitches.

On her website, the blog *Sunshine in my throat*, Rosa Menkman's *Glitch Studies Manifesto* is available in different versions, including a Power Point presentation, a ten-point version, and a revised eight-point version, which has been published in the *Video Vortex Reader II: moving images beyond YouTube* (2011). Besides minor changes, the two statements have not been deleted, but included in the other eight.

"1) The dominant, continuing search for a noiseless channel has been – and will always be – no more than a regrettable, ill-fated dogma.
2) Dispute the operating templates of creative practice; fight genres, interfaces and expectations!
3) Get away from the established action scripts and join the avant-garde of the unknown. Become a nomad of noise artifacts!
4) Employ bends and breaks as a metaphor for différance. Use the glitch as an exoskeleton for progress.
5) Realize that the gospel of glitch art also reveals new standards implemented by corruption.
6) Force the audience to voyage the acousmatic videoscape.
7) Rejoice in the critical trans-media aesthetics of glitch artifacts.
8) Employ Glitchspeak (as opposed to Newspeak) and study what is outside of knowledge. Glitch theory is what you can just get away with!" (Menkman 2011, 346)

In her first claim Menkman makes a stand against such statements made by Jeff Papows, promising that glitch-free media, protocols, hardware or software could be created. The followers of such a belief in progress she calls "the naive victims of a persistent upgrade culture" (ibid., 339), which are constantly searching for the Holy Grail of perfection. Clearly she expresses her wish for imperfection and calls for art against fashion and the monopolisation of aesthetics that try to domesticate glitches through software, filters, or plug-ins. Referring to Marshall McLuhan's concept of "hot" and "cool" media (McLuhan 1964, 22), she distinguishes between "hot" and "cool" glitches: between forms that, on the one hand, function as design and as final products and do not require the active participation of recipients; and, on the other hand, those glitches that are the products of an avant-garde and that are constantly in motion and reveal opportunities for personal and active construction of meaning beyond conventions (Menkman 2011, 340ff.). Only in "cool" glitches Menkman sees a possibility for freedom and for a technological democracy, and it is the artist's challenge to discover new forms in the uncertain noise of an old, disintegrating constellation. Therefore the generation of glitches is an artistic practice, action and strategy, and the noise artist and nomad of artifacts can use three opportunities to explore the noise. These chances Menkman mentions in statement three of her manifesto: "during encoding-decoding (compression); feedback; or when a glitch (an unexpected break within the flow of technology) occurs" (ibid., 346).

Despite the artistic engagement, the manipulations between encoding and decoding, and besides the feedback, the glitch is something sudden and unexpected, which implicates the hope for something new. According to her definition, a glitch is independently from a particular medium an experience that produces a difference between a familiar, conventional, known form and a new, unnamed one. These changes can lead to technological, political, economic consequences. By definition, a real glitch is temporary, processual, ephemeral, and cannot be controlled. And so it is a punctual phenomenon, an in-between and in a certain way a thing without definition: "But once the glitch is named, the momentum – the glitch – is gone... and in front of my eyes suddenly a new form has emerged" (ibid., 341). And so even the talking about glitches, "Glitchspeak" (ibid., 344) and glitch studies should always reflect the other side of thinking, excluded by theories and discourses. Thus, glitch studies should continuously lead to new formulations: "Glitch studies is a misplaced truth; it is a vision that destroys itself by its own choice of and for oblivion. The best ideas are dangerous because they generate awareness" (ibid., 345).

The presentation of fractures and the revealing of the inner working of a medium by cool glitches Menkman does not euphorically describe as a possibility for a media revolution, but as critical media awareness. From her point of view glitch artifacts lead to "critical trans-media aesthetics" (ibid., 343). On the one hand, they enable us to perceive a ruined medium, in an unexpected state, from which something new can arise, and on the other hand, these aesthetics would reflect and criticise media genres, interfaces and user expectations. To what extent, however, even a real, cool glitch really can break and transform a medium and not merely formal possibilities inside a medium, that has to be discussed in more detail.[4]

Besides the call for artistic glitch production, it is exciting that these unexpected glitches seem to be independent media events which can only be experienced, observed and described by producers, users and recipients; which eventually can be used, but not controlled by them. Apart from the artistic challenge there exists a utopian dream and the hope that in the confrontation of unusual protocols and programmes, media themselves draw attention to their other sites and to new forms not created merely by artists and programmers, but generated independently by actions and perhaps the thinking of images and sounds.

---

4 | See e.g. Niklas Luhmann (1996, 83): "The difference between meaning and world is formed for this process of the continual self-determination of meaning as the difference between order and perturbation, between information and noise. [...] A preference for meaning over world, for order over perturbation, for information over noise is only a preference. It does not enable one to dispense with the contrary". With Luhmann glitch art probably would be an experimental game with forms which are invisible but always possible, however, the playing with forms never arrives at 'matter'. Not the medium is changing, but its forms (Luhmann 2000, 118).

The Cinema of Game Glitch Attractions

It is undoubtful that in the last years new digital aesthetics emerged that until today have only been sparsely theorised. Digital, compressed, moving and partly moving, coded video images involve a new visual syntax that could be called "post-photogrammatic" (Thomas Y. Levin 2011)[5]; a new visibility of the technological scenery, of a coded background of images and sounds; aesthetics of compression artefacts, glitch art or datamoshing that implicate new differences between moving and still elements and between the viewing of colour and shape (see Holl 2009, 72ff.). Besides the question of the revolutionary impact of glitches and their importance for media theory, historiography, or for our understanding of states and structures of technology, and besides possible doubts if glitches really make a difference, it is for sure that in different media glitches produce images never seen before.

A simple fact that applies not only for game glitches, but for all the glitch videos available on the internet, is that their temporary and ephemeral forms are made visible via videos. The documentation of noise such as image noise produces images of noise, and particularly video images which are circulating on video sharing websites. That is, the glitches are, even if they are transitory, presented in a captured, filmic form through which the breaks can be observed under new conditions. We need different media in order to perceive and remediate the randomness, the noise and interferences. Glitch videos are, no matter what media, always a genre and on the internet they are left to endless repetitions. In search for game glitches we come across websites like *Gamerglitch.com* or *Glitchblog.com*. These websites mainly present videos that were uploaded on *YouTube* and that share different types of glitches.

Referring to Wey-Han Tan (2010) such a use of video and computer games can be defined as "second order gaming", that is as a playful strategy and to some extent also as an educational or instructional intention to show the borders and hidden possibilities of a game and a medium in the sense of Rosa Menkman.

According to Aldo Tolino and his dissertation *Gaming 2.0 – Computer Games and Cultural Production* (2008), in his taxonomy of "ludic artifacts" these documentaries can be classified under different categories as user-generated content. In this categorisation, Tolino notes the activities that can be developed by users beyond a game and its rules. The exploration, production, and the release of game glitch videos bring with it new competition, other ways of expression, performance opportunities, and a new community for gamers and glitchers. In game glitch videos, the exploration of the unknown, the break and the curiosi-

---

[5] | See the video of the lecture held by Thomas Y. Levin: Datamoshing as Syntactic Form. Reading Digital Video Compression Algorithm Hacking.

ties are presented as a gaming experience of its own, which makes the 'normal' primary goal of a game a minor matter. The gamers generate unseen images and show them to a community, which is not necessarily the same network of a game. By breaking the boundaries of a game, gamers create new aesthetical value and new vocabulary that distinguishes between different types of glitches. Thus, for example on *Glitchblog.com* the link 'glitchwords' offers a list with probably all kinds of game glitches—and I would like to mention just a few:

"*clipping* (n) - when a player passes through geometry or textures in a game environment
crash (n) - when a game freezes or ceases to run as intended; a game-ending glitch
exploration (n) the act of travelling outside of the normal bounds of a game environment
game-ending glitch (n) - a glitch that forces the player to restart their game console, prevents normal progress, or forces a player to load a prior game save to continue progress
OoB (adj) - out of bounds; the condition of being outside of the normal bounds of the game environment
out of the level (n) - the condition of being outside of the normal bounds of the game environment
under the level (n) - the condition of having fallen beneath the normal bounds of the game environment; sometimes referred to as 'falling through the map'"
(http://glitchblog.com/glitchwords)

Here, we can distinguish between positive, neutral, and negative glitches. Glitches that can help a gamer to gain advantages or to reach a game's target perhaps easier or faster; glitches that have no influence on the gameplay, but lead to another experience inside or outside a game's world, for instance an exploration that causes no advantage; and glitches that produce unexpected effects and can bring a game to an undesired end, crash, and restart. What they look like depends, above all, on the kind of game environment they are happening in, whether it is a 2D or 3D game, an action game such as an Ego-Shooter or a Jump'n'Run.

The glitches that are mostly recorded with capture cards, but also with handheld video cameras, differ in their sophistication. Some of them, produced by regular and 'professional' glitchers and glitch teams, often do not just show long takes and a single shot from a character's perspective, but they are edited with music, credits, and titles, voice over, or inserts, which sometimes even show controller and button combinations in order to instruct how glitches can be achieved. Some videos are clearly made as tutorials for communities, such as the videos of *TeamLAG*—"Life's a glitch"—who urge to comment and upload new versions of glitches.[6] Other gamers document their findings without much effort and drown in the masses of *YouTube* videos, staging themselves without their own website and without logos, such as *Machinima.com*.

When glitches are recorded, edited, uploaded, and embedded on websites, they are, that is obvious, no longer part of a game. And gamers who e.g. create tutorials are not only gamers, but they become film-makers, and especially in the case of handheld video cameras they do not just document the game, but also their own gaming, and at the same time, they document more or less consciously their own documentation. Even if the videos are not explicitly intended as tutorials, the gesture of showing is visible in all the glitch videos. Even if indirectly, all the videos stimulate experimental gaming and new glitch videos. But besides this tutorial aspect, we can generally ask what kinds of videos are produced in the transition from game to video and to the internet. Unlike most machinima videos the glitch videos do not tell any stories. They build no narration, but show, on the one hand, ways through which glitches can be achieved, and, on the other hand, the aesthetic impact of glitches; unusual images that—and that is often said in the *TeamLAG* videos—just should be enjoyed. Often they are less about awareness and more about the beauty of disorder, the wish to disorient the protocols of a game and to create exceptional images that have also found a place in art galleries, such as the still images of the game glitch photographer Robert Overweg.[7]

When Teresa Rizzo discusses Tom Gunnings famous text on *The Cinema of Attractions* (Gunning 2000), she argues that "[t]oday many of the clips on video-sharing sites like *YouTube* bear a remarkable similarity to these early films. They also address the audience directly, are exhibitionist and are frequently sensational and shocking" (Rizzo 2008). While she doesn't explicitly talk about glitch videos, they also fit her description.

Gunning, in his analysis of early film before 1906 and prior to a period of 'narrativisation' from 1907 to 1913, observes a cinema that is more interested in exoticism and in exhibitionism than in voyeurism and storytelling. This avant-garde cinema is about the spectacle of opening the filmic space. Instead of self-enclosed fictional worlds, its films value the presentation of different perspectives, which includes the look at the camera by actors, establishing contact with the audience. The fictional world of the film is ruptured for a chance to solicit the attention of the audience and to show the spectator the new possibilities of cinema—and above all, the possibility of showing. Besides the moving image on the screen, the technical conditions of the cinematic apparatus and its tricks are a spectacle. As in Eisenstein's concept of the attractions, these early films play with moments of irritation, shock and surprise in a dialogue between

---

6 | See TeamLAG's *YouTube* channel under [www.youtube.com/user/TeamLAG].
7 | See Robert Overweg: *glitches* [http://www.shotbyrobert.com/?page_id=191].

the moving image and the masses. Instead of a diegesis these films highlight incoherent, illogical attractions, in order to stimulate the engagement of the new masses of cinema. The roots of this "cinema of attractions", Gunning adds, can be found in amusement parks, and it exists until today in recent spectacle cinema, that always presents its latest effects and newest upgrades.

Certainly, these characteristics of the "cinema of attractions" can easily be found in game glitch videos. They are not narrative, but present surprising effects, addressing the gamers and spectators and showing them the constructedness of games. Another common feature is the up-to-dateness, which can be found in early actuality and non-fiction films and also in the game documentaries. It is always a challenge for gamers and glitchers, not just to walk through the games as fast as possible, but with every new game the search for unseen glitches and more attractive attractions becomes a new contest.

Teresa Rizzo emphasises that the possibilities of media practices related to *YouTube* not only expand the concept of the 'cinema of attractions', but create unique media-specific forms: *YouTube* attractions. And she describes three special kinds: firstly, videos that show trains and railway lines, secondly, dance videos, and thirdly, remediation videos. And the concept of remediation, as described by Jay David Bolter and Richard Grusin in their book *Remediation: Understanding New Media* (2000), seems to be a useful approach, when we understand remediation as a meaningful interaction between media such as film, computer or video game, and the internet, and as a process of appropriation and transformation of different forms in various media. For Teresa Rizzo remediation is central to the aesthetics and experience of the attractions on video-sharing sites like *YouTube*: "Remediation is a way of showing off the force of the medium" (Rizzo 2008). Thus we can understand Menkman's "critical transmedia aesthetics" not only as a glitch producing interaction of different media, but as a communication that transfers and translates them into the language of other media, changing and pushing the glitches to further critical insights. This movement into other spatial environments and media arrangements therefore happens at different levels. And each layer can be seen as uncharted territory for the production of new attractions and for new experiments to break the borders of a limited gameplay and of common playing fields of media.

A Game Space Odyssey: Acousmatic Videoscapes

In the film GAMER (USA 2009, Mark Neveldine/Brian Taylor) the mind-controlled protagonist John Tillman alias Kabel has to fight himself through levels of a violent real multi-player online shooter called 'Slayers'. In order to gain his freedom, Kabel and his gamer Simon have to shoot their way out of the game's boundaries to reach the outside world where Kabel can kill the evil game creator Ken Castle. There are different forms of those breakout or jailbreak films, in which protagonists are trapped in virtual or game worlds and have to find their way back to the more or less real outside world; and of course, there are the films without playing fields, in which characters travel between different media and end up in books, films, or in television programmes: THE MATRIX (USA 1999, The Wachowski Brothers), THE PURPLE ROSE OF CAIRO (USA 1985, Woody Allen) or VIRTUOSITY (USA 1995, Brett Leonard)—or, probably the most popular video game film, TRON (USA 1982, Steven Lisberger)[8]—just to mention a few.

Computer games are not normally designed for those breakouts and gamers are not intended to reach the outside of the bounds of the game environment. But in a 'real' gameplay the glitches might be traces of this cinematic and perhaps even transmedial desire to break free from real or virtual limits. The breaks and the production of 'different' images can not always be observed in such concrete aesthetic attractions as shown in game glitch videos. In her video RADIO DADA (2008) Rosa Menkman created a loop "out of nothing but the image that feedback created".[9] This non-narrative, transmedia work with abstract attractions of feedback and the interferences of radio frequencies Menkman mentions in point six of her manifesto, when she postulates an education of the audience or at least a necessary mediation of these images: "Force the audience to voyage the acousmatic videoscape". The images that arise from the repetitive self-perception of a camera let us perceive an outside of media and signals, that cannot be attributed to anything specific. Menkman: "The glitches in RADIO DADA create an acousmatic videoscape in which I can finally perceive an output outside of my goggles of speed, transparency and usability" (Menkman 2011, 343). Referring to RADIO DADA Menkman demands that by showing "acousmatic videoscapes" the audience should be forced to see, interpret, and understand the inner working of a medium and the possibility of new structures: "The new structures that unfold themselves can be interpreted as a portal to a utopia, a paradise-like dimension, but also as a black hole that threatens to destroy the technology as I knew it" (ibid.).

In Menkman's concept the "acousmatic videoscape" is not merely an acoustic event, but it should be understood as a visual phenomenon. According to Pierre Schaeffer (1966), to whom she refers, and also according to Michel Chion (1994, 71ff.) acousmatic sounds are those sounds whose sources (and Schaeffer refers to Pythagoras) are hidden behind a curtain, that is, that they are not visible—hidden behind a speaker or sounds that are recorded and played from tape or a CD. In the case of images, acousmatic images could be those images

---

8 | A film that recently got the sequel TRON: LEGACY (USA 2010, Joseph Kosinski) and has thus been continued under contemporary media conditions and with brand new 3D attractions.

9 | See Menkman's video description on her Weblog (Menkman 2008).

and their recordings, whose sources are uncertain and from which we do not know where they come from or if they are mere synthetic products without source. In the feedback of Menkman's video, in which the image gets stuck in its self-observation, we can also perceive the gesture of showing the possibility of showing the perception of perception. But without knowing the technical arrangements of RADIO DADA, this experience remains a visual one, and—if we do not describe every recorded image as 'acousmatic'—it is unclear, which of these images are hidden or revealed. Without knowing the production conditions, we cannot distinguish between inside and outside, between interior and exterior or between the inner world of a medium and another world behind a curtain. There is no chance for discrimination.

The term of 'acousmatic sound' has already been discussed in order to explain image and sound relations in games (see e.g. Stockenburger 2006, 191ff.). But how could we use Menkman's idea of the "acousmatic videoscape" and of visual "acousmatic events" in order to analyse the other side of games and the documentations of game glitches? In cinematic contexts the term has been developed and applied most prominently by Michel Chion when describing relations between images and sounds. But to what extent can we talk about paradise-like dimensions or black holes when we analyse the spaces of game glitches and the filmic spaces of their documentations, adopting Chion's concept of "acousmatic zones" (Chion 1994, 66ff.)?

Chion distinguishes between three separate zones where sound may come from in a film (ibid.)—the "visualized zone" and two "acousmatic zones": first, the sound within the image field, the 'onscreen sound' with a visible source; second, the sound in the 'hors-champ', the 'offscreen sound' outside the image field, i.e. the source is not visible, but it could appear in the image at any time; and third, the sound that comes from the nondiegetic zone, for example a film's soundtrack. In the "visualized zone" the visible and the audible meet, while the "acousmatic zones" remain invisible. When there are transitions between these three boundaries, it is important to recognise the relationship between what we see and what we hear. Only on the basis of the images we can say when sounds are visualised and when they are "acousmatic" (Chion 2003, 127). This spatial distinction is important in order to be able to identify acousmatic events at all. When we apply it on Menkman's concept of "acousmatic landscapes" and on games, then it could be possible that we have to deal with images that originate from visual offscreen or nondiegetic zones that have nothing in common with the images of a game. But how do they become visible?

What is striking is that Chion describes that there exist filmic characters which are able to travel between the 'visualized' and the 'acousmatic zones'. Since the invention of sound film, Chion argues, acousmatic presences can emerge who exist as mere voices without visual bodies in the images, who are not yet visualised and only move within the "acousmatic zone". Such an acousmatic presence that exists only as a voice, Chion calls "acousmêtre" (ibid., 128), that is, a character, who could not be seen yet, because he or she remained only in the 'hors-champ' or in the off, in the "acousmatic zones". Referring to Fritz Lang's DAS TESTAMENT DES DR. MABUSE (THE TESTAMENT OF DR. MABUSE, Germany 1933), Chion explains that entire films can depend on the acousmêtre question, his appearance and his "de-acousmatization" (ibid., 130). His strength and power are his ubiquity and his overview of the events in the "visualized zone". Through "de-acousmatization", that is when the voice enters the onscreen and a body in the images, this invisible person, monster or mastermind, loses his ubiquitous power. Chion's concept is therefore one that, on the one hand, regards the zones of film, and, on the other hand, also a specific presence, which can arise in the tension between image and sound, visibility and invisibility, and whose characteristics can change depending on his location.

Referring to Chion and Menkman, in the case of game glitches I would argue that, not in all but in special cases, we can observe and describe a new form of "acousmatic zone" and a new type of "acousmêtre". Not an acousmêtre who initially exists as a voice and loses the overview and his power when he steps into the picture, but a *visible acousmêtre* who could also be called a *'visumêtre'*, a visual being that can cross over into acousmatic videocapes and show the viewer the transitions between and the visible areas beyond the playing field. Through 'clipping', 'OoB', 'out of the level' or 'under the level' gamers and spectators of glitch videos experience an environment beyond the maps, grids and textures. When the breakouts from playing fields do not lead to abstract compression artefacts, then it can happen that a character either falls deeper into the void under a level, or that he can explore the unknown outside of a game, sometimes even re-enter the gameplay at a different point and thus maybe gain an advantage (Consalvo 2007, 114ff.). In some cases the fall through the map causes a black hole from which there is no way out. But other glitches create new rules and allow to explore the normally invisible space beyond the game—or rather, a space beyond and within the game; an in-between, not a place beyond the medium, but new forms that can lead to new movements and rules; and this space can quite assume a 'paradise-like dimension' aesthetically.

An example for a positive glitch is the video ESCAPING FROM JAIL GLITCHING STYLE (2010) by Spikeeee1337. Here the protagonist of the game PRISON BREAK: THE CONSPIRACY (2010, ZootFly), company agent and prisoner Tom Paxton, can break out of prison through a persistent back-and-forth movement between a bunk bed and a toilet. The so caused glitch allows him to leave the building and fly around in the darkness outside the game's map and borders. Finally, after a short flight across the dark space and around the transparent prison, he re-enters the normal game architecture, where he can leave the level through a door with an exit sign. Another random example for a glitch that shows a transition into another world of images, is TeamLAG's L.A. NOIRE: OUT AND UNDER THE

Figure 1a + 1b: Screenshots from L.A. NOIRE: OUT AND UNDER THE MAP (2011, TeamLAG) featuring the game L.A.NOIRE *(2011, Rockstar Games).*

MAP (2011). Here, in a game that itself pushes the boundaries between game and film by showing long cinematic sequences, Detective Cole Phelps can glitch easily through the grid by just running against a hill. On the other side of the game he can stroll around between floating houses and trees and run on an invisible ground into the void under the city (fig. 1a + 1b).

Even if these images are not as abstract and radical as Menkman's *RADIO DADA*, I would argue that we also have to deal with "acousmatic videoscapes" here. The utopian character of these views may not be as strong as in other "hot" glitches of the "critical trans-media aesthetics", considering that it is 'only' a game, but I think that some of Menkman's claims are also satisfied in these attractions. Game glitchers constantly try to break the boundaries of games in order to discover other, invisible spaces and the 'madness' of the medium. As nomads of noise artifacts they break the linear narratives and corrupt expectations and genres. They create new vocabularies, "Glitchspeak", and do not rest on their findings, but with every new game they search anew for glitches and unusual image worlds. They do not create filters or design, but they show the audience constant transformations and the knowledge that every game can be glitched. Through the documentation and the transition from game to online video, they create communities that constantly present new attractions of "critical trans-media aesthetics".

Glitch Over

In every medium and also in video and computer games, there exist other forms of exclusion and invisibility. In the example of game glitches we see that the breakouts of game characters and gamers can lead to different "acousmatic zones": either one from which a character can come back or an outside with no chance for "de-acousmatization", so that the game is permanently disabled and a gamer can only escape by restart. Thus, the games create the possibility of different acousmatic realities: an acousmatic world where you get an unreal look behind the scenes of the game—like Western cities consisting only of facades—and where you either get caught or from where you can return. But also other image worlds are conceivable that have nothing to do with the architecture of a particular game, its landscapes or objects, and that are radically different, new realities that cannot be integrated into previous ones.

In the games these worlds can be discovered by another kind of guide than the glitch artist. When characters break through the boundaries and reach acousmatic spaces, then we are dealing with another form of acousmatic being. In the character movements we always can perceive the movements and the act of showing of a gamer who moves the camera and the pictures like a film-maker. He guides the game character and our vision. In the game glitch documentaries the gamer who talks to us from the "acousmatic zone" is not just a narrator, but a new type of acousmètre who shows us the "acousmatic videoscapes". He is a voice that establishes a relationship to the images and creates a close connection to the game character that is obviously not the gamer himself, but his other body in the images which itself may not be an acousmètre, but at least an *acousmètre avatar*.

As an artistic or terrorist act a glitch can be understood as a successful attempt to disorient a form, a programme or a controlled course of a medium. But it can also be a phenomenon that happens without human influences, as deviation and disorientation of media itself, that gets deformed when an element, a figure, function or form, such as a game character, gets lost in a kind of *off-form* or, in the case of games, *hors concourse*; a space and new form that can put an ordinary form across by, for instance, showing a different perspective of usually invisible grids or maps. So, perhaps we could say, that a glitch is a possibility of self-(dis)orientation of media in order to perceive and observe itself and its forms through a new form. Seeing it that way, it is a reflexive and emancipatory moment of media trying to be different, perhaps 'better' or 'out of order'.

A definition of a real glitch could be, that it is something of which we do not know yet what it is and when it happens; and from which those who hope for it, expect that it is different. But when it occurs, we expect from it that it is not what we expected, that it remains without definition. For theory that would mean that we could not handle true glitches without taming them in descriptions. Real glitches cannot be observed, only the documentation of their images and sounds and the talking about them. At best, we can think about glitches with the glitches, as a theory that must play with the constant break and even with the other side of thinking and discourse. In this spirit, a glitch could also be described as an artistic or academic gesture that wants to guide an audience between the thin lines and broad abysses between logic, sense, knowledge, or truth, and madness, disorder, and everything excluded from established forms and formats. A glitch is a permanent rupture with common definitions and theoretical approaches. Regarding such a vanishing object any analysis trying to explain glitches always appears narrow-minded and conventional.

Besides the upgrade culture's belief in progress, the new developments in video and computer games, and the hope for more and more detailed maps, higher resolutions, more human character movements or facial expressions using ever-improving motion capture processes, there is the hope for the constant disorientation of these improvements and perfections, a joy over dysfunction, the beauty of break and the utopia of new media realities. Possibly this other side of video, cinema, game, or soon augmented reality will partly also be integrated and aesthetically incorporated into templates and media narratives. But even then, it will remain the job for glitchers to discover new ways out and detours away from this appropriations, in order to break established orders and embrace the permanent odyssey.

Bibliography

Ayto, John (1998): *The Oxford Dictionary of Slang*. Oxford/New York: Oxford University Press.
Bolter, J. David/Grusin, Richard (2000): *Remediation: Understanding New Media*. Cambridge: MIT Press.
Cascone, Kim (2000): *The Aesthetics of Failure*. Web. Retrieved from: [http://www.hz-journal.org/n3/cascone.html]; access: 2012/10/10.

Chion, Michel (1994): *Audio-Vision. Sound on Screen.* New York: Columbia University Press.

Chion, Michel (2003): Mabuse – Magie und Kräfte des acousmêtre. Auszüge aus 'Die Stimme im Kino'. In: Epping-Jäger, Cornelia/Linz, Erika (eds.): *Medien/Stimmen.* (Mediologie, Vol. 9). Köln: DuMont, 124–159.

Consalvo, Mia (2007): *Cheating. Gaining Advantage in Videogames.* Cambridge: MIT Press.

Geimer, Peter (2010): *Bilder aus Versehen. Eine Geschichte fotografischer Erscheinungen (Fundus-Bücher 178).* Hamburg: Philo Fine Arts.

Gunning, Tom (2000): The Cinema of Attraction: Early Film, Its Spectator, and the Avant-Garde. In: Stam, Robert/Miller, Toby (eds.): *Film and Theory: An Anthology.* Malden/Oxford: Blackwell, 229–235.

Holl, Ute (2009): Vom Kino Eye zur You-Tube. In: *CARGO Film/Medien/Kultur,* 03/2009, 72–74.

Kelly, Caleb (2009): *Cracked Media: The sound of malfunction.* Cambridge: MIT Press.

Luhmann, Niklas (1996): *Social Systems.* Stanford: Stanford University Press.

Luhmann, Niklas (2000): *Art as a social system.* Stanford: Stanford University Press.

McLuhan, Marshall (1964): *Understanding Media: The Extensions of Man.* New York: McGraw Hill.

Menkman, Rosa (2008): *Radio Dada.* Web. Retrieved from: [http://rosa-menkman.blogspot.com/2008/04/radio-dada.html]; posted: 2008/4/20; access: 2012/10/10.

Menkman, Rosa (2009): *The use of artifacts as critical media aesthetics.* Web. Retrieved from: [http://aboutrosamenkman.blogspot.com/2009/03/publications.html]; posted: 2009/09; access: 2012/10/10.

Menkman, Rosa (2009/10): *Glitch Studies Manifesto.* Web. Retrieved from: [http://www.slideshare.net/r00s/glitch-studies-manifesto]; posted: 2010/02/01; access: 2012/10/10.

Menkman, Rosa (2011): Glitch Studies Manifesto. In: Lovink, Geert/Somers Miles, Rachel (eds.): *Video Vortex Reader II: Moving Images Beyond YouTube.* Amsterdam: Institute of Network Cultures, 336–347.

Moradi, Iman (2004): *Glitch Aesthetics.* Dissertation, School of Design Technology, Department of Architecture, The University of Huddersfield. Web. Retrieved from: [http://www.oculasm.org/glitch/download/Glitch_dissertation_print_with_pics.pdf]; posted: 2004/01/27; access: 2012/10/10.

O'Reilly, David (2009): *Datamoshing is so over.* Web. Retrieved from: [http://www.davidoreilly.com/2009/02/datamoshing-is-so-over]; posted: 2009/02; access: 2012/04/15.

Papows, Jeff (2011): *Glitch. The hidden impact of faulty software.* New York et al.: Prentice Hall.

Rizzo, Teresa (2008): *YouTube: the New Cinema of Attractions.* Web. Retrieved from: [http://scan.net.au/scan/journal/display.php?journal_id=109]; posted: 2008/05/01; access: 2012/10/10.
Schaeffer, Pierre (1966): *Traité des objets musicaux.* Paris: Le Seuil.
Stockburger, Axel (2006): *The Rendered Arena. Modalities of space in video and computer games.* Web. Retrieved from: [www.stockburger.at/files/2010/04/Stockburger_Phd.pdf]; access: 2012/10/10.
Tan, Wey-Han (2010): Playing (with) Educational Games – Integrated Game Design and Second Order Gaming. In: Sonvilla-Weiss, Stefan (ed.): *Mashup Cultures.* Wien/New York: Springer, 223–283.
Tolino, Aldo (2008): *Gaming 2.0 – Computer Games and Cultural Production.* Web. Retrieved from: [http://io-noi-aldo.sonance.net/gaming-2-0/Gaming_2_0_Thesis_lowres.pdf]; access: 2012/10/10.

Web Sources

GamerGlitch.com: *Video Game Glitches, Exploits and Easter Eggs.* Web. Retrieved from: [http://gamerglitch.com]; access: 2012/10/10.
GlitchBlog.com. Web. Retrieved from: [http://glitchblog.com]; access: 2012/04/15.
Machinima. Web. Retrieved from: [www.machinima.com]; access: 2012/10/10.
Menkman, Rosa: *Sunshine in my throat.* Web. Retrieved from: [http://rosa-menkman.blogspot.com]; access: 2012/10/10.
Overweg, Robert: *Glitches.* Web. Retrieved from: [http://www.shotbyrobert.com/?page_id=191]; access: 2012/10/10.

Films

Das Testament des Dr. Mabuse (The Testament of Dr. Mabuse, Germany 1933, Fritz Lang)
Gamer (USA 2009, Mark Neveldine/Brian Taylor)
The Matrix (USA 1999, The Wachowski Brothers)
The Purple Rose of Cairo (USA 1985, Woody Allen)
Tron (USA 1982, Steven Lisberger)
Tron: Legacy (USA 2010, Joseph Kosinski)
Virtuosity (USA 1995, Brett Leonard)

Games

L.A. Noire (2011, Rockstar Games)
Prison Break: The Conspiracy (2010, ZootFly)

Web Videos

Datamoshing as Syntactic Form. Reading Digital Video Compression Algorithm Hacking (2011/11/22). Lecture by Thomas Y. Levin held at the University of Cologne. Web. Retrieved from: [http://www.zfmk.uni-koeln.de/cologne medialectures/programm/13-thomas-y-levin]; access: 2012/10/10.
Escaping from Jail Glitching Style (posted by Spikeee1337). Web. Retrieved from: [https://www.youtube.com/watch?v=GY9cP3oPPKI]; posted: 2010/03/19; access: 2012/10/10.
Evident Utensil (posted by Data Mosher). Web. Retrieved from: [http://vimeo.com/3139412]; posted: 2009/02/08; access: 2012/10/10.
How to Datamosh (posted by Data Mosher). Web. Retrieved from: [http://www.youtube.com/watch?v=tYytVzbPky8]; posted: 2009/02/24; access: 2012/10/10.
L.A. Noire: Out and Under The Map (posted by TeamLAG). Web. Retrieved from: [http://www.youtube.com/watch?v=qBGGVUpj1qg]; posted: 2011/05/21; access: 2012/10/10.
Please Say Something (posted by David O'Reilly). Web. Retrieved from: [http://vimeo.com/3388129]; posted: 2009/02/26; access: 2012/04/15.
Radio Dada (posted by Rosa Menkman). Web. Retrieved from: [https://www.youtube.com/watch?v=hRwkD6vTPjA]; posted: 2009/09/02; access: 2012/10/10.
Welcome To Heartbreak (posted by Nabil Elderkin). Web. Retrieved from: [http://vimeo.com/4578366]; posted: 2009/05/10; access: 2012/10/10.

Image Source

Figure 1a + 1b: Screenshots from *L.A. Noire: Out and Under the Map* (posted by TeamLAG, 2011) featuring the game L.A.Noire (2011, Rockstar Games). Retrieved from [https://www.youtube.com/watch?v=qBGGVUpj1qg]; access: 2012/10/10.

Captivating Screens
On 'Manipulation Aesthetics' as Style and Topos

BENJAMIN EUGSTER

"DO NOT BE AFRAID" –
OF CONVERGENCE CULTURE IMPERATIVES!

In the summer of 2011, the German TV channel *Pro7* broadcasted a commercial that, in all its simplicity, is hard to define. The sequence of various overexposed shots conveyed an enigmatic charm.[1] The commercial was neither explicitly positioned among the programme previews, nor did it feature any particular product or brand. Thus, it remained uncertain as to what its function was and what its imagery alluded to: Playing children, dolphins breaking waves, a mother kissing her baby (fig. 1), and other over-stylised views of nature were supported by the repetitive and soothing sentence "Do not be afraid". A website with the same wording (*habt-keine-angst.de*) was the only concrete information provided at the end of the spot. Viewers were left wondering whether what they just saw was simply an odd insurance commercial or an exuberantly 'positive' iconography of a Scientology campaign (see e.g. SCIENTOLOGY AD: *"LIFE"*, Churchof Scientology 2009). When I saw it myself for the first time, I was caught between the ambivalent delight of witnessing something uniquely bizarre and the more discomforting suspicion and disappointment that it might be just another viral marketing campaign vying for attention. Anyhow, it became evident that the spot aimed at a particular reaction by its spectator. In the following discussion I will describe the relation between this kind of obtrusiveness and the particular way the spot is arranged. How does the structure of audiovisual media relate to the conception of their manipulative impact? I will characterise the underlying enigmatic aesthetics as 'manipulation aesthetics'. Manipulation here stands for a certain audiovisual insistence that either dares the viewer to make sense of what he or she sees or calls for concrete action as in the given case. However

---

1 | The commercial can be watched on *YouTube*: HABT KEINE ANGST (PRO 7) (posted by ARGRep, 2011).

Figure 1

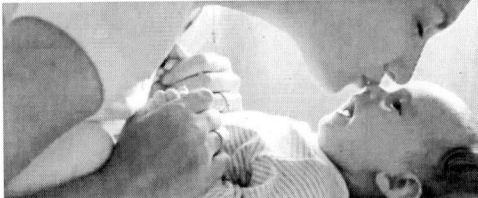

Figure 2

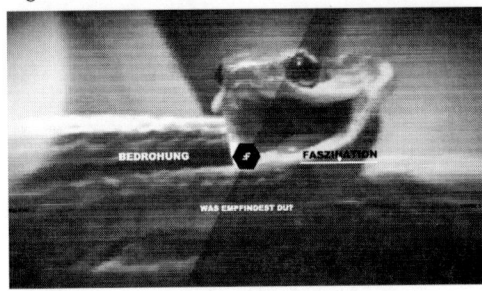

much I tried to resist enquiring further, the sound of the sentence "do not be afraid" was stuck in my head, urging me to cross the border of the televisual medium and type in the URL on my laptop.

The "flow of content across multiple media platforms" (Jenkins 2006, 2) that Henry Jenkins describes as "convergence culture" by far grasps more than the postmodern media hybrids, invisible processes of collaborating media industries, and the barely perceivable shifts from one medium to another.[2] "The migratory behaviour of media audiences" (Jenkins 2006, 2) becomes manifest in every single action and thought transcending the sole channel, screen, or tube in front of the media participants. Transmedial migration in the given example of *habt-keine-angst.de* is not reflected only by me and my urge to go online and figure out what was behind the luring mantra stuck in my head. Since the removal of the homepage, many recordings and variations of the webpage's interface have been uploaded to *YouTube* by anonymous users. The following descriptions are based on two sources that captured different parts of the homepage. The video *Habt-keine-angst.de – "Wer bist du*? by user magmafack (2011) covers all of the interactive questions of the personality test but skips the 'evaluation' of his choices. The video *Rebell – habt-keine-angst.de (Pro7)* by the user MaryLilianMary (2011) isolates this evaluation, which I will refer to as the 'rebel sequence'. On the website, the user is confronted with an interactive surface that consists of an audiovisual questionnaire introduced by a shortened version of the TV spot. However, the online version of the spot differs slightly from the previous one seen on a flat screen TV. A structure of horizontal lines gives an impression of a CRT (cathode ray tube) TV screen surface. This transmedial aesthetic suggests an idea of materiality that is empirically linked to the TV screen. As soon as the TV spot is over, a pair of glaring red lips aspirates the sentence "It is time for progress". A button with the inscription "I am not afraid" appears and invites the user to affirm the progression. After the user pushes the button, a

---

2 | See Daniela Olek's article in this volume.

written reply "We want to get to know you" initiates a series of questions more or less vaguely related to the looped video content in the background. For instance, the first two questions about the user's age and number of siblings are supported by a scene of playing children from the TV spot. This associative linkage gains further significance in the next steps when the user is asked to react to the image shown in the background. Question three (fig. 2) has to be answered with the felt sentiment towards the video of a hissing snake. The user's options 'Threat' and 'Fascination'

Figure 3

Figure 4

seem to influence her decision and classification within a dichotomous scheme. The options in question four ('Boredom' or 'Security') support an even harsher juxtaposition when the user is asked to react to the image of two parents playing with a child. All the questions are separated by short extracts from the TV spot, which are titled with associated concepts such as 'Goodness', 'Hope', 'Life' and 'Luck'. In the end of this associative survey, the user is categorised as 'Rebel'. This verdict is followed by an aggressive forty second montage highlighting a strong visual tension that radically contrasts with the harmonic imagery in the rest of the campaign. The montage culminates in a trailer of the science-fiction series V – THE VISITORS (Canada/USA 2009-2011, ABC) with direct reference to TV channel *Pro7*.

The fact that everything turned out to be some kind of a viral campaign after all is not of concern here. Rather the manifold online replies suggest a close aesthetic analysis of both the conserved TV material and the users' individual interpretations of what they saw. Isolation of the evaluative 'rebel sequence' on the homepage is particularly significant because it strongly contrasts the rest of the campaign and takes its treatment of manipulation aesthetics to a new level. Most strikingly, this intensification sets in when the stylistic standards of digital imagery are challenged by technical disturbance. At the beginning of the sequence, one of the female characters in the series turns around and looks straight into the camera. Her face is evenly lit and she is set against a sombre, chaotic backdrop with a straying crowd of people. But as her gaze hits the viewer, it is distorted by a pseudo-glitchy mosaic effect (fig. 3). Several loops of the distorted movement emphasise aesthetic disturbance and coincide acoustically with a stuttering of the last word in the sentence "No remorse for errors, errors, errors" (MaryLilianMary 2011; transl. B.E.).[3] This alteration is followed by an intensification of the devices of manipulation aesthetics. The subtle striation is taken to an explicit level when computer displays or filmed monitors with a TV test pattern and news-footage are displayed. When one of those screens within the scene is turned off, such traits of transmediality bring the essence of their condensed material to the fore (fig. 4).

The disparate montage in all the three videos plays a decisive role in the aesthetic convergence of the different media observed above. Not only does the montage merge different media in a single frame, but the combination of seemingly unrelated images enables a visual stream that highlights its own impact on the viewer. Both the disparate montage and the aesthetic media convergence help in establishing the idea of a spectator's direct manipulation by a visual dispositive that constitutes the mimicked phantasms of 'brainwashing' or 'propaganda'. These devices need to be integrated into a broader historic framework of an audiovisual discourse on media manipulation. How can one describe the convergence process that takes place when a television spot provokes an online search and the website in turn imitates the TV screen's visuality? Certainly, these mutual inscriptions can no longer be regarded as mere self-reflections of the medium. Rather, they reflect different media aesthetics and different modes of spectatorship through a practical transfer of style across media production and consumption.

AESTHETICS OF PHANTASMATIC MEDIA IMPACTS

The modifications in user generated recordings and uploads on video platforms open up novel possibilities of a reception based analysis. Even the most immaturely commented video and the most mutilatingly remixed movie scene increases information and enhances the complexity and relevance of the subject. A user's video reaction to the 'Do not be afraid' campaign illustrates what I mean by this. The video with the title '*HABT KEINE ANGST (EXTREM)*' (Aschitaka14 2011) has a very simple structure. A short intertitle with the comment "This video may harm your sickness [sic], only watch it at your own risk" (Aschitaka14

---

3 | Original citation: "Keine Reue für Fehler" (*REBELL – HABT KEINE ANGST.DE (PRO7)*, Mary LilianMary 2011).

2011; transl. B.E.)[4] introduces the 'Do not be afraid' mantra. The underlying hypnotic movements of a set of black and white concentric circles (fig. 5) emphasise the intrusive character of the the mantra and the ten minute original video. Despite the spelling and grammar mistakes in the introductory warning and its obvious ridicule of both the ad campaign and the user watching it, this video tells us more about how the campaign is perceived than the closest iconographic analysis would. The video is not reduced to a simple optical illusion but rather tries to grasp a mode of spectatorship that relies on an interaction between the acoustic and the visual, and between the video's kinetic energy and the spectator's state of mind. Without drifting off to esoteric concepts of spiritual perception, I want to stress two characteristics of such a mode of spectatorship.

Figure 5

Figure 6

First, the experimental nature of this video is particularly striking. It appears (and the comments below the video indicate so) that some of the users actually exposed themselves to this dispositive for the whole ten minutes and experienced an intense optical impression. This subjective experience may result in a distorted view of everything outside the monitor's frame or in mild dizziness from concentrating on the centre of the concentric circles. Second, the associative use of this optical effect alludes to the spiral's connotative dimension as a symbol of chaos or hypnosis. Thus, by combining the acoustic background of the TV spot with a dispositive of explicit mental manipulation, the user draws an analogy between the phantasmatic effect (brainwashing) of the original video

---

4 | Original citation: "Dieses video könnt krankheitsschädigend [sic] wirken deswegen ist das anschauen auf eigener Gefahr!!!" (*Habt keine Angst (EXTREM)*, Aschitaka142011).

and the symbolically imagined (complete hypnosis) or subjectively experienced (mild dizziness) effect of the spiral.

Three different levels of experience converge in this experimental mode of spectatorship: the visual pleasure of the optical toy, the affective impact of the dispositive on the human sensorium, and the intellectual association of both with one another. It appears that this playful use of pre-cinematographic optical illusions never completely gave way to the more complex visual media that developed in the last two centuries. Tom Gunning indicates in his influential article, *Cinema of Attraction: Early Cinema, its Spectator and the Avant-Garde*, that this pre-cinematographic mode of spectatorship has been present throughout the history of cinema (Gunning 2006, 27). The extent to which sensationalist manners of early cinematic attractions prevail becomes evident in action movie blockbusters and in artistically daring adventures of the avantgarde. On the other hand, narratively embedded distortions in dream sequences or hallucinations, have been relatively neglected. These sequences do not simply transgress certain stylistic norms for narrational purposes, rather they include a visual pleasure that is inherently experimental. The culmination of cinematographic, lived, and phantasmatic experience in a very similar optical illusion should clarify the relation between media phantasms and transmediality.

In Walter Ruttmann's movie, BERLIN: DIE SINFONIE DER GROSSSTADT (BERLIN: SYMPHONY OF A GREAT CITY, Germany 1927), a spinning spiral appears in three different contexts. The prototypical city symphony film is divided into five acts, from an awakening city in the first act to the metropolitan night life by the fifth. The editing pace during the second act increases and thereby intensifies urban businesses to such a degree that the movie has to resort to aesthetic measures other than sober realistic cinematography. The rapidity and agitation of the editing transfers to the camera movement: Two shots of a typewriter keyboard rotate in opposite directions and create an optical effect that is replaced by a spinning spiral in the end of the second act. While use of the spiral makes complete sense within the dramaturgical structure, its effect does not end here. It represents a visual stimulus that targets the viewers' somatic experience of urban nervousness through cinematographic movement. Thus, this optical toy that causes dizziness and disorientation, not only affects the spectator's imagination but also her nerves. The early 20th century discussion on neurasthenia and film (Kreimeier 2011, 77ff) highlights a strong correlation between a discursive construction of media phatasms and a medium's ascribed psychophysiological impact. Another scene in the third act features the same spiral as an optical toy in a showcase and suggests an embeddedness of the optical toy within a modern media culture of sensationalism and self-affection. Thus, the spiral is not an exclusively symbolic element in the film, but an everyday instrument of affect transfer itself. This enables Ruttmann to use it both as an impact targeting the spectator's nervous system and as an expression of the hectic city at the same time. Notably, the last appearance of the spiral in the film is closely tied to the state of mind of a suicidal woman jumping off a bridge. But the spiral of chaos has also been celebrated as an expression of modernity in another abstract movie. The anagrammatic spiral in Marcel Duchamp's ANÉMIC CINÉMA (France 1926) exemplifies the dialectical relation between orientation and disorientation. In his recent book, *Le Corps Du Cinema*, Raymond Bellour attributes a particular tension to the spiral in Duchamp's film (Bellour 2009, 339) that is significant to my understanding of manipulation aesthetics. The spiral's movement prevents the spectator from focusing on the centre. Yet, this point of fixation attracts the viewer's gaze like a vortex, while everything around starts to blur.

In order to understand the transmedial processes triggered by one simple TV spot, I will trace back as to how particular modes of spectatorship and phantasms of media manipulation led to the aesthetic transgressions that range from a simple trick of a spinning spiral to the complexly edited brainwash sequences in the narrative film. Further analysis will deepen our understanding of the two main aspects of manipulation aesthetics. First, a stylistic and topical identification of the presented audiovisual material with the televisual or filmic apparatus prevails through most of the examples. Second, it is a certain editing style that makes any 'brainwash scene' so distinct from the rest of a movie or TV programme. Given the context of this publication, I suggest a re-evaluation of the terms of orientation and disorientation and their moral bias. By looking at the following examples of brainwashing sequences in films, it becomes apparent that the obsolescence of the temporal dichotomy of orientation is the result of resolved disorientation. In the given examples, disorientation does not precede orientation. On the contrary, mental manipulation of the imaginary viewer is induced by a complicated interrelation of strong orientation of the user's gaze towards the screen (here onwards referred to as 'fixation') and her disorientation and cluelessness within the medium's content (here onwards referred to as 'distraction').

Who's (Still) Afraid of the Apparatus?

The modern nervous spirit of the metropolis Berlin is a rather subtle example of an external force that controls the media's desired impact. The introduction of a controlling entity is thus a decisive step from early examples of media impact to elaborated media phantasms of mind control and subliminal propaganda. The many 1960s and 1970s films dealing with brainwashing are rooted in the topos of hypnosis that used to be ubiquitous in the 1920s. The two axes along which the parallel between cinema and hypnosis gained popularity in early film theory are the fixation of the spectator's eye on a particular object and the simultaneous isolation and distraction from everything around. Such theories, proposed by anti-cinema writers like the German psychiatrist Robert Gaupp (1912), were reflected in cinema. Therefore, hypnosis offers a broad field of interactions between film style and film phantasms. A critical revision of hypnosis as a metaphor of film theory and as an actual historical media phantasm is found in the works of Schweinitz (2010), Andriopoulos (2008) and the previously mentioned Bellour (2009). Schweinitz' work provides a close analysis of continuous changes within this early filmic topos. While earlier examples oppose the hypnotised and the hypnotist on a horizontal stage, later examples such as Vampires – Les Yeux qui Fascinent (The Vampires – Hypnotic Eyes, France 1916, Louis Feuillade) and Dr. Mabuse – Der Spieler (Dr. Mabuse – The Gambler, Germany 1922, Fritz Lang), depict the eyes frontally. The screen takes the place of the hypnotist and the audience is directly confronted with the source of mind control.

    This basic cinematic phantasm of the cinematic screen captivating the spectator undoubtedly came back into fashion in the paranoid thrillers of the late 1960s and early 1970s. Be it the iconic blepharostat of Kubrick's A Clockwork Orange (UK 1971), the maoist garden party of Frankenheimer's The Manchurian Candidate (USA 1962), or Patrick McGoohan's secret agent Number 6 of The Prisoner (UK 1967–1968, ITV) being tricked in numerous ways, the mind controllers are omnipresent on the screen. Stanley Kubrick's A Clockwork Orange gives a good understanding of how the idea of a closed cinematic apparatus was subverted in narrative films. In the movie's acclaimed brainwashing scene, the protagonist Alex is tied to a chair and forced to watch a montage of Ludwig Van Beethoven's Ninth Symphony with Nazi propaganda footage. Shots of his fixed head and unbarred eyes are opposed to 'ultraviolent' projections on the screen. The supervising doctors in the frontal and symmetrical shots of the projection room suggest a test arrangement that is very typical for this kind of scientific depiction of mind control and has its roots in concrete psychological experiments in this area (Meteling 2007, 233ff). This combination of external supervision and medial fixation undoubtedly reverberates in the online survey of *habt-keine-angst.de*. However, in the 1960s, the media controllers were neither obscure hypnotists like Dr. Mabuse, nor seemingly friendly invaders from another planet like in V – The Visitors. It is the government that turns against its own people in order to remain in power. This threat from within comes along with the shift from exotic controlling entities to the media of everyday life (cinema, television and later even the LED projector of the conference room). With its stylistic interpretation of media manipulation and conspirative implications, the brainwash scene in A Clockwork Orange gives insights into the cinematic apparatus as it is described by Jean-Louis Baudry (1974) a few years later. Cinema's function within an ideological framework of the state apparatus is reflected in the concrete microcosm of the audience situation:

"No doubt the darkened room and the screen bordered with black like a letter of condolence already present privileged conditions of effectiveness – no exchange, no circulation, no communication with any outside. Projection and reflection take place in a closed space, and those who remain there, whether they know it or not (but they do not), find themselves chained, captured, or captivated." (Baudry 1974, 44)

What can be found here at the peak of psychoanalytical film studies is a very similar description of the media practice as Robert Gaupp already used in 1912 (Gaupp 2002, 110). The fixation of the body as a predisposition for the hypnotic state is linked to the semi-conscious experience that the filmic dispositive allows. The spectator is depicted both physically and mentally chained. While the pervasiveness of the manipulation in some of these films is guaranteed by the person not knowing about the ongoing manipulation (THE PRISONER, THE MANCHURIAN CANDIDATE), in other films, this state of receptivity has first to be induced by more intense means than the sole fixation and isolation of the depicted audience. The flickering screen and the sound of the rolling film reel are described as reinforcing factors in early cinema's nervous impacts (Gaupp 2002, 110) and are progressively replaced by ever more intrusive strategies. Brainwashing in movies like THE PARALLAX VIEW (USA 1974, Alan Pakula) is not restricted to the protagonist's physical and mental fixation. The content of what the protagonist sees is itself modified in order to have a stronger impact on his mind. The alternation of illuminated and black frames is reinforced by an intensified montage in general. The rapid change of diverse imageries is sought to captivate the viewer's attention.

MONTAGE AND MENTAL DISTRACTION

At the beginning of the notorious testing sequence in the Parallax Company, a pitch black room is shown with a slowly dimming spotlight directed at a chair in the centre of the image. Then, a very calm and slow voice reads the following instructions while the film's protagonist makes himself comfortable (fig. 7): "Just sit back, nothing is required of you; except to observe the visual material that is presented to you". A few seconds later, a calm musical score sets in and the montage sequence that confronts the protagonist fills the broad Panavision screen. A range of still images are presented in a similar order as the *habt-keine-angst.de* online survey. But unlike the 'Do not be afraid' mantra, the authoritative voice in THE PARALLAX VIEW stops playing a role as soon as the series of visual impacts has begun. The first shot in the five-minute sequence consists of white capital letters 'LOVE' on a black background. Family photos and more captions like 'MOTHER', 'FATHER', 'ME', or 'GOD' follow and are always combined with associated images. Especially in context of the iconography with the

Figure 7

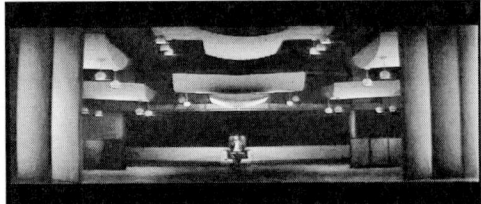

Figure 8

family (fig. 1 and fig. 8) and the topic of security, the TV spot shares a striking resemblance to this sequence.

However, the spectrum of imageries is completed first by captions of a different kind, like 'MONEY', 'ENEMY', 'COUNTRY', and 'HAPPINESS' before the established visual categories are progressively mixed up. In the end, clear-cut titles fall away entirely and the editing follows harsh contrasts or visual similarities rather than thematic coherence.

This internal distraction of the viewer's gaze and mind foretells the interactive classification of the online survey. Every new still prompts a new association just as each intertitle in the survey feeds new suspicions of what the campaign might be about. In his reading of THE PARALLAX VIEW, Arno Meteling describes this "semantic shifting" (Meteling 2007, 245) as a constriction of possible interpretations that calls upon the spectator for her "political identification" (ibid., 246). It is tempting to read the iconicity of the explicit titles and photographs in this way. But in this example, shouldn't it rather be regarded as what enables the manipulation? Is it not the feeling that there is some implicit meaning behind the random combination and recombination of images and topics that lies at the core of a paranoid thriller? As these mixed-up categories call for some kind of rational resolution, both the protagonist and the movie's spectator get carried away by a plethora of possible combinations in the visual material. Distracted from her fixation within the visual and ideological apparatus, the last thing she would question is the meaningfulness of the given categories. Therefore, I pledge for an understanding of this kind of montage as a phantasmatic construct in its own right: heightened visual diversity and rhythmic density, rather than an intricate riddle that tricks the viewer into believing in an overly complex meaning behind it.

A closer look at these settings of a manipulatable viewer, the stylistic recourse to editing styles similar to Sergej Eisenstein's reflexological conceptions of film reception does not come as a surprise. According to his early writings on film editing, the human mind works analogous to the filmic structure and thereby allows the latter to manipulate the former. Meaning is created as soon as two different images collide and get recombined in the spectator's mind. This function of the intellectual montage is best illustrated by a scene from Oktyabr (October, Russia 1928) that tries to deconstruct the meaning of religion by combining seemingly unrelated sanctuaries and idols of different religions (see Goodwin 1993, 87). Arno Meteling begins his article *Mind Control and Montage* with a torturing sequence from the TV series Lost (USA 2004–2010, HBO) that is reminiscent of Eisenstein's intellectual montage. In the episode *Not in Portland* (S3/E07) the teenage boy Carl is tied to a chair in the mysterious room number 23 and rapid drum'n'bass music dominates the acoustic background. Similar to the tin gods, masks, and idols in Oktyabr, a series of doll faces and exotic idols are cast against the wall by a digital projector. Although this mimicry characterises the applied montage technique as a stylish stimulus rather than a decodable riddle, I will not dichotomise these levels. A semantic-hermeneutic approach as presented by Meteling clearly reaches its limits here: "As this very specific test arrangement appears only cursorily and does not add fundamentally to the episode's line of action, we can assume that it is an allegorically emptied scene" (Meteling 2007, 231f; transl. B.E.).[5] On the one hand, this assertion reduces the narrative maze of a mystery series to the logical coherence of one simple episode. On the other hand, it underestimates the ludic processes of the illusion of meaningfulness: Simply everything becomes important and potentially relevant to the viewer in a mystery series like Lost. In a scene like the one in room 23, this principle meets its formal equivalent. In consequence, there is no such thing as an "allegorically emptied scene" (ibid.) in the bigger picture, no matter how randomly the scene avails itself of a wide range of phantasms and media. Actually, a broad range of interpretations for this scene can be found quite easily if one crosses the border of the televisual medium and joins the game of a forensic participatory culture.[6] On YouTube and in different fan forums, user modified videos with a reversed and decelerated version of this scene can be found (e.g. Only Fools, Backwards Lost, dabestdefense 2007). They indeed manage to reveal interesting cues to its narrative relevance. If the scene is played backwards, in the beginning, a deep voice says "Only fools are enslaved by time and space" and thereby predicts the complicated and abundantly random leaps in time in the fifth season. But is it the task of film studies to join this game of decoding?

---

5 | Original citation: "Da diese sehr spezifische Versuchsanordnung aber nur kursorisch in Erscheinung tritt und auch nicht zum Thema des Handlungsstrangs der Folge wird, lässt sich vermuten, dass es sich um eine allegorisch entleerte Szene handelt" (Meteling 2007, 231f.).
6 | See the article by Jason Mittell in this volume.

The New Polemics of Discontinuity and Media Convergence

All of the above examples are embedded in a broader or narrower web of narratives: on one side the brainwashing scene that takes place somewhere within hours and hours of LOST episodes and fan discussions; on the other side the VISITORS TV ad that is only linked to its multimedia surrounding as it brings change to the spectator's role, taking them from a 'passive' viewer to an 'active' web user. The developed set of characteristics of manipulation aesthetics allows us to now look at more complex and less self-explanatory examples. With new ways of digital editing and boundless availability of audiovisual material, new aesthetic expressions of how users think about media begin to emerge. Nevertheless, a subgenre like the video mashups of 9/11 footage seems to meld the different strategies of manipulation aesthetics that were developed so far with the specificity of digital aesthetics. Rapid editing, confused iconography, and the preoccupation with conspiracy discourses call for a closer reading. The fuzzy corpus of sometimes baffling, and sometimes outrageous videos marked the beginning of my attempts to conceptualise audiovisual negotiations of brainwash phantasms, digital editing styles, and both explicit and implicit transmediality. Conscious of the problematic notion of 'genre' in the context of online video cultures, I focus on one particular user (heavyplastician) and his applied aesthetic forms and iconographies. Even though there are a number of YouTube videos treating footage of the 9/11 attacks as the subject of contemporary conspiracy theories, I would only loosely relate the user heavyplastician to the revisionist "9/11 truth movement" (Wind Meyhoff 2009, 61ff) behind such speculations. How does the phantasmatic conception of mainstream media influence the work of users that try to deconstruct disseminated media contents and the ideological role of mass media? The underlying premise of these video mashups relates to a very simplistic criticism: Because the mainstream media are lying, it is up to the participatory media to debunk their explanations of historic events. Unlike other videos of the so called "no plane movement" (Olmsted 2009, 255), the elaborated mashups of heavyplastician do not try to convince the spectator by fastidiously analysing every second of TV footage to support the notion that no plane ever touched the World Trade Centre. Rather than appealing to the spectator's rationality, the hallucinatory videos seem to appeal to subliminal receptiveness in a complex mimicry of phantasmatic manipulation devices. They utilise the same aesthetic strategies that they accuse television of. In order to unmask mainstream media's WEAPONS OF MASS HYPNOSIS (heavyplastician 2008), they make use of the same strategies of manipulation: audiovisual fixation and mental distraction. One example of this can be found in the user's video THINK KARTOONZ (heavyplastician 2009), which drags the viewer into a vortex of almost undecipherable superimpositions and a nightmarish mixture of post 9/11 popular culture.

The video starts with a flickering screen on which the logo "Heavy Plastic" and the slogan "Mashing-up Others!" appear in two rows; the former mimicking the *YouTube* logo, and the latter written in the well-known *Walt Disney* font. The video continues with a rotating globe slowly increasing between four different screens within the screen: a cross with a computer war game, a rectangle with changing views of the 9/11 attack, a triangle with news broadcast on a war scene, and a circle with an esoteric *YouTube* talk show (fig. 9). This kind of split screen highlights its own imagined mediality when the whole image is slightly distorted by a 'magnetic' interference. Irrespective of their differing indexicality, these four dimensions are conjoined in a montage and get mixed up completely after the globe covers the full image. One of the main polemic strategies of this video is to discredit used historical television material: Jammed between cartoon scenes and modified logos of different TV stations (e.g. NoTV instead of MTV), footage of the exploding plane is moved into the realm of fantasy and fiction. In his paper *The Consequential Narrative: Comics and the Unwritten Stories of the Modern Media Platform* Gabriel S. Moses refers to a similar strategy of a "stream of seemingly non-sequitur transitions" (Moses 2012, 307), which he deems typical for "today's alternative news broadcast" (ibid.). This is exemplified by the strong affinity of conspiracy videos to certain polemics of discontinuity in reference to the far more outreaching movie ZEITGEIST by Peter Joseph (USA 2011).

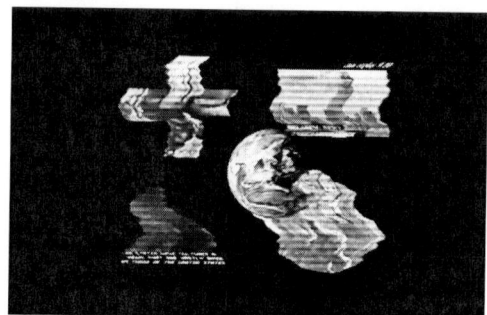

Figure 9

Figure 10

The merge of disparate material is intensified by the editing pace and the increasing use of superimpositions throughout the video. This stratification is the result of converging media aesthetics enabled by excessive digital assemblage techniques and reminds us of transmedial inscriptions encountered in examples like the online campaign of V – THE VISITORS. Whereas the split screen technology in fig. 9 is a very explicit reference, the imitation of television screens or of damaged VHS videos (fig. 10) opens up the tension between low resolution digital videos and mimicked analogue artefacts. Beyond the split of orientation and disorientation, these digital strategies take audiovisual discourse of manipulation aesthetics to the extreme. In its reference to other media, this video mashup exploits the same stylistic aberrations like the 're-bel sequence'. THINK KARTOONZ strengthens its own visual density by explicit references to analogue media and implicit inscriptions of analogue artefacts. These televisual aesthetics stand in for the manipulatable state of mind of a hypothetical spectator. As there is no narrative framing or an explicit test subject as in paranoid thrillers on brainwashing, the user's own experience of media practices is addressed. Rapid editing and excessive use of superimpositions reminds us of the hours lost while channel surfing. They incorporate an audience that is lulled by their fixated gazes and the alternating TV programmes. What I called manipulation aesthetics are simply the shadows that follow changes throughout media history and leave their traces in depictions of the demonised new paradigms of spectatorship. In order to understand these, there is no way around questioning the orienting function of science itself. Sometimes there is a need to obey the most mundane and obscure imperatives in order to get behind such processes of converging audiovisual cultures. Especially when audiences are deemed the most attentive, film and media scholars ought to question their own role the most. The hypnotic mantra voice-over that reappears in the mashup from 2009 should be an invitation to indulge and get lost in the merge of images: "Now what we need to do is just concentrate, we just need to think, is to concentrate on images" (THINK KARTOONZ 2009).

BIBLIOGRAPHY

Andriopoulos, Stefan (2008): *Posessed. Hypnotic Crimes, Corporate Fiction, and the Invention of Cinema*. Chicago: University of Chicago Press.

Baudry, Jean-Louis (1974): Ideological effects of the basic cinematographic apparatus. In: *Film Quarterly*, Vol. 28, No. 2, 39–47.

Bellour, Raymond (2009): *Le Corps du cinéma: Hypnoses, émotions, animalités*. Paris: P.O.L.

Gaupp, Robert (1912): Der Kinematograph vom medizinischen und psychologischen Standpunkt. In: Kümmel, Albert/Löffler, Petra (eds.) (2002): *Medientheorie 1888–1933*. Frankfurt a. M.: Suhrkamp, 100–114.

Goodwin, James (1993): *Eisenstein, Cinema and History*. Urbana: University of Ilinois Press.

Gunning, Tom (1986): The Cinema of Attraction: Early Film, its Spectator and the Avant-Garde. In: *Wide Angle*, Vol. 8, Nos. 3–4, 63–70.

Jenkins, Henry (2006): *Convergence Culture: Where Old and New Media Collide.* New York: New York University Press, 1–24.

Kreimeier, Klaus (2011): *Traum und Exzess. Die Kulturgeschichte des frühen Kinos.* Wien: Zsolnay.

Meteling, Arno (2007): Mind Control und Montage: The Ipcress File – A Clockwork Orange – The Parallax View. In: Krause, Marcus/Pethes, Nicolas (eds.): *Mr. Münsterberg und Dr. Hyde.: Zur Filmgeschichte des Menschenexperiments.* Bielefeld: transcript, 231–252.

Moses, Gabriel S. (2012): The Con-sequential Narrative: Comics and the Unwritten Stories of the Modern Media Platform. In: Baleva, Martina/Reichle, Ingeborg/Schultz, Oliver Lerone (eds.): *Image Match. Visueller Transfer, ‚Imagescapes' und Intervisualität in globalen Bildkulturen.* Paderborn: Wilhelm Fink, 295–308.

Olmsted, Kathryn (2009): *Real Enemies. Conspiracy Theories and American Democracy, World War I to 9/11.* Oxford: Oxford University Press.

Schweinitz, Jörg (2010): Hypnotismus, früher Film: Übertragungen. Ein psychologischer Diskurs des 19. Jahrhunderts im medialen Transfer. In: Kleihues, Alexandra/Naumann, Barbara/Pankow, Edgar (eds.): *Intermedien: Zur kulturellen und artistischen Übertragung.* Zürich: Chronos, 457–476.

Wind Meyhoff, Karsten (2009): Kontrafaktische Kartierungen: Verschwörungstheorie und der 11. September. In: Poppe, Sandra/Schüller, Thorsten/Seiler, Sascha (eds.): *9/11 als kulturelle Zäsur: Repräsentationen des 11. Septembers 2001 in kulturellen Diskursen, Literatur und visuellen Medien.* Bielefeld: transcript, 61–80.

Web Videos

Habt-keine-angst.de "Wer bist du ?" (posted by magmafack). Web. Retrieved from: [http://www.youtube.com/watch?v=jJwD3J8nsnQ]; posted: 2011/06/25; access: 2012/10/10.

Habt keine Angst *(EXTREM)* (posted by Aschitaka14). Web. Retrieved from: [http://www.youtube.com/watch?v=i3C3cypcrQc]; posted: 2011/06/30; access: 2012/10/10.

Habt Keine Angst *(Pro 7)* (posted by ARGRep). Web. Retrieved from: [http://www.youtube.com/watch?v=6I5GtCrIiAA]; posted: 2011/06/19; access: 2012/10/10.

Only Fools, Backwards Lost - 03x07 - Not in Portland (posted by dabestdefense). Web. Retrieved from: [www.youtube.com/watch?v=mVCFbUPPZRo]; posted: 2007/02/10; access: 2012/10/10.

REBELL - HABT-KEINE-ANGST.DE *(PRO7)* (posted by MaryLilianMary). Web. Retrieved from: [http://www.youtube.com/watch?v=aA1KfJlHl_A]; posted: 2011/06/24; access: 2012/10/10.

SCIENTOLOGY AD: *"LIFE"* (posted by ChurchofScientology). Web. Retrieved from: [http://www.youtube.com/watch?v=5ku4I_WBEZ4]; posted: 2009/06/29; access: 2012/10/10.

THINK KARTOONZ (posted by heavyplastician). Web. Retrieved from: [http://www.youtube.com/watch?v=KImc2_kAelI]; posted: 2009/01/01; access: 2012/10/10.

WEAPONS OF MASS HYPNOSIS (posted by heavyplastician). Web. Retrieved from: [http://www.youtube.com/watch?v=S55ZToruJqA]; posted: 2008/02/14; access: 2012/05/13.

FILMS

A CLOCKWORK ORANGE (UK 1971, Stanley Kubrick)
BERLIN: DIE SINFONIE DER GROSSSTADT (BERLIN: SYMPHONY OF A GREAT CITY, Germany 1927, Walter Ruttmann)
ANÉMIC CINÉMA (ANEMIC CINEMA, France 1926, Marcel Duchamp)
DR. MABUSE – DER SPIELER (DR. MABUSE – THE GAMBLER, Germany 1922, Fritz Lang)
OKTYABR (OCTOBER, Russia 1928, Sergej M. Eisenstein)
THE MANCHURIAN CANDIDATE (USA 1962, John Frankenheimer)
THE PARALLAX VIEW (USA 1974, Alan J. Pakula)
VAMPIRES – LES YEUX QUI FASCINENT (VAMPIRES – HYPNOTIC EYES, France 1916, Louis Feuillade)
ZEITGEIST (USA 2007, Peter Joseph)

TELEVISION SERIES

LOST (USA 2004–2010, HBO)
THE PRISONER (UK 1967–1968, ITV)
V – THE VISITORS (Canada/USA 2009–2011, ABC)

IMAGE SOURCES

Figure 1: Screenshot from *HABT KEINE ANGST (PRO7)* (posted by ARGRep). Retrieved from: [youtube.com/watch?v=6I5GtCrIiAA]; access: 2012/07/23.

Figure 2: Screenshot from HABT-KEINE-ANGST.DE "WER BIST DU ?" (posted by magmafack). Retrieved from: [youtube.com/watch?v=jJwD3J8nsnQ]; access: 2012/07/23.

Figure 3+4: Screenshots from REBELL - HABT-KEINE-ANGST.DE (PRO7). Retrieved from: [youtube.com/watch?v=aA1KfJlHl_A]; access: 2012/07/23.

Figure 5: Screenshot from HABT KEINE ANGST (EXTREM) (posted by Aschitaka14). Retrieved from: [youtube.com/watch?v=i3C3cypcrQc]; access: 2012/07/23.

Figure 6: Screenshot from BERLIN: DIE SINFONIE DER GROSSSTADT (D 1927). DVD-Source: Edition Filmmuseum.

Figure 7+8: Screenshots from THE PARALLAX VIEW (USA 1974). DVD-Source: Paramount Home Entertainment.

Figure 9+10: Screenshots from THINK KARTOONZ (posted by heavyplastician). Retrieved from: [youtube.com/watch?v=KImc2_kAelI]; access: 2012/07/23.

Negotiating Boundaries

TV for the Post-TV Generation?[1]
How Transmedia Television Series Yearn for Another Type of Audience

DANIELA OLEK

Observing contemporary television series, we detect narrations that are no longer confined to television itself but expand towards other media.[2] For example ABC's LOST (USA 2004–2010) is one of the first television series which is distributed and told further predominantly online besides its regular broadcasting. Although it is classified as a "test case for the marriage between new technology and creative content" (Fernandez 2006; cited by Ross 2008, 19) because of its extreme use of such techniques[3], today, television series are watched 'outside the box' by default. That's why by labelling LOST as 'TV for the post-TV generation' the questions of what the structural changes of contemporary television series are and which repercussions they have on viewers arise immediately.

---

1 | This phrase was coined by Stephen Poniewozik in *Time Magazine* in 2006 describing ABC's LOST.

2 | This statement could be read on several levels—among others on a technological one. Television series no longer have to be watched exclusively on TV, but can be received on DVD, as a stream on the internet or as a download, respectively; thus, their reception is no longer confined to the TV set and the programme. The medium and its special form of reception no longer have to be a decisive factor if we talk about television series. But instead of analysing this technological transformation, this article focuses on the narrative expansion by using different media forms at once.

3 | In 2009, I researched LOST under the premise of intermedia effects (for further reading see Olek 2011). This contribution seeks to advance the results of this research on a universal basis and with a focus on (dis)orientation. It has already been proved by other researchers that the concept of narration crossing media borders is not limited to such a highly complex television series as LOST (see e.g. Mittell 2012; Piepiorka 2011).

As a catchphrase, 'post-TV' stands for the on-going developments in media landscapes which are characterised as media convergence—another catchphrase. According to Henry Jenkins (2006, 282), media convergence is "[a] word that describes technological, industrial, cultural and social changes in the way media circulates within our culture [...] [and] refers to a situation in which multiple media systems coexist and where media flows fluidly across them". This highly complex, unfinished process has many noticeable effects on most different ranges. One of them is that television, considered to be the most popular source of entertainment for a long time, has got severe competition. Digital media, like the computer in combination with the internet, opened the way to new technological infrastructures which enabled these media to remediate all kinds of pre-existing media (see Münker 2009, 20; Bolter/Grusin 1999). With the internet becoming a part of our everyday life the structural change of public communication has established it as "*the* medium of the masses in the 21st century" (Münker 2009, 19; transl. D.O.).[4] As a result people's attention is distracted from 'old' media and directed to the 'new' ones which in turn threaten the existence of the 'institution television' in its prevailing form. Although there is a slight and general growth in viewership shown in current surveys (see Zubayr/Gerhard 2012), the watching hours of the advertising-relevant group of the 14- to 29-year-olds are definitely much lower than those of elder viewers (see Peters/Niederauer-Kopf/Eckert 2012, 73). At the same time the internet is used more and more for entertainment and not only to provide information (see Busemann/Engel 2012, 133). Not least because of the migratory behaviour of this group, the mentioned 'post-TV generation', television needs to reinvent itself. Since media convergence is not an exploitation of the 'old' by the 'new', but rather an innovate impact on pre-existing media and their forms (see Bolter/Grusin 1999), television programmes need to be modified and developed further. Consequently, television series told across several media platforms, the transmedia television series, are one of these modifications.

Telling television series across several media not only by distributing videoclips involves deep structural transformation. The series have to be organised as networks so that cross-border story worlds can occur. In many cases these narrative elements will be found in the World Wide Web, but they are also present in analogue media like books or comics. These processes must not be understood as a repetition of already aired information, but as an addition to and expansion of the story world of the individual television series. In sum, the story unfolds across diverse media platforms, thereby establishing a distinct form of narration that is called 'transmedia storytelling' according to Jenkins (2006, 95) and that is often employed by producers and/or marketing departments. By making

---

4 | Original citation: "[D]ie Dynamik des Web 2.0 [hat] das digitale Netz [...] zu *dem* Medium der Massen für das 21. Jahrhundert werden lassen" (Münker 2009, 19).

use of several media platforms for the narration or reception at once, televisual series are no longer restricted to linearity referring to the TV medium. Besides the core text narration, additional parts of the story are widespread over several platforms and have to be searched and gathered by the viewer. Hence, textual systems that used to be primarily enclosed are opened up and the narration is spatially[5] constructed. To perceive the story as a whole the viewer[6] has to take a more active role than merely watching an episode. He has to follow the narrative parts on the several platforms and in doing so he creates his own path and order of the storyline. As a result he is embedded as an integral part within the storytelling process. Undeniably, such a construction has a huge potential to disorient the viewer, given he realises the transmedia expansion and has an interest in participating.[7]

In the coming paragraphs I want to analyse how this potential of spatially constructed narrations is concerning current transmedia television series: Which strategies are offered by the text so that the viewers are able to orient themselves? And, hence, what type of activity is trigged by such a kind of narration? To describe this systematically, the hypertext model will be used as a template. While there are other suitable concepts, the hypertext will provide us with one of the most useful patterns to observe the transformed textual organisation of television series. Depending on Marie-Laure Ryan's (2004, 356) argumentation that new media evoke new modes of storytelling, it will be assumed in this paper that the mentioned transformations are based on the interaction of media and their forms; or more specifically: They are consequences of the impact of the internet and its textual organisations.[8]

---

5 | With my colleague Christine Piepiorka I am working on a project about the impact of spatialisation on seriality by applying Michel de Certeau's sociological conceptions on spatiality (for further reading see Olek/Piepiorka 2012).

6 | Concerning transmedia television series, it is problematic to talk about the viewer as such, because experiencing a transmedia narration implies being a reader, a player, or a user all at once besides being a viewer. Up to now, there is no adequate term which covers all these facets. Hence, all these terms will be used in this paper, if I talk about the corresponding media forms. But it has to be emphasised that the whole context should always be kept in mind.

7 | Because this aspect is essential for the functioning of transmedia television series, some parts of the audience are excluded from this argumentation. Thus, if I talk about viewers in this contribution I only mean the ones who are aware of and take part in the transmedia network.

8 | Of course, I am aware of other media or forms (e.g. video games etc.) which are influencing conventional media and their narrative modes as well; with regard to the topic of (dis)orientation, the hypertext model will give us a broader range of possible answers.

The Hypertext Concept

Contrary to the linear structure of conventional television texts, which should be ideally received from beginning to end, hypertexts consist dominantly of modules organised in a non-linear way. Defined as "networks of textual fragments [...] connected by links" (ibid., 340) a hypertext needs to be read on an electronic device:

"The use of hypertext is most appropriate when 1. The content of the document is a large body of information logically organized and structured into multiple units or fragments; 2. These units are loosely associated with another, though not necessarily in a sequential manner; 3. A user or reader of the document only needs one unit or fragment of the content at any one time." (Shneiderman 1989; cited by Yoo 2007, 47)

Neither the number of fragments nor their sequence is set so that everything is changeable and all concepts of a chronological or causal organisation have to be abandoned. The fragments are structured like a network and can be received in any order, without a defined entry or exit point. The inner structure of each fragment, however, still remains linear—because a successful communication act maybe still requires a somehow coherently presented context.[9] Besides the mere transmission of information, the fragments are used as annotations, comments, explanations, references, and so on. But these fragments alone are not the hypertext. To become one, fragments have to be linked to each other. By activating the more or less visible junctures (see Storrer 2000, 228) a new fragment appears on the screen. Given that there are many links in every fragment which are associated in an arbitrary manner[10], the users are offered lots of choices in exploring the different itineraries through the hypertext. Hence, the reception can be seen as a dynamic construction process, because the users construct their own texts by clicking on links. But these constructed texts do not have to cover

---

[9] | If a communication act is intended to be successful, the content has to be presented coherently. Providing and receiving information is and remains a successive flow because speech has to be transmitted successively (see Storrer 2000, 239). Because of the hypertextual diversity, general statements are problematic. Depending on the communication goal, the construction of individual fragments (or of the whole hypertext, respectively) can vary significantly, so that fictional hypertexts are often more complex than informing ones.

[10] | Basically every element of a hypertext—a word, a graphic and so on—can be a link. Ontologically links are "tag[s] of electronic positions in a text on a screen" (Suter 2005; transl. D.O.; original citation: "eine Markierung einer elektronischen Textstelle auf einem Bildschirm") consisting of an anchor and a destination at least (see Olek 2011, 19ff.).

the complete hypertext; it is rather seemingly complete because of the user's perception. While a classical audiovisual narration requires cognitively active recipients, the hypertext demands actually active ones. Based on Ryan's (2001, 210ff.) definition of interactivity which can range from purely selective (the activation of a link among others) to productive (e.g. posts or comments), it can be said that the hypertext recipient has to be interactive. By identifying a link he has to decide whether to stay in this particular fragment, to jump to another now or later, or to go backwards, while always having to remember where his position is within the text, provided that he wants to. Thus, the decision for movement depends on the interest of the user.

In general, the aim of the communication act is essential for constructing hypertexts. Their structures differ considerably from one another: Hypertexts may assume the shape of a rhizome[11] by building up networks without beginning or end and without a constructed centre; they may evolve into a labyrinth or a more hierarchical form—like a tree; or they may be linear. For example, hypertextual narrations, so-called hyperfictions, have to be more coherent[12] than an online encyclopaedia. Instead of the complete abandonment of linearity, the presentation of the story (which is comparable with the plot level in linear media narrations) has been transformed in hyperfictions (see Ryan 2004, 354ff.): "Many hypertexts [...] exemplify [...] a 'storyworld'. Storyworlds, which contain multiple narratives, demand active readers because they only disclose their stories in response to the reader's action" (Landow 2006, 245). Contrary to prevalent printed narrations, the presentation is not chronological and causal on the whole, but the story in hyperfictions unfolds spatially and can be designed multidimensionally (see ibid., 221). These multiple narratives are potentially infinite and linked with each other (see ibid.), so that the narration spreads out ramifiedly. The goal of hyperfiction should be "followability" according to Land-

---

11 | Gilles Deleuze and Félix Guattari (2005 [1977], 36f.) have been using the concept of the rhizome, understood as a web of roots, as a metaphor for forms of 'knowledge organisation' in the postmodern age. But with regards to the specific characteristics, it has to be said that these concepts, the rhizome and the hypertext, are not completely congruent with each other (see Landow 2006, 58f.). As, for example, rhizomes are never hierarchical, the separation between production and reception cannot be maintained with this concept.

12 | The literature offers two differentiated approaches defining coherence in hypertexts: on the one hand, coherence within the reception process results from the user's 'walking through' the networked text and from his own sense making; on the other hand, coherence is planned during text production. The latter is more applicable to hyperfictions because they are no "story-generating machine[s]" (Ryan 2004, 342), but more similar to jigsaw puzzles whose text fragments need to be pieced together by the user. This activity refers more to the reconstruction of a planned story.

ow (ibid, 223), which means that the story should be comprehended in spite of diverse story lines, discontinuities, or diversions. The user has to follow the story by moving through the fragments, by exploring them, keeping everything in mind, searching for new ones, and making sense of information often given coincidentally and unrelated. He has to organise these bits of information by the known principles of chronology and causality (see Ryan 2004, 341). But the more open a narration is constructed, the more difficult it is to understand it. And without any guiding or hierarchy and in combination with the sheer bulk of information, user disorientation is possible and even likely. Thus, especially in hypernarrations the options are limited and depending on the previous path through the text (see Seibel 2002, 230).

THE PROBLEM WITH EXTENDED STORY WORLDS

Coming back to answer the question why transmedia television series are capable of disorienting their viewers, it is necessary to have a close look at how they are constructed by analysing some examples. Although there are no generalities in designing such a narration, besides the mentioned presentation 'out of the box', there are some often used forms.

Several television series use comic strips, which are available either online or as a book, to continue selected story elements, to deepen the story itself or to further develop the characters. For instance, since 2010 TRUE BLOOD (USA 2007–, HBO) has bridged each season break with a comic book series (see Huehner/Tischmann 2010). In the first volume the action takes place in one of the show's main locations: the bar Merlottes, which is the workplace of the protagonist Sookie Stackhouse. Seven main characters are trapped there by a spirit who feeds on shame and they have to tell their most embarrassing secrets to survive. Thus, by using the comic form the viewer receives key information about the characters that helps to understand their actions within the television plot. Another example for using comic strips to extend the story world (but in a different way) is Joss Whedon's BUFFY THE VAMPIRE SLAYER (USA 1997–2003, The WB/UPN). After the show's final televised season, the seventh, the series was continued within comic books setting in a year after the final events (the destruction of Sunnydale) and picking up the loose plot lines (see Whedon/Jeanty 2007–2010). This eighth season was published in 40 issues between 2007 and 2011 and is now followed by a ninth one. Besides elaborating prevailing plots or characters, comic strips can also be used to establish new narrative elements which will be assimilated by the television plot afterwards.

NBC's HEROES (USA 2006–2010), for instance, introduced the new character Hana Gitelman in their graphic novels during its first season (see fig. 1).

Figure 1: Hana Gitelman's 'way from the comic book into the television text'.

Hana's character is developed within four online issues[13], so-called chapters, on the official NBC website[14] between December 2006 and January 2007, and first appears within the show in February 2007 (S1/E16). She is introduced by her abilities: Hana Gitelman acts as a living transmitter and receiver and can receive and send electronic messages. Before her physical appearance, she contacts another character via an instant messenger on an unplugged laptop. Because of the short on-screen appearance, only a reader of the graphic novels is able to perceive the introduction of this character and is aware of the whole meaning.

Although all these examples show slightly different ways of expanding story worlds, the overall function of using another narrative medium is to establish new plots—which, however, could also be told on television. Picking up the hypertext concept, the establishment of new plots (understood as narratives linked together by elements like characters) may also lead to the emergence of multi-dimensional stories.

---

13 | See *Wireless. Part One* [http://www.nbc.com/heroes/novels/novels_display.shtml?novel=13], *Wireless. Part Two* [http://www.nbc.com/heroes/novels/index.shtml?novel=14], *Wireless. Part Three* [http://www.nbc.com/heroes/novels/index.shtml?novel=15)], *Wireless. Part Four* [http://www.nbc.com/heroes/novels/index.shtml?novel=16].

14 | The online comic issues were published during the seasons and continue to be available on the official website after the show's cancellation. The seven to nine pages long comics are provided in PDF and Flash format [see http://www.nbc.com/heroes/novels/novels_library.shtml].

Figure 2: Screenshot from the website 'Buy More' from NBC's CHUCK.

But transmedia extensions do not have to be exclusively narrative.[15] Other—elementarily digital—forms are used to enhance the story world itself without being merely narrative. These can be fictional websites, so called "simulation sites" according to Will Brooker (2009, 54), which present elements of the television plot as factual within the internet. These sites are often—but not exclusively—accessible without any clue of its fiction and interconnected with others.

Figure two is a screenshot of a simulation site from NBC's CHUCK (USA 2007-2012)—the online presence of the fictional multimedia store 'Buy More' which is one of the settings within the fictional universe. This website simulates factual online multimedia stores by using similar layouts and menu structures. However, there is also the NBC logo and trademark, a link leading back to the show's website, and links to the service terms and the privacy policy of the broadcaster, each pointing to the website's fictionality (and its promotional

---

15 | Another narrative form are the so called 'webisodes', short episodes about two to five minutes long which are streamed mostly on the official broadcaster's websites. Indeed, there is little scope to develop new plots which is the reason why they are not analysed fully in this paper. They are also used to deepen the story world and its characters or to tell previous events. For example, amongst others LOST used it for the presentation of events which took place directly before the pilot; and USA Network created LITTLE MONK in which childhood stories of Monk as an awkward but talented kid are presented (see [http://www.usanetwork.com/series/littlemonk]).

Figure 3: Screenshot from Barney Stinson's Blog.

character). Other simulation sites do not have such markers, like BREAKING BAD'S (USA 2008–, AMC) donation website.[16]

Another often used digital form are blogs. In general, they are used to give another perspective on the screened action, to comment on it or deepen it. By this pretended self-presentation the characters seem to gain some added value, an off-screen (quasi private) personality and psychological depth. Examples can be found in the TRUE BLOOD universe: One of the marginal characters, Jessica Hamby, uses a blog to post about her life as a 'teenage vampire'.[17] Another example is a blogging website referring to HOW I MET YOUR MOTHER (USA 2005–, CBS), on which one of the protagonists, Barney Stinson, presents his view of the events within the series.[18] Suggesting that he writes about his experiences (which the viewers may have watched on television), the story world is extended by the addition of a new perspective. But the posts are not limited to the on-screen action, they are also presenting several further topics. Besides reading the blog posts, the users get more information about the fictional person Barney

---

16 | See [http://www.savewalterwhite.com].
17 | See [http://www.babyvamp-jessica.com].
18 | See [http://www.cbs.com/shows/how_i_met_your_mother/barneys_blog]. Written by screenwriter Matt Kuhn (see Gelman 2008), this blog is a good example for a differentiated structure and regular updates.

Stinson, his books[19] (which can be bought), or about the motivational posters which are part of the decoration of the character's on-screen office (see fig. 3). Moreover, the character is further differentiated by integrating social media into his transmedia construction: Barney Stinson has a *Facebook* profile[20] and a *Twitter* account.[21]

In addition, blogs crucially modify the reception process: While the television show and the comic books are still confined, the user is able to encounter the story world by using the web extensions. Hence, the borders between fiction and reality begin to blur. Although the recipient is aware that he engages himself with a staged world, the hypertextual experience is the crucial innovation. The user can explore the different sites, can activate links, can jump to others and, thus, can move through parts of the fictional universe and 'interact' with it. Furthermore, blogs or other social networking devices like *Facebook* enable something very interesting: They not only allow for the described interconnectedness, they offer some kind of multiway communication. In fact, everyone can comment on the individual posts.

While a transmedia television series is not a pure hypertext[22], because the show still is clearly the established centre, its transmedial fragmentation reproduces hypertextual structures. The exemplarily shown transmedia extensions all enhance the core text: First of all, by continuing the story in other media, the temporal limits of television are transcended. Fragmenting the story and disposing these fragments on diverse platforms at once interferes with the successive mode of narration and facilitates a non-linear organisation. While the arrangement is more or less linear within each transmedial extension (a comic strip, for example, is designed in a more consistent manner than a blog) their simultaneous and parallel availability and their accessability in any order leads to the emergence of a narrative network. The previously given examples illustrate the usage of the transmedia fragments as annotations, explanations, or references. Currently these extensions are not mandatory to understand the television show. But all these various narratives multiply the narration and further its ramification. As a result, there is a bulk of information on different media platforms instead of a coherent, confined television show. Although the recipient is allowed to walk through and to explore the narrative spaces, the threat of getting lost within them arises. Searching for dispersed narrative fragments combined with an increasing number of them thus may lead to a disoriented recipient:

19 | Stinson/Kuhn (2008).
20 | See [http://www.facebook.com/pages/Barney-Stinson/10569236108].
21 | See [https://twitter.com/broslife].
22 | Even if the beginning of a story or the end is narrated within a transmedia fragment, so that the show's plot is not the origin, television series cannot be called rhizomatic (see Olek 2011, 55f.).

Every new bit of information can draw his attention to another fragment so that he has to decide every single time whether to stay in this particular fragment, to jump to another now or later, or to go backwards, while always having to remember what he wanted to look for. In addition, the potential of viewer disorientation increases through the many fan produced workings. Particularly many of them can be found on the internet: Fans create websites, which stand next to official ones, or use character names to set up *Facebook* or *Twitter* accounts (currently, there are six Barney Stinsons on *Twitter*). Also, there do not have to be any markers to verify the fragments as official productions and, furthermore, some plots can be contradictory to the others without being non-official.[23]

This mode of non-linear storytelling also requires a different mode of reception compared to the common watching of a television show. As mentioned before, watching the show is furthermore a significant part of experiencing transmedia universes. But moreover, the recipients have to be prepared for engaging themselves with different reception contexts. They have to act like internet users, (video game) players, and readers all at once. Basically, they have to be participants who want to explore and search for other media extensions. The concept of dispersing narrative fragments over several media platforms seems to be based on the presumed migratory behaviour of the desired advertising-relevant target group—the post-TV generation. They should be picked up where they are expected—mostly on the internet. That is why each fragment is coherent in itself and—according to the introduced hypertext theory (see above), but also consistent with Henry Jenkins (2006, 95)—functions as an individual entry point into the story world of each television series. Providing that the 'new' recipients are familiar with hypertextual strategies, orientation can be the result of their everyday practice. They are accustomed to navigate through digital spaces by clicking on links, searching for dispersed bits of information, and assembling them to make sense.

But the producers would risk too much if they only counted on modified habits of younger recipients. Therefore, they create strategies to guide all of the interested recipients through the transmedia universes: first of all by offering special websites for each television series. Besides common production information like cast, episode guides, or video streams of each episode, a transmedia extension can be embedded (like Barney's Blog on CBS' How I Met Your Mother website) or the particular link is offered (like the one to Babyvamp Jessica's page on HBO's True Blood website). Consequently, current network websites function as portals into the transmedial world. Another strategy to gain the viewers' attention and to direct them outside of the box, is the referencing

---

23 | Under the premise of the hypertext-concept, fan-created texts can be seen as parts of the transmedia story world because hypertexts are open systems which allow for participation by linking new textual fragments to it.

during the broadcast or within the televised plot. For example, in How I Met Your Mother the characters often talk about websites they created or the blog Barney writes. Exactly these sites can be found by the viewers if they go online.[24] Some of the websites link to other transmedia extensions like simulation sites or—holding on to the How I Met Your Mother blog example—promote books which can be bought and which transfer the fiction into the recipients' reality. In general, narrative elements like the mentioned websites, the setting[25], or individual characters can be used as an orientation guide.[26] If the recipient discovers another extension and recognises a particular element, regardless of the starting point, he will connect both fragments as a result. To explore the transmedia universe further, the recipient can follow these elements into different contexts. In addition, the mentioned social networking devices are not only used to extend the story world, they are helpful as orientation tools, too. If someone is linked to such a profile, he receives posts and additional information regularly without searching for it, thus being guided to one of the transmedia fragments subsequently. Particularly important within the orientation context are the fan created wikis which come up with nearly every television series. Besides the general articles about the series, its seasons, its characters etc., they gather all the dispersed transmedial fragments and analyse and classify them within the narrative universe.

In conclusion, to understand a television show there is no 'desperate need' for additional information and the mentioned 'blessings of the hypertexts additional information'—in most cases. At the moment, the television show as such still is the main narration—or like the Lost producers' said "the mothership" (Lachonis 2007). But members of the post-TV generation, who assumedly do not watch TV according to a schedule, will find and follow the series and its extensions. The reinvention (and re-orientation) of television, which results in modified ways of narration in this case, could be comprehended as a search for an audience which is no longer confined by television.

---

24 | Particularly How I Met Your Mother is a good example how new media forms are used. Besides using blogs, *Facebook*, or *Twitter* there are several simulation sites online. In general, every time a website is mentioned within the television show, it can be found on the internet (see e.g. [http://itwasthebestnightever.com], [http://slapcountdown.org]).

25 | The bar 'Merlotte', for example, has its own *Facebook* profile without any 'fiction markers'. It looks like any regular company (or restaurant) profile (see [https://www.facebook.com/merlottesbarandgrill/info]).

26 | See the contributions of Jason Mittell and Christine Piepiorka in this volume, too.

Bibliography

Bolter, Jay David/Grusin, Richard (2000): *Remediation: Understanding New Media.* Cambridge: MIT Press.

Brooker, Will (2009): Television Out of Time: Watching Cult Shows on Download. In: Pearson, Roberta (ed.): *Reading Lost: Perspectives On a Hit Television Show.* London/New York: I. B. Tauris, 51–72.

Busemann, Katrin/Engel, Bernhard (2012): Wandel der Mediennutzungsprofile im Zeitalter des Internets. In: *Media Perspektiven* 3, 133-146.

Deleuze, Gilles/Guattari, Félix (2005 [1977]): *Tausend Plateaus.* Berlin: Merve.

Gelman, Vlada (2008): Boning Up on the ›Bro Code‹. Web. Retrieved from: [http://www.tvweek.com/blogs/blink/2008/08/boning_up_on_the_bro_code.php]; posted: 2008/08/22; access: 2012/10/10.

Jenkins, Henry (2006): *Convergence Culture: Where Old and New Media Collide.* New York: New York University Press.

Lachonis, Jon (2007): *BuddyTV Interviews Lost's Damon Lindelof and Carlton Cuse – and Gets Answers!* Web. Retrieved from: [http://www.buddytv.com/articles/lost/more/buddytv-interviews-losts-damon-4766.aspx]; posted: 2007/03/07; access: 2012/10/10.

Landow, George (2006): *Hypertext 3.0: Critical Theory and New Media in an Era of Globalization.* (Rev. ed.). Baltimore: John Hopkins University Press.

Mittell, Jason (2012): *Complex TV: The Poetics of Contemporary Television Storytelling.* Pre-publication edition. Media Commons Press. Web. Retrieved from: [http://mediacommons.futureofthebook.org/mcpress/complextelevision]; access: 2012/10/10.

Münker, Stefan (2009): *Emergenz digitaler Öffentlichkeiten: Die Sozialen Medien im Web 2.0.* Frankfurt a. M.: Suhrkamp.

Olek, Daniela (2011): *Lost und die Zukunft des Fernsehens. Die Veränderung des seriellen Erzählens im Zeitalter von Media Convergence.* Stuttgart: Ibidem.

Olek, Daniela/Piepiorka, Christine (2012): To Be Continued ... Somewhere else. Die Auswirkungen struktureller Räumlichkeit auf die Serialität im Kontext transmedialer Serien. In: Spangenberg, Peter M./Westermann, Bianca (eds.): *Im Moment des ‚Mehr'.* Münster: Lit, 75–93.

Peters, Bärbel/Niederauer-Kopf, Kerstin/Eckert, Matthias (2012): Die individualisierte Fernsehnutzung. In: *Media Perspektiven* 2, 72-77.

Piepiorka, Christine (2011): *Lost in Narration: Narrativ komplexe Serienformate in einem transmedialen Umfeld.* Stuttgart: Ibidem.

Poniewozik, James (2006): *Why the Future of Television is Lost.* Web. Retrieved from: [http://www.time.com/time/magazine/article/0,9171,1538635,00.html]; posted: 2006/09/24; access: 2012/10/10.

Ross, Sharon Marie (2008): *Beyond the Box: Television and the Internet.* Malden/Oxford: Blackwell Publishing.

Ryan, Marie-Laure (2004): Will New Media Produce New Narratives? In: Ryan, Marie-Laure (ed.): *Narrative across Media: The Language of Storytelling*. Lincoln: University of Nebraska Press, 337–359.

Ryan, Marie-Laure (2001): *Narrative as Virtual Reality: Immersion and Interactivity in Literature and Electronic Media*. Baltimore: John Hopkins University Press.

Storrer, Angelika (2000): Was ist "hyper" am Hypertext? In: Kallmeyer, Werner (ed.): *Sprache und neue Medien*. Berlin: De Gruyter, 222–249.

Seibel, Klaudia (2002): Cyberage-Narratologie: Erzähltheorie und Hyperfiktion. In: Nünning, Vera/Nünning, Ansgar: *Erzähltheorie transgenerisch, intermedial, interdisziplinär*. Trier: Wissenschaftlicher Verlag Trier, 217–236.

Stinson, Barney/Kuhn, Matt (2008): *The Bro Code*. New York: Fireside.

Suter, Beat (2005): *Der Hyperlink in der Lektüre: Pause, Leerstelle oder Flucht?* Web. Retrieved from: [http://dichtung-digital.org/2005/2/Suter/index.htm]; posted: 2005/02. access: 2012/10/10.

Yoo, Hyun-Joo (2007): *Text, Hypertext, Hypermedia: Ästhetische Möglichkeiten der digitalen Literatur mittels Intertextualität, Interaktivität und Intermedialität*. Würzburg: Königshausen & Neumann.

Zubayer, Camille/Gerhard, Heinz (2012): Tendenzen im Zuschauerverhalten. In: *Media Perspektiven* 3, 118-132.

Comics

Huehner, Mariah/Tischman, David (2010): *True Blood*. San Diego: IDW.

Whedon, Joss/Jeanty, George (2007–2011): *Buffy the Vampire Slayer. Season 8*. Milwaukie: Dark Horse.

Whedon, Joss/Jeanty, George (2012–): *Buffy the Vampire Slayer. Season 9*. Milwaukie: Dark Horse.

Web Sources

Babyvamp Jessica. Web. Retrieved from: [http://www.babyvamp-jessica.com]; access: 2012/10/10.

Barney's Blog/Barney Stinson Blog. Web. Retrieved from: [http://www.barneystinsonblog.com]; access: 2012/10/10.

Buy More (NBC CHUCK). Web. Retrieved from: [http://buy-more.net]; access: 2012/10/10.

CBS HOW I MET YOUR MOTHER: *Barney's Blog*. Web. Retrieved from: [http://www.cbs.com/shows/how_i_met_your_mother/barneys_blog]; access: 2012/10/10.

Facebook: Barney Stinson. Web. Retrieved from: [http://www.facebook.com/pages/Barney-Stinson/10569236108]; access: 2012/10/10.

Facebook: Merlotte's Bar and Grill. Web. Retrieved from: [https://www.facebook.com/merlottesbarandgrill/info]; access: 2012/10/10.

HBO TRUE BLOOD: *Jessica's Blog.* Web. Retrieved from: [http://www.hbo.com/true-blood/index.html#/true-blood/inside/extras/social/jessicas-blog.html]; access: 2012/10/10.

itwasthebestnightever (CBS HOW I MET YOUR MOTHER). Web. Retrieved from: [http://itwasthebestnightever.com]; access: 2012/10/10.

NBC HEROES: *Graphic Novel Library.* Web. Retrieved from: [http://www.nbc.com/heroes/novels/novels_library.shtml]; access: 2012/10/10.

NBC HEROES: *Graphic Novel Chapter 13: Wireless. Part One.* Web. Retrieved from: [http://www.nbc.com/heroes/novels/index.shtml?novel=13]; access: 2012/10/10.

NBC HEROES: *Graphic Novel Chapter 14: Wireless. Part Two.* Web. Retrieved from: [http://www.nbc.com/heroes/novels/index.shtml?novel=14]; access: 2012/10/10.

NBC HEROES: *Graphic Novel Chapter 15: Wireless. Part Three.* Web. Retrieved from: [http://www.nbc.com/heroes/novels/index.shtml?novel=15]; access: 2012/10/10.

NBC HEROES: *Graphic Novel Chapter 16: Wireless. Part Four.* Web. Retrieved from: [http://www.nbc.com/heroes/novels/index.shtml?novel=16]; access: 2012/10/10.

Slapcountdown (CBS HOW I MET YOUR MOTHER). Web. Retrieved from: [http://slapcountdown.org]; access: 2012/07/24.

Twitter: Barney Stinson (@Broslife). Web. Retrieved from: [https://twitter.com/broslife]; access: 2012/10/10.

USA Network: LITTLE MONK. Web. Retrieved from: [www.usanetwork.com/series/littlemonk]; access: 2012/10/10.

TELEVISION SERIES

BREAKING BAD (USA, 2007–, AMC)
BUFFY – THE VAMPIRE SLAYER (USA, 1997–2003, The WB/UPN)
CHUCK (USA, 2007–2012, NBC)
HEROES (USA, 2006–2010, NBC)
HOW I MET YOUR MOTHER (USA, 2005–, CBS)
LOST (USA, 2004–2010, ABC)
MONK (USA, 2002–2009, USA Network)
TRUE BLOOD (USA, 2007–, HBO)

Image Sources

Figure 1: Screenshot from *Wireless Part Four* (NBC Heroes, Graphic Novel Chapter 16). Retrieved from: [http://www.nbc.com/heroes/novels/index.shtml?novel=16]; access: 2012/10/10.

Figure 2: Screenshot from the Website *Buy More* (NBC Chuck). Retrieved from: [http://buy-more.net/]; access: 2012/10/10.

Figure 3: Screenshot from *Barney Stinson Blog*. Retrieved from: [http://www.barneystinsonblog.com/]; access: 2012/10/10.

Re-orienting Romantic Comedy
Genre Negotiations in Richard Linklater's BEFORE SUNRISE

KATJA HETTICH

The title of this paper may immediately raise the following question: Does BEFORE SUNRISE (USA/Austria/Switzerland 1995, Richard Linklater) actually count as a romantic comedy? The romantic comedy is one of mainstream Hollywood's most successful and enduring vehicles and, as such, is widely regarded as "the most conventional and conservative of all genres" (Deleyto 2009, 3), with a very distinctive plot-driven narrative. BEFORE SUNRISE, by contrast, may be considered marginally mainstream in the popularity it gained as a cult film for Generation X, but it is still a small-scale niche film with an unorthodox, minimalist plot made by independent auteur Richard Linklater, whose oeuvre includes films as experimental as SLACKER (USA 1991) or WAKING LIFE (USA 2001). Nonetheless, I would argue that BEFORE SUNRISE, despite its obvious differences from typical mainstream romantic comedy, is undeniably constituted by and constitutive of genre expectations. Following Rick Altman's *Semantics/Syntactics Approach to Film Genre* (1986), I maintain that Linklater's film renews the romantic comedy genre by applying and adjusting its conventional orientation system to align it with that of another framework: namely that of independent cinema.

The implications and the validity of this assumption will be explored in seven sections: The first section will review some genre conventions that BEFORE SUNRISE appropriates, making it likely that the spectator will read the film, to some degree, against the backdrop of romantic comedy. After a brief outline in the second section of how genre expectations determine the spectator's orientation during the film viewing, the third section will explore the impact of two key conventions—a crisis to overcome and a guaranteed happy ending—on both the traditionally linear narrative of the romantic comedy's trajectory and on the viewer's engagement. The fourth section will, first, examine to what extent the absence of these two key tropes from BEFORE SUNRISE raises serious doubts as to its labelling; then, I will suggest that these hesitations may be explained by means of Rick Altman's theory of genre innovation. The fifth section will compare the label of 'romantic comedy' with that of 'indie film', focussing on their functions as orientation systems to which the film viewer aligns his expectations. The sixth section will finally set out how BEFORE SUNRISE attributes new meaning to romantic comedy by replacing its linear trajectory with a movement mode that could be described as *flânerie*, before the seventh section will conclude this essay by summarising its results.

VIENNESE HOLIDAY: *BEFORE SUNRISE* AS ROMANTIC COMEDY

Admittedly, BEFORE SUNRISE is certainly not likely to attract the casual film viewer who is in search of a typical romantic comedy. Still there is some evidence to suggest that spectators will tend to perceive the film against the background of the genre. Its paratexts already provide them clear indications in this direction (e.g. the trailer, featuring the cheerful *Lemonheads* love song "Into Your Arms" and showing the couple falling in love and having fun together). And after all, one has to admit that the film fits very well under the broadest definition of a romantic comedy as "a film which has as its central narrative motor a quest for love, which portrays this quest in a light-hearted way and almost always to a successful conclusion" (Jeffers McDonald 2007, 9).

To give a short plot summary: BEFORE SUNRISE is about the fourteen-hour romance between two strangers in their early twenties after a chance meeting on a train. The French grad student Céline is on her way back to Paris after visiting her grandmother in Budapest. The American tourist Jesse is on the last leg of his Euro-rail trip right before taking a flight back to the U.S. Wishing to continue their stimulating conversation and flirtation he talks her into leaving the train with him. They spend the night strolling through Vienna, flirting and talking about their pasts, their momentary situation, their fears and their hopes for the future—and mainly about love. As they take leave of each other the next morning, they spontaneously decide to meet again six months later, before parting and continuing their travels back home.

In short, the whole story of BEFORE SUNRISE is nothing more than this very "quest for love" mentioned in the rom-com definition above: It is all about two protagonists searching for soul-mate-ship and intimacy by wandering around and sharing their thoughts and feelings. And sure enough, Céline and Jesse's flirtatious night-time stroll through summery Vienna is also likely to light up the spectator's heart as he is invited to share the positive emotions the youthful lovers experience in their growing bond, just as he will join in their laughter that dissipates feelings of awkwardness and inhibition that naturally accompany the courtship situation. It is true that Céline and Jesse go their separate ways in the end, which is not what one would usually expect as a typical 'successful conclusion' to a romantic comedy, yet the fact remains that this ending is represented in a light-hearted way and thus still likely to be interpreted as a positive outcome.[1]

Beyond its main topic and its overall tone, BEFORE SUNRISE displays more specific characteristics of the romantic comedy genre, in particular plot elements, setting and characters. Céline and Jesse's night together is based on a common rom-com staple: the 'meet cute', a contrived situation that gives two strangers the opportunity to become attached to one another (Jeffers McDonald 2007, 12). Their first encounter in the train suggests their immediate emotional connection. It follows a love-at-first-sight scenario, indicated by shot-reverse-shots of close-ups that emphasise their shared meaningful and seductive glances. And Jesse's spontaneous proposal creates the particular situation in which he and his girl spend a whole night together in a foreign city where they have nothing else to do than to grow close.

BEFORE SUNRISE also features an emblematic genre setting. First of all, it is set in a city, which is generally the genre's preferred location (ibid., 11). It is, no less, a European city that is prone to be considered a particularly romantic location. Second, the picturesque sites the foreigners Céline and Jesse visit and the open-hearted residents who cross their paths seem to embody the "magic space" removed from ordinary life as well as the "benevolent context" that Celestino Deleyto describes as crucial engines of the transformation the romantic comedy's protagonists have to undergo in order to be ready for deep commitment (2009, 30ff.). Third, Linklater's Vienna also gives Céline and Jesse an adequate location for what Stanley Cavell considers to be required in the rom-com's coupling process: Nothing more than a transitional stopping-off place, it is the perfect "setting [...] in which the pair have the leisure to be together, to waste time together" (1981, 88).

In terms of character configuration, Céline and Jesse correspond closely to the conventions of romantic comedy. They are young, good-looking and likely to enlist the audience's sympathies. Their slightly antagonistic characterisation follows another common genre rule (Jeffers McDonald 2007, 16): As a rather down-to-earth but indecisive American male, on the one hand, and a more spirited and decisive French female, on the other, they seem to complement each other perfectly. Furthermore, the film's minimalist narrative takes to the extreme "the genre's traditional dual focused narrative" (Krutnik 1998, 22): It follows its equal main characters not only on parallel tracks, but sets them throughout the film literally on the very same track as they walk through the streets of Vienna.

The description of BEFORE SUNRISE so far seems to suggest that it fits quite neatly into romantic comedy patterns, except for two variations. First, it basically extends the initial 'boy meets girl' situation over the entire length of the feature and leaves out all the complications the protagonists (and the emotion-

---

1 | This point will be discussed in more detail in the concluding section of this article.

ally involved viewer) usually have to confront. Second, it leaves us with an open though still rather light-hearted ending. The crux, however, is that these two narrative alterations do not merely change the final outcome. As I will point out in what follows, the way in which the narrative is modified and the happy ending is suspended is liable to question and eventually to adjust the whole orientation system of both the narrative trajectory and the audience's expectations, and consequently, the whole idea of romance and of romantic comedy conveyed by this film.

GENRES AS ORIENTATION SYSTEMS

Given the wide variety of possible issues to be raised in the context of genre criticism, it is first of all important to be clear about what is meant here by 'genre'. Rather than assuming a restrictive definition of genres as fixed and ahistorical categories with specific inherent qualities, this paper will draw on a reception-focused conception of genres as fluid processes which are open to constant negotiation and variation in the interaction between film-makers, films, and audiences. Adopting the semio-pragmatic approach suggested by Francesco Casetti (1999), genres can be seen as "a collection of shared rules that allows the film-maker to use established communicative formulas and the viewer to organise his own system of expectations" (ibid., 271). In this perspective, genres establish, according to Thomas Schatz' widely used phrase, a sort of "tacit 'contract' between film-makers and the audience" (1981, 16) that is satisfied if the generically implied expectations are met. The contract metaphor is, however, prone to entail some misunderstandings, since it evokes an idea of the generic experience as determined by previously fixed and even enforceable rules. To stress the preliminary character of generic agreements, it seems therefore more useful to consider genres to be orientation systems that are subject to continued adjustment during the reception process.

The orienting functions of genres can be depicted in both a spatial and a temporal dimension. Speaking in spatial terms, genres have a triple function. First, they define boundaries for probable audience expectations: They set limits on the kind of characters, events, settings, stylistic features, etc. that the film viewer is prepared to accept as suitable with the inherent probability system of a specific genre. Taking his cue from Tzvetan Todorov's theory on the fantastic (1973), Steve Neale states that generic "systems of expectations and hypothesis involve a knowledge of—indeed they partly embody—various *regimes of verisimilitude*—various systems of plausibility, motivation, justification, and belief" (1990, 161; emphasis added). To give an example: Characters suddenly bursting into a song would seriously challenge the generic verisimilitude of a thriller whereas such behaviour is considered perfectly appropriate and believable in a musical.

Second, genres direct the film viewer's interpretation activities during the viewing process. Generic knowledge tells him that the plot is liable to follow certain directions rather than others and, hence, orientates him towards assumptions and attitudes that are more useful in making sense of the film than others.

Third, genres hold out prospects not only of predictable plotlines, but also of distinctive gratifications spectators may derive from their emotional engagement with each genre. In this context, Vinzenz Hediger and Patrick Vonderau (2005), focusing on the functions of genres in film marketing, consider them to be "maps of pleasures" (transl. K.H.) that allow the filmgoer to keep the orientation in the vast landscape of products offered by the film industry.[2]

In some sense, all these, metaphorically spoken, spatial features of generic orientation also include a temporal dimension in that they prompt the audience to anticipate what would be likely—and like*able*—to happen in the future. The film viewer's forward-looking activities not only concern upcoming developments, but also the satisfaction he hopes to achieve when his genre expectations will finally be fulfilled.

In order to provide a background for a closer consideration of the transformations the romantic comedy genre undergoes in BEFORE SUNRISE, the next section will summarise some general characteristics of the orientation system of romantic comedy.

THE ORIENTATION SYSTEM OF ROMANTIC COMEDY

In general, romantic comedies are still quite faithful to what is considered one of the main features of classical Hollywood's story construction: narrative linearity, consisting in "a linkage which resembles a game of dominos, each dangling cause matched by its effect in the following scene" (Bordwell/Staiger/Thompson 1985, 64). This causal chain of events creates a narrative drive that constantly incites the spectator to form hypotheses about what happens next. Furthermore, as Patrick Keating (2006) reminds us, linear narratives are particularly suitable to incite not only anticipatory assumptions about possible outcomes, but also anticipatory emotions. According to Murray Smith's theory of character engagement (1995), we get emotionally involved with films through allegiance

---

2 | Original citation: "Als Verzeichnisse zu erwartender Gratifikationen sind Genres gleichsam *Landkarten des Vergnügens*: Sie verhalten sich zum Film wie Landkarten zur Landschaft, insofern sie eine hinreichend genaue, aber keine erschöpfende Darstellung des Unterhaltungsangebotes geben" (Hediger/Vonderau 2005, 241; emphasis added).

and alignment with characters, causing us to evaluate the narrative situation in response to their individual condition, their values and their needs. In short, sympathising with a protagonist will prompt us to hope that he will reach his goal and to fear, in the face of obstacles that may arise, that he won't.

Turning now to the question of how linearity, in this sense, affects the orientation system of romantic comedies, it appears that the linear and emotionally loaded progress towards the happy ending is a distinctive quality of the genre. Romantic comedies are usually aimed at forming an intense allegiance to likeable main characters and at making the viewer realise that there is only one way to fulfil their inner needs: Their quest for love has to come to a successful conclusion. Even if the protagonists themselves may not realise it from the beginning, the generically informed film viewer will identify them instantly as the perfect romantic couple. And their final reunion, thus being the overarching goal, is the generically inevitable orientation point for both the causal chain of events and the audience's cognitive and emotional engagement.[3] The happy ending is not only the culmination point of this process; even its anticipation affects the experience of the film as a whole. Within the reassurance that, in the end, everything will be alright, the spectator can, even in face of upcoming obstacles to the couple's happiness, fully enjoy his compassionate suffering with them. In this context, the happy ending turns out to be much more than just an accessory plot element. When it comes to the romantic comedy, the happy ending is a generically required orientation principle that guides the narrative trajectory as well as the film viewer's cognitive and emotional experience. It is also the prior condition that has to be met so that he receives the promised gratifications.

As a consequence, romantic comedies usually develop a strong forward thrust: Once kicked off by the protagonists' first meeting, the narrative motor is set in motion, persistently driving forward until the final destination—the assured happy ending—is reached. The typical plot development plays a major role in this: Usually, the lovers-to-be have to overcome obstacles, misunderstandings, and uncertainties before they can consummate their love. It could be said that these complications are indeed an indispensable part of the very concept of Hollywood linearity as described above. As Keating argues:

"Obstacles are not simply breaks in the forward progress of the story. They are essential tools of Hollywood narrative as a system for producing emotions. While conventions like goal orientation are means toward the end of coherence, they are also

---

3 | In a way, this is true for all kind of romance films, even for romantic dramas which do not result in a happy ending. May those films culminate in smashing all hope of a positive solution; the plot still gravitates towards the vision of the couple's union—even if it does so in form of an anticlimax.

means toward the end of emotional experience. When the lovers kiss at the end of a romance, we are not happy simply because the narrative has achieved maximum coherence; we are happy because we can celebrate the culmination of a long process of hopeful anticipation." (2006, 8)

It is worth noting that the obligatory complications on the path to generic happiness do not only enhance the narrative drive and intensify the emotional experience. Showing how the protagonists have to undergo a process of overcoming obstacles, increasing self-awareness and self-transcendence also conveys an ideology that is still at the heart of the genre, despite its manifold transformations: the idea of romantic love as an almighty and transformative power.[4]

DISORIENTING ROMANTIC COMEDY?

Let us now, against this background, take a closer look at BEFORE SUNRISE and its seemingly marginal deviations from romantic comedy conventions. In contrast to the rom-com's inexorable trajectory towards an 'always and forever', the narrative progression in BEFORE SUNRISE is rather undetermined. It even comes to somewhat of a standstill—the film remains at the initial meeting and refuses to cross this threshold from which the typical romantic comedy picks up pace. Céline's and Jesse's affair begins as love at first sight—and stays that way until the film ends. Certainly, the plot covers some moments that are common landmarks in a relationship, such as their first kiss on the Ferris wheel and their making love in a public park. But fundamentally, the characters do not undergo any development during the course of the film, neither as individuals nor as a couple. Nor are there any complications to overcome beyond some minor disturbances.[5] They meet, they fall in love, they have a romantic night together, and they part—leaving each other and the film viewer with only the vague promise that they will meet again.

In fact, BEFORE SUNRISE does treat a multitude of issues that cross the lovers' path through a typical romantic comedy: falling in love, first dates, relationship crises, jealousy, separations and wrong partners, even marriage and childbirth. But none of these topics (except for 'falling in love') is actually *lived* by the char-

---

[4] | Frank Krutnik notes: "Conceptualisations of love may constantly be in flux—along with the broader configurations of romance, sexuality, gender identity and marriage—but the genre routinely celebrates it as an immutable, almost mystical force that guides two individuals who are 'made for each other' into one another's arms. Love is shown triumphing over all manner of obstructions [...]" (2002, 138).

[5] | E.g. the little controversy over the supposedly impromptu verses the street poet writes from a word given to him by Céline.

acters during the film; they are merely the subject of their conversations. Moreover, these conversations express Jesse and Céline's clearly pessimistic view in regards to the capacity of romantic love to endure, as does the fact that they back away from pursuing the path of the romantic comedy. Throughout the film, long-term relationships and marriage are associated with an inevitable, gradual loss of affection and bonding. The recurrent theme of scepticism about the persistence of romantic love is already established in the first scene, which opens with a shot of a quarrelling couple in their forties: Even for non-German speakers the embittered and even overtly aggressive nature of their dialogue is palpable.[6] The scene takes on even more significance considering that it is precisely this negative example of partnership that sets the narrative in motion in the first place, since it is the Austrians' heated argument that prompts Céline to take a different seat—just across the aisle from Jesse.

We can see, thus, that BEFORE SUNRISE, not only deprives the audience of the romantic comedy's usual trajectory and an assured happy ending for the couple; the film even denies, in multiple ways, the very premise of romantic comedy: the faith in ever-lasting love and reconciliation.

Considering these fundamental transgressions of rom-com conventions leads us back to the introductory question: Are we, notwithstanding, justified in labelling BEFORE SUNRISE a romantic comedy? Let us take a step back and reflect again on the constitutive and stable elements of romantic comedy, independent from the ideological implications the genre may carry in a precise moment of its history. I would argue that the genre's label itself is quite revealing and leads us back to the widest definition of the genre. Come what may, it is simply inconceivable that anyone would consider a film a romantic comedy if this film fails to meet two conditions independent of any particular plot development: A romantic comedy has, first, to focus on the topic of *romance*, and second, it has to treat this subject in a *comic* manner, creating a blissful atmosphere in which the representation of a 'love relationship' is associated with positive emotions.

As we have seen in the first section of this paper, BEFORE SUNRISE meets both of these conditions—which begs the question of what makes us, nevertheless, intuitively hesitate to define the film as a 'proper' romantic comedy. In the search for a solution to this dilemma, Rick Altman's landmark essay on genre criticism from 1986 provides fruitful suggestions. Adopting Altman's terminology, these two features can be subsumed under the genre's obligatory *semantics*, the "text's material" (Altman 1986, 37), whereas the association of the rom-com's indispensable topic and tone to a specific narrative trajectory or certain ideological implications can be considered constitutive elements of its conventional *syntax*, that is to say "the structures into which they are [usually] arranged" (ibid.). Altman

---

6 | In the Anglophone original version of the film, the couple's German dialogue is not subtitled.

suggests that genre innovations mostly emerge through the combination of the syntax of one genre with the semantics of another (ibid., 36). This gives reason to consider whether the seemingly contradictory nature of BEFORE SUNRISE might indeed be explained by the fact that it combines essential rom-com semantics with syntactic features of another genre.

COMPETING ORIENTATIONS:
ROMANTIC COMEDY VS. INDEPENDENT CINEMA

To find out which other genre influences the particular orientation system of BEFORE SUNRISE, it proves helpful to recall the initial reason that made us hesitate to label the film a romantic comedy: its association with independent cinema. For the purposes of this essay, it certainly makes sense to attribute generic qualities to independent cinema, in view of the fact that the 'indie' character of a film can be defined not only in terms of economics, but also through the aesthetic strategies, ideological implications and distinctive viewing experiences the audience associates with the label. Consequently, as notes Geoff King, "'[i]ndependent cinema' is itself a term that asserts a distinction from the Hollywood mainstream [...] and one that has sometimes, if loosely, implied the status of something like a genre—or collection of genres—in its own right" (2005, 195). It can be argued that a film's association with the 'indie' label has the same effect as categorising it within a particular genre: it raises particular expectations regarding verisimilitude and potential gratification. In this respect, independent cinema can be regarded as a generic framework whose syntactic features are, in BEFORE SUNRISE, combined with the basic semantics of romantic comedy.[7]

In this context, it is useful to turn once more to Todorov's concept of verisimilitude, and to examine it in more detail. Todorov actually distinguishes two types of verisimilitude that come into play when it comes to genre experiences: *generic verisimilitude*, on the one hand, and *cultural verisimilitude*, on the other. Whereas generic verisimilitude informs the recipient of what is likely to happen in a work of fiction due to the inner norms of the genre it belongs to, cultural verisimilitude refers him to the norms and values of the social world outside the

---

7 | Support for this interpretation comes from one of the most interesting recent publications on the romantic comedy: In his book *The Secret Life of Romantic Comedy* (2009), Celestino Deleyto discusses BEFORE SUNSET (USA 2004, Richard Linklater), the sequel film to BEFORE SUNRISE, in the context of the increasing intersection between mainstream Hollywood production and independent cinema in the past years. Advocating a more flexible conception of the alleged notoriously 'conservative' rom-com genre, he relates Linklater's auteur film and the romantic comedy in terms of cross-fertilisation rather than antagonism.

fiction (Todorov 1981, 118f.). This distinction is, however, not to be understood in a way that either of the two types of verisimilitude equates to some sort of 'objective reality' or 'absolute truth'. To highlight this key point of his argument, Todorov refers to Aristotle's concept of mimesis, pointing out that, even in the case of cultural verisimilitude, "the verisimilar is not a relation between discourse and its referent (the relation of truth), but between discourse and what readers believe is true [...], [that means,] to public opinion. The latter is of course not 'reality' but merely a further discourse, independent of the work" (ibid.).

Simplistically, one could say that these two regimes of verisimilitude correspond to the different expectations spectators have to the two conflicting orientation systems between which BEFORE SUNRISE oscillates: that of romantic comedy, on the one hand, and that of independent film, on the other. In their capacity as genre films, romantic comedies are expected to provide a certain kind of comfort by presenting, to borrow a phrase from Lévi-Strauss' structural study of the myth (1968), imaginary solutions to real-life problems. That being so, the distinctive gratifications expected from genre films often derive from their refusal to meet cultural verisimilitude insofar as they reconcile issues and contradictions that are, according to the rules of public discourse, unlikely to be reconciled. Neale states: "[...] it is often the generically verisimilitudinous ingredients of a film—those elements that are often least compatible with regimes of cultural verisimilitude [...] that constitute its pleasure and thus attract audiences to the film in the first place" (1990, 163). Each genre has its own imaginary way of dealing with particular issues societies or individuals have to face in a particular cultural and historical context.

The romantic comedy, for its part, is suited, first, to loosen up the feelings of inhibition and fear that usually accompany modern individuals' approaches to matters of love, desire and intimacy, and second, to reconcile themselves to the constraints that the social institution of marriage imposes upon them. Thus, portraying the protagonists compromising their individuality in the eventual formation of the romantic couple and their integration into the social community transmits a strong sense of harmony and festiveness—a positive feeling that can be considered the gratification the audience hopes to derive to see its generic expectations fulfilled.[8]

The special appeal of independent cinema, however, seems to stand in direct contrast to the generic escapism from real-world problems that is generally associated with mainstream cinema. Filmgoers usually expect independent films to address the very issues that inhabit the real world and to reflect their own

---

8 | In this regard, the romantic comedy is, despite the genre's transformations and variations in the course of film history, still deeply rooted in the Shakespearean New Comedy where Northrop Frye (1949) sees the origins of this "spirit of reconciliation" with society.

experiences in an unembellished though artistically intensified manner.⁹ They claim an 'authenticity' that implies a high degree of loyalty to the norms of cultural verisimilitude, more precisely to a paradigm that can be loosely identified as 'realism': "In any case, one of the central features of the contemporary independent discourse, although by no means shared by all so-called independent movies, is a realistic vocation" (Deleyto 2009, 156).

Taking all these aspects together, the fundamental distinction between independent and genre cinema, in terms of audience expectations, can be summarised as follows: Broadly speaking, spectators hope to find in the generic verisimilitude of mainstream films a beneficial distraction from real-life problems, whereas it is, on the contrary, precisely the independent cinema's orientation towards the cultural verisimilitude, hence the 'realistic' discourse, that makes audiences evaluate the fictional representation as satisfactorily valid and thus pleasurable. It is my assumption that it is precisely the tension and, in some way, the eventual reconciliation of these differing orientation systems that contributes to the special appeal of BEFORE SUNRISE as a romantic comedy.

RE-ORIENTING ROMANTIC COMEDY

At this point, it must be emphasised once again that the generic pact between film-maker and film viewer does not need to be regarded as a preliminary fixed and binding contract, but as a flexible orientation framework that leaves sufficient room for variations. Casetti reminds us, however, that there is a condition to be followed so that the generic pact remains unbroken: "These variations are something that the film must openly negotiate with its viewer" (Casetti 2002, 28). In other words: In the end, a genre movie has to live up to audience expectations in order not to break the mutually agreed generic pact, but it can, in the course of the movie, adjust the spectator's orientation towards aspects and gratifications that are different from those he expected at the outset.

It is obvious that the absence of essential orientation markers, such as the overcoming of obstacles and the happy ending, may have a deep impact on the generic experience of BEFORE SUNRISE and could risk disappointing the film view-

---

9 | This claim on truthfulness does not necessarily exclude stylistic artificiality, quite the contrary. Geoff King states that independent film-makers mostly choose two directions to distinguishing their work from typical mainstream cinema, "either in making greater claims to verisimilitude/realism, or in the use of more complex, stylised, expressive, showy or self-conscious forms" (King 2005, 10). I maintain, however, that this is not even a question of selecting one solution over the other since the formal experiments demonstrate the awareness of the film's illusional character and, by this means, conform to the realistic discourse on the nature of art.

er who is prepared to watch the film against the background of assumptions and expectations forged by romantic comedy. This means that if BEFORE SUNRISE invites the audience off the beaten path of romantic comedy, the film has to offer another way to sustain its orientation through the cinematic journey and to ensure its generic satisfaction. If the film makes allusions to rom-com conventions while, at the same time, deliberately disappointing the involved expectations, the question becomes: How and by what means does the film adjust the generic orientation system of the romantic comedy in order to avoid the viewer's complete disorientation and, thus, dissatisfaction?

The distinction between a genre's semantics and its syntax gives exceedingly helpful suggestions for answering this question and for shedding light on the seemingly bi-directional orientation devices the viewer of BEFORE SUNRISE is confronted with. In light of Altman's theory, the co-existence of the competing references to the romantic comedy and the independent film can be described as follows: Linklater's film draws on the romantic comedy's most essential semantics as it broaches the topic of love in a decidedly cheerful way and thus associates the idea of romance with positive emotions. It separates, however, these semantics from the syntax that is traditionally associated with them. Following Altman's suggestion that "individual texts establish new meanings for familiar terms only by subjecting well-known semantic units to a syntactic redetermination" (ibid., 39), it could be argued that BEFORE SUNRISE establishes a new meaning of the 'romantic comedy' by combining its familiar semantics of gratifying romance with an unusual syntax.

It can be agreed that the film actually lacks the typical rom-com syntax as described above. Certainly, as far as the narrative order is concerned, its trajectory is perfectly linear in that the events of the plot proceed in a chronological order from the beginning to the end. Still it lacks the typical forward thrust, and the trajectory even stops at a certain point. Hence, it does not fulfil the archetypical narrative arc of romantic comedy, nor does its representation of romance meet the conditions of romantic love implied in the conventional rom-com trajectory. But if BEFORE SUNRISE does not comply with the condition of linearity in the described sense—how must one conceive the syntactic structure to which it aligns its representation of romance?

As already indicated, the most striking difference of BEFORE SUNRISE, compared to a conventional rom-com, is its narrative minimalism. The film consists of a casual sequence of scenes that depict virtually no action, that serve no immediate narrative purpose and that make no obvious contribution to a causal chain. The film's narrative principle is symbolically pictured in the pivotal scene in which Céline and Jesse play pinball in a bar. The pinball machine's seemingly random movement makes it a kind of *mise en abyme* for the film's narrative trajectory: Once set in motion, the ball moves in contingent trajectories, following impulses for spontaneous changes in direction—just like the protagonists move back and forth through Vienna, and just like their dialogues constantly shift due to their chance encounters with strangers and to their random observations, thoughts, and memories.

In order to point out the essential difference between the narrative mode which characterises BEFORE SUNRISE, on the one hand, and the rom-com's linearity with all its implications, on the other, it seems productive to apply the aesthetic figure of the *flâneur*, as introduced by Charles Baudelaire (1863). Transcending the poles of a goal-oriented linearity and a non-linear disorientation, the *flâneur* deliberately eschews the constraint of orientation altogether. In this regard, the concept of *flânerie* describes even more than just the film's narrative principle. Not only can Céline's and Jesse's aimless wandering through the city be described as *flâneuresque*, but also their refusal to tie their romance to the pursuit of a specific goal in the future. They enjoy their walks as well as their romantic get-together just for the sake of the moment itself, without heading to a specific destination. Moreover, just as the Baudelairean *flâneur* distances himself from the spectacles he witnesses while strolling through the city, Jesse and Céline distance themselves from the spectacle of love relationships that they only touch on in their conversations. By this means, their brand of *flâneuresque* romance allows them to meander through the space of romantic love without really diving into it and without risking the eventual disenchantment that seems—in terms of the 'realistic' discourse supported in the film—unavoidable.

Similarly, BEFORE SUNRISE allows the spectators to enjoy a warm-hearted and cheerful love story without having to face the unpleasant 'truth' that the pleasurable feelings he derives from the genre require—in terms of cultural verisimilitude—an escapist self-deception. To a certain extent, the combination of rom-com semantics and 'indie' syntax allows him, thus, to have it both ways: to enjoy, on the one hand, the affective gratifications associated with romantic comedy, and on the other hand, the satisfaction of witnessing a 'realistic' piece of life, which he expects to get from independent cinema.

COMING TO AN ENDING

In conclusion, it can be argued that BEFORE SUNRISE stretches the genre of romantic comedy in new directions by replacing its conventionally linear syntax by the *flâneuresque* syntax of independent cinema. Following Altman's assumption that the textual meaning of a film as a whole is "constructed by virtue of the syntactic bonds established between [the] primary elements" (1986, 38)—its semantics—, BEFORE SUNRISE engages the spectator to adjust the meaning he or she is accustomed to ascribe to the romantic comedy genre, namely the promotion of an idea of 'romantic love' as indispensably relying on continuance. By this means, he is offered an opportunity to experience the cinematic representation of heart-warming romance independently from the condition of the couple's everlasting togetherness.

Thus, BEFORE SUNRISE gives rise to a significant discussion of the conception of 'true' love as conveyed by the traditional rom-com, as well as the conception of the romantic comedy genre itself. It presents a story in which romantic love is celebrated not despite but because of its ephemeral, fugitive and contingent nature—as a deep feeling whose magic lies in the moment itself rather than in the anticipation of its persistence through eternity. Correspondingly, the film celebrates the uplifting experience of romantic comedy, by orienting the viewer towards an intense experience of the present tense instead of an anticipated future.

However, there is one slight caveat to that: Structurally, a film will never be able to freeze the moment forever. Sooner or later, the film must choose a point to end. And this choice presents a ticklish task for BEFORE SUNRISE as a romantic comedy, even after having relativised the significance of the ending.

In the course of the film, Jesse and Céline repeatedly agree that their night in Vienna will be their only time together and that they will never meet again afterwards. When they touch on the question of a potential reunion, Céline insists on their initial decision, claiming that they should "just be rational adults about this", and Jesse wonders why people actually think that "relationships are supposed to last forever". Yet, their longing glances and shy gestures indicate that, in this case, the medium of their self-deception could in fact be the 'realistic discourse' rather than the romantic comedy genre. Consequently, it does not come as a huge surprise that the precarious moment of the closing scene involves a subtle plot twist: Just before Céline's train leaves, the two agree to meet again, in six months' time, at the same place.

In view of the characters' ambiguous attitude towards 'romantic love', which is noticeable in the contradiction between their spoken opinions and their nonverbal expression, their change of mind does, in terms of the verisimilitude established during the film, not seem completely improbable. It is, however, not predictable either. Moreover, their final agreement by no means represents a clear indication of a common future. Rather, the to-and-fro of their date arrangement as well as the composition of the film's epilogue[10] raise some doubts upon the question of whether their reunion will actually occur.

I would argue that this ambiguity is the absolute precondition for the renegotiated generic pact to be fulfilled: It is the only way of reaching an ending where all expectations that were raised by the film's orientation devices are met.

---

10 | After their final kiss, we are shown Céline and Jesse going their ways, staring pensively into space, and the film closes with a thought-provoking epilogue: a sequence of long shots present the locations in which their nightly romance took place—by day, empty and, even if still picturesque, somewhat disenchanted.

With the couple's common future in doubt—but still possible—the verisimilitudes and gratifications of both of the established orientation systems are neither entirely realised nor completely thwarted[11], and both 'indie' enthusiasts and rom-com fans can be content.

Ultimately, BEFORE SUNRISE is a true genre film as it indeed offers an imaginary solution for a significant real-life problem of its (postmodern) era: In its 'indie' representation of romantic comedy, the contradictory ideas of love conveyed by popular culture, on the one hand, and by the 'realistic' discourse, on the other, are finally reconciled. While dealing with an issue that is essentially at the heart of all romantic comedies since the 1970s—the widening chasm between sober skepticism and romantic longing—BEFORE SUNRISE develops its own coping strategy.[12] It offers a compromise that might even present an overarching truth about real-life romance. In between the romantic conception that true love lasts forever and the 'realistic' assumption that love eventually dies lies a truth that applies to every relationship experience: Maybe love will last, maybe it won't. We just cannot know while it is lasting.

---

11 | This question of how the sequel film BEFORE SUNSET not only pursues Céline's and Jesse's story, but also rewrites the ending of the initial film could not be explored in this study, but it would provide an intriguing topic for further examination.

12 | The majority of post-classical rom-coms create a sense of self-consciousness or an ironic double-bind to enable spectators in the postmodern "age of lost innocence" (Eco 1985, 67) to engage once again in the discourse of romantic love—a tendency that is currently even enforced by overtly meta-fictional films such as STRANGER THAN FICTION (USA 2006, Marc Forster). Whereas the 'nervous romances' of the late 1970s (e.g. ANNIE HALL, USA 1977, Woody Allen) express a pessimistic view of love but still celebrate a "wistful nostalgia for the 'whole romantic thing'" (Krutnik 1998, 19) through sentimental references to old romance films and love songs, the so-called 'new romances' (Neale/Krutnik 1990, 171ff.) or 'neo-traditional romances' (Jeffers McDonald 2007, 85ff.) of the 1980s and the 1990s (e.g. WHEN HARRY MET SALLY... (USA 1989, Rob Reiner), PRETTY WOMAN (USA 1989, Gary Marshall) or SLEEPLESS IN SEATTLE (USA 1993, Nora Ephron)) use self-reflexive strategies in order to reaffirm the traditional idea that romantic love, despite all doubts, indeed can lead to a happy marriage. Frank Krutnik describes the underlying assumption as follows: "Even though the old certainties have been tarnished, these films propose that it is better to believe in a myth, a fabrication, than have nothing" (1998, 30).

Bibliography

Altman, Rick (1986): *A Semantic/Syntactic Approach to Film Genre.* In: Grant 2010, 27–41.

Baudelaire, Charles (1863): *Le Peintre de la vie moderne.* In: *Œuvres Complètes, II.* (ed. by Claude Pichois). Paris: Gallimard, Bibliothèque de la Pléiade, 1975–1976, 683–724.

Bordwell, David/Thompson, Kristin/Staiger, Janet (1985): *The Classical Hollywood Cinema: Film Style and Mode of Production to 1960.* New York: Columbia University Press.

Cavell, Stanley (1981): *Pursuits of Happiness: The Hollywood Comedy of Remarriage.* Cambridge (MA)/London: Harvard Film Studies.

Casetti, Francesco (2002): *Communicative Negotiation in Cinema and Television.* Milano: VeP.

Deleyto, Celestino (2009): *The Secret Life of Romantic Comedy.* Manchester/New York: Manchester University Press.

Eco, Umberto (1985): Postmodernism, Irony, the Enjoyable. In: Eco, Umberto: *Reflections on The Name of the Rose* (transl. by William Weaver). London: Secker & Warburg, 65–72.

Frye, Northrop (1948): *The Argument of Comedy.* New York: Columbia University Press (English Institute Essays, ed. by D. A. Robertson, 1949).

Grant, Barry Keith (ed.) (2010): *Film Genre Reader III.* Austin: University of Texas Press.

Hediger, Vinzenz/Vonderau, Patrick (2005): Landkarten des Vergnügens. Genre und Filmvermarktung. In: Hediger, Vinzenz/Vonderau, Patrick (eds.): *Demnächst in Ihrem Kino. Grundlagen der Filmwerbung und Filmvermarktung.* Marburg: Schüren, 240–249.

Jeffers McDonald, Tamar (2007): *Romantic Comedy: Boy Meets Girl Meets Genre.* London/New York: Wallflower.

Keating, Patrick (2006): Emotional Curves and Linear Narratives. In: *The Velvet Light Trap*, No. 58, 4–15.

King, Geoff (2005): *American Independent Cinema.* London/New York: Wallflower.

Krutnik, Frank (1998): Love Lies: Romantic Fabrication in Contemporary Romantic Comedy. In: Deleyto, Celestino/Evans, Peter William (eds.): *Terms of Endearment. Hollywood Romantic Comedy of the 1980s and 1990s.* Edinburgh: Edinburgh University Press, 15–36.

Krutnik, Frank (2002): Conforming Passions? Contemporary Romantic Comedy. In: Neale, Steve (ed.): *Genre and Contemporary Hollywood.* London: BFI, 130–147.

Lévi-Strauss, Claude (1968): The Structural Study of Myth. In: Lévi-Strauss, Claude: *Structural Anthropology.* Harmondsworth: Penguin, 206–231.

Neale, Steve/Krutnik, Frank (1990): *Popular Film and Television Comedy*. New York: Routledge.
Neale, Steve (1990): Questions of Genre. In: Grant 2010, 160–184.
Smith, Murray (1995): *Engaging Characters. Fiction, Emotion, and the Cinema*. Oxford: Clarendon Press.
Todorov, Tzvetan (1973): *The Fantastic: A Structural Approach to a Literary Genre* (transl. by Richard Howard). Cleveland/London: Case Western Reserve UP.

Films

ANNIE HALL (USA 1977, Woody Allen)
BEFORE SUNRISE (USA/Austria/Switzerland 1995, Richard Linklater)
BEFORE SUNSET (USA 2004, Richard Linklater)
PRETTY WOMAN (USA 1989, Gary Marshall)
SLACKER (USA 1991, Richard Linklater)
SLEEPLESS IN SEATTLE (USA 1993, Nora Ephron)
STRANGER THAN FICTION (USA 2006, Marc Forster)
WAKING LIFE (USA 2001, Richard Linklater)
WHEN HARRY MET SALLY... (USA 1989, Rob Reiner)

NARRATIVE MAZES

Televisual (Dis)Orientation

Serial Orientations
Paratexts and Contemporary Complex Television

JASON MITTELL

Throughout its history, we might consider 'accessibility' to be a defining feature of most commercial American television. Per the medium's commercial strategies for advertiser-supported programming, any programme's success would be judged by its ability to attract, retain, and grow its viewership, which could then be converted into the currency of Nielsen ratings and sold to advertisers. The programming strategies that emerged to support this system of popular appeal have been termed "least objectionable content" or more dismissively, "lowest common denominator". In short, a television storyteller's first job is to avoid alienating potential viewers. At the base level of narrative comprehension, the industry demands that television be easy enough to follow in order to make sense to casual viewers. However, in the mode of narrative complexity I have discussed elsewhere, television series often challenge the ease with which a casual viewer might make sense of a programme, inviting temporary disorientation and confusion, allowing viewers to build up their comprehension skills through long-term viewing and active engagement (Mittell 2006).

In this essay, I will consider how viewers make sense of complex television's serial forms through practices of orientation and mapping, primarily through the creation of orienting paratexts. Arguably, most orientation practices involve paratexts, whether in the tangible form of maps and lists, or more ephemeral processes of conversation, as orienting ourselves in relation to a narrative world places us outside the core text itself. These paratexts are distinct from transmedia paratexts that explicitly strive to continue their storyworlds across platforms (see Gray 2010; Evans 2011). Instead, such orienting practices exist outside the diegetic storyworld, providing a perspective for viewers to help make sense of a narrative world by looking at it from a distance—although as with all such categorical distinctions, actual practices often muddy such neat dichotomies. Orientation is not necessary to discover the canonical truth of a storyworld, but rather to create a layer atop the programme to help figure out how the pieces fit together, or propose alternate ways of seeing the pieces that might not be suggested by or contained within the original narrative design. The act of linking a text to a paratext[1], whether official or viewer-created, changes the way we see the original, and thus this essay maps out many ways that a complex serial is transformed through the act of paratextual extension, often with the explicit goal of making 'sense' of the original.

In the internet era, we are surrounded by an array of paratextual information, much of which is not designed specifically in support of a series. In a telling quote, David Simon, creator of THE WIRE (USA 2002–08, HBO) and TREME (USA 2010–, HBO) explains to critic Emily Nussbaum the usefulness of creating television in the contemporary media environment:

> "'Fuck the exposition... Just be. The exposition can come later.' [Simon] describes a theory of television narrative. 'If I can make you curious enough, there's this thing called Google. If you're curious about the New Orleans Indians, or 'second-line' musicians—you can look it up.' The Internet, he suggests, can provide its own creative freedom, releasing writers from having to overexplain, allowing history to light the characters from within." (Nussbaum 2010)

While few would point to Simon's series as robust examples of online paratextual activity, especially as compared to cult programmes like LOST (USA 2004–10, ABC) or BUFFY THE VAMPIRE SLAYER (USA 1997–2003, The WB/UPN), his description of the internet's expositional usefulness highlights how creators can outsource backstory and cultural references to a pre-existing and highly accessible paratextual realm. In turn, the internet can be used as a site to develop and share vast paratextual resources designed specifically to help orient viewers of ongoing serials. The key point is that television shows are not treated as standalone, self-contained texts by either their creators or fans, but rather exist in a media landscape where online paratexts are always part of a viewer's potential intertextual flow. The paratexts explored in this essay are more specifically tied to their source texts than Simon's evocation of *Google*, traversing the boundary between fan-created extensions and official industrial products—while there are obvious differences between such variants of paratexts and many fans certainly do regard them differently based on source. Thus it is important to think of both official and unofficial paratexts as part of the same spectrum of viewing practice, rather than as necessarily opposed to and separate from one another (see Dena 2008).

In thinking about the range of orientation practices that television viewers embrace today, we encounter a mass of strategies and paratextual modes that can be rather disorienting. So to understand the scope of orientation, we need to first understand the aspects of narrative that might invite or require orient-

---

1 | See also the contribution of Daniela Olek in this volume.

ing, attempting to organise viewers' comprehension, interpretation, analysis, and intertextual expansion. A simple definition of serial narrative—*a television serial creates a sustained narrative world, populated by a consistent set of characters who experience a chain of events over time*—presents four basic storytelling facets that might require orientation: *time, events, characters, and space*.[2] These four landmarks provide a top level set of categories for how viewers make sense of television narratives—to comprehend an ongoing story, we need to be able to follow each of these elements, and for many complex television programmes, such paratexts are a useful strategy for viewers to orient themselves.

Temporal Orientation

The first category of time is arguably the most central aspect of serial narrative, as seriality is defined by manipulating time as a storytelling variable—we consume the story in installments defined by the creators and experience mandatory gaps between episodes and seasons to process the narrative. The three layers of story time, discourse time, and screen time, as discussed elsewhere, each potentially require orientation practices (Mittell 2007). The last of these seems most obvious, but it points to a central issue in viewer orientation: We need to know when an episode is on, and in what order we are supposed to watch them. Traditionally in American television, the order in which episodes air was a minor concern for primetime programmes, as networks might choose to air episodes in unusual timeslots or sequence depending on their competition or other mitigating factors—in some cases, like Firefly (USA 2002–03, Fox), a network might change the episodic sequence in a way that damages viewer comprehension and enjoyment. Syndicated reruns often aired a series out of its original sequence, meaning that viewers were likely to encounter a programme in haphazard order, and thus storytellers adapted to the lack of guaranteed sequence by avoiding story arcs that surpass the length of a given episode, a practice that still lives on in most episodic police procedurals and many sitcoms.

With the profusion of cable channels and other viewing technologies in the 1990s and beyond, the industry developed ways to orient viewers' sense of screen time, notably through the onscreen Electronic Programme Guide. Viewers adapt their own ways of navigating screen time by cataloguing episodes and airdates on websites like *epguides.com* or show-specific fansites, and employ technologies like the Digital Video Recorder to structure their viewing. And the rise of boxed sets or downloadable purchases provides another technology to orient viewers to screen time, as the structure of seasons and episode order are foregrounded, often in ways that assert an original intended sequence rather

---

2 | See also the contribution of Christine Piepiorka in this volume.

than network reordering. Together, we see the use of *schedule as orientation* to help viewers master a base chronology of screen time that while seemingly obvious, is essential to being able to comprehend an ongoing complex serial.

While screen time follows a fairly rigid set of boundaries and structures, discourse time is much more variable and free-flowing, especially in shows with complex chronology.³ Understanding how nested flashbacks, replays, flash forwards, and other atemporal shifts play out on shows like HOW I MET YOUR MOTHER (USA 2005–, CBS) or FLASHFORWARD (USA 2009–10, ABC) requires dedicated attention to details and chronicling of markers of temporal continuity, often through elaborate plot summaries on official network or fan websites. LOST's complex chronology led to numerous graphic and textual representations proliferating both on and offline, including both fan-created images and officially sanctioned paratexts on ABC's website or in DVD releases. Shows do not need to embrace time travel to warrant such use of *chronology as orientation*, as fans of a series like BATTLESTAR GALACTICA (USA 2004–09, Sci Fi) chart its narrative through diagrams that help guide viewers to understand both the sequence of events and temporal relationship between various onscreen representations.

Discourse time refers to the sequence and selection of the narrative material presented to the audience, while story time comprises the actual events taking place in the narrative universe. For shows with tight chronology, reconciling between story and screen time can be a challenge, requiring strategies to orient the show's timeframe. For instance, BREAKING BAD (USA 2008–, AMC) lacks the sci-fi temporal play of LOST, but it is important to keep in mind that the events of the first four seasons only take up one year of story time to grasp the consequences, pacing, and stakes of dramatic events that remain fresh in characters' minds. For the historical realism of MAD MEN's (USA 2007–, AMC) 1960s to resonate, fans use timelines to parallel the fictional events with historical moments that are mentioned in the show or left unsaid in the subtext. Such use of *calendaring as orientation* helps us follow an unfolding narrative in a way that foregrounds a realist sense of a persistent storyworld with consequences and history, a fairly new development in television narrative.

Even when the storyworld is not realistic in the least, mapping chronology and calendars can be a crucial orientation strategy. Probably the most complicated timeline on contemporary television is the "timey-wimey" playfulness of DOCTOR WHO (UK 2005–, BBC), especially in the title character's ongoing relationship to fellow time-traveller River Song. Fans have created numerous visual representations of the bidirectional relationship experienced by River and The Doctor, attempting to match-up their experiences and chart the key moments in their story, a strategy that the characters themselves perform on the show by synching up their journals and memories whenever they meet. Of course this

---

3 | See the contributions by Julia Eckel and Matthias Brütsch in this volume.

is not the exclusive domain of fans, as the BBC produced their own orientation material in the form of an online video chronicling River Song's story narrated from her own perspective and timeframe.[4] This video highlights how the process of orientation is an element of both official and unofficial production, and can be presented in a range of media, not just graphic timelines or textual lists.

One of the most interesting ways that fans create orientation tools is through the use of video remixes, recasting the temporality of the original series in innovative ways. Two LOST projects speak to the varied approaches fans take to remixing chronology. In the online video LOST: THE SYNCHRONIZING by NDHatch (2008), a fan took footage depicting various moments around the plane crash from across three seasons and multiple perspectives, editing them together via split screen in the style of 24 (USA 2001–10, Fox) to synch the chronology and highlight how these moments converge into the show's most important narrative event. At a larger scale, another fan created *ChronologicallyLost.com* to distribute his re-edited version of the series in chronological order in 45 minute episodic installments, starting with the origin of Jacob and The Man in Black from ACROSS THE SEA (S6/E15), and moving forward through the island's time jumps, character flashbacks, plane crash, escape and return, and finally ending with the final season's flash sideways as an epilogue. While I doubt that such extensive remix projects work to orient confused viewers like a timeline or map, they do serve as analytic forms of orientation, providing insights via rethinking the show's narrative timeframe.

So like any complex taxonomy, we need more than one axis to categorise practices of viewer orientation—it's not just 'what' is being oriented (time vs. space), but also 'how' the orientation proceeds. One type of orientation practice aims for *recapitulation*, summarising narrative material in a straightforward manner like the calendar or chronological list of events. Another practice embraces a mode of *analysis*, exploring narrative material via a representational mode, typically a visual map or video, that offers an analytic dimension to the representation that goes beyond recapitulation. While analytic orientations aim to better understand what is happening within the text, orientations of *expansion* look outward extratextually to connect the series with other realms beyond the core programme, whether it is another fictional series or aspects of the real world. These three modes, which certainly can blur and blend together, can be applied to the various aspects of narrative temporailty, creating a matrix of orientation practices.

---

4 | This video aired on the BBC programme DOCTOR WHO CONFIDENTIAL (UK 2005-2011, BBC) in the U.K. on October 1st , 2011, (S6/E13, *WHEN TIME FROZE*) and is described by Anders 2011.

PLOT ORIENTATION

These three modes of orientation practice can be applied to other narrative dimensions beyond time as well. Narrative events are closely linked to time, as they are typically thought about in terms of "what happens when", and attempting to orient oneself to story events often involves chronology and temporal causation. *Plot recapitulations* are commonplace orientation tools, whether the now ubiquitous "previously on" segments preceding most episodes discussed elsewhere (Mittell 2010), or write-ups on official network websites or fansites aiming to provide a clear summation of an episode's narrative events. Such textual recaps are abstractions as well, as the conversion of televisual material into prose is just as much of a transformation as visual or video remixes, and the rise of humorously tinged recaps on sites like *Television Without Pity*[5] suggest how orientation can also be a creative act (Andrejevic 2008). However, some *event analyses* detach narrative events from their chronology to create a different perspective on the story, such as lists of character deaths found on various series wikis to more visual depictions, like an infographic poster documenting DEXTER'S (USA 2006–, Showtime) dozens of murders, charting weapons, motives, and interrelations between victims (see fig. 1). Such analytic reinterpretations take a series of narrative events and explore them for greater understanding of causality, significance, or even basic comprehension, and can be pursued within the realm of various media forms. For instance, BREAKING BAD'S *END TIMES* (S4/E12) left some ambiguities as to who was responsible for poisoning a child; a fan took to *YouTube* to offer an interpretation of the narrative events to (correctly) argue that Walter White was responsible, piecing together scenes from the episode providing clues and evidence that proved what would only be revealed in the next episode. Such analytic abstractions and reinterpretations function as sites of forensic fandom, enabling viewers to make greater sense or propose new explanations of the narrative events beyond chronology and recapitulation, a tendency we can see even more acutely in analyses of THE SOPRANOS' (USA 1999–2007, HBO) ambiguous finale *MADE IN AMERICA* (S6/E21).

Plot expansions aim to contextualise the events of a series into a larger intertextual web, most typically by connecting what happens in a fictional series to the real world. For instance, TREME depicts life in post-Katrina New Orleans, with many fictionalised versions of real people and events; bloggers and journalists, most notably Dave Walker from the *New Orleans Times-Picayune*, catalogue and analyse the programme's cultural references, working to orient viewers to the factual basis of the fictional events. More rare are paratextual examples trying to connect the narrative events from one series to another fictional world beyond the moments where a programme itself cues its own intertextuality, as with

---

5 | See [http://www.televisionwithoutpity.com/].

HAPPY DAYS (USA 1974–84, ABC) references on ARRESTED DEVELOPMENT (USA 2003-06, Fox)—but in the paratextual realm, no orientation practice is as disorienting as the Tommy Westphall Universe theory. In the legendary conclusion to 1980s series ST. ELSEWHERE (USA 1982–88, NBC), it was revealed that the entirety of the medical drama existed in the imagination of Tommy, an autistic child staring into a snowglobe. Because the series had a number of crossover episodes and intertextual references with other programmes like CHEERS (USA 1982–93, NBC), HOMICIDE: LIFE ON THE STREET (USA 1993–99, NBC), and THE BOB NEWHART SHOW (USA 1972–78, CBS), fans have posited that all of these other fictions are figments of Tommy's imagination as well. Fans catalogue these crossover events and create elaborate maps of an intertextual multiverse—as of 2012, the grid lists 282 programmes ranging from I LOVE LUCY (USA 1951–57, CBS) to THE WIRE. While such orientation practices are certainly not designed to actually help viewers truly make sense of fictional worlds, as

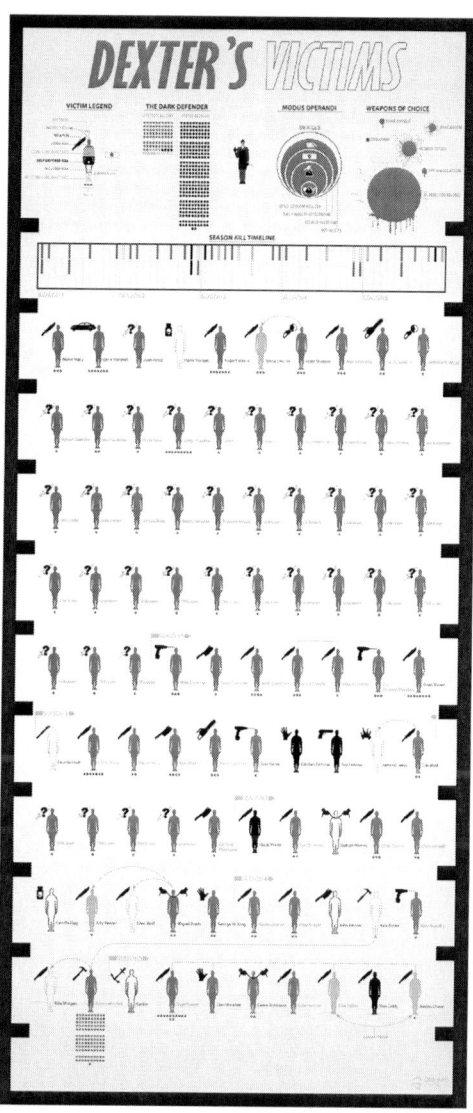

Figure 1: Graphic designer Shahed Syed charts DEXTER *to categorise the title character's murder victims as an example of an analytic paratext.*

the theory is clearly meant to be taken as playfully ludicrous, I would argue that fans do take it seriously—they get immersed in the intertextual web and passionately argue about interpretations concerning the validity of various connections. They know it's not 'real', even within the fictional worlds of television, but many seriously embrace the practice of creating expansive paratexts as if it were 'real', playfully undertaking hypothetical analysis and conjecture similar to recent forms like alternate reality games (Booth 2010).

CHARACTER ORIENTATION

The third type of narrative orientation seeks to understand a programme's cast of characters. For vast, sprawling series like THE WIRE, it is hard work keeping track of who's who amongst the dozens of characters, many only known by nicknames or left unseen for long stretches of episodes. *Character guides*, whether found on official websites or tie-in books, or fan-created wikis or guides, offer convenient overviews of *dramatis personae* in a manner common to theatre goers; the baseline goal of such guides is to orient us to the cast, connecting faces with names and dramatic functions. *Character analyses* typically visualise narrative aspects via alternate means as a way of mapping relationships, developments, and personalities. For instance, LOST DVDs contained an interactive character guide to chart out the often coincidental connections between characters, and fans made similar maps to highlight inter-character links. Analytic commentary can be mixed with a character guide, as on *Lostpedia* and other fan sites that probe the complex histories and relationships featured on the series.

While certainly many fan paratexts aim for character reinterpretation, such as fan fiction and remix vids, I would not call most of those 'orientation practices' per se, as they are less focused on making sense of the existing narrative world than expanding them into other possibilities. A common mode of such fan creativity is intertextual expansion, bringing characters from multiple storyworlds together into a shared universe, a genre called "crossover fic". It is fairly rare to see such *character expansion* clearly functioning as an orientation practice, although one example is a fun case of intertextuality: A number of fans have adopted the alignment system from the classic role-playing game *Dungeons & Dragons*, which charts a character's morality on dual axes of good to evil and lawful to chaotic, and mapped them onto the cast of various television series. Examples range from ARRESTED DEVELOPMENT's dysfunctional Bluth family to the array of 1960s businessmen from MAD MEN, but probably no show is more apt for such intertextual orientation than THE WIRE, given its thematic emphasis on morality and codes of conduct. Mapping out the characters on a game-based alignment chart invited discussion on blog comment threads over the meaning of lawfulness and chaos in the context of THE WIRE, and whether characters like Avon and Omar can be seen as anything but evil due to their murderous ways. Such intertextual expansion is an invitation to rethink our impressions of the original series, orienting ourselves to a new way of categorising and grouping the characters, as well as creating intertextual resonances by connecting contemporary characters to mythic figures from the game's medieval fantasy setting.

Spatial Orientation

The final aspect of narrative that might require orientation is the most common to the practice of mapping: a spatial storyworld. While practices of mapping are well-suited to spatial orientation, it would seem that space is the dimension of television narrative that needs the least outside help for viewer comprehension. While temporality, plotting, and characterisations have all become more complex in contemporary television, spatial storytelling is still fairly conventional and straightforward. Most programmes follow well-established filmic conventions for orienting viewers spatially in any scene, with little sense of purposeful ambiguity and playfulness. If anything, space is the storytelling dimension that television is most willing to cheat on to maximise complexity in other realms; for instance, 24's dedication to maintaining strict chronology and pseudo-real-time narration frequently forced the series to create spatial implausibilities, traversing Los Angeles or Washington DC traffic and geography at unrealistic speeds. While many fans will try to make sense of muddled chronology or plot continuity, such geographical incoherence in navigating a story space is typically only recognised by natives of a given city searching for spatial realism, suggesting that in the process of consuming serialised television, temporal consistency trumps spatial coherence.

Nevertheless, both viewers and the industry do invest energy in creating spatially orienting paratexts for television series. For shows that feature a fantasy space, orientation maps are helpful paratexts to ground viewers in the show's mythology, a common practice found in previous media like Tolkien's novels of Middle Earth that included maps. We can see a televisual parallel to this in the opening credits of Game of Thrones (USA 2011–, HBO), which present an animated map of the series's fantasy world Westeros that changes each week to orient viewers where that episode's action will take place; additionally HBO's website provides an interactive map charting out each episode's events and linking the map to characters and their genealogies. Maps are more typically presented outside a programme's core text, as with Battlestar Galactica publishing a poster-size map of its cosmos, outlining the Twelve Colonies of Kobol with detailed mythological information and graphic depiction not covered by the show; the poster was even signed by series writer Jane Espenson as a marker of canonical authenticity. For fantasy series that do not produce their maps, fans typically fill the gaps, as typified by the vast array of Star Trek (USA 1966–69, NBC) cartography that spans the franchise's multiple series, and frequently facilitates fans moving from creating unofficial orientation paratexts into joining official production teams. Such fan mapping is part of a larger facet of affirmative fan productivity that Bob Rehak has labeled "blueprint culture", as fans work to document the canonical facts established by a fantastic fictional franchise.[6]

For programmes based here on Earth, no tool has been more important to spatial orientation practices than *Google Maps*, as both fans and production teams create custom maps for dozens of series to show both shooting locations and addresses for fictional story sites, ranging from THE WIRE's realistic Baltimore to VERONICA MARS' (USA 2004–07, UPN/The CW) fictional Southern California town of Neptune overlayed with its real San Diego shooting locales. An interesting example is SEINFELD (USA 1989–98, NBC), as even though it was filmed primarily in Los Angeles, its New York City locale is a powerful part of the show's narrative experience. Thus both Sony, the show's production studio, and fans have created their own SEINFELD-themed Google Maps—while the map on Sony's site features glossier visuals with embedded videos, not surprisingly the fan version is more comprehensive, including more than twice as many locations. Such maps then can translate into embodied practice, as fans explore the locales of their favourite series as part of the growing realm of media-themed tourism, with popular tours of places like THE SOPRANOS' New Jersey or the MAD MEN "Time Machine" Tour of New York. The SEINFELD case is particularly interesting in blurring fact and fiction, as Kenny Kramer, Larry David's old neighbour who was the inspiration for the Cosmo Kramer character, entrepreneurially created Kramer's Reality Tour that brings fans around New York to see the real places that inspired SEINFELD's fictional version of the city, as filmed in Los Angeles. Unlike other media tourism like the New Zealand tours of "Middle Earth" via the LORD OF THE RINGS (USA/New Zealand 2001–2003) filming locations, when television tourism focuses on an ongoing serial, it adds another experiential dimension, as fans may explore a space where they anticipate future narrative developments or even hope to see filming on-location. In these cases, maps and tours function less to orient fans to the fictional worlds than to extend those fictions into their real lives and allow them to momentarily inhabit their favourite storyworlds (see Couldry 2007; Torchin 2002).

An interesting case study of using mapping within an ongoing series is LOST, which created a fantasy setting of a fictitious island whose geography is central to the narrative, and is also grounded within the interesting real-world island of its Hawaii shooting locale. Given the show's huge participatory fanbase, it is not surprising that fans have created a detailed Google Map of Hawaii, with shooting locations catalogued by season, character, and fictional locale—and it's equally unsurprising that Hawaiian travel companies offer LOST tours as well. *Google Maps* also hosts a collaborative map of every real world locale referenced

---

6 | See Bob Rehak's *Graphic Engine* blog for his in-process writing on the topic (Rehak 2012).

on Lost and its copious transmedia extensions, highlighting the show's global reach despite nearly everything being shot in Hawaii. *Google Maps* is less helpful in orienting us to the fantasy geography of the show's central location, although a number of fans have used it to chart potential sites for the mysterious island, including the use of the show's mythological numbers of 4, 8, 15, 16, 23, and 42 as geographic coordinates. But Lost's forensic fandom is most active in its attempts to map the internal geography of the show's fantastic island, requiring platforms beyond *Google Maps*.

Unlike BATTLESTAR GALACTICA, the producers of Lost did not give us a clear rendering of the show's fictional geography—although the virtual island created for the videogame Lost: Via Domus (2008, Ubisoft) attempted to create such a virtual map—but maps are a central obsession of various characters and do appear onscreen quite frequently. Such brief appearances were copiously catalogued by the forensic fans at *Lostpedia* and numerous other fan sites dedicated to decoding the world of Lost, but no map is as indicative of how such practices straddle the line between orientation and disorientation as the cultural life of what fans have termed the "blast door map". In the episode LOCKDOWN (S2/E17), John Locke found himself trapped in an underground bunker with his leg pinned under a blast door. For a few moments, a black light turns on, revealing a hand-painted map (see fig. 2) on the back of the door that we see onscreen for no more than six seconds. The information contained within the map, as decoded collectively by fans only hours after the episode aired, pointed to deep mythological clues that resonated both in the show and across the transmedia extensions. John Locke himself attempts to reconstruct the map's geographical revelations, but fell far short of what fans accomplished, aided by freeze-frame screengrabs, image manipulation software, and collective discussion forums. The map would reappear in transmedia versions four times with slight alterations and additional information, outlasting its role in the series itself. Through their forensic fandom, viewers got a preview of future hatches still to be revealed, references to the backstory of the Hanso family and the Black Rock ship, and other minor clues to forthcoming puzzles.

However, I would contend that the blast door map's least successful function concerned spatial orientation, as the map provides little sense of scale or relationship between the outlined stations and the places we had seen on the island. Instead, the map functions more like a roster of places, names, and clues scrawled onto a wall, a to-do list for fans anticipating what might be revealed in future episodes. It also provides a window into a number of character subjectivities, visualising the mentalities of the map's two authors-to-be-named later, Radinsky and Inman, who chronicle their limited mythological knowledge and island explorations under duress, as well as orienting us to John Locke's obsessive quest to make sense of the briefly seen images. The map also charts narrative time and events, as we try to situate the drawing's creation into the island's backstory and our own limited knowledge of the history of the DHARMA Initiative. Thus as fans worked to decode the multiple versions of the map, they arguably were less engaged with questions of spatial orientation than attempting to understand the embedded representations of a fictional storyworld, refracted by still to-be-discovered characters and events.

This is not to say that LOST fans did not seek to create maps to spatially orient the island. A wide range of fan-created island maps emerged throughout the series, including illustrated schematics, topographic charts, and even 3D simulations. Like the schematics of the Enterprise, these are clearly attempts to render an unreal fantastic story space via the tools and assumptions of scientific realism. While we never saw LOST's island explicitly change its shape or topography, we did see it move through time and space in a manner that suggests that realistic geography was low among the show's priorities. The show's commitments were more to the flexible realm of the fantasy genre than any notion of realism, yet fans strived to map a consistent geography onto the island; such

Figure 2: LOST's 'blast door map' appeared on television for only a few seconds, but lived on within fan communities and transmedia extensions, as with this hidden blacklight image on the back of the official LOST jigsaw puzzles.

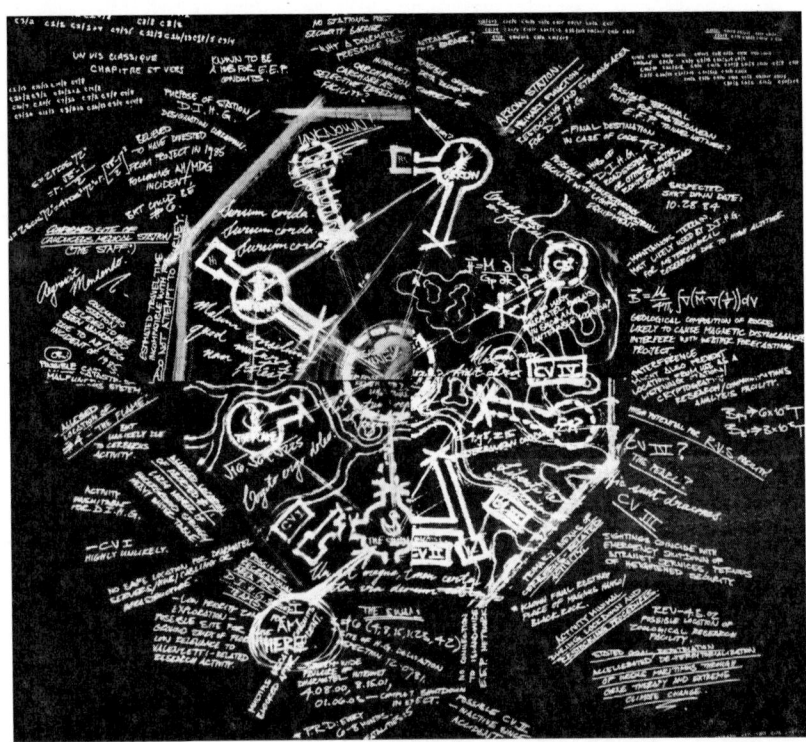

conflicts between the rational realms of science fiction and more spiritual and irrational concerns of fantasy were an echo of one of LOST's main thematic debates between science and faith that became a key point of contention in its finale.

DIMENSIONAL ORIENTATION

LOST points towards one final dimension of orientation that transcends time and space: the concept of dimensions themselves. As narrative complexity has opened up possibilities of time and space in serialised storytelling, it has occasionally explored notions of parallel worlds or multiple dimensions, issues that have emerged more commonly in complex films like LOLA RENNT (RUN LOLA RUN, Germany 1998, Tom Tykwer), SLIDING DOORS (UK/USA 1998, Peter Howitt), and INCEPTION (USA 2010, Christopher Nolan). Multiple dimensions can emerge in specific episodes of shows like COMMUNITY (USA 2009–, NBC) or BUFFY THE VAMPIRE SLAYER, or even as serialised plot arcs as on FRINGE (USA 2008–13, Fox), LIFE ON MARS (UK 2006–07, BBC), or ONCE UPON A TIME (USA 2011–, ABC), but the final season of LOST was one of the highest profile television examples of such storytelling—abandoning the flashback structure typical of the show's first three seasons, the fourth season's flash forwards, and the fifth season's frequently jumping time travelling, the sixth season introduced what producers and fans called "flash sideways". In almost every episode, action would toggle between the endgame being played out on the island, and a seemingly parallel dimension where Flight 815 never crashed, most of the characters had drastically different lives, and seemingly the island was sunk at the bottom of the ocean. Not surprisingly, forensic fans were both frustrated with and excited by the challenges of orienting themselves to this dimension, especially since the actual explanation for what the world was and how it related to the main storyworld were not revealed until the final minutes of the series finale. Scanning the edit history and discussions on *Lostpedia* on the entry for the *Flash Sideways Timeline* documents dozens of fans working for months, debating issues of chronology, character, and even ontology for this aspect of the story—and finally when all was revealed, arguing over whether to delete the whole article due to the temporal ambiguities that remain in the sideways dimension.

The case of LOST's sixth season points to one of the particular challenges that emerges at the intersection of narrative complexity and seriality: as storyworlds grow more complicated and challenging, they require greater attention to ensure comprehension. But orientation practices for an ongoing serial are charting out a storyworld that is still evolving as they are being created and consumed, forcing viewers to try to map a moving terrain. Viewers watched hours of flash sideways stories without knowing how to orient themselves to this fictional world relative to the core storyworld that many fans had invested a great deal of time and energy mapping and documenting. Especially for fans who watched the season in its original airing, the weekly gaps between episodes provided ample time for speculation and attempted orientations, aiming to map a coherent explanation onto the unspecified time and space of the flash sideways. While few examples are as acute as Lost, a danger of all complex serials is that we will not realise what is vital for maintaining our orientation until all of a show's mysteries and outcomes are revealed, and by that time it might be too late for fans to care.

What do these categories of orientation practices teach us about how we consume complex television? First, it is significant that they are happening at all, as standing as proof not only that viewers are actively engaging in television viewing (which we have known for decades), but that today's television outright demands that viewers stretch beyond the time and space of their initial viewing to try to make sense of what they have seen. It's not just that audiences are active, but that texts are explicitly activating, designed to stimulate viewers, strategically confuse them, and force them to orient. These orientation practices also help us understand the ways that television has embraced narrative complexity, and the areas where it might still look to develop. Clearly there has been much experimentation with complex plots and time schemes, and character relationships have always been a fertile ground for serial complexity. However, there is comparatively little experimentation in terms of innovative spatial storytelling, so if we were to predict where another wave of narrative innovation might come, we might look to how serial storytelling plays with space.

For many television viewers, series that demand drilling into transmedia, consulting maps or reference materials, or otherwise require orienting paratexts to ensure comprehension set too high of a bar to entry to attract audiences sufficiently large enough to sustain themselves within the commercial television marketplace, despite rare exceptions like Lost. Given that television has traditionally been regarded (if not actually functioned) as a medium allowing for low engagement and passive attention, the rise of complex programming that encourages paratextual play and expansiveness does not meet many people's expectations for how they watch television and what they hope to take away from it. There are certainly viewers who avoid complex series for fear of the implied time commitments and need for external 'homework' that counter their goals of television offering more relaxing and low-impact pleasures, especially when compared to other media that are regarded as more serious (literature, some music) and/or participatory (games, other music). But we need to recognise the particular viewing possibilities offered by complex series, not to hierarchise complexity over conventionality, but to highlight how contemporary television broadens the possible textual pleasures and corresponding modes of engagement available to viewers, fostering a mode of forensic fandom that appears to be an essential type of 21st century media consumption.

Bibliography

Anders, Charlie Jane (2011): *River Song's Chronology on Doctor Who, from River's Own Point of View*. Web. Retrieved from: [http://i09.com/5845981/river-songs-chronology-on-doctor-who-from-rivers-own-point-of-view]; posted: 2011/10/03; access: 2012/10/10.

Andrejevic, Mark (2008): Watching Television Without Pity: The Productivity of Online Fans. In: *Television & New Media*, Vol. 9, No. 1, 24–46.

Booth, Paul (2010): *Digital Fandom*. New York: Peter Lang Publishing.

Couldry, Nick (2007): On the Set of THE SOPRANOS: 'Inside' a Fan's Construction of Nearness. In: Gray, Jonathan/Sandvoss, Cornel/Harrington, C. Lee (eds.): *Fandom: Identities and Communities in a Mediated World*. New York: New York University Press, 139–148.

Dena, Christy (2008). Emerging Participatory Culture Practices Player-Created Tiers in Alternate Reality Games. In: *Convergence: The International Journal of Research into New Media Technologies*, Vol.14, No.1, 41–57.

Evans, Elizabeth (2011): *Transmedia Television: Audiences, New Media, and Daily Life*. London: Routledge.

Gray, Jonathan (2010): *Show Sold Separately: Promos, Spoilers, and Other Media Paratexts*. New York: NYU Press.

Mittell, Jason (2006): Narrative Complexity in Contemporary American Television. In: *The Velvet Light Trap*, No. 58, 29–40.

Mittell, Jason (2007): Film and Television Narrative. In: Herman, David (ed.): *The Cambridge Companion to Narrative*. Cambridge: Cambridge University Press, 156–71.

Mittell, Jason (2010): Previously On: Prime Time Serials and the Mechanics of Memory. In: Grishakova, Marina/Ryan, Marie-Laure (eds.): *Intermediality and Storytelling*. Berlin: De Gruyter, 78–98.

Nussbaum, Emily (2010): Pugnacious D: THE WIRE Creator David Simon on His New HBO Series, TREME. *New York Magazine*, April 4. [http://nymag.com/arts/tv/features/65235/]; access: 2012/10/10.

Rehak, Bob (2012): *Graphic Engine*. Web. Retrieved from: [http://graphic-engine.swarthmore.edu/?tag=blueprint-culture]; access: 2012/10/10.

Torchin, Leshu (2002): Location, Location, Location. In: *Tourist Studies*, Vol. 2, No. 3, 247–266.

Web Sources

Lostpedia: *Timeline*. Web. Retrieved from: [http://lostpedia.wikia.com/wiki/timeline]; posted: 2008/09/09; access: 2012/10/10.

ChronologicallyLost.com. Web. Retrieved from: [http://www.chronologicallylost.com]; access: 2012/10/10.

TelevisionWithoutPity.com. Retrieved from: [http://www.televisionwithoutpity.com]; access: 2012/10/10.

TELEVISION SERIES

24 (USA 2001–10, Fox)
ARRESTED DEVELOPMENT (USA 2003–06, Fox)
BATTLESTAR GALACTICA (USA 2004–09, Sci Fi)
BREAKING BAD (USA 2008–, AMC)
BUFFY THE VAMPIRE SLAYER (USA 1997–2003, The WB/UPN)
CHEERS (USA 1982–93, NBC)
COMMUNITY (USA 2009–, NBC)
DEXTER (USA 2006–, Showtime)
DOCTOR WHO (UK 2005–, BBC)
FIREFLY (USA 2002–03, Fox)
FLASHFORWARD (USA 2009–10, ABC)
FRINGE (USA 2008–13, Fox)
GAME OF THRONES (USA 2011–, HBO)
HAPPY DAYS (USA 1974–84, ABC)
HOMICIDE: LIFE ON THE STREET (USA 1993–99, NBC)
HOW I MET YOUR MOTHER (USA 2005–, CBS)
I LOVE LUCY (USA 1951–57, CBS)
LIFE ON MARS (UK 2006–07, BBC)
LOST (USA 2004–10, ABC)
MAD MEN (USA 2007–, AMC)
ONCE UPON A TIME (USA 2011–, ABC)
SEINFELD (USA 1989–98, NBC)
THE SOPRANOS (USA 1999–2007, HBO)
ST. ELSEWHERE (USA 1982–88, NBC)
STAR TREK (USA 1966–69, NBC)
THE BOB NEWHART SHOW (USA 1972–78, CBS)
TREME (USA 2010–, HBO)
VERONICA MARS (USA 2004–07, UPN/The CW)
THE WIRE (USA 2002–08, HBO)

WEB VIDEOS

LOST: THE SYNCHRONIZING (posted by NDHatch). Web. Retrieved from: [http://www.youtube.com/watch?v=0ILPnh4mOK0]; posted: 2008/01/25; access: 2012/10/10.

Films

INCEPTION (USA 2010, Christopher Nolan)
LOLA RENNT (RUN LOLA RUN; Germany 1998, Tom Tykwer)
SLIDING DOORS (UK/USA 1998, Peter Howitt)
THE LORD OF THE RINGS 1–3 (USA/New Zealand 2001–2003, Peter Jackson)

Games

LOST: VIA DOMUS (2008, Ubisoft)

Image Sources

Figure 1: Infographic by Shahed Syed. Retrieved from: [http://www.shah3d.com/posters/dexters-victims/]; updated 2011; access: 2012/10/10.

Figure 2: Image from the LOST jigsaw puzzles, released by TDC Games from 2006-07. Image retrieved from Lostpedia: [http://lostpedia.wikia.com/wiki/Jigsaw_puzzles]; access: 2012/10/10.

You're Supposed to Be Confused![1]
(Dis)Orienting Narrative Mazes
in Televisual Complex Narrations

CHRISTINE PIEPIORKA

In recent years, a transformation of televisual serial narratives has led to a new and widely discussed phenomenon named "narrative complexity".[2] The term was coined by Jason Mittell in 2006, but was not defined in full detail at that time; thus I have analysed complex serials and determined specific characteristics by an analysis of the so-called 'narratively complex serials' in my book *Lost in Narration* (2011). In my point of view the specific characteristics of this serial form include complexity of the look and televisuality, characters, story arcs, time, genre, intertextuality, self-reference and transmediality.[3] Furthermore, the implications of this paradigm shift in TV-presentation and in narration are, of course, essential for the ongoing reconceptualisation and (self-)understanding of the viewer. But this article will neither put the focus on a viewer behaviour (that may lead to an abolition of the binary opposition of media text and consumer) nor on concepts of participatory culture in transmediality, nor even on viewer practices of orientation. Instead, the present paper is initiated by a quote by Steven Johnson talking about narratively complex serials: "[...] and then you realize that you're supposed to be confused" (Johnson 2005, 77). With this quote Johnson refers to the recent developments in serial narration and—in my point

---

1 | This phrase was coined by Steven Johnson in his book *Everything Bad is Good for You* describing complex television (Johnson 2005,77).

2 | These shows offer an alternative to conventional television narratives and represent new modes of television storytelling: As experiments of innovative narrations, they include pre-existing as well as innovative narrative elements, which will be described in more detail in this article.

3 | The named characteristics are not intended to be exhaustive: Not every complex serial exhibits every single characteristic and not every named serial is as complex as others that are mentioned.

of view—the upcoming pressing question: How and by which characteristic does narrative complexity produce a demand of cognitive orientation or an incurrence of disorientation?

To analyse a possible orienting and disorienting potential of narrative complexity, I have to examine the ambivalent phenomenon of '(dis)orientation' a little further. 'Confusion', the term Johnson uses concerning the cognitive demands that televised narratives place on their viewers, is the state of being bewildered or unclear in one's mind about something (Oxford Dictionary 2010). In other words, the person who is confused is disoriented. In the field of psychology orientation is a function of the mind involving awareness of three dimensions: time, place, and person/own personality (Baars/Gage 2010, 257). Vice versa—disorientation is a cognitive state in which the senses of time, place, and recognition of people or even oneself encounter difficulties.

Additionally, to follow up the asked question concerning disorientation in narratively complex serials, it is necessary to think about the term 'narration'. A narrative is defined as "a chain of events in cause-effect relationship occurring in time and space" (Bordwell/Thompson 2001, 60). Causality in time and space (which is constructed by places) therefore is central, while characters occur as the agents of causes and effects. Time, place, and characters/persons thus build a narrative network of information that is readily understandable by a complex sequence of perceptive, cognitive processes, which finally work out a coherent story.[4]

This definition exhibits useful similarities between narratological and psychological elements of orientation, because both seem to rely on the same bases: time, place, and person. Therefore it is on the dice to ask how a narration can cause disorientation for the viewer with regard to time, place, and person[5]: Which orienting or disorienting functions and potentials do the characteristics of narrative complexity have and what are the consequences for the understanding of narration? How does a narratively complex serial oscillate between offering orientation and being a confusing narrative maze? The named elements of orientation (time, place, person) will therefore be examined in reference to the mentioned characteristics of narrative complexity. In contrast to Mittell's chapter in this volume this analysis will not focus on viewer behaviour caused by disorienting elements of serials, but wants to get to the crux of the matter: the core text. Hence, the paper will examine the intratextual elements of the serial

---

4 | The narration is "the moment-by-moment process that guides us in building the story out of the plot" (Bordwell/Thompson 2001, 60). In order to make sense of a narration, Bordwell initiates the distinction between story and plot.

5 | The terms 'time' and 'place' shall refer to the time and place within the narration. Accordingly, the term 'person' does not mean the own personality of the viewer but the recognition of persons/characters appearing within the narration.

(televisuality, characters, story arcs, time) and opens up for extratextual elements of narrative complexity (genre, intertextuality/self-reference, transmediality) to finally argue the effect of the dissolution of traditional narrative structures generated by the interplay of narratively complex (dis)orientations.

TELEVISUALITY AND THE LOOK

The first of all narrative complexity characteristics I want to to examine regarding (dis)orientation, is televisuality and the look of those serials. The style of classical narrations typically encourages the spectator to construct a coherent, consistent time and space for the story action (Bordwell 1986, 26f.). This includes a limited number of particular technical devices organised into a stable paradigm and ranked according to plot demands: staging, camera work, sound etc. (Mittell 2009, 177ff.), while narrative complexity offers distinctive visual features, which are not situated under these classical maxims. In contrast, the style used in some narratively complex serials recalls the term "televisuality" by John T. Caldwell (1995).[6] This complexity of style is distinctive for complex narratives and can lead on to a (dis)orienting function of style.

The opening credits of the serial DEXTER (USA 2000–, Showtime), for example, show every detail of Dexter's morning routine in intensive colour and in extreme close-ups: shaving, cutting meat, frying eggs, squeezing an orange, putting on clothes. But because of the created look, the viewer perceives the activities of Dexter's morning routine in a different light. They become the activities of a serial killer: cutting meat, shedding blood, pulping entrails, putting on a burial gown. The credits indicate an orienting function as well as a disorienting one. Confusion is created by the look of the morning routine because it can be connected to something completely different. It raises the question which the viewer has to ask during the whole serial and which confuses him again and again: Is Dexter the good guy or the bad guy? But it creates an orienting effect as well because of the immediate presentation of both parts of the ambivalent character Dexter at the very beginning of each episode. The opening credits therefore mirror it: He is a hero as a cop and the villain as a serial killer. This merges both of his personalities and highlights that the viewer is (dis)oriented concerning the dimension of person, whereby this does not mean a personal disorientation, but a disorientation concerning characteristics of the protagonist.

---

6 | Televisuality is summarised by Kolker as follows: "The term [...] describe[s] the complexity of style that, beginning in the 1980s, began to inscribe television images with a richness of detail and flourish of color and special effects" (Kolker 2009, 200). Thereby the "style itself became the subject" (Caldwell 1995, 5) and culminated in a "fetish for effects" (Caldwell 1995, 5).

Another example including spatial and person-related disorientation is the often mentioned opening scene of the serial Lost (USA 2004–2010, ABC), which is an utterly disorienting serial and can be named as one of the most complex narratives up to the present day. In the first episode there is no establishing shot to offer any orientation of place to the viewer. An extreme close-up of a wide opened eye constitutes the exposition of the serial, so the viewer has no knowledge about the person whose eye he sees yet. The framing prevents that we catch sight of the person whose eye it is. After a point-of-view-shot from the perspective of this eye causing disorientation (because the viewer does not know where the action takes place, he can just assume that it is a part of a jungle or a forest), a crane shot from the treetops the viewer has seen before from below follows: A man is lying on the floor of a jungle. This leads to the assumption that this is the man whose eye the viewer has seen at the very beginning. This disorientation is highlighted by the following long tracking shots and jump cuts showing the man running through the jungle, searching for something, for orientation, like the viewer himself. After he stops running, the camera shows the terrified man, not the beach he has arrived at. After a long tracking shot we are able to look at what he sees: a crashed plane. The scenery at the beach is like a spectacle—to the man and to the viewer: Sound and image produce many fragments of a chaos, out of which the viewer has to build up the whole situation. Right from the beginning, the man seems to be confused and disoriented about place and person, when he catches sight of persons at the beach. He is seemingly not aware of some of the dimensions of orientation. Even the viewer is not because he experiences what the protagonist does: disorientation about place and persons.

A distinct temporal orientation with simultaneous spatial and person-related disorientation caused by an overflow of information and image may be noted in 24 (USA 2001–2010, FOX). It includes a dis- and orienting look in terms of visual effects. An inserted digital clock offers a temporal key for orientation: Narrative time and discourse time are in line and suggest a kind of pseudo-liveness, which is highlighted by the on-screen-text "events occur in real time"(S1/E01). This eye-catching liveness is stressed by splitscreens, which offer a huge range of information. The visualised simultaneity of different scenes may be confusing concerning the senses of recognition of people and places, but is held together by the clock and therefore by the orientation of time.

COMPLEXITY OF CHARACTERS

Characters are the vehicle and most important carriers of the causal events of a story (Thompson 1995, 57) and thus a significant characteristic of narrative complexity and important for orientation within a narration. In classical narrations, the protagonists are presented as psychologically defined individuals (Rayner/Wall/Kruger 2001, 67). Narratively complex serials additionally seem to use them to establish confusion by enhancing the quantity as well as the quality (which means the depth) of the characters. The multiplicity of protagonists forms a network of characters, which opens a spectrum of simultaneous stories. Narrative complexity combines a numerous cast, followed over an extended period of time, with a depth of characters provided by well-defined backstories.

The retrospective construction of the characters in LOST is an example for the level of quality. The characters are constructed through flashbacks and nearly their whole past is stated. By this the viewer gets a kind of orientation concerning characters: What are the motivations in the past for their actions in the present or future? From this depth of the protagonists an impression of psychologically rounded characters originates (Nelson 1997, 47). This is extended through the noticeable use of character names, which can offer indications of background or intertextuality (Butler 2002, 56).[7] The producers of LOST mentioned that "every single name on the show has purpose and meaning" (Gilbert 2005). For example, many names in LOST refer to philosophers. One example is the character John Locke, who is named after the philosopher of the same name. In his opinion every human is born into a 'Tabula Rasa' and resembles a blank slate (Specht 2007, 35). 'Tabula Rasa' is a synonym for a new beginning and that is what it is for the character John in the episode TABULA RASA (S1/E03). He starts his new life after the plane has crashed on the island of LOST cured from his paraplegia. Similar references are made by character names like Desmond David Hume[8], Danielle Rousseau, and Michail Bakunin[9], which offer the possibility of orientation concerning the character's opinions, backgrounds, psychology, and relationships.

Furthermore, the quantity of characters and therefore a multilayered network of relationships is essential for many complex narratives.[10] In LOST, there are fourteen to thirty-five protagonists.[11] The number of supporting actors amounts to twenty. Therefore, the interpersonal network is highly sophisticated.

---

7 | Intertextuality will be discussed later on in the category 'intertextuality and self-reference'.

8 | This is a reference to the philosopher David Hume. In the serial character Desmond Hume is affected by John Locke like philosopher David Hume was by John Locke.

9 | This is a reference to Jean Jacques Rousseau and Michail Alexandrowitsch Bakunin. The characters are members of competing groups as well as Bakunin was a critic of J.J. Rousseau's philosophy.

10 | Not every narratively complex serial works with such a complex character network; to name already mentioned serials: 24 and DEXTER.

11 | The amount of protagonist depends on the definition of protagonist; it differs between different analyses of LOST.

The protagonists of Lost have already met each other by chance in their daily life, in institutions, or through friends before their plane crashed.[12] The viewer is urged to retain orientation within this network and thus concerning persons/characters.[13] The narration offers this orientation through flashbacks of each character and of their relationships, but requires a high level of attention from the viewer to avoid his disorientation.

Story Arcs

The next characteristic of narrative complexity I use to attribute a (dis)orienting potential to, is the multitude of story arcs.[14] To achieve a meaningful analysis of story arcs, a proper differentiation of types of stories and their story arcs has to be made, resulting in a categorisation of series, serials, and complex serials.

Series include an episodical narration, which is indicated by narrative closure at the end of each episode and a mostly linear progression (Creeber 2004, 8ff.) (fig. 1). Every episode is self-contained with autonomous storylines, there are no coherences connecting it to the next episodes (e.g. by continued story arcs). The viewer is able to view the episodes in any order and thus is generally oriented about the dimensions of time, place and person, not least because especially the persons do not change dramatically during a season in contrast to time and place.

A serial operates with continuous story arcs and therefore with an open, future-oriented story (Mikos 1994, 137). The story arcs of different episodes refer back to each other (fig. 1). Hence, the order of the episodes is specified as ongoing, because the episodes are not self-contained. Instead they are constituted as one part of a bigger, coherently narrated story. This story is often distinguished by an arc of tension which reaches beyond the maximum of three episodes followed by a so called 'wash up' as the last act of a storyline (Mielke 2006, 563). Therefore, it is important for the viewer to know about the events and thus about

---

12 | A very interesting edit of the chance meetings in the past is the *YouTube*-Video Lost: In preparation of season 5: Connections.

13 | Different charts, created by viewers, present the highly complex relationships of the protagonists and supporting actors. Those viewer-created charts can be seen as viewer practices of orientation. One very detailed and well-done chart is: Krzywinsk, Martin (2010): Lost – The Web of Intrigue. For more examples concerning viewer practices of orientation reference is made to Jason Mittell's article in this volume.

14 | A 'story' is a bundle of 'story arcs' or 'storylines', which are happening one after another, simultaneously, alternating or parallel (Miller 1980, 44). Story arcs are also, but not exclusively, influenced by character amount, depth of character, and their relationships.

Figure 1: Classical structure of series and serial.

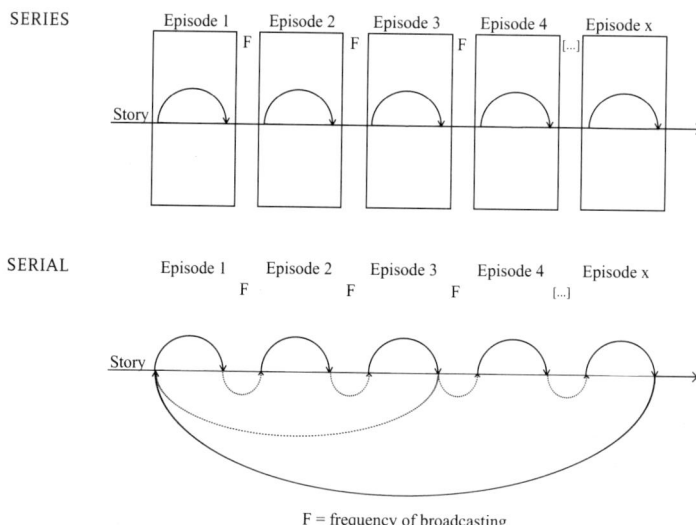

F = frequency of broadcasting

the story arcs of the previous episode. To offer orientation to the viewer concerning time, place, and person, the exposition of an episode begins in most cases with a recapitulation that summarises the story arcs (ibid., 564).

Of most interest in this article is the hybrid of the aforementioned forms: the narratively complex serial, which is indicated by a high amount of story arcs, depending on a high amount of characters with own story arcs and backstories and a non-linear progression. Hence, narrative complexity does not just oscillate between series and serials like the cumulative narratives.[15] Furthermore the story arcs are denoted by a high amount of storylines, which emanate from different episodes and refer back to each other. The absence of an arrow (fig. 2) at the end of each episode represents the absence of any closure.

The different lines all represent narrative connections between episodes: Some are connected directly, some connections skip one or more episodes. The number of storylines can vary, thus an episode can include a wide spectrum shown in parallel storylines. A season operates as a bundle of narrative units, which are taken together as a coherent segment. Considering one isolated epi-

---

15 | Cumulative narratives are characterised by a closed structure of each episode, but a small number of story arcs overlap episodes, which includes background stories and character developments. Hence, this form enables occasional viewers to watch the series as well as frequent viewers who have more interest in character development. Thus both the advantages of series and serials are included. See Piepiorka (2011) for details.

Figure 2: Structure of narrative complexity and narratively complex seasons.

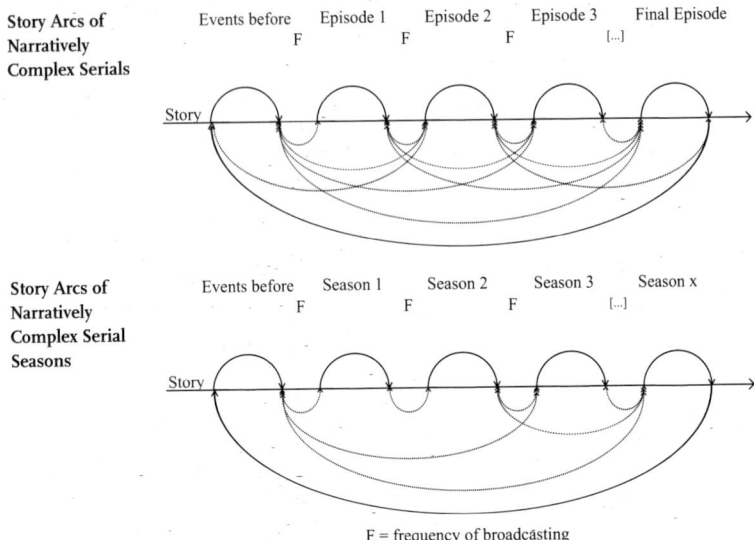

F = frequency of broadcasting

sode, it becomes very clear how complex any single one of them can be. Just to give an impression: In episodes one to six of season one, Lost develops thirty-three story arcs, while episode four alone consists of nine of them. Only two of those are introduced and closed in that episode (Reinecke 2007, 123).[16] LOST is an extreme example for the highest complexity of story arcs, but serials like HOW I MET YOUR MOTHER (USA 2005–, CBS) also exhibit interwoven elements—even though they emerge more from details than from whole story arcs, (like, for example, the yellow umbrella of the kids' mother, which is mentioned again and again like a golden thread of the story). And as if that was not enough: Narrative complexity is constituted by the fact that some narrative connections are first shown in the first episode and not finished until the last episode of the same season. Story arcs do not only skip one season, they even skip seasons (fig. 2).

The viewer has to be able to make cognitive connections between the different story arcs of the serial's story to reconstruct it as a whole and he has to retain orientation concerning place, person, and time of the story arcs. Therefore Bill Carter is not wrong when he describes these types of narration as a "you've-got-to-see-it-every-week-drama" (Carter 2006). Only if the viewer does watch it consistently, he can reach the cognitive state in which the senses of time, direction, and recognition of people and places are not dulled.

---

16 | This result is, however, not representative due to the small number of analysed episodes for a serial of six seasons with 121 episodes. Nevertheless it makes the model developed here very clear.

COMPLEXITY OF TIME

The temporal disorientations that Julia Eckel (2012) describes in her book about "non-linear narratives in contemporary cinema"[17], are very useful for analysing a feature of narrative complexity on television as well, because she is working with manipulations of time, space, and causality, too. In contrast to *Classical Narration*[18] the non-linear plot deviates from the standard, so that it is open for a play with temporality (Eckel 2012, 8).

Firstly two nearly conventionalised breaks of chronology and of time are to be mentioned: flashback and flashforward (in the form of recounting or enactment or enacted recounting (Bordwell 1985, 78)). One serial example is when the viewer watches two kids sitting on a couch and hears a man say: " I will tell you an incredible story, the story of how I met your mother" (How I MET YOUR MOTHER, S1/E01). Afterwards the narration shows the life of the narrating man in his mid-twenties. So the whole series is kind of an enacted flashback, which is—at the same time—by the use of a voice-over during the whole episode an enacted recounting. From S1/E02 on, due to the caption "2030" it is clear that the kids are sitting on the couch in the year 2030. Thus, from the kids' perspective, every episode is a flashback, the present of the series is 2030 and the told stories are in the past. But from the 20th century-viewer's perspective the telling man or narrator and his kids are in the future and the narration and the man in his mid-twenties are in the present.

For LOST, flashes in both directions are striking attributes. As already mentioned concerning the complexity of characters, every character's past is constructed via flashbacks.[19] The more interesting game of using both flashes is presented by LOST (S3/E22) when we are witnesses of a dialogue between the

---

17 | For a summary of this concept, see also Julia Eckel's article in this volume.

18 | The story model of *Classical Narration* by David Bordwell (1985,156ff.) describes a norm of narration, in which story and plot exhibit a kind of well-established set of guidelines for a decent compression of time and space (Elsaesser/Hagener 2007, 113). By using this scheme time, space, and causality and with it the construction of the story are coherent and readily understandable.

19 | They are subjectively motivated explanations for their behaviour on the island and thus allow the retrospective constructions of the characters. Many flashbacks of a person's past are introduced by close-ups of his or her eyes, thus the flashbacks get a marker of their own and therefore an intraserial convention is established. However, unmarked flashbacks evoke a kind of disorientation concerning time, too. S2/E01 shows the morning routine of character Desmond. This seems to happen in present time, but after the arrival of character Locke, the viewer can establish a connection to a former episode showing this arrival. Therefore the viewer can classify it as a flashback, but only if he knows the specific mentioned episode.

characters Jack and Kate, which does not take place on the island. Because of this setting (outside of the island) as a marker for flashbacks, the viewer is oriented in time: It must be a flashback. But as soon as Jack is saying "we have to go back to the island" it is very clear that our orientation of time has been clouded: It is a flashforward.

And there are more complex uses of time structures. The reversed time (see Eckel's article in this volume) is opposed to the linear order of plot-elements. At first appearance LOST does not offer such a time structure, but while the main arcs on the island are going ahead in linear causality (A to B), the flashbacks of the character Kate, for example, are presented backwards. The explanation for the first shown flashbacks is presented in the next flashbacks (d to a).[20] Initially the viewer is disoriented and has to put these flashbacks together in the correct order to understand Kate's backstory and to be oriented in time and causality.

Multi-perspectival time, according to Eckel (ibid.), is the result of a character-based multiperspectivity. Hence, it is a period narrated from different perspectives connected to different persons. S2/E07 of LOST, for example, uses this time variation. So far, the whole series has told about 48 days of one group of plane crashed people until we see the same 48 days of another group of people. This becomes clear when both groups clash into each other. The plot shows the same period of time consecutively, but in the story both periods take place simultaneously.

The encapsulated time category (ibid.) includes mimeographed and nested time-dimensions. In the manner of DOCTOR WHO, in LOST the whole island is travelling through time and space. Every time travel is initiated by a white flash, but the 'when' is not indicated. This multidimensionality through up to fourteen time dimensions is one of the most extreme forms of temporal disorientation. If the protagonists are asking "when are we now?" after a time travel, it is a mirror of the viewer's feeling. He looses nearly every possibility to orientate in the time of the island. Just details of the setting, like the clothes or cars, are providing indications which are not missed only by very attentive viewers.

The same features that Eckel states for non-linear movies thereby apply to serials: The mentioned structures of time transgress with norms and deman the cognitive ability of the viewer to orient himself in time while being confronted with time complexities that he is not used to in life or in fiction.[21]

---

20 | For example S1/E03 shows that a marshal arrests Kate. But only then in S1/E12 the reason for this arrest is shown: a bank robbery. S1/E22 then specifies the reason for the robbery.

21 | Even if it is not a dissolution of continuity or linearity (because of completeness), Real-Time has to be mentioned in the category of time complexity, too. Nevertheless, it is an unusual time use in televisual narrations: simultaneity of narrative time and discourse time. This is disclosed by the title of the serial 24, which does not describe

Genre-Hybrids

After having analysed the intratextual elements of narrative complexity, I continue with the extratextual elements, which can also lead to narrative (dis)orientations. First, I start with the classification of media texts in groups of same attributes—which means: genre. The classification of media texts under a genre is an important piece of information and a possibility of orientation for viewers concerning their programme selection (Turner 2003, 4ff.).[22] Viewers connect specific expectations with a genre (Rayner/Wall/Kruger 2001, 57), because it is "a horizon of expectations" (Todorov 1990, 18f.). Television shows which cannot be classified generically are genre-hybrids. Genre-hybrids are the combination of different genre conventions and assumptions, "which makes each genre norm richer and more vibrant through clever practices of fusion" (Mittell 2004, 150f.).

BUFFY THE VAMPIRE SLAYER, for example, mixes serial and series[23] as well as conventions of different genres like horror[24], action, romantic teenage drama[25], science-fiction, high school drama and even musical[26] (Recht 2011, 18f.). "It highlights and draws upon generic assumptions as they are placed in juxtaposition with other genres" (Mittell 2004, 150). This statement applies as well to a serial like VERONICA MARS (USA 2004–2007, UPN), which mixes crime, drama, and mystery with romance and comedy or to BREAKING BAD (USA 2007–, AMC) which combines genres like crime, black comedy, social satire, and family drama. There are lots of examples of genre-hybrids —not only in narratively

---

the content of the serial as most titles do, but the structure of time it uses. Furthermore, the split screen produces a simultaneity of events, which demands a rapid change of attention from the viewer. This is stylised in 24 more than in any other serial before and may reflect the just-in-time-style of life of the 21st century.
22 | See also the contribution by Katja Hettich in this volume.
23 | The first episodes of the show are characterised by typical elements a series like a 'villain of the week' and therefore by an episodical narration with narrative closure. But after a few episodes the show changes into a serial: The characters are subjects of a development and the episodes refer to each other because of multiple temporally non-linear story arcs.
24 | Most of the time, the horror genre presents female characters as victims of a male monster, who are saved by a male monster killer. In Buffy, the female character is the killer. Thus, the show plays with genre conventions and has successfully adapted the horror genre to the demands of a serial drama (Horrocks 2009, 7ff.).
25 | This is highlighted in the heroine's consecutive relationships with Angel, Riley, and Spike.
26 | See S6/E07: ONCE MORE WITH FEELING.

complex serials—which emerge more and more, letting them become a norm themselves.

But the 'new' norm of genre-hybrids that features narrative complexity mostly can, of course, cause disorientation itself, because the viewers are not able to assign a television show into a conventionalised genre and therefore an uncertainty occurs about any expectations they are supposed to have.

INTERTEXTUALITY AND SELF-REFERENCE

Two more striking characteristics of the focused serial forms are intertextuality and self-reference—which are elements with distinct orienting potential. Like Julia Kristeva (1972) mentioned in accordance to Saussure's semiotic relationships of signs to each other, already existent mediatexts can be part of a new one; They can be intertextual. According to Kristeva a mediatext is a "mosaic of quotes" and a "[...] transformation of existing texts" (ibid., 348; transl. C.P.).[27] Thus, intertextuality means to shape the meaning of a text by other texts.[28]

One form of intertextuality is the similarity between two stories and their story arcs, like Jason Mittell mentioned in an interview: "LOST is a wood of intertextuality" (Piepiorka 2011, 154ff.). The narration of the serial evolves along a "cast-away-topos" (Drangsholt 2009, 210) as a 'robinsonade', an intertextual reference to *Robinson Crusoe* (1719).[29] Likewise, LOST shows parallels to *Lord of the flies* (1954).[30]

Equally, VERONICA MARS is a serial that demands a high degree of intertextual competence of its viewer (Emmerton 2011, 128) and imitates an already-known story arc: a murder of a young blond girl shakes up the town and is brought to

---

[27] | Original citation: „Jeder Text baut sich als Mosaik von Zitaten auf, jeder Text ist Absorption und Transformation eines anderen Textes" (Kristeva 1972, 348).

[28] | The term intertextuality has been transformed many times since Kristeva defined it; for example Gérad Genette (1982, 93) considers the term 'transtextuality' as more inclusive than 'intertextuality' and develops a systematic typology of transtextuality: Intertextuality (direct quotation, allusion, plagiarism), paratextuality (relations between a text and its paratexts which frame the text like introduction etc.), metatextuality (critical commentary of a text about another), hypertextuality (relation between a text and a hypotext as a transformed, elaborated or extended version). Here intertextuality only means *to shape the meaning of a text by other texts*.

[29] | Both texts describe the life of the survivors of a travel accident who are as a result stranded on an island.

[30] | A group of survivors on a paradisical island is electing a leader, building huts, making beacons, hunting wild boars and escaping a beast on the island. There are many more similarities of media texts which cannot be mentioned entirely here.

justice by the main characters. Thus, the whole serial is a homage to TWIN PEAKS (USA 1990–1991, ABC)—one of the first series mentioned dealing with narrative complexity.[31] On top, both serials are dedicated to the same genre 'noir television', which falls squarely within the 'film noir tradition'[32] (Thomas 2006, 59): VERONICA MARS is 'neo-noir' by mixing elements of noir with other genres, like the teen drama. Settings, plots, and characters takes the idea of duality and with it of 'noir' into the show (ibid., 60) and open up a reference to already seen serials in that genre.

Another form of intertextuality are the visual and oral hints of media texts: for example, the books which a character reads. LOST shows a lot of books read by the character Sawyer and is thus full of allusions concerning meanings of different narrations.[33] GILMORE GIRLS (USA 2000–2007, The WB), although not that complex, is a very good example as well, which exhausts this type of intertextuality by citations of literature and movies. The direct citation is an often used form, for example when the character Hurley in LOST cites: "Dude, that beer is sitting there since before Rocky 3, maybe even 2. It is poison by now" (S3/E10). Hence, he draws attention to the age of that beer by using an intertextual reference to the production year of a movie. Not a direct citation, but a more subtle reference of intertextuality can be found in the episode titels of season three of VERONICA MARS, which are named after literary and cinematic media texts and videogames.[34] These examples exhibit the possible concentration of intertextual references, which leaves no room not to think about them and to connect the media text's meanings.

The viewer can orientate himself along those references by embedding some parts of the narration in a greater context. Every viewer who knows about those other mediatexts can put a new significance to the series. Thus, intertextuality is an invitation to rethink the meaning of the narration and to conduct one's own

---

31 | Mittell (2006, 30) mentions early accounts of innovative strategies, which he suggests to be the antecedents of contemporary narrative complexity in MAGNUM, P.I. (USA 1980-1988, CBS), ST. ELSEWHERE (USA 1982-1988, NBC) and TWIN PEAKS.
32 | Duality is a characterisation in noir as well as an anti-hero trying to walk a straight path, corrupt authority figures, and the ambivalence of characters struggling with the coexistence of opposing attitudes (Thomas 2006, 59f.).
33 | See e.g. Spangler 2006.
34 | S3/E05 *PRESIDENT EVIL* (videogame: RESIDENT EVIL, Capcom/Virgin Interactive, 1996; movie: RESIDENT EVIL, USA, 2002, Paul W.S. Anderson) S3/E07 *OF VICE AND MAN* (book: *Of Mice and men*, 1937, John Steinbeck), S3/E06 *HI, INFIDELITY* (book: *High Fidelity*, 1995, Nick Hornby; movie: HIGH FIDELITY, USA/UK, 2000, Stephen Fears), S3/E08 *LORD OF THE PI´S* (book: *Lord of the Flies*, 1954, William Golding; movie: LORD OF THE FLIES, 1963, Peter Brook), S3/E16 *UN-AMERICAN GRAFFITI* (movie: AMERICAN GRAFFITI, USA 1973, George Lucas) etc.

research beyond the initial viewing experience (Emmerton 2011, 128). But if the viewer does not have the frame of reference of those other media texts, he is missing a level of narrative complexity.

Interestingly, some of the media texts themselves demonstrate an ironic self-reference regarding their disorienting properties, just to name one example: Lost's Hurley (S5/E11) refers to the complexity of time in a dialogue with Miles. With the words "That´s very confusing!" Hurley speaks for the viewers and begins a question-response-game concerning the time confusions in the narration as well as of the narration. This orientates the viewer, who learns that he is not the only one who is confused or lacks orientation in time. Additionally Miles offers a kind of temporal orientation for Hurley as well as for the viewer.

Transmediality

Classical narrations induce the viewer to fill-in the accruing gaps, while they are offering or retaining information for the construction of the story (Bordwell 1985, 55). The hermeneutic code (Barthes 1970, 30) permanently produces new questions and opens up gaps in the narrative structure. The search for the cues in narratively complex serials does not only take place within the narration, but is expanded by its 'transmedia storytelling'[35]: The textual and narrative design is not solely limited to the original medium, but the boundaries of media may be exceeded (Jenkins 2006, 95). According to this, not the repetition of the existing content in different media is essential, but a content extension across media

Figure 3: Hypertextuality/Transmediality.

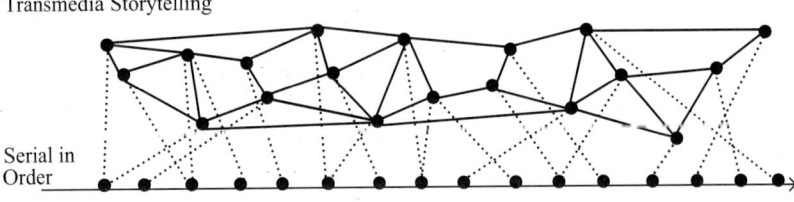

---

35 | Jenkins defines it as follows: "A transmedia story unfolds across multiple platforms, with each new text making a distinctive and valuable contribution to the whole. In the ideal form of transmedia storytelling, each medium does what it does best—so that a story might be introduced in a film, expanded through television, novels, and comics; its world might be explored through game play or experienced as an amusement park attraction" (Jenkins 2006, 95f.).

boundaries, and thus a representation of an independent continuing element. The content is not only summarised in other media, but the narrative world is extended (Mittell 2009, 434). Therefore, in the field of transmedia storytelling the 'worldbuilding' is essential: Transmedia narrations are not based on an individual character or plot, but on a complex fictional world. This can be seen in the producer-created and viewer-created extensions of the original text, in which the narration is continued. Transmedia storytelling thus represents the extension of the narrative universe (ibid.).

In connection with transmediality it is essential to think about reception—although this paper focuses on the intra- and extratextual elements of core text—because transmediality has direct influences on narration and its reception and orientation in it. There are two levels of narratively complex reception. Firstly, the viewer receives the serial or core text by watching the episodes in a significant order (arrow in fig. 3); secondly and additionally, he uses the second level of transmedia storytelling (spots in fig. 3) by perceiving webisodes, mobisodes, graphic novels, books, fictive websites, internet platforms, videogames etc.[36]

The viewer has the possibility to consume and connect the elements (black lines in fig. 3) to get information, which can be used to understand the complex narration in a better way. He gets the task of building connections between the series and the transmedia elements (dotted lines in fig. 3). Like Daniela Olek (see her article in this volume) mentions, we can understand this construction as a simulation of a hypertext.[37] In compliance with hypertext-theories, texts are non-linear fragments, which are connected to each other and are structured like a network (Nelson 1980, 2), as we see at the top of fig. 4. Apart from that,

Figure 4: Simulation of hypertextuality in serial's story arcs.

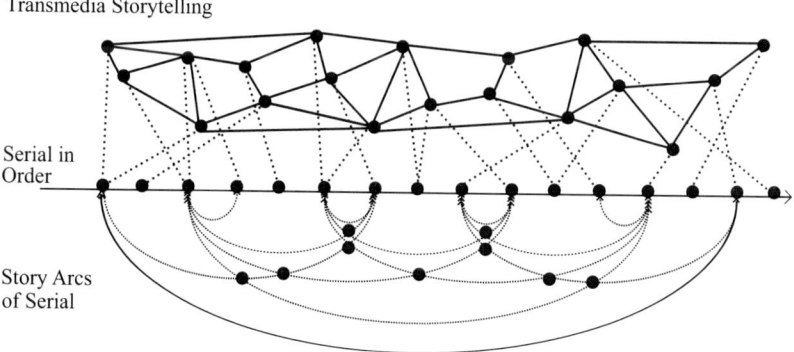

---

36 | For a detailed typology of those narrative extensions, see Askwith 2003 as well as Piepiorka 2011.
37 | See also Olek 2011.

the serial mirrors or simulates this existing virtual hypertext of the transmedia universe (see the bottom of fig. 4).

The building of hypotheses and filling in of gaps is not limited to the televisual narration itself, it takes places in and outside the narration by using information of the intramedial and transmedial serial. In view of the overload of information, the viewer—or in this case user—of the transmedia world has to ask: Where do I get information about the series, what do I search for, do I know the found information or how do I have to connect it? He has to orientate himself concerning place, time, and person while he uses the network of information.

Lost in Narration, Lost in Space

To orientate oneself seems to be difficult both within and even outside of the television frame. Narratively complex television evokes a potentially (dis)orienting narrative by using different intra- and extratextual practices, as it has been highlighted in this article on the basis of categories of narrative complexity. Indeed, this phenomenon can be described as an effect of the dissolution of traditional narrative structures and at the same time evokes a viewer concept based on (dis)orientation in narrative complexity. Complex television programmes invite temporary disorientation, allowing viewers to build up their comprehension skills by active cognitive work. Thus, every viewer has his own way to (re)gain orientation within the serials and the transmedia world: The serial offers different accesses and meanings to the viewer, thus making him experience the story world and the orientation in it in another way. The viewer has to retain orientation concerning place (Which island are we on?), person (Who knows whom in this character network?), and time (flashes, present or time travel?). This produces a kind of loss and recovery of oneself: Sometimes the viewers seem to be *lost in narration*. Therefore the complexity and expansiveness of serials forces viewers to engage in television viewing and activates them to develop practices of orientation to ensure comprehension of the narrative. Complex forms thus appear to be narrative mazes, with the goal of supposed disorientation and a request for ongoing intra- and extratextual re-orientation concerning time, place, and person.

In his article in this volume Jason Mittell refers to the upcoming question of spatiality in narration and diegetic space. But I think this approach has to go further to an abstract level of structure: Narratively complex serials place events/story arcs on different mediaplatforms, thus creating seemingly spatially fragmented narrations. The viewer connects these intraserial and transmedial information collected from different places with each other and constructs the whole narration in the first place. Thus, the movement through and the collection of information within the transmedia universe are essential for transmedia narration. The transmedia space is constructed and set by the media, but requires movement from place to place by the viewer to complement the space and with it the narration.[38] Hence, the recipient moves within a structural space of narration. Thereby the question of spatiality does not only apply to a diegetic space within narration, but metaphorically to the spatial structure of narrations as such: a spatialisation of narration in which the viewer has to find orientation to not be *lost in space*.

Bibliography

Askwith, Ivan (2003): *Television 2.0: Reconceptualizing TV as an Engagement Medium*. Massachusetts: Massachusetts University, Master thesis.
Baars, Bernard J./Gage, Nicole M. (2010): *Cognition, Brain, and Consciousness: Introduction to Cognitive Neuroscience*. Burlington (MA): Academic Press/Elsevier.
Barthes, Roland (1970): *S/Z*. Frankfurt a. M.: Suhrkamp.
Bordwell, David (1985): *Narration in the Fiction Film*. London: Methuen & Co Ltd.
Bordwell, David (1986): Classical Hollywood Cinema: Narrational Principles and Procedures. In: Rosen, Philip (ed.): *Narrative, Apparatus, Ideology. A Film Theory Reader*. New York/Oxford: Columbia University Press, 17–34.
Bordwell, David/Thompson, Kristin (2001): *Film Art: an Introduction*. New York: McGraw-Hill.
Butler, Jeremy G. (2002): *Television-Critical Methods and Applications*. New Jersey: Lawrence Erlbaum.
Caldwell, John T. (1995): *Televisuality: Style, crisis and authority in American television*. New Brunswick/New Jersey: Rutgers University Press.
Carter, Bill (2006): *Don't Touch That Dial*. New York Times, Web. Retrieved from: [http://query.nytimes.com/gst/fullpage.html?res=9502E6D7173FF93AA15753C1A9609C8B63&sec=&spon=&&scp=1&sq=touch%20that%20dial%20by%20bill%20carter&st=cse]; posted: 2006/10/29; access 2012/10/10.
Creeber, Glen (2004): *Serial Television*. London: British Film Institute.
Defoe, Daniel (1719): *Robinson Crusoe*. London: W. Taylor.
Drangsholt, Janne Stigen (2009): World without end or beginning: structures of displacement in Lost. In: *New Review of Film and Television Studies*, Vol. 7, No. 2, 209–224.

---

38 | In a forthcoming research, Daniela Olek and I will further investigate this approach of a "spatialisation of narration" and its consequences for seriality (see also Olek/Piepiorka 2012).

Eckel, Julia (2012): *Zeitenwende(n) des Films: Temporale Nonlinearität im zeitgenössischem Erzählkino.* Marburg: Schüren.

Elsaesser, Thomas/Hagener, Malte (2007): *Filmtheorie zur Einführung.* Hamburg: Junius.

Emmerton, Lisa (2011): This Teen Sleuth´s Tricks Aren´t just for Kids: Connecting with an Intergenerational Audience. In: Wilcox, Rhonda V./Turnbull, Sue (eds.): *Investigating Veronica Mars: Essays on the Teen Detective Series.* Jefferson: MacFarland & Co, 123–137.

Fiske, John (1987): *Television Culture.* London/New York: Routledge.

Genette, Gérard (1982): *Palimpseste. Die Literatur auf zweiter Stufe.* [Original: "Palimpsestes. La littérature au second degré"], Frankfurt a. M.: Suhrkamp.

Gilbert, Matthew (2005): The games people play with names. The Boston Globe, Web. Retrieved from: [http://www.boston.com/ae/tv/articles/2005/02/10/the_games_people_play_with_names?pg=full]; posted: 2005/02/10.; access: 2012/10/10.

Golding, William (1954): *Lord of the flies.* London: Faber & Faber.

Hornby, Nick (1995): *High Fidelity.* London: Gollancz.

Horrocks, Adrian (2009): The First Horror Soap: the innovative genre mix of Buffy the Vampire Slayer. In: *Necronomicon Book Five: The Journal of Horror and Erotic Cinema,* 7–20.

Jenkins, Henry (2006): *Convergence Culture: Where Old and New Media Collide.* New York/London: New York University Press.

Johnson, Steven (2005): *Everything Bad is Good for You.* New York: Penguin Group.

Kolker, Robert Phillip (2009): *Media Studies: An Introduction.* Oxford: John Wiley & Son Ltd.

Kristeva, Julia (1972): Bachtin, das Wort, der Dialog und der Roman. In: Ihwe, Jens: *Literaturwissenschaft und Linguistik. Ergebnisse und Perspektiven.* Vol. 3. Frankfurt/M: Athenäum, S. 345-375. [Original: Bakhtine, le mot, le dialogue et le roman. In: *Critique* 33/239, 438-465.]

Krzywinsk, Martin (2010) *Lost – The Web of Intrigue.* Web. Retrieved from: [http://www.wired.com/magazine/2010/04/ff_lost/all/1]; posted 2010/04; access: 2012/10/10.

Mielke, Christine (2006): *Zyklisch-serielle Narration - erzähltes Erzählen von 1001 Nacht zur TV-Serie.* Berlin: Walter de Gruypter.

Mikos, Lothar (1994): *Es wird dein Leben! Familienserien im Fernsehen und im Alltag der Zuschauer.* Münster: MAkS.

Miller, William C. (1980): *Screenwriting for narrative in film and television.* Ohio: Hastings House.

Mittell, Jason (2004): *Genre and Television.* New York: Routledge.

Mittell, Jason (2006): Narrative complexity in Contemporary American Television. In: *The Velvet Light Trap,* No. 58, 29–40.

Mittell, Jason (2009): *Television and American Culture*. New York: Oxford University Press.

Nelson, H. Theodor (1980): *The Hypertext*. Sausalito (CA): Mindful Press.

Nelson, Robin (1997): *TV Drama in Transition. Forms, Values and Cultural Change*. New York: Palgrave Macmillan.

Olek, Daniela (2011): *Lost und die Zukunft des Fernsehens: Die Veränderung des seriellen Erzählens im Zeitalter von Media Convergence*. Ibidem: Stuttgart.

Olek, Daniela/Piepiorka, Christine (2012): To Be Continued ... Somewhere else. Die Auswirkungen struktureller Räumlichkeit auf die Serialität im Kontext transmedialer Serien. In: Spangenberg, Peter M./Westermann, Bianca (eds.): *Im Moment des ‚Mehr'*. Münster: Lit, 75–93.

Oxford University Press: *Confusion*, Web. Retrieved from: [http://oxforddictionaries.com/definition/confusion]; posted: 2010/04; access: 2012/10/10.

Piepiorka, Christine (2011): *Lost in Narration: Narrativ komplexe Serienformate in einem transmedialen Umfeld*. Ibidem: Stuttgart.

Rayner, Phillip/Wall, Peter/Kruger, Stephen (2001): *Media Studies: The Essential Introduction*. New York: Routledge.

Recht, Markus (2011): *Der symphatische Vampir*. Frankfurt a. M.: Campus.

Reinecke, Markus (2007): *TV-Serien als Megamovies. Die US-Serie Lost als Beispiel einer neuen Seriengeneration*. Hamburg: Diplomica.

Spangler, Bill (2006): The Lost Book Club. In: Card, Orson Scott (ed.): *Getting Lost*. Dallas: Benbellas Books, 45–54.

Specht, Rainer (2007): *John Locke*. Münnchen: Beck.

Steinbeck, John (1937): *Of Mice and Men*. New York: Covici-Friede.

Thomas, Rob (2006): *Neptune Noir. Unauthorized Investigations into Veronica Mars*. Dallas, Texas: BenBella Inc.

Thompson, Kristin (1995): Neoformalistische Filmanalyse. In: *montage/av*, Vol. 4, No. 1, 23–62.

Todorov, Tzvetan (1990): *Genres in discourse*. Cambridge: Cambridge University

Turner, Graeme (2003): The Uses and Limitation of Genre. In: Creeber, Glen (ed.): *The Television Genre Book*. London: British Film Institute, 4–6.

TELEVISION SERIES

24 (USA 2001–2010, FOX)
BREAKING BAD (USA 2007–, AMC)
BUFFY – THE VAMPIRE SLAYER (USA 1997–2003, The WB)
DEXTER (USA 2000– , Showtime)
GILMORE GIRLS (USA 2000–2007, The WB)
HOW I MET YOUR MOTHER (USA 2005–, CBS)
LOST (USA 2004–2010, ABC)

Magnum P.I. (USA 1980–1988, CBS)
St. Elsewhere (USA 1982–1988, NBC)
Twin Peaks (USA 1990–1991, ABC)
Veronica Mars (USA 2004–2007, UPN)

Films

American Graffiti (USA 1973, George Lucas)
Lord of the Flies (USA 1963, Peter Brook)
High Fidelity (USA/UK 2000, Stephen Fears)
Resident Evil (USA 2002, Paul W.S. Anderson)

Web Videos

Lost: In preparation of season 5: Connections (posted by manueunam). Web. Retrieved from: [http://www.youtube.com/watch?v=sjqLgkV50Do]; posted 2008/08/29; access: 2012/10/10.

Games

Resident Evil (1996, Capcom/Virgin Interactive)

Image Sources

Figure 1: Piepiorka 2011, 79f.
Figure 2: Piepiorka 2011, 84.
Figure 3: Piepiorka 2011, 111.
Figure 4: Piepiorka 2011, 145.

Filmic Incoherences

Amazing Maze

On the Concept of Diegese, Possible Worlds, and the Aesthetics of Illness

NELE UHL

Scenario: A new computer game developed by Allegra Geller for the company Antenna Research, called *eXistenZ*, is presented to a small number of invited guests and journalists. The players are connected to the virtual world of the game via the video game console, which is physically connected to the nervous system of the players by a *bioport*. During the presentation Allegra is attacked by a man from the audience. She manages to escape with the inexperienced marketing trainee Ted Pikul. In order to repair the console, damaged by the assault, they both have to connect to it and play *eXistenZ*. They enter a virtual reality and Ted is soon unable to differentiate reality from a new level of the game. Within this virtual world, Ted and Allegra start playing a similar game, which takes them into a virtual world within the virtual world. The worlds they enter become more and more surreal. When they awake in a world that seems to be reality to them, the situation gets out of hand and Allegra kills Ted. But the film does not end there. The mind-game is taken to another level: Ted and Allegra wake up once more, this time in a room with several other people, all of them connected to a game called *transCendenZ*. It is only now that the audience wakes up to the fact that what they had taken for reality was in fact merely a level of the computer game *transCendenZ*.

But how can the protagonists of EXISTENZ (Canada/UK 1999, David Cronenberg), the film outlined above, as well as the audience be sure as to what is real? Or is it rather a virtual world within the already fictional world of the film? What remains is the recipients' disorientation, caused by the lack of re-establishment of a fictional order, one which draws a clear line between virtuality and cinematic reality. But how can the maze of worlds created by the film be put into words in order to understand the way the film is playing with the recipients' orientation or disorientation?

The Concept of Diegese

Etienne Souriau provides a term which he introduced in the early 50s in a lecture on *The Structure of the Filmic Universe and the Vocabulary of Filmology—Diegese*.[1] Souriau's term ‚Diegese' refers to "everything one considers depicted by the film, and what is part of the reality implied by its meaning" (Souriau 1951, 237; transl. N.U.)[2], or "everything that happens, according to the fiction presented by the film and what is implied by this fiction, if taken for reality" (ibid., 240; transl. N.U.).[3] According to Souriau the understanding of the diegetic is realised in a mental act, based on what appears on the screen (see ibid., 238f.).

Souriau's term, however, remains a term rather than a fully developed concept of Diegese. Given the example of eXistenZ, it becomes clear that films can cover more than the reality implied by their meaning. In addition, the definitions of Diegese as the notion of the narrated world (see Wulff 2007, 39ff.; Fuxjäger 2007, 17ff.; Hartmann 2007, 54ff.) or as "the fictional world of the film" (Bordwell 1985, 16) are also equally misleading, since the term 'world' conveys the idea of a self-contained spatiotemporal system. The film eXistenZ, however, establishes a multitude of self-contained worlds. As a means of describing fictional cinematic worlds the term 'Diegese' obviously fails to go into sufficient depth. For the term 'Diegese' to be useful for the theory of fiction in film studies, it must be developed into a more detailed concept.

The film eXistenZ provides an excellent example to do this. Hans-Jürgen Wulff describes the notion of Diegese as "the spatiotemporal relations of the narrated world, its model-like unity, the spatiotemporal universe of the characters" (Wulff 2007, 5; transl. N.U.)[4], thereby providing an approach as to how Diegese as a concept of fictional worlds can be further differentiated. Understanding space and time as basic categories of organisation, description, and

---

1 |In this paper the term 'Diegese' will be used rather than the English translation 'Diegesis' in order to differentiate clearly from the Greek 'diêgêsis', which means narrative/explanation. Anton Fuxjäger points out that although the function of narrative lies in communicating the notion of a narrated world, it is not the same as narrative discourse.

2 | Original citation: "[...] tout ce qu'on prend en considération comme représenté dans le film, et dans le genre de réalité supposé par la signification du film [...]" (Souriau 1951, 237).

3 | Original citation: "[...] tout ce qui est censé se passer, selon la fiction que présente le film; tout ce que cette fiction impliquerait si on la supposait vraie [...]" (Soriau 1951, 240).

4 | Original citation: "[...] die raumzeitlichen Beziehungen der erzählten Welt, ihre modellhafte Einheit, das räumlich-zeitliche Universum der Figuren [...]" (Wulff 2007, 5).

cognition of worlds allows for a promising analysis of the Diegese of eXistenZ from these perspectives.

In the debate on space and time in film, the main focus often lies on the dualism of screen/story (see Souriau 1997, 143) and narration time/narrated time (ibid., 144; Metz 1972, 38; Bordwell 1985, 44ff.). In this article, however, the only aspects analysed will be the space and time *of the story*: the diegetic space and the diegetic time. Souriau attaches particular importance to the aspects of space and time in the mental construction of Diegese. Several convincing examples can be found in the work of Anton Fuxjäger: When a film is set in town X, the recipients are aware that this city will comprise more streets than those shown in the film. The houses in the streets seen in the film will consist of more than frontages, they will contain flats, will have gardens maybe a backyard. The same goes for the diegetic time. When a small boy appears in a scene only a few minutes later as a grown man, the recipients will be aware of a 20 to 30 year leap in diegetic time (see Fuxjäger 2007, 18). Whereas diegetic time has to be generally linearly reconstructible, the narrative entities of the film are not bound by linearity. The recipients have to supplement the more or less sparse information on diegetic space and time provided by the film's text and structure it into a coherent and logical notion of the narrated world—the Diegese according to Souriau.

But the Diegese of eXistenZ comprises more than just a single diegetic space and a single diegetic time which the recipients have to reconstruct. The film opens up four different diegetic worlds, consisting of four diegetic spaces and four diegetic times—all part of the Diegese of the film. At least three of these diegetic worlds are virtual worlds within the realm of a computer game. More precisely: one of the diegetic worlds is created by the computer game *transCendenZ*. Two more are created by the virtual computer game *eXistenZ*—which itself is part of the diegetic world within the game *transCendenZ*. Who would be surprised at the recipients' disorientation about the nature of the film's Diegese? It is only at the end of the film that the fourth of the diegetic worlds is presented. It pretends to be "the reality implied by its [the film's, N.U.] meaning" and which—following Souriau—contains "everything that happens, according to the fiction presented by the film and what is implied by this fiction, if taken for reality".

The problem is quite clear: Diegese cannot be equated with the film's immanent reality. A more promising approach would be to differentiate between *Diegese* and *Diegetic Reality* since these two terms are not always synonymous. Whereas the Diegese is the film's universe, which can comprise one or more worlds—possible and impossible—the Diegetic Reality is the fictional reality within the Diegese. It is the characters' reality, the level of cinematic facts—i.e. the physical world which the characters live in and which is coherent and consistent. Although there are many examples of films where the Diegese contains just one singular diegetic world and can thus be equated with the Diegetic

Reality, there are just as many examples that present multiple diegetic worlds, but only one of them will be the Diegetic Reality. It is up to the recipients to pinpoint this Diegetic Reality. Especially in films like eXistenZ the recipients are encouraged to organise the diegetic worlds presented to them into a hierarchy; and to identify the diegetic world most likely to be the Diegetic Reality based on the information given by the film. Although the plot twist at the end of eXistenZ—which exposes everything previously seen as virtual diegetic worlds—provides an answer, doubts remain as to whether or not the alleged Diegetic Reality is not just another virtual diegetic world of just another computer game.

Diegese is therefore understood not so much as the notion of the narrated world but rather as a fictional universe which can comprise multiple diegetic worlds, only one of which can represent the Diegetic Reality. These diegetic worlds can be further specified and it is worth considering Wulff's thoughts on the layer-structure of the diegetic in this respect. For Wulff, the Diegese consists of four mutually coordinated sub-layers: a *physical world*, a *cognitive world*, a *social world*, and a *moral world* (see Wulff 2007, 40). Each layer can work independently from the others and may differ from the extra-fictional world. Wulff's ideas on the Diegese as a physical world and as a cognitive world are particularly interesting. Due to physical qualities such as gravity and consistency, the Diegese can be understood as a *physical world*. As long as recipients are presented a consistent world with clear-cut physical qualities, they can adapt themselves to a world that is not their own.[5] The narrated world is also conceptualised as the cognitive world of the characters. According to Wulff, the characters of a film usually have a collective perception of their world—although there are also examples where characters do not completely share one cognitive space (see Wulff 2007, 42).

Of special importance for this paper is the cinematic representation of hallucinations or dreams playing with the characters' different cognitive worlds, which disorient the recipients of unreliably narrated films like Fight Club (USA/Germany 1999, David Fincher), The Sixth Sense (USA 1999, M. Night Shyamalan) or A Beautiful Mind (USA 2001, Ron Howard). It also has to be taken into account that a character's dreams within the Diegetic Reality can represent consistent diegetic worlds which at the same time can be physical, cognitive, social, and moral worlds. For example, little Max in Where The Wild Things Are (USA/Australia/Germany 2009, Spike Jonze) steps into a new diegetic world on the island of the wild things, which is completely different from the Diegetic Reality of the film (life with a mother who cannot cope and a sister who ignores him). This new diegetic world can also be specified with Wulff's four sub-layers. The

---

5 | Thus recipients can accept the diegetic realities of films like Harry Potter (USA/UK/Germany 2001-2011, Chris Columbus, Mike Newell, Alfonso Cuarón, David Yates) or The Lord Of The Rings (USA/New Zealand 2001-2003, Peter Jackson), because they are self-consistent, i.e. free of contradictions.

cinematic text makes it clear that the diegetic world represented by the island of the wild things is a dream of little Max.

This example illustrates that Wulff's differentiation may be useful but more applicable to diegetic worlds *within* the Diegese than to the Diegese *as a whole*.

As can be seen from the film examples eXistenZ and Where The Wild Things Are, several diegetic worlds—which are located within the Diegese separate from the Diegetic Reality—can be *bound*. That is to say that they are mentally produced by one or several characters or that they are, as in eXistenZ, attached to a computer game. The Diegese of a film can also comprise *loose* diegetic worlds, which means that they are detached from the perception of one or more characters or from objects they have been created by. This can be illustrated by the example of Lola Rennt (Run Lola Run Germany 1998, Tom Tykwer) where the Diegese comprises three *loose* parallel diegetic worlds which cannot be defined as some character's dreams or hallucinations.

In short: For Diegese to be a useful tool of description in the theory of fiction, it has first to be conceptualised:

- There has to be differentiation between the Diegese of a film and its Diegetic Reality. Although the Diegetic Reality, "the reality implied by its meaning", is *in toto* part of the Diegese, the Diegese is not necessarily *identical* with the Diegetic Reality.
- The Diegese can comprise multiple diegetic spaces and times which can together form multiple diegetic worlds. These diegetic worlds are self-consistent with regard to space and time. Every diegetic space can be subject to a diegetic time of its own.
- Thus several diegetic worlds apart from the Diegetic Reality can be potentially located within the Diegese of a film. They can be either *bound*, i.e. to the mental production of a character within the Diegetic Reality, or *loose*.
- Every diegetic world within the Diegese of a film is at the same time a physical world, a cognitive world, a social world, and a moral world. It is independent on all levels and not necessarily identical to the world outside the fiction.

The Concept of Diegese and the Possible-worlds Theory

In recent years, the so-called possible-worlds theory has entered research on fictionality in film (see Kaczmarek 2007, 134). In its current use it is identical in many aspects to the above-mentioned concept of Diegese. Originally a philosophical theory developed by analytic philosophers such as Saul A. Kripke (1963), Jaakko Hintikka (1969) or Nicholas Rescher (1979) on the basis of Gottfried Wilhelm Leibniz' idea of "the best of all possible worlds" (Leibniz 1986, 96f.), it has been applied to literature and narrative theory by theorists like Umberto Eco (1984), Thomas G. Pavel (1986) Marie-Laure Ryan (1991) or Lubomír Doležel (1998). This narratological possible-worlds theory, especially the model of possible worlds as developed by Ryan, which describes the modal structure of narrative universes, is—although timidly—applied in film studies.

Eva Laass refers to Ryan's possible-worlds theory to describe the "different perspective-dependent possibilities of perception and representation of the fictional world and to explain the effect of narrative unreliability" (Laass 2006, 259) in MULHOLLAND DRIVE (France/USA 2001, David Lynch). Analysing THE SIXTH SENSE and THE OTHERS (France/Spain/Italy/USA 2001, Alejandro Amenábar), Dominik Orth resorts to the possible-worlds theory to describe the narrated worlds and correlates them to the theory of unreliable narration (Orth 2006, 252ff.).

Both Laass and Orth apply the possible-worlds theory to subdivide the worlds presented in the films into a *textual actual world* and other *possible worlds*. In this way, they can locate the reliable, the fictional reality of the films, to expose the possible worlds as unreliable representations. The correlation with the concept of Diegese as presented in this paper is obvious. It might be questioned why one should work with the terminology of Diegese when the possible-worlds theory has already introduced such a concept, which only has to be adapted to the specifics of film as a medium. This theory, however, is far from homogeneous, and it is worth taking a look at its development to make clear the problems inherent in the current scientific use of this theory.

With his idea of "the best of all possible worlds" Leibniz stressed that in every point in time, an event could have taken a different turn from the one it did, which would have led to a totally different historical development. These possible developments circle the *actual* world as unrealised *possible* worlds. Based on this modal system, the US logician Saul A. Kripke developed a model of possible worlds (*m-model*) to explain the logic of counterfactual conditionals. This model allows one to determine which events in history did not actually happen but would have been possible and which events have to be considered as impossible (Kripke 1980, 111ff.). In this sense, forecasts and possible worlds are closely connected, as every forecast is—in all possible worlds—in itself either true or false. From this, the modal condition of a proposition can be deduced. All possible worlds share one center of reference: the actual world—or, in the words of Leibniz, "the best of all possible worlds" as a standard measure for the possibility, necessity, or contingency of propositions.

Such an alternative world could only be considered *possible* (from a philosophical point of view) if it has an accessibility relation to the actual world, otherwise it is an *impossible* world (Surkamp 2002, 155). From a modal logics point of view, accessibility means compliance to the laws of logic. As Ryan puts it:

"The boundary between possible and impossible worlds depends on the particular interpretation given to the notion of accessibility. The most common interpretation associates possibility with logical laws; every world that respects the principles of non-contradiction and the excluded middle is a PW." (Ryan 2005, 446)

This interpretation greatly expands the accessibility relation between an actual and a possible world since every conceivable world is possible as long as it is self-consistent. However, this notion deviates from the original idea of the possible-worlds theory as developed by Leibniz and Kripke. Kripke comments on this as follows:

"I will say something briefly about 'possible worlds'. [...] In the present monograph I argued against those misuses of the concept that regard possible worlds as something like distant planets, [...] or that lead to spurious problems of 'transworld identification'. Further, if one wishes to avoid the *Weltangst* and philosophical confusions that many philosophers have associated with the 'worlds' terminology, I recommended that 'possible state (or history) of the world', or 'counterfactual situation' might be better." (Kripke 1972, 15; original emphasis)

He is clearly pointing out here that possible worlds are always just possible states of the actual world. For example, in the actual world of the recipients, trees cannot speak. Thus, a hypothetical world where trees can speak can only be an impossible one because this does not comply with laws of logic. It must be noted that compliance with laws of logic in this case does not mean consistency (if all trees in a hypothetical world could speak—if speaking trees were introduced by law—a speaking tree would not be inconsistent), but compliance with the laws of logic of the actual world *within the hypothetical world*. Only in this case can a hypothetical world be recognised as a 'possible state of the world'.

Ryan's model of the *Modal Structure of Narrative Universes* is also based on interpreting accessibility relation in terms of consistency. She conceives the fictional universe of literary texts as a modal system consisting of a textual actual world (TAW) and other possible worlds (PW). According to Ryan, possible worlds can be sub-divided into *K(nowledge)*, *W(ish)*, *O(bligation)* and *I(ntention)* worlds as well as Fantasy-universes (*f-universes*). F-universes have a special status as, in contrast to the *KWOI worlds*, they create new independent world systems, which are the dreams, hallucinations and fictional stories of the characters (Ryan 1991, 730f.).

"These constructs are not simply satellites of TAW, but complete universes, and they are reached by characters through a recentering. For the duration of a dream, the dreamer believes in the reality of the events he or she experiences, and the actual world of the dream takes the place of TAW." (Ryan 1991, 119)

This model is obviously relevant and useful as it considers multiple fictional and self-consistent worlds which can comprise narratives and enables the localisation of a narrative reality. At the same time, this concept is detached from the idea behind the possible-worlds theory, which makes Ryan's reference to Leibniz and Kripke seem very questionable. Using the possible-worlds theory to set films like the LORD OF THE RINGS trilogy or the HARRY POTTER series in relation to the reality outside the film (see Orth 2006, 289; Krützen 2010, 44) appears even more problematic since *possible*, in this case, is reduced to a mere lip service (see Kaczmarek 2007, 132). One way to avoid this problem is to work with the concept of Diegese as suggested in this paper: to replace *textual actual world and possible worlds* with Diegetic Reality and *bound* or *loose* diegetic worlds. This allows Diegese to provide the theory of fictionality with a concept for compiling and describing fictional universes which does not depend on problematic reference to Leibniz and Kripke or on the burden of such a heterogeneous theory.

INCONSISTENCY OF THE DIEGETIC REALITY IN JEAN-CLAUDE LAUZON'S *LÉOLO*

A very interesting example for an unusual Diegese is represented by LÉOLO (France/Canada 1992, Jean-Claude Lauzon)—a film which confuses its recipients in many ways and exposes them to major problems regarding the aspect of naturalisation. Interestingly, many of the discrepancies inherent in the filmic narration only become clear after multiple viewings. At first, it seems possible for the recipients to mentally construct the Diegetic Reality in LÉOLO as any confusion arises from the numerous perplexing moments within the plot itself. It is only after multiple viewings that the discrepant information inherent in the cinematic text is recognised as a principal pattern so that the constructed Diegetic Reality collapses and eventually appears impossible. It is worth using the concept presented in the first part of this paper to examine the Diegese of the film to determine which elements of the cinematic narration are responsible for the impossibility of a Diegetic Reality. In LÉOLO, the mental construction of the Diegese is disturbed due to disparate information but the recipients are not completely disoriented. This is a unique feature of this film since it is not just 'playing a game' with the recipients nor does it address or reflect the issue of its own unreliability.

On the first viewing, everything in LÉOLO seems to be clear. A 10-year-old boy tells about his life in a dysfunctional and poor family in Mile End/Montreal, Canada. His whole family, apart from his mother, display mental problems and are in psychiatric treatment. Léolo's father is driven by a faecal obsession and administers laxatives to his family on a weekly basis; Léolo's brother Fernand lives only for body building; the two sisters Rita and Nanette are at the psychiatric clinic almost all the time and their brutal grandfather sexually assaults the young neighbour Bianca. It is no wonder that little Léo Lozeau escapes into his fantasies in which his mother was not made pregnant by his father but by a tomato that was ejaculated on by a Sicilian farm worker. Since this daydream, Léo insists on being called Léolo Lozone—because of his alleged Italian origin. His daydreams alleviate the pain of his tragicomic reality which he writes down meticulously and immediately throws away. An old man, called the *tamer of verses* collects Léolo's notes and archives them. When Léolo himself collapses at the end of the film and is treated in the clinic for schizophrenia, it seems like the sad but logical end to a broken family.

After an initial review, the Diegese of the film can be subdivided in two diegetic worlds: a *bound* diegetic world established by Léolo's daydream about his alleged conception, and a Diegetic Reality—Léolo's everyday life with his family. The *bound* diegetic world of the dream is not only consistent and defined by the space and time given in the subtitles ("Somewhere in a valley in Sicily..." and "Some days later in America ..."), but is also presented as coherent by the "cinematic narrator" (Chatman 1990, 211). This is not the case with the alleged Diegetic Reality: Due to contradictions in the information the recipients are given regarding the diegetic space and time, the Diegetic Reality appears inconsistent and therefore has to be considered as impossible.

Irreconcilable discrepancies prevent the reconstruction of a linear diegetic time in a Diegetic Reality. Recipients are bound to fail in attempts to figure out the time span of the film. Léolo does not show any sign of physical development, suggesting that the time span is approximately one year. In contrast to this, Léolo's brother Fernand seems to have aged several years. He is introduced as a 14-year-old boy who—after a traumatic experience—makes fear his single motivation in life and as a consequence starts excessive body building. He goes through a physical transformation and turns into a monstrous muscleman. The divergent development of these two characters is particularly evident in the 20th minute of the film. Léolo is sitting writing next to skinny Fernand, who is training with home-made weights in the chicken coop. The camera pans through an impressive 360° panoramic view of the room, starting and ending with a close-up of the two boys. Léolo looks just the same as in the first picture of the scene whereas Fernand has become a muscular young man. Although the film does not give any information on his age after his transformation, one might guess that the time span is five to ten years. In an interview, Jean-Claude Lauzon mentions that Fernand has been training for ten years altogether (Racine 1992, 121). This means several years elapse during the camera pan but Léolo does not age at all.

Another problematic aspect is the exact timing of the loosely aligned sequences. Taking Fernand's development as a point of reference could serve as orientation for the recipients but proves to be misleading. In the 26th minute of the film, Léolo and his siblings are playing in the paddling pool. In this sequence, Fernand appears as a skinny boy which suggests that this event has obviously happened *before* his metamorphosis. The grandfather, annoyed by the children, tries to drown Léolo in a rage until Léolo's mother beats him with a frying pan. Cut. The whole family is seated in the common room of the psychiatric hospital—the grandfather bears signs of the pan attack with his head bandaged and a black eye. Relying on the consistency of time and space, the hospital meeting must have happened directly or only a few days after the attempted murder against Léolo. The camera pans over the family members assembled in the room, slowly one after the other, but the recipients now see Fernand sitting there as a muscular man: an inconsistency which makes the reconstruction of the linear diegetic time impossible.

Another example: At the beginning of the film, in the eighth minute, Léolo is reading by the light of the refrigerator *L'avalée des avalées* by Réjean Ducharme. The book plays an important role throughout the film, and its subheading "I dream therefore I am not" becomes Léolo's credo. In this scene, his brother appears as a pubescent boy, suggesting that the scene has taken place before Fernand's transformation. The subjective voice-over explains to the recipients that he had never wondered how the book had come into the house. It is actually not until the 23rd minute of the film that the *tamer of verses* places it inside the house. However, it is confusing that the latter, while going through the rubbish bins in the same sequence, finds notes by Léolo describing his brother's transformation. After that, the old man goes to see Léolo's mother and uses the book to fix a wobbly table leg. This is the *ex post* explanation for the recipients as to how the book came into the Lozeaus' house. At the same time, this contains discrepancies of the plot which make it impossible to reconstruct the time structure of the story. It is obvious that the book must have come into the house *after* Fernand's metamorphosis but at the beginning of the film, *before* Fernand's metamorphosis, the book is already there.

Another inconsistency is inherent to the diegetic space in the assumed Diegetic Reality. The diegetic world of the daydream established at the beginning of the film has, in this respect, great influence on the further understanding of the film. At the end of the daydream, the voice-over admits that since this daydream, Léolo insists on being called Léolo Lozone and confesses that this dreamed diegetic world influences his reality. Since the bound diegetic world of the daydream is marked both visually as well as by the voice-over, the film dictates an interpretation that eventually does not work out. The recipients expect later daydream sequences to be unambiguously marked with clear borders between the Diegetic Reality and a potential daydream world. But there is no such separation and thus no orientation for where the Diegetic Reality ends and where Léolo's daydream world begins. At some stages of the film such separations result from the plot's inner logic. When Léolo awakes in his room in the

63rd minute of the film and enters Sicily by walking through his wardrobe, the recipients can clearly see that they are inside Léolo's dream world. However, this is harder to distinguish in all the other scenes that seemingly represent the Diegetic Reality of the film. As explained before, the recipients are confronted with discrepancies of time which make a consistent diegetic world impossible. Therefore, the recipients are not able to clearly allocate the scenes containing inconsistencies in time to either the Diegetic Reality or a *bound* diegetic world. This problem is due to the fact that the *bound* diegetic world is well marked at the beginning of the film so the recipients are aware of what *cannot* be part of the Diegetic Reality, but that no distinct Diegetic Reality is designed as a counterpoint allowing scenes to be unambiguously assigned. Instead, the recipients are confronted with a conglomerate of diegetic worlds which eventually proves to be impossible to unravel.

Aesthetics of Illness

The question remains as to the purpose and function of such an inconsistent Diegetic Reality. In trying to answer this, it is worth analysing Léolo's medical condition which becomes evident at the end of the film. When Léolo is brought to the psychiatric hospital, a nurse gives him Largactil, a neuroleptic for the treatment of schizophrenia and hallucinations, the film therefore suggesting that Léolo suffers from one of these disorders. Here the question arises as to what possibilities the medium of film has to represent illness. It has at its disposal numerous channels of communication that could be used for this purpose. Illness, however, is usually dealt with on the plot level as, for example, in RAIN MAN (USA 1988, Barry Levinson), MY LIFE WITHOUT ME (Spain/Canada 2003, Isabel Coixet) or BIUTIFUL (Mexico/Spain 2010, Alejandro González Iñárritu). But there are also films like FIGHT CLUB or BLACK SWAN (USA 2010, Darren Aronofsky), in which the protagonist's illness—his/her hallucinations or delusions—can be experienced by the recipients through an implicit narrative authority, which makes them visible. In these cases, illness is not only thematised but the recipients can participate in the respective progression of the disease by means of internal focalisation. Regarding the Diegese of these two films, it can be assumed that sooner or later a Diegetic Reality will be constructed without significant difficulties and will be recognised as such due to the disease symptoms visually presented by the camera. The Diegese is spared the illness in so far as it can be reliably reconstructed and all the information given in the cinematic text can be placed in a Diegetic Reality, in further character-dependent diegetic worlds or in subjectively distorted cognitive worlds of the characters. LÉOLO conveys the protagonist's schizophrenia in a more profound way. At this point, the Diegese of the film is significantly affected by the illness, as becomes evident from the subsequent presentation of Léolo's distorted view of the world. According to the Federal Psychotherapists' Association of Germany, schizophrenia can be characterised in the following way:

"The literal translation for schizophrenia—'split personality disorder'—has led to misunderstandings and incorrect use of the term 'schizophrenic' in the everyday language. Schizophrenia has got nothing to do with a split personality as fictionalised in 'Dr. Jekyll and Mister Hyde'. The term rather describes the disintegration of subjective thinking and the perception of reality." (BPTK 2012; transl. N. U.)[6]

In the context of LÉOLO, this definition can be fruitfully correlated to the characteristics of the cinematic narration and the resulting Diegese, since the film represents Léolo's schizophrenia by all available means. As the subjective voice-over assumes Léolo's perspective to narrate the film, conveying to the recipients his view on the fictional reality, the discrepancies can then be understood as indications of Léolo's loss of touch with reality. Blurring the boundaries between Diegetic Reality and the diegetic world of Léolo's daydream is a consistent representation of his distorted perception of reality.

Illness in filmic adaptation is usually represented by a juxtaposition of norm and deviation. The illness in FIGHT CLUB for example, conveyed by the cinematic narrator, is opposed to the norm—a Diegetic Reality—in contrast to which the illness is presented as a problem with an explicitly negative connotation. What makes the cinematic realisation of Léolo's illness different is the absence of problematisation of the protagonist being schizophrenic as there is no confrontation between norm and deviation. Because of the inconsistency of the Diegetic Reality, the recipients cannot compare what has been seen to any norm. It is not possible to distinguish to what extent Léolo's potential schizophrenic hallucinations influence what is happening and when reality is being shown. In this way, it is only the aesthetic potential in LÉOLO, which lies in the protagonist's schizophrenia, which counts. The film presents a view of the world which follows a schizophrenic logic that can be experienced and understood by the recipients because they were also convinced at first by the verisimilitude of what was presented. Léolo's schizophrenic thinking can only produce an inconsistent Diegetic Reality since his view of reality is *per definitionem* unreliable. Thus, the

---

6 | Original citation: "Schizophrenie bedeutet in der wörtlichen Übersetzung ‚Spaltungsirresein', was zu Missverständnissen und falscher Verwendung von ‚schizophren' in der Alltagssprache geführt hat. Denn Schizophrenie hat nichts mit einer gespaltenen Persönlichkeit zu tun, wie sie in ‚Dr. Jekyll und Mister Hyde fiktional verkörpert wird. Der Begriff beschreibt vielmehr das Auseinanderfallen von persönlichem Denken und Wahrnehmen und der Realität" (BPTK 2012).

deviation of Léolo from the norm of how cinematic Diegese is usually constructed has to be considered as systematic and comprehensible.

Conclusion

It became clear, that the concept of Diegese—including a Diegetic Reality and additional *loose* or *bound* diegetic worlds—constitutes an extremely valuable tool to describe and unravel the tangled paths of filmic worlds. Thus it provides the audience orientation even in the case of disorienting world constructions. Furthermore it offers the possibility to bypass the problematic terminology of the possible-worlds theory, which is always connected to the origin ideas of philosophers like Leibnitz or Kripke.

Although there are some films without a way out of the diegetic maze, as seen in the analysis of Léolo, the concept of Diegese helps to re-orient within the confusion by understanding why some films cannot be understood.

Bibliography

Bordwell, David (1985): *Narration in the Fiction Film*. London: Methuen.
Chatman, Seymour (1990): *Coming to Terms. The Rhetoric of Narrative in Fiction and Film*. Ithaca (NY): Cornell University Press.
Doležel, Lubomír (1998): *Heterocosmica. Fiction and possible worlds*. Baltimore: Johns Hopkins University Press.
Eco, Umberto (1984): *The Role of the Reader: Explorations in the Semiotics of Texts*. Bloomington: Indiana University Press.
Fuxjäger, Anton (2007): Diegese, Diegesis, diegetisch. Versuch einer Begriffsentwirrung. In: *montage/av*, Vol. 16, No. 2, 17–37.
Hartmann, Britta (2007): Diegetisieren, Diegese, Diskursuniversum. In: *montage/av* 16/2, 53 - 69.
Helbig, Jörg (ed.) (2006): *"Camera doesn't lie". Spielarten erzählerischer Unzuverlässigkeit im Film*. Trier: Wissenschaftlicher Verlag Trier, 283–307.
Hintikka, Jaakko (1969): *Models for Modalities. Selected Essays*. Dordrecht: D. Reidel.
Kaczmarek, Ludger (2007): Allyfying Leibniz. Einige Aspekte von Kompossibilität und Diegese in filmischen Texten. In: *montage/av*, Vol. 16, No. 2, 131–145.
Kessler, Frank (2007): Von der Filmologie zur Narratologie. Anmerkungen zum Begriff der Diegese. In: *montage/av*, Vol. 16, No. 2, 9–16.
Kripke, Saul A. (1963): Semantical Considerations on Modal Logic. In: *Acta Philosophica Fennica* 16, 83–94.

Kripke, Saul A. (1980): *Naming and Necessity*. Cambridge: Havard University Press.
Krützen, Michaela (2010): *Dramaturgien des Films. Das etwas andere Hollywood*. Frankfurt a. M.: Fischer.
Laass, Eva (2006): Krieg der Welten in Lynchville. Mulholland Drive und die Anwendungsmöglichkeiten und -grenzen des Konzepts narrativer Unzuverlässigkeit. In: Helbig 2006, 251–284.
Leibniz, Gottfried Wilhelm (1986): *Die Theodizee von der Güte Gottes, der Freiheit des Menschen und dem Ursprung des Übels*. Frankfurt a. M.: Insel-Verlag.
Metz, Christian (1972): *Semiologie des Films*. München: Fink.
Orth, Dominik (2006): Der unbewusste Tod. Unzuverlässiges Erzählen in M. Night Shyamalans THE SIXTH SENSE und Alejandro Amenábars THE OTHERS. In: Helbig 2006, 283–307.
Pavel, Thomas G. (1986): *Fictional Worlds*. Cambridge: Harvard University Press.
Racine, Claude (1992): Jean-Claude Lauzon. It is an image that I have retained from infancy (transl. by Jim Leach). In: Melnyk, George (ed.) (2008): *The Young, the Restless, and the Dead. Interviews with Canadian Filmmakers*. Waterloo: Wilfrid Laurier University Press, 117–129.
Rescher, Nicholas (1979): The Ontology of the Possible. In: Loux, M. (ed.) *The Possible and the Actual: Readings in the Metaphysics of Modality*. Ithaca (NY): Cornell University Press.
Ryan, Marie-Laure (1991): *Possible Worlds, Artificial Intelligence, and Narrative Theory*. Bloomington: Indiana University Press.
Ryan, Marie-Laure (2005): Possible worlds-Theory. In: *Routledge Encyclopedia of Narrative Theory*. New York: Routledge.
Souriau, Étienne (2007 [1951]): Die Struktur des filmischen Universums und das Vokabular der Filmologie. In: *montage/av*, Vol. 16, No. 2, 140–157.
Surkamp, Carola (2002): Narratologie und Possible-Worlds Theorie: Narrative Texte als alternative Welten. In: Nünning, Ansgar/Nünning, Vera (eds.): *Neue Ansätze in der Erzähltheorie*. Trier: Wissenschaftlicher Verlag Trier, 153–183.
Wulff, Hans J. (2007): Schichtenbau und Prozesshaftigkeit des Diegetischen: Zwei Anmerkungen. In: *montage/av*, Vol. 16, No. 2, 40–51.

Web Sources

Bundes Psychotherapeuten Kammer (BPTK): *Schizophrenie*. Web. Retrieved from: [http://www.bptk.de/patienten/psychische-krankheiten/schizophrenie]; access: 2012/10/10.

Films

A Beautiful Mind (USA 2001, Ron Howard)
Biutiful (Mexico/Spain 2010, Alejandro González Iñárritu)
Black Swan (USA 2010, Darren Aronofsky)
eXistenZ (Canada/UK 1999, David Cronenberg)
Fight Club (USA/Germany 1999, David Fincher)
Harry Potter 1–7 (USA/UK/Germany 2001–2011, Chris Columbus, Mike Newell, Alfonso Cuarón, David Yates)
Léolo (France/Canada 1992, Jean-Claude Lauzon)
Lola rennt (Run Lola Run, Germany 1998, Tom Tykwer)
Mulholland Dr. (France/USA 2001, David Lynch)
My Life Without Me (Spain/Canada 2003, Isabel Coixet)
Rain Man (USA 1988, Barry Levinson)
The Sixth Sense (USA 1999, M. Night Shyamalan)
The Others (France/Spain/Italy/USA 2001, Alejandro Amenábar)
The Lord of the Rings 1–3 (USA/New Zealand 2001–2003, Peter Jackson)
Where the Wild Things Are (USA/Australia/Germany 2009, Spike Jonze)

Ants, Games, Brains
The Complexity of Reality in Darren Aronofsky's π

KATHRIN ROTHEMUND

Max Cohen, the protagonist of Darren Aronofsky's film π (USA 1998), who is a socially troubled but brilliant mathematician and computer scientist, spends his days searching for a way to calculate the future developments of the stock market. Trapped in his little apartment, which is mostly occupied by the humongous computer and which is sealed off from the outside through several locks, Max's daily routines and his compulsive behaviour are structured around anxiety attacks, headaches and the statement of assumptions.

Throughout the course of the film π Max gets more and more entangled into a vortex of logic, computer viruses, Kabbalah, numerology and game play while his paranoia and hallucinations slowly take over his perception of reality until reality and imagination become seemingly indistinguishable. Shot in high contrast black and white, the film's aesthetics result in an artistic and grainy look with a fast-paced montage. Close-ups of spirals, numbers or symbols are followed by subjective shots representing Max's view on his surroundings or images focusing on the mimic expression on the protagonist's face. Max also comments on several scenes through voice-over by which the spectators get an inside into the protagonist's mind.

His quest for a 216-digit number turns more and more into an obsessive journey into his own brain, resulting in a metaphorical scene in which Max drills into his skull during one of his attacks, before turning into a pleasant and quiet young man sitting outside on a bench and interacting charmingly with a young girl from his apartment building in the final scene of the film. Leaving the astounded spectators behind with uncertainty about the actual outcome of the film and about what really happened throughout the previous 80 minutes, the movie can only be reconstructed by looking thoroughly at its relationship with the filmic representation of reality. When considering self-reflexive gestures of the film it becomes obvious that the narration is not only set out to disorientate the spectators but it also offers clues, patterns and formulas to detect the structure of the film and to help to re-orientate. In order to disintegrate the incoherence and blanks of filmic narrative the viewers have to reconstruct Max Cohen's reality piece by piece, shot by shot. Therefore, Aronofsky's π is a movie that elaborates on the conditions of filmic reality and perception by referencing film historical notions of the medium's capability of depicting outer reality. Playing with self-reflexive references and by transgressing classical divisions of subjective and objective presentations of the diegetic world the film π asks for a very specific integration of the spectators into the progress of narration.

With a reference to François Truffaut's famous account of the Nouvelle Vague Thomas Elsaesser describes a "'certain tendency' in contemporary cinema" (2009, 14). This group of films—mainly consisting of transnational independent movie productions that fluctuate easily between cult movies and art house cinema—sets out to establish a new relationship—"a new contract between spectator and film" (ibid., 37):

"What once was 'excessively obvious' must now be 'excessively enigmatic,' but in ways that still teach (as Hollywood has always done) its audience 'the rules of the game' of how a Hollywood film wants to be understood, except that now, it seems, at least as far as the mind-game film is concerned, the rules of the game are what the films are also 'about,' even more overtly than before." (ibid.)

Labelled as *mind-game films* those movies can be characterised by their "delight in disorienting or misleading spectators" (ibid., 15). Prominent examples, that tend to play games with protagonists as well as audiences, are MEMENTO (USA 2000, Christopher Nolan), FIGHT CLUB (USA/Germany 1999, David Fincher), THE SIXTH SENSE (USA 1999, M. Night Shyamalan), SLIDING DOORS (UK/USA 1998, Peter Howitt), LOLA RENNT (RUN LOLA RUN, Germany 1998, Tom Tykwer) or more recently INCEPTION (USA 2010, Christopher Nolan). Darren Aronofsky's film π can be added to this group of films not only due to its cinematic borderline status between art film, independent movie production, and international success story but especially because of its affinity to complexity and its fundamental approach to detecting the inner core of reality.[1]

---

1 | Darren Aronofsky's later films such as REQUIEM FOR A DREAM (USA 2000), THE FOUNTAIN (USA 2006), THE WRESTLER (USA 2008) or his most recent film BLACK SWAN (USA 2010) also offer complex storytelling methods with a tendency towards non-linearity, intertwining story-arcs and in-depth elaborations on the character's identities and their struggle surviving in estranged and often hostile surroundings. THE WRESTLER is the only one of Aronofsky's films in which reality is in a fairly fixed and unquestioned state. In his other films either different time zones (THE FOUNTAIN), dream worlds and drug hallucinations (REQUIEM FOR A DREAM), or phantasmagoria (BLACK SWAN) deliberately question or even decline the notion of an objective reality.

In order to inquire the aspect of reality and its filmic representation in context of the complexity of narration and in order to solve some of the incoherences offered by the film π I will go back in the history of film theory to reread Siegfried Kracauer's *Theory of Film: The Redemption of Reality* (1960). Confronting his approach with the film π and interrogating the physicality of reality in it, I will go beyond his approach by including more recent theories on the relationship of complexity, film, brain, and perception. This way I want to show how reality is not solely captured in photographic or cinematic images but instead fabricated by a complex and dynamic system of parts, connections and indetermination. According to that, reality cannot be understood as limited to physicality or materiality as Kracauer proposes but has to be extended by a mental dimension. The complexity of such a broader reality in π undermines and at the same time strengthens Kracauer's theory.

Complexity

But first of all, how to describe complexity when the term as well as the concept itself are rather complex (Nowotny 2005, 15)? The constant ambivalence between highly complex systems and their explicability—which necessarily needs reduction—is a central feature of complexity. Furthermore, the various fields of study dealing with complexity (from biology, physics, and mathematics to social sciences, economics, and philosophy) all offer new and differentiating insights into the problem (Urry 2005, 1ff.). Therefore, any definition of the term inevitably falls behind the actual phenomenon but is still necessary to at least access the problem. An approach to complexity can be taken by using Edgar Morin's rather additive but catchy description:

"At first glance, complexity is a fabric (complexus: that which is woven together) of heterogeneous constituents that are inseparably associated: complexity poses the paradox of the one and the many. Next, complexity is in fact the fabric of events, actions, interactions, retroactions, determinations, and chance that constitute our phenomenal world. But complexity presents itself with the disturbing traits of a mess, of the inextricable, of disorder, of ambiguity, of uncertainty." (Morin 2008, 5)

Several features of complexity become obvious here. Most important are the interactions between various elements that turn entities into a dynamic texture—a "fabric" as Morin puts it. In Morin's remarks liveliness and microstructure of complex systems become evident. Furthermore, complexity has a time-dimension of change and emergence with recursive tendencies, which is leading to non-linearity. Apart from that, any complex system "is made up of uncertainty, indetermination and random phenomena. Complexity is, in a sense, always about chance" (ibid., 20).

What Morin describes as chance is elsewhere defined as chaos. Chaotic systems cannot be mistaken for disorderly systems but have to be understood as systems that are assembled by too many parts to be accounted for which are at the same time showing arbitrary behaviour: "Here is a typically complex idea in the sense that we have to bring together two notions—order and disorder—that logically seem to exclude each other" (ibid., 41). Central to the notion of complexity is always the interconnectedness of the one and the many—whether considering non-linearity, chaotic structures, or recursive practices—or as Morin would say: "This is the primary complexity; nothing is really isolated in the universe. Everything is interrelated" (ibid., 84).

By transferring aspects of complexity onto modes of storytelling several features become evident. Elsaesser easily dismisses the aspect of complex storytelling in his remarks on the mind-game film as too narrow in its way of recognising the films' idiosyncrasy because of its negligence of the spectators' involvement in the (re)construction of narration in most of the concepts on narrative complexity. I instead would like to rehabilitate the term 'complexity' not only as the central feature of the film π but also as a mode of understanding this "certain tendency" of contemporary cinema through its features of emergence and dynamic and as a necessary enhancement to realist approaches in film theory.

Elsaesser's scepticism and his early dismissal of the concept of narrative complexity lies grounded in the various assumptions of an evolution of narration towards more elaborated levels. Several scholars consider narrative complexity to be a more sophisticated, more innovative use of conventional storytelling. But as Elsaesser rightly criticises for example David Bordwell's approach of forking path narratives (Bordwell 2002), complex storytelling goes beyond a mere revision and updating of basic filmic storytelling principles. Instead it offers a mode of rethinking narrative cinema in general—especially when a film such as π is about complexity on a formal as well as on the content level. Some scholars even go as far as to attribute "anti-narrative elements" to complex narratives (Poulaki 2011, 13f.). Deliberate incoherence becomes a significant aspect of contemporary narration that transgresses the enigmatic or the undetermined but poses the tasks for spectators of merging elements, re-evaluating premises and uncovering patterns.

Looking at π, I would argue that the film's narration is not only dominated by cyclic or spiral instead of linear storytelling but questions the possibility of representation of an outer reality while posing the complex quest for a formula to grasp the inner core of our world—a formula, which the protagonist as well as the film itself want to detect and envision. While the protagonist wants to explain patterns in nature by reducing the complexity of the world to a simple string of a 216-digit number, the film becomes more and more complex through the reciprocity of various systems of world explanation such as science, religion and philosophy. In doing so, the narration itself fluctuates between complexity and reductionism while reflecting both principles without necessarily taking sides in the end.

LEAVES STIRRED BY THE WIND

The protagonist's world in the film π is structured around a number of personal notes and suppositions that are presented to the viewers through Max's voice-over and are illustrated by images of the protagonist and his surroundings. These descriptions are formulas that enable the viewers to access the diegesis—almost like manuals to the film. As an introduction Max Cohen recounts a personal note. He is telling us about a loss of vision in early childhood and its later recovery, which is followed by a set of assumptions. He announces:

"14:45: Restate my assumptions.
1: Mathematics is the language of nature.
2: Everything around us can be represented and understood through numbers.
3: If you graph the numbers of any system patterns emerge. Therefore, there are patterns everywhere in nature."
(π, 00:03:08-00:03:35)

Max Cohen, the scientist, sets out to reconnoitre the world by using his scholarly approach of deduction and by transferring his perception into mathematic language in order to cope with reality. Just as film in general transforms any extra-filmic actions into its own 'formula'—consisting not of numbers but of cinematic images and sound—and creates its own patterns through montage, Max wants to transform the complex system of the stock market into a very specific formula. In order to do so, he does not limit his research to the analysis of share price but he tries to find similarities "everywhere in nature".

While the narration is presented, the visual imagery fluctuates between seemingly subjective shots, head-on shots presenting the main protagonist and more distant shots following—almost surveying—Max Cohen on his way through the streets of his neighbourhood in New York City. Finally, he is shown sitting on a bench and looking at leaves stirring in the wind while the voice-over narrator tries to strengthen his assumptions through a list of evidence, such as epidemics, population phenomena as well as other examples deriving from nature.

Right there at the beginning—the movie will come back to that scene of Max sitting on the bench looking at the leaves at the end of the plot—, the movie π refers to one of the earliest incidents in film history of evoked assumptions to what film is capable of and what film signifies. 'The leaves stirred by the wind' references LE REPAS DE BÉBÉ (BABY'S DINNER, France 1895, Auguste Lumière/Louis Lumière), one of the short films of the Lumière brothers' first public screening in 1895, about which several observers noted that it was not the ordinary dinner scene in the foreground but the branches moving in the wind in the background that actually drew their attention to it. Siegfried Kracauer uses this very specific incident to introduce his *Theory of Film: The Redemption of Physical Reality*:

"Films come into their own when they record and reveal physical reality. Now this reality includes many phenomena which would hardly be perceived were it not for the motion picture camera's ability to catch them on the wing. And since any medium is partial to the things it is uniquely equipped to render, the cinema is conceivably animated by a desire to picture transient material life, life at its most ephemeral. Street crowds, involuntary gestures, and other fleeting impressions are its very meat. Significantly, the contemporaries of Lumière praised his films – the first ever to be made – for showing 'the ripple of the leaves stirred by the wind'." (Kracauer 1960, ix)

In this quote the ephemerality as well as the motion of reality is stressed and Kracauer points at the film's capability of capturing a very specific quality of our surroundings which enables the film to represent a reality not perceivable through ordinary perception—"the rendering of a reality made more real by the use of aesthetic device" (MacCabe 1986, 181). By using Henri de Parvilles expression of the trembling leaves (Kracauer 1960, 31) Kracauer evolves his theory of film as a realistic approach to the medium in order "to call attention to the (semi-)transparency of the filmic medium" (Elsaesser/Hagener 2010, 3).

π not only questions this mode of filmic representation of reality on its structural as well as presentational level but a very specific complexity of its filmic reality becomes evident already within the first five minutes. When π offers the visual reference to the medium's origin during its opening while at the same time situating it within a sequence of highly subjective shots and the expression of personal thoughts on the sound level it evokes a discussion of the film's capacity to represent reality, because if one goes beyond Kracauer then "both third- and first-person shots are equally 'real,' equally dependent on the audience's understanding the logic of their presentation" (Kawin 1978, 192). Hence, representation of reality in π's sense—and in mind-game films in general—has to include the representation of physical as well as mental reality. Bruce Kawin therefore offers the concept of the "mindscreen" where filmic reality has to be understood as a "personalized world, one that both incorporates the emphases and distortions of its organizing intelligence and expresses the mind's relation to its materials" (ibid., 84). Luring the viewers into a filmic texture of Kabbalah mythology, stock market theory, game philosophy as well as subjective perception and interpretation of reality, π can be seen as a filmic contemplation of what reality means as well as what role cinema plays into the disentangling of complex thought. Amplified by the numerous visual metaphors as well as the reduced imagery through the absence of colour, the film π therefore offers a filmic commentary on complexity and perception. In order to unravel some of the film's puzzles and to be able to re-orientate within π's complex diegesis the following analysis of the film will be structured around three metaphors introduced by some remarks on realist film theory.

Redemption of Reality

The relationship between content and form has always been a reflexive one. Considering one without the other is impossible but theorists may accentuate one of the two as dominant to the other. While Sergej Eisenstein, Rudolf Arnheim or, more recently, the neo-formalists around David Bordwell and Kristin Thompson highlight the film as a construction and focus on its means of representation, other theorists such as Siegfried Kracauer and André Bazin consider film to offer a more or less transparent view onto an extra-filmic reality (Elsaesser/Hagener 2010, 3/15).

Kracauer himself stresses this difference when he distinguishes a realistic from a formative tendency of film-making. The former—exemplified by the Lumières—"convey[ed] the impression of actuality" (Kracauer 1960, 34) while the latter—exemplified by Georges Méliès—"ignored the workings of nature out of the artist's delight in sheer fantasy" (ibid., 32). This rather simplistic division between the two tendencies has been criticised a lot and actually also partly taken back by Kracauer himself when he made clear that formal aspects are important for the film—as long as they serve the overall goal of "pictur[ing] transient material life" (ibid., ix). For Kracauer, staging and creating illusions undermines the film's main quality of being able to record and reveal physical reality. The recording function, which is a fundamental element in Kracauer's apprehension of film, can best be understood by capturing movement as for example in chases, dancing, or through the obvious absence of motion (ibid., 41ff.). In a broader sense, this recording function constitutes the representation of reality by filmic means. This representation is then determined by realism:

"[R]ealism is mainly a word used in order to describe the relationship between representations and a physical and social 'reality' exterior to such representations. [...] realism does not imply that what has been represented is true and 'real' in all aspects. It only implies that the representation is experienced as being a concrete representation that is, or might be true." (Grodal 2002, 68)

For Kracauer this representation has to be as close to material reality as possible and this is why he stresses the importance of the photographic for film. In many ways, this favouring of the photographic leads to the central disorientation in mind-game films because the actual status of the images becomes fragile—if not to say undetermined. If reality and complexity become the content, how can the cinematic record and reveal those two without elaborating on the formative?

In context of the film π, the revealing function seems more important to look at than the recording function—not only because it is comparable to the formula Max Cohen is looking for in the film but also because the revealing aspects leaves room for expanding Kracauer's theory from the physical to the mental reality. Revealing means uncovering "things normally unseen; phenomena overwhelming consciousness; and certain aspects of the outer world which may be called 'special modes of reality'" (Kracauer 1960, 46). Even though Kracauer considers the revealing function as secondary to the recording function, the film's possibility to "discover" (ibid.) things is highly important in the context of mind-game films and especially in π because Max Cohen's quest of detecting the formula has to be considered as a metaphor for the film's quest in general of recording and revealing content through formal representation.

So now what can the cinematic discover in π? First, ants will be central to the introduction of complexity and the filmic representation of parts—the single shot. This will be followed by a more structural look into the game-play of the film on two levels: On the one hand, the film uses the game of Go as a central motif within the narration and on the other hand, the syntax of the film will be in focus in order to look into the rules of playing. Finally, the brain will become the dominant metaphor for the construction of narration and the perception of 'mental' reality. From ants to brains there are many things to look at more closely.

Ants

First of all, film can reveal things normally unseen, which include very small and very big as well as transient things and blind spots of the mind (ibid., 46ff.). Looking at π the importance of close-ups becomes evident because many of the shots are determined by a proximity of the camera to the recorded, which leads to the magnification of ordinary things in Max Cohen's surroundings. Those close-ups try to display or to decipher the patterns of nature the protagonist is looking for by making use of their revealing function:

"Any huge close-up reveals new and unsuspected formations of matter; skin textures are reminiscent of aerial photographs, eyes turn into lakes or volcanic craters. Such images blow up our environment in a double sense: they enlarge it literally; and in doing so, they blast the prison of conventional reality, opening up expanses which we have explored at best in dreams before. It is not the big close-up alone which changes familiar sights into unusual patterns. Like it, diverse cinematic techniques and devices draw on shots of physical reality to evolve pictures or combinations of pictures which deviate from the conventional image of that reality." (ibid., 48)

Kracauer himself hints at the patterns that can be detected through the transformation of small things onto the big screen because the spectators are enabled to expand the exploration or reality into scrutinising the images.

In π, some of the most outstanding and at the same time irritating close-ups are of a single ant that populates the computer's heart: the computer chip. Technology and nature intertwine at that moment and the ant pronounces the computer's aspiration towards becoming a living entity with an own consciousness. Through its movement around the computer parts and by attracting Max's attention and distracting him from his work on the stock market the ant becomes a disturbance and an interruption of Max's technical and schematic processes of perception and contemplation.

Ants are also a recurring motif for complexity scholars because their interaction in groups and their tactics in colonising offer the possibility for basic research on emergent or complex systems (see for example Johnson 2001, 29ff.). Even though ants are "rather simple creatures" (Mitchell 2009, 4) as single entities, their group dynamic and their interaction become highly complex and effective. So the single ant in π signifies an absence, a blank, because its isolated appearance contradicts the ant's nature as part of a colony. Once in π only one ant appears it can be seen as prospect of a process of colonising. One wants to follow its path back to the colony and trace its origin. Just as Max is digging deeper into patterns of complexity that surface in symbols of spirals, the golden ratio or Fibonacci numbers, the single ant references through its existence the super-organism that a whole ant colony embodies and which will become more apparent later in the film when more and more ants are present in the sink, occupying the brain which is lying there. By highlighting the single ant through several close-ups the film offers just one of many self-reflexive metaphors.

Close-ups in general hint at complexity's special relationship between the one and the many because:

"[I]n its preoccupation with the small the cinema is comparable to science. Like science, it breaks down material phenomena into tiny particles, thereby sensitizing us to the tremendous energies accumulated in the microscopic configurations of matter. These analogies may well be related to the nature of film. It is quite possible indeed that the construction of the film image from shots of minute phases of movement favors the reverse tendency toward decomposing given wholes." (Kracauer 1960, 50)

By dissecting Max Cohen's world through the frequent use of close-ups, by scrutinising the details of nature, by getting closer to the numbers on the screen the camera wants to make visible what is to be found underneath the surface of objects and entities. But the film goes beyond the 'decomposing' because the montage offers the possibility to let various close-ups interact, react and progress through the succession in time—and here the game comes into play.

Games

Max does not only look closely at objects or symbols to discover the relevant patterns in nature but he has to come up with the right connections and references in order to construct the formula. The film offers a good explanation of this in a scene where Max and his mentor Sol discuss the ancient board game Go:

> *"Sol:* The ancient Japanese considered the Go-board to be a microcosm of the universe. Although, when it is empty it appears to be simple and ordered the possibilities of game play are endless. They say no two Go-games have ever been alike, just like snowflakes. So the Go-board actually represents an extremely complex and chaotic universe and that is the truth of our world, Max. It can't be easily summed up with Math. There is no simple add.
> *Max:* But as the Go-game progresses the possibilities become smaller and smaller. The board does take on order. So now all the moves are predictable. So...
> *Sol:* So? So?
> *Max:* So maybe—even if we are not sophisticated enough to be aware of it—there is a pattern... an order underlying every Go-game. Maybe that pattern is like the pattern in the stock market, the Torah, these 216 numbers...
> *Sol:* This is insanity, Max.
> *Max:* Or maybe it is genius. I have to get that number!"
> (π, 00:29:26-00:30:31)

While Sol, who has come in contact with the mysterious 216-digit number before Max and considers it to be the moment in which the computer machine becomes aware of its own existence and therefore gains consciousness, wants to stop Max to go further with his research, Max is looking at the dynamics of a complex system to detect a way to anticipate actions and reactions. The lines on the Go-board between the tokens become more and more interesting for Max. He goes beyond the one towards the many by connecting the information he has gained through the observation of nature. This becomes also evident in a metaphorical shot when Max overlays a picture of Leonardo da Vinci's *Vitruvian Man* with a diaphanous drawing of the golden spiral (see fig. 1). Revealing becomes superimposing and the question of interconnecting points, relationships and layers becomes apparent.

But as Sol points out, Max faces a sheer insoluble problem here because the amount of information is just too vast:

"Science postulates principles bearing the nature of the universe or some dimension of it, deduces their implications, and tries to verify them by experiment and observation. The physical universe being indefinable, this is an endless process, involving ever new hypotheses, ever new verifications. Facts emerge which do not conform to the original propositions; consequently, more fitting propositions must be evolved and again tested, and so on. It is a process which can also be described as a continuous to-and-fro movement between the hypothesized qualities of complex entities and the observed qualities of their elements (which partly elude direct observation, though). The similarity between this movement and the editing sequence long shot–close shot–long shot, etc., consists precisely in their common aspiration to comprehend, each in its way, large ensembles and eventually nature itself." (Kracauer 1960, 52)

π does not necessarily use a common sequence of long shot–close shot intervals as mentioned here by Kracauer but it uses frequently sequences of close-ups intermitted by images of Max Cohen looking at objects. These intervals stress the observational mode as well as the revealing function of the camera even more because every representation is shown in the need for an observer—just as Max as an observer of his surrounding needs the observation of the spectators: "The cinema, then, aims at transforming the agitated witness into a conscious observer" (ibid., 58).

What is characteristic for the film π as well as several other so-called mind-game films is not only the awareness for the observation of the filmic sound and images by spectators but also the non-linearity of montage. Instead of signifying

Figure 1: Screenshot from π.

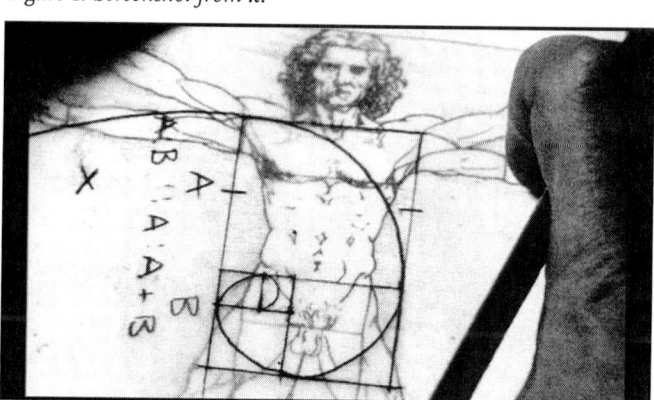

a chronological succession of time the arrangement of shots in π is rather in a procedural manner of recursive operations. Assumptions and observations are constantly revised and fed back into the machine to revise the formula and to come closer to the actual patterns, which are presumably underneath everything. Complex storytelling has an order of telling things but this order does not follow coherent notions of causality, spatiality or temporality. It rather offers reflexive and associative montage sequences just as the succession of close-ups in the film π suggests. So the spiral—one of the central metaphors Max uses to explain the complex patterns in nature—becomes the central structure of montage in π. The film returns to several incidents, sequences or images just to exhibit the difference in repetition. No cyclic revision is made but the 'restating', the adjusting or the extending of those reoccurring moments is stressed. Therefore, with a limited number of 'montage-rules' the filmic 'game' shows the sheer endless innovation and transformation of imagery and sound.

Brains

In order to process all the information consisting of elements, connections, dynamic interactions, and emergence that any complex system proposes a 'machine' is necessary. In π two of those 'machines' interact and correlate: the computer in Max's apartment and the human brain. While the computer seems to become more and more human because of the increasing amount of mysterious mucilage between the hardware and the moaning that actually comes from Max's next-door neighbour, Max's mind seems to be very technical in the sense that he appears emotionally deprived and highly logically structured. All his behaviour comes across being compulsive and following the strict succession of choreographed operations.

Throughout the course of the film, the brain becomes a major object of interest, which culminates in one scene in an underground station where Max discovers a brain lying on the stairs of a platform (π, 00:32:59 00:35:47). After one of his fits he sees a man standing at the next platform looking away from him. The other seems to be Max's alter ego but he wears the outfit of an orthodox Jew, which references his upcoming engagement with mythology and the numerology of the Kabbalah. Trying to follow the man he rushes to the other side but only finds a trace of blood leading to the brain. He approaches the pulsating brain and pokes it with a pen. This moment can be considered a moment of epiphany in the film. Whenever he touches the brain with the pen the sound suggests a fast approaching train, which is finally made visible at the third occurrence. If one considers the montage of this scene with its alternation of close-ups of the brain and medium shots looking at Max while he is looking at the brain, the scene becomes highly self-reflexive, not only as a moment of recognition and self-awareness but also as a moment of the overwhelming capacity of film capturing such a moment. Just like in the big myth of another Lumière movie—during the screenings of L'Arrivée d'un Train à La Ciotat (Arrival of a Train at La Ciotat, France 1896, Auguste Lumière/Louis Lumière) spectators presumably jumped up and tried to escape the approaching train—the realist impression of an approaching train grabs Max right at the moment of the most intense contact with the brain. As if the film would become self-aware of its possibilities at that moment it denounces any clear distinction between fantasy, hallucination, dream, and reality in that particular scene. Instead it replaces it with contemplation on the reality of the mental: "The mind reaches out to film and finds its own landscape, a version of its own process" (Kawin 1978, 192). Max physically explores the brain—and also his head in one other central scene towards the end of the film. This becomes a metaphor to the revealing of mental reality. The brain is physically present which references the materiality Kracauer asks for—only to finally replace it with cinematic images of thought—or as Deleuze (1989) would argue: The film as medium offers an own philosophical approach to cognition and thinking.

Max Cohen's quest to unravel the complex maze, which might lead in the narration of the film to an understanding of the inner core of nature, becomes less and less important throughout the course of the narration and finally even totally unanswerable. By the open ending of the final scenes—Max destroys the paper sheet with the last account of the 216-digit number and then drills into his skull before the screen turns black and we see Max in one last scene sitting back at the bench in the park, looking at the leaves stirred by the wind, not being able to do complex mental arithmetic (anymore)—the film refuses to re-orientate the spectators on the content level. Instead the film offers a revocation of classical concepts of filmic reality. Its disorientation of spectators is at the same time a reorientation of filmic capacities. Elaborating self-reflexively on what film is by interrogating filmic means of representation within a narration about the re-presentation of the world's complex fabric offers the possibility to revise earlier film theories such as Kracauer's *Redemption of Reality* and expand them towards complex thought. The presentation of a first-person consciousness by the protagonist Max Cohen and by the film itself through subjective images, voice-over and mindscreens (Kawin 1978, 12) become equally valid of offering of insights on world-perception.

To conclude, I want to quote from Gille Deleuze's *Time Image* in which he expresses the inseparable relationship between the inside and the outside of reality, which is made visible in π and which shows to what extent reality has to be expanded over and above the physical. The two sides of the inside (mental reality) and the outside (physical reality) encounter in the moment of perception and cognition. Revealing reality cannot be removed from becoming aware of the act of observation.

"The identity of world and brain, the automation, does not form a whole, but rather a limit, a membrane which puts an outside and an inside in contact, makes them present to each other, confronts them or makes them clash. The inside is psychology, the past, involution, a whole psychology of depths which excavate the brain. The outside is the cosmology of galaxies, the future, evolution, a whole supernatural which makes the world explode. The two forces are forces of death which embrace, are ultimately exchanged and become ultimately indiscernible." (Deleuze 1989, 206)

Therefore, a division between subjective and objective representation becomes obsolete and the film π shows that especially on the formal level reality has to be expanded to the mental according to its filmic revealing function as well as to the aspect of perception through the spectators. So when Max finally drills into his own skull—when he forces the outside reality into his brain beyond the underground station—the override takes place. The genius calculator inside his brain is removed but he is finally capable of ordinary social interaction and achieves a changed perception of his reality.

Bibliography

Bordwell, David (2002): Film Futures. In: *SubStance. A Review of Theory and Literary Criticism* ,Vol. 31, No. 1, 88–104.

Deleuze, Gilles (1989): *Cinema 2. The Time-Image*. London: The Athlone Press.

Elsaesser, Thomas (2009): The Mind-Game Film. In: Buckland, Warren (ed.): *Puzzle Films. Complex Storytelling in Contemporary Cinema*. Malden/Oxford/Chichester: Wiley-Blackwell, 13–41.

Elsaesser, Thomas/Hagener, Malte (2010): *Film Theory. An Introduction Through the Senses*. New York/Oxon: Routledge.

Grodal, Torben (2002): The Experience of Realism in Audiovisual Representation. In: Jerslev, Anne (ed.): *Realism and 'Reality' in Film and Media. Northern Lights. Film and Media Studies Yearbook 2002*. Copenhagen: Museum Tusculanum Press, 67–92.

Johnson, Steven (2001): *Emergence. The Connected Lives of Ants, Brains, Cities, and Software*. New York/London/Toronto/Sydney: Scribner.

Kawin, Bruce F. (1978): *Mindscreen. Bergman, Godard, and First-Person Film*. Princeton: Princeton University Press.

Kracauer, Siegfried (1960): *Theory of Film: The Redemption of Physical Reality*. Oxford/London/New York: Oxford University Press.

MacCabe, Colin (1986): Theory and Film: Principles of Realism and Pleasure. In: Rosen, Philip (ed.): *Narrative, apparatus, ideology. A Film Theory Reader*. New York: Columbia University Press, 179–197.

Mitchell, Melanie (2009): *Complexity. A Guided Tour.* Oxford: Oxford University Press.
Morin, Edgar (2008): *On Complexity.* Cresskill: Hampton Press.
Nowotny, Helga (2005): The Increase of Complexity and its Reduction. Emergent Interfaces between the Natural Sciences, Humanities and Social Sciences. In: *Theory, Culture & Society,* Vol. 22, No. 5, 15–31.
Poulaki, Maria (2011): *Before or Beyond Narrative? Towards a Complex Systems Theory of Contemporary Films.* Amsterdam: Dissertation University of Amsterdam.
Urry, John (2005): The Complexity Turn. In: *Theory, Culture & Society,* Vol. 22, No. 5, 1–14.

Films

BLACK SWAN (USA 2010, Darren Aronofsky)
FIGHT CLUB (USA/Germany 1999, David Fincher)
INCEPTION (USA 2010, Christopher Nolan)
L'ARRIVÉE D'UN TRAIN À LA CIOTAT (ARRIVAL OF A TRAIN AT LA CIOTAT, France 1896, Auguste Lumière/Louis Lumière)
LE REPAS DE BÉBÉ (BABY'S DINNER, France 1895, Auguste Lumière/Louis Lumière)
MEMENTO (USA 2000, Christopher Nolan)
π (USA 1998, Darren Aronofsky)
REQUIEM FOR A DREAM (USA 2000, Darren Aronofsky)
LOLA RENNT (RUN LOLA RUN, Germany 1998, Tom Tykwer)
SLIDING DOORS (UK/USA 1998, Peter Howitt)
THE FOUNTAIN (USA 2006, Darren Aronofsky)
THE SIXTH SENSE (USA 1999, M. Night Shyamalan)
THE WRESTLER (USA 2008, Darren Aronofsky)

Image Sources

Figure 1: Screenshot from π (USA 1998). DVD-Source: Arthouse Collection.

Narrative Re-orientation

Navigation in Complex Films
Real-life Embodied Experiences
Underlying Narrative Categorisation

MIKLÓS KISS

David Bordwell ponders upon questions of cinematic understanding based on real-life experiences the following way: "Recognizing the contents of realistic images [...] depends heavily upon our everyday perceptual abilities. Similarly, filmic storytelling relies upon cognitive dispositions and habits we've developed in a real-world context" (Bordwell 2011). The present paper focuses on one of these cognitive dispositions, based on embodied experiences, which we bring into our film viewing. I highlight the real-life skills of orientation and navigation in particular and their consequences on our evaluations and categorisations of different storytelling experiences; that is of differently felt complexities caused by diversely complex storytelling practices. Following an overview of recent discussions on complexity in film narratives, my reasoning aims to encompass two areas. Providing a theoretical framework, first I will recall the well-researched role of embodied·cognition in mapping narrative experiences[1]; claiming a key relevance for skills of orientation and navigation as ecological foundations for narrative comprehension. Second, I will bring this explanation of embodied-cognitive dispositions into the field of narrative categorisation. Once the overlap is recognised between used skills of orientation and navigation, both in real-life environments and narrative structures, one can make these explanations useful for contributing to the vague, still continuous debates on the categorisation of narrative complexity (Ramírez Berg 2006; Cameron 2008; Buckland 2009 vs. Thompson 2001; Bordwell 2006; Grodal 2009).

---

1 | That is, the extensions of elementary *source-path-goal* schemata (Lakoff 1987; Johnson 1990; Fauconnier/Turner 2002; Gallese/Lakoff 2005) to categorical thinking and narrative reasoning (Slors 1998; Menary 2008).

The Problem with Categorising Narrative Complexity

Different definitions of the (filmic) narrative often result in malleable theories, producing somewhat inconsistent, or at least arbitrary, groupings of movies. Narrative study, or better studies of cinema, have established a vast amount of categories, such as classical (Bordwell/Staiger/Thompson 1985) and *post-classical* forms of storytelling (Wyatt 1994, 15ff.; Elsaesser/Buckland 2002), *historical-materialist, art-cinema, parametric,* and *classical* narrations (Bordwell 1985), as well as *simple*, and *complex*, (Aristotle 1987; Bordwell 2002) and recently even *puzzle narratives* (Buckland 2009). Bordwell provides the best attempt to untangle the obvious incongruities or overlaps inherent in these categories. In his *Three Dimensions of Film Narrative* (Bordwell 2008, 85ff.), he does not specifically focus on the problem of categorisation, but still addresses the question indirectly when he distinguishes between narrative dimensions of *storyworld, plot structure,* and *narration*. Although Bordwell's input is efficient and powerful in the practice of film analysis, it remains abstract and vague as a justification for narrative categorisation.[2] The problem with this seemingly "hairsplitting taxonomy," as even Bordwell calls it (ibid., 92), is its inefficiency in meting out justice among, and to justify within, the above listed categories in relation to cinematic narratives. To illustrate the problem, firstly I will introduce the idea of narrative complexity, and its debated relation to traditional classifications. Although arguing for the relevance of this discussion, I will point out the debate's practical shortcomings, and offer an alternative solution that handles narrative complexity in a theoretically more justified manner.

The clear prominence of the recent (from the early 1990s) cinematic tendency of storytelling complexity is underlined by the academic debate (from the early 2000s) on the evaluation and theorisation of the trend. From the popularisation of non-linear storytelling (approximately from Quentin Tarantino's RESERVOIR DOGS (USA 1992), but definitely from his PULP FICTION (USA 1994)), numerous theoretical contributions appeared explaining the renewed[3] narrative phenomenon that is still influential in contemporary cinematic and televisual[4] representations. The theoretical treatment is divided into two fairly distinct groups. On

---

[2] | The taxonomy, admitted by Bordwell himself, is better in answering the question of "What is *a* narrative?" than giving definition of "What is Narrative?" (Bordwell 2008, 88). His early recognition is still valid that "[t]here are virtually no theoretical studies of the representational dimension of film narrative" (Bordwell 1985, xii).

[3] | Importantly, the *Tarantino-Effect* refers not to the invention (see classic film noir's complex narratives in the 1940s and 50s), but to the popularisation of "narrative pyrotechnics" (Ramírez Berg 2006, 13), causing some "competitive showing-off" (Staiger 2006, 2) among certain film-makers.

[4] | See Jason Mittell's forthcoming book on *Complex Television*.

the one hand, Kristin Thompson (2001) and David Bordwell (2006) adhere the new storytelling trend to classical tradition (Bordwell/Staiger/Thompson 1985) and downplay the significance of narrative complexity.[5] On the other hand, Allan Cameron (2008) and Warren Buckland (2009) "disagree with Bordwell's contention that 'offbeat storytelling' has become 'part of business as usual' in Hollywood" (Cameron 2008, 5), and claim that "the majority of forking-path/multiple draft/puzzle films are distinct in that they break the boundaries of the classical, unified mimetic plot" (Buckland 2009, 5). Bordwell's assertion that post-classical films' strategies are only intensified and use more complex versions of techniques that are inherently present in classical narratives (2002a; 2002b; 2006, 121ff.), is already relativised in Edward Branigan's (2002) and Kay Young's (2002) early responses. While Branigan lists and exemplifies more radical kinds of narrative complexities well beyond Bordwell's cases, Young, pondering the diverse cognitive effects of narrative manipulations, also relativises Bordwell's simplified points. Soothing the opposition, there are also the careful 'in-betweeners,' like Charles Ramírez Berg and Elliot Panek, who, while recognising the trend, formulate their assessments as rhetorical questions, such as "Do these films represent a movement, trend, cycle, or possibly something bigger, more profound, and potentially more significant? A new kind of film storytelling?" (Ramírez Berg 2006, 8), or temper their predictions, for example, "Whether this group of non-traditional films constitutes a genre or a new mode of narration will only be known after an in depth analysis of how narration works in these films" (Panek 2006, 65). In 2002 Buckland and Thomas Elsaesser were also cautious of addressing the unfolding tendency (although they went further, announcing a 'post-post-classical' paradigm): "The 'work' of classical narrative [...] is becoming, it seems, the 'play'-station of the post-postclassical. This, *if true*, would indeed demand the shift to a different paradigm" (Elsaesser/Buckland 2002, 79; emphasis added).

In 2009 Buckland, reconsidering his previous standpoint, returns to the question. His *puzzle film* concept, aiming to deal with the now inexorably dominant experience of cinematic complexity, this time without *ifs* or any reservation, claims a distinct narrative category beyond Bordwell's all-embracing classical label. With his proposed term, which "names a mode of filmmaking that cuts across traditional filmmaking practices" (Buckland 2009, 6), Buckland unwittingly enters the problems of narrative categorisation. His *puzzle film* category, covering "a popular cycle of films from the 1990s that rejects classical storytelling techniques and replaces them with complex storytelling" (ibid., 1), offers a necessary but crude reflection on contemporary storytelling trends. In its vague

---

5 | See Bordwell's latest articulation of his firm standpoint in relation to Tomas Alfredson's Tinker Tailor Soldier Spy (France/UK/Germany 2011), explaining narrative complexity as "unconventionally conventional" (Bordwell, 2012).

definition, *puzzle film* apparently traverses Bordwell's dimensions that these films activate interest both in *plot structure* ("the arrangements of the parts") and *narration* ("the moment-by-moment flow of information" (Bordwell 2008, 90)): "[T]he complexity of puzzle films operates on two levels: narrative and narration" (Buckland 2009, 6). Bordwell's *narration* and *plot structure* becomes Buckland's *narrative* ("simple or complex *story*"), and *narration* ("the complex *telling*"), respectively (ibid.). Put simply, cinematic complexity ultimately can manifest itself in two different ways. An overwhelming story, for example, by the employment of multiple subplots, can be labelled as a complex narrative (from Christopher Nolan's INCEPTION (USA/UK 2010) to Sang-soo Hong's DAIJIGA UMULE PAJINNAL (THE DAY A PIG FELL INTO A WELL, South Korea 1996)). Another option, such as the strategy of plotline complication, exemplifies complex narration as manipulation of storytelling (from Nolan's MEMENTO (USA 2000) to Michel Gondry's ETERNAL SUNSHINE OF THE SPOTLESS MIND (USA 2004)). Buckland's primary interest tends towards this latter, structural and compositional playfulness, and therefore centres on Bordwell's second dimension of plot structure.[6] Since the possible combinations of narrative segments result in different plot-complexities, following Buckland's summary, one may distinguish between *simple*, *complex*, and *puzzle*-like narrative arrangements.

For Buckland the relatively high degree of complexity in *puzzle films*' plot structures qualifies the term *puzzle film* as a distinct narrative category. Following the logic in Buckland's train of thought: If "Bordwell does not feel the need to go beyond Aristotle's conception of complexity," while "puzzle films go beyond Aristotle's sense of complexity" (Buckland 2009, 1), then *puzzle film* seems to stand out as a distinct mode of filmic representation, where "the arrangement of events is not just complex, but complicated and perplexing; the events are not simply interwoven, but *entangled*" (ibid., 3). The definition's palpable subjectivity, using far from precise adjectives like *complex, perplexing, entangled*, or *interwoven*, is reinforced by the broad selection of presented case studies in Buckland's anthology. His collection presents analyses that lump together movies with completely different levels and dimensions of created and felt complexity, such as LOST HIGHWAY (France/USA 1997, David Lynch), LOLA RENNT (RUN LOLA RUN, Germany 1998, Tom Tykwer), SUZHOU HE (SUZHOU RIVER, Germany/China 2000, Ye Lou), OLDEUBOI (OLDBOY, South Korea 2003, Chan-wook Park), etc. If one agrees that these films trigger different experiences of felt complexity, then one should categorise them by reflecting on this sensed diversity. My dissatisfaction of placing these films within a single category, necessitates formulating the question of *how to supply a more objective, rational framework to the problem of narrative categorisation related to the experience of storytelling complexity?*

---

6 | "[W]e can treat narrative as a *structure*, a particular way of combining parts to make a whole" (Bordwell 1985, xi).

NARRATIVE COMPLEXITY'S RELATION TO EMBODIED-COGNITIVE FUNCTIONS

Beyond their incongruent evaluations about the living trend of complex narratives, all the contributions listed above have something in common. Namely, they all avoid the difficulty and trouble of delivering a clear-cut explanation for their argument, treating their subject safely by explaining the trend's media archaeological, that is industrial and technical context, or by simply providing extensive taxonomies of complex storytelling techniques. The seemingly competing arguments, which "locate a film's complexity—or non-complexity—at a different level" (Simons 2008, 112), actually limit the assessment of complexity to typologies. All the approaches listed above seem to diagnose the trending strategy in contemporary films, but all fail to scrutinise the recognised complexity in its core function within the viewing experience. Narrative complexity's essence is not an abstract structure mapped by narratologists' descriptive methods, but a sensed confusion explained by *cognitive poetics* (Tsur 2008; Stockwell 2002; Grodal 2002, 2009). In order to provide an objective framework, one needs to understand 'complexity' by its caused effect on one's embodied-cognitive experience. Complexity opposes simplicity, where their relative difference is a feeling (e.g. the feeling of something as being complex) resulting from differences of cognitive efforts invested in handling variously demanding incoming information. If human cognition is a problem solving activity (Eysenck/Keane 2005, 1), then the required amount of invested cognitive effort is approximately proportional to the degree of the given situation's—evoked and felt—complexity. The overlap is obvious between the function and effect of complexity in real-life's direct access, and in the mediation's indirect experience: If any incoming stimulus' relative complexity causes sensed cognitive confusion in reality (relative along some imaginary axis of 'simplicity-complexity'), then *narrative complexity* stands for a temporary or prolonged cognitive confusion evoked by diverse storytelling media's challenging compositional practices. In the same way that physiological, psychological, perceptual, or environmental constraints and contexts test our real-life abilities to cope with their aggregate complexity, similarly, representational, narrative, stylistic, generic, etc. choices place the filmic experience on an imaginary axis of 'simplicity-complexity', too. While classical narration's strategy of mimetic realism results in easy-to-follow stories, art-cinema or puzzle-like complex narrations' deliberate break with the mimetic tradition concludes in diverse levels of sensed confusion. Bordwell recognises, but downplays the relevance and effect of narrative manipulation. For him complexity, caused by storytelling's departure from the mimetic tradition, challenges but does not alter the experience.[7] Quite the reverse, Buckland evaluates narrative complexity as deliberate confrontation with our cognitive functioning. He talks about a new kind of experience, certainly beyond the one that classical narratives can offer. For him *puzzle films* represent a brand new attitude when playing with complexity that is challenging their viewers' cognitive capabilities, sometimes only for the sake of the challenge.[8] With this part-conclusion—that complexity's quality is best measured by framing its effect on the level of cognitive experientiality—we are still not closer to the solution of our main concern, but at least we have a more appropriate formulation of the problem we are faced with. Looking at the question from the experiential side, the difference between intact, challenged, and broken cognitive processes becomes crucial for my forthcoming argument on underlying narrative categorisation.

What is at stake here is to understand the viewer's relative ability to comprehend, follow, and even map different complexities of narratives, which are manifested through different complexities of storytelling compositions. At this point a practical question arises: *What are the components and machineries of such a viewing skill?* A feasible answer requires proving at least two hypotheses. Firstly: The differences in varying intricate narrative structures' felt complexities are based on differences of experiences which deal with diversely complex, that is cognitively confusing situations in reality. Secondly: Among the embodied-cognitive skills, which maintain this ecological overlap between real-life and film-viewing capabilities of dealing with complexity, orientation and navigation play a key role in providing rational arguments for explaining and categorising complexity's narrative manifestations.

Both hypotheses rely upon proven explanations of embodied experientiality's role in film viewing. Arguments are based on the supposed overlap between real-life and narrative experiences, where orientation and navigation skills, using elemental embodied schemata, appear as one of the core abilities for this overlap.[9] In order to test the argument, and to reveal these overlapping functions, I will start with a brief listing of three dimensions where orientation and navigation play a key role.

---

7 | His seminal article (Bordwell 2002a) lists seven conventions that compensate complex narratives' challenges, thus ensuring the cognitive economy on the level of their experience.

8 | Elsaesser argues similarly in Buckland's anthology on the trend of the *mind-game films*, which are "movies that are 'playing games'" (Elsaesser 2009, 14), or Steven Johnson and Jason Mittell on the narratively complex television practices that are providing *cognitive workouts* (Johnson 2006, 14), thereby increasing problem-solving skills, eventually mobilising *forensic fans (*Mittell 2009).

9 | See Mark Johnson on the emergence of embodied schemata by spatial means (Johnson 1990, 18ff.).

First and foremost, orientation and navigation is vital in *real-life physical environments*. Model research was done in 1948 by Edward C. Tolman, coining the expression *cognitive map*, while M. Jeanne Sholl and Harry Heft present recent, ecological-based extensions of Tolman's insights in Juval Portugali's anthology *The Construction of Cognitive Maps* (1996).[10]

Secondly, viewers use their real-life skills of orientation during mapping of, and navigation in *film-diegetic spaces*. This specific interest in storyworld organisation elucidates the film viewer's ability to immerse into, then follow and understand the spatial settings and setups of fictional worlds' constructed storyspaces. While Daniel G. Morrow, Gordon H. Bower and Steven L. Greenspan (1989), or James E. Cutting (2007) deliver ecological-evolutionary and physio-cognitive insights of the question, Marie-Laure Ryan's *Narrative Cartography* (2003) provides an illuminating case study on the processes and results of such an interest.[11] Driven by similar interest in storyworld-space, Steven Jacobs (2007), closely reading Alfred Hitchcock's carefully built storyworlds, provides insights not only for architectural, but also for dramaturgical interests in films. Jacobs' inferred floor-maps offer more than dry descriptions of architectural setups: The meticulously reproduced storyworlds reveal well-planned narrative functions, like a case of a spatially determined suspense in Hitchcock's NORTH BY NORTHWEST (USA 1959). There is an obvious procedural overlap between strategies of orientation and navigation in real-life physical, and film-diegetic illusory environments. The correspondence is obvious as no one has specific organs or skills for mapping film-space beyond the biologically given ones. This ecological overlap ensures the effectiveness of cinema's most profound trick of turning the two-dimensional reality of the canvas into an illusion of three-dimensional realism. Next to these apparent similarities one has to be aware of clear differences, too. The disassociation of mind and body is responsible for self-evident differences in the experiencing process, as for example, climbing a real mountain and watching somebody who is climbing a mountain are not the same experiences.[12]

---

10 | According to them, human navigation is dependent on two types of orientation structure: One of them is a disembodied, overview-like traditional cognitive map-representation of *optic-space*. The other type is an embodied, participatory map route with sequentially organised perspective structure, offering *haptic-space*. The two orientating possibilities appear as a user choice of view in smartphones' mobile navigation applications.

11 | Ryan asked a group of high school students to draw a map of the diegetic world of Gabriel García Márquez's novel *Chronicle of a Death Foretold*. Comparing the created maps by reviewing their overlapping graphical features, Ryan drew consequences on the spatial triggers of the text.

12 | This difference is at stake in the debate between Gregory Currie (1995) and Buckland (2003). While Currie rejects the idea of a viewer that participates and navi-

Figure 1a + 1b: Harry Heft's model (1996, 118), which explains the continuous, nested hierarchy of path units in real-life orientation shows strong organisational similarities with David Bordwell's and Kristin Thompson's plot segmentation method (2008, 69) for analysing Victor Fleming's THE WIZARD OF OZ *(USA 1939).*

Path from Home to Post Office	
Path from Home to Newsstand	Path from Newsstand to Post Office
Vista 1	Vista 2	Vista 3

THE WIZARD OF OZ: PLOT SEGMENTATION
C. Credits
1. Kansas
    a. Dorothy at home, worried about Miss Gulch's threat to Toto
    b. Running away, Dorothy meets Professor Marvel, who induces her to return home
    c. A tornado lifts the house, with Dorothy and Toto, into the sky
2. Munchkin City
    a. Dorothy meets Glinda, and the Munchkins celebrate the death of the Wicked Witch of the East
    b. The Wicked Witch of the West threatens Dorothy over the Ruby Slippers
    c. Glinda sends Dorothy to seek the Wizard's help
3. The Yellow Brick Road
    a. Meeting the Scarecrow
    b. Meeting the Tin Man
    c. Meeting the Cowardly Lion
4. The Emerald City
    a. The Witch creates a poppy field near the City, but Glinda rescues the travelers
    b. The group is welcomed by the City's citizens
    c. As they wait to see the Wizard, the Lion sings of being king
    d. The terrifying Wizard agrees to help the group if they obtain the Wicked Witch's broomstick
5. The Witch's Castle and Nearby Woods
    a. In the woods, flying monkeys carry off Dorothy and Toto
    b. The Witch realizes that she must kill Dorothy to get the Ruby Slippers
    c. The Scarecrow, Tin Man, and Lion sneak into the Castle; in the ensuing chase Dorothy kills the Witch
6. The Emerald City
    a. Although revealed as a humbug, the Wizard grants the wishes of the Scarecrow, Tin Man, and Lion
    b. Dorothy fails to leave with the Wizard's hot-air balloon but is transported home by the Ruby Slippers
7. Kansas—Dorothy describes Oz to her family and friends
E. End credits

Still, similarities are expected to be dominant; elucidated by recent explorations of neural and physiological processes of immersion and identification (see research on mirror neurons by Francesca Garbarini and Mauro Adenzato (2004), or by Paul Elliott (2010)).

Thirdly, from the perspective of my main purposes, the most important task is to highlight the role of one's orientation and navigation skills while 'mapping' *narrative plot-structures*, especially when confronted with comprehensive difficulties of differently complex storytelling constructions. However the expression 'mapping narratives' sounds like a metaphor, the claim that orientation and navigation *in* narrative structures is perhaps more than a figure of speech is not an issue anymore. Proofs came in several steps as conclusions of different researches and methods. Among these probably the most influential is George Lakoff and Mark Johnson's seminal linguistic investigation on embodied experientiality, concluding in the following well-known statement: "[B]odily experiences give rise to image-schematic structures of meaning that can be transformed, extended, and elaborated into domains of meaning that are not strictly tied to the body" (Johnson 1990, 44f.). As fundamentally bodily

---

gates in fictional worlds *from the inside*, Buckland argues for an embodied immersion that places the spectator into the fictional space by a mental representation of his or her own body image.

experiences convert and solidify into abstract concepts, similarly one can trace the bodily origins of our analytical thinking's abstract results, too. Following this bi-directional logic, one's orientation in narrative constructions' abstract spaces is a result of *blendings* (Fauconnier/Turner 2002) from neuro-physiologically existent image-schematic experientiality to analytical thinking.[13]

Vittorio Gallese teamed up with Lakoff himself and delivered the theory's neuroscientific explanation. Their conclusion—"abstract reasoning in general *exploits* the sensory-motor system" (Gallese/Lakoff 2005, 19)—connects real-life bodily functions with analytical cognition. Other psychological contributions, bringing the transformations, extensions and elaborations of bodily experiences to narrative-related directions, were presented by Marc Slors, who argues for "a crucial role to the body in the narrative coherence of successive perceptual contents" (Slors 1998, 74). His laconic deduction, "there can be no psychological continuity without bodily continuity" (ibid., 77), creates a significant link between real life's existing and film's virtual continuities. In another psychological study, similar to the one of Slors, Richard Menary also combines embodied-cognitive underpinnings with narrative issues. In his talkatively entitled *Embodied Narratives* Menary delivers an ultimate conclusion: "[O]ur narratives are structured by the sequence of embodied experiences" (Menary 2008, 75). Slors and Menary's embodied accounts on psychological continuity ultimately link the abilities of real-life orientation (see Harry Heft's mentioned ecological theory) with analytical skills of narrative segmentation. Bordwell and Thompson articulate the same idea, although less scientifically reasoned but as an apt intuition, through a telling metaphor:

"Analyzing a film is a bit like investigating a building's design. When we walk through a building, we notice various features – the shape of the doorway, the sudden appearance of an immense atrium. [...] Similarly, we experience a film scene by scene [...]. Movies don't come equipped with blueprints, however, so we have to make our own." (Bordwell/Thompson 2008, 431f.)

This train of thought claims a direct, neuroscientifically proven, relation between one's real-life navigation skills understood as sequential embodied experience (Heft), and one's narrative comprehension, which is determined by possibilities of navigating *in* plot structures' different sequential complexities (Bordwell and

---

13 | Monika Fludernik—introducing her *prototype theory*—argues similarly as follows: "Prototype theory stresses how whole/part relationships and back/front, right/left, up/down orientations [...] not only play a crucial role for our immediate body experience but from there are apt to infect our categorical thinking and effect repercussions even on the level of entirely 'abstract' areas of reasoning" (Fludernik 1996, 18).

Thompson).[14] While Menary and Slors are interested in the question "how the thoughts, feelings, and perceptions of the minimal embodied and ecologically embedded self give rise to narratives" (Menary 2008, 75), my inquiry looks at this relation from the viewer's side, asking: *How are these different narratives understood and categorised through actual embodied experiences?*

PUZZLE FILMS' RELATIVE COMPLEXITY

In the following section I reconsider the debated categories of narrative complexity through the introduced theory, claiming that these categories are rooted in our embodied real-life experientiality using everyday skills of orientation and navigation. This re-categorisation will take shape through specific film examples and previous arguments delivered by Bordwell, Buckland, and Elsaesser from the narrative perspective, and Menary, Slors, and Grodal from the embodied-cognitive side. Going back to Buckland's introduction of different narrative complexities, distinction is made between *simple, complex*, and, allowing Buckland's own contribution, *puzzle plots*.

Considering *simple plots* a prominent example, used both by Buckland (Elsaesser/Buckland 2002, 26ff.) and Grodal (2009, 222), could be John McTiernan's DIE HARD (USA 1988), providing seamless chronology, straightforward action-reaction-based causality, character-integrity, and—tight—narrative continuity and coherency. All these attributes make the film *classical* (perhaps *post-classical*—the distinction points to another long and vague theoretical negotiation). While for Elsaesser *simple plots* are "[e]xcessively obvious" (Elsaesser 2009, 37), for Grodal they don't provide any epistemological uncertainty (Grodal 2009, 222). Taking the viewers' embodied rootedness as blended real-life experiences seriously, simple plots, by offering apparent paths with clearly positioned obstacles, create effortlessly mappable plot-trajectories without challenging the viewers' orientation and navigation skills.

Following Buckland and still remaining within the Aristotelian paradigm, *complex plots* are "simple plots with the additional qualities of 'reversal' and 'recognition'" (Buckland 2009, 2). For complexity Aristotle uses the term *peplegmenos*, which literally means *interwoven*. The focal aim of complex narratives is not about providing a seamless and straightforward experience. Complex films' adherence to the traditional mimesis-based plot-structuring norms is not pri-

---

14 | Heft's analogy between real-life navigation and segmentation while listening to music is easily applicable to the analytical experience of watching connected sequences of moving images: "perceiving music is consistent with the view that a fundamental form of navigation, wayfinding, is a process of perceiving a temporally structured visual event, namely, a path of travel" (Heft 1996, 120).

mary; the classical rules are subordinated to other interests. By designing inviting narrative environments for mental challenges and "cognitive workouts" (Johnson 2006, 14), complex plots offer a forensic playground as a playful and participatory experience for the viewer. For Aristotle, as well as for Bordwell, complex plots are still classical. What makes these films still classical is their *narrative coherency*, that takes care of a balanced *cognitive economy* on the level of experience. I add here, that at the end of this experience plot-wrinkles are ironed out, interwoven paths integrate, revelations arise, and thus the complicated plot provides a puzzle with challenged, but possible solutions. The challenged viewing is tantamount to an embodied experience of orientation and navigation in a labyrinth without clear paths and vistas, but with a possible exit as a 'resolution'. Although it requires heightened cognitive investment (such as extended memory-working, mental rotation, and other mental constituents of cognitive mapping), the invested energy pays off. The viewers' plot-arrangement concludes in a relatively complex, but rational and coherent *cognitive map* of the diegesis, which is ready to host our embodied immersion.

Buckland's ambition is to introduce a third, distinct category of plot-complexity, a *puzzle plot*, which, according to him,

"far exceeds Aristotle's meaning of complex plot. [...] The 'puzzle plot' is, I would argue, the third type of plot that comes after the complex plot. A puzzle plot is intricate in the sense that the arrangement of events is not just complex, but complicated and perplexing; the events are not simply interwoven, but *entangled*." (Buckland 2009, 1ff.)

For Buckland, *puzzle films* constitute a "post-classical mode of filmic representation" (ibid., 5), while Bordwell downplays their narrative complexity keeping them within the classical paradigm. Consequential to my references, while puzzle plots are, for Thomas Elsaesser, "excessively enigmatic" (Elsaesser 2009, 37), according to Torben Grodal, they cause "epistemological uncertainty" (Grodal 2009, 223). Buckland's indication of differentiating new trends in film narratives from Aristotelian and Bordwellian complexity seems to be reasonable; however his take on the question is too generous as it addresses complexity as a relative feeling. As my introduction pointed out, it is hard to contain all the film examples of his anthology within one single category. His definition is right, but his examples are too extensive in that only certain *puzzle films* seem to form a category beyond complex plots. A more restricted film selection could make up a more accurate group, offering not only relatively complex, but uncompromisingly confusing experiences. These re-selected films' narrative strategies, such as their ambiguities, mutual exclusivities, and paradoxes, are not compensated by any "trade-off between innovation and norm" (Bordwell 2002a, 103) that normally ensures a cognitively manageable experience (ibid., 90), but keep the viewer in a perplexed state ceaselessly. From this definition, films like Lynch's LOST HIGHWAY, Lars von Trier's FORBRYDELSENS ELEMENT (THE ELEMENT OF CRIME, Denmark 1984), Michael Walker's CHASING SLEEP (Canada/USA/France 2000), or loop-narratives, for example Christopher Smith's TRIANGLE (UK/Australia 2009) or Nacho Vigalondo's LOS CRONOCRÍMENES (TIMECRIMES, Spain 2007), could form that distinct category, better called *riddle plots*, which, providing riddles without solution, would go beyond some of the *puzzle films*' 'simple complexity'.[15] The analytical trouble of segmenting these films' unnatural plots is related to the difficulty of one's navigational immersion not only within the uncanny storyworlds, but also *in* the tricky narrative designs. The problem clearly exemplified by the viewers' persistent willingness in, but at times unsatisfying struggle of—cognitively or/and graphically—mapping the confusing experience.[16]

SPECIFYING RIDDLE FILM THROUGH AN EMBODIED THEORY OF NARRATIVE COMPLEXITY

Buckland's hunch that claims a distinct category for the trend and goes beyond 'traditional' complexity, seems to be correct but not precise enough. A necessary sub-division of his all-embracing label of *puzzle film* both enables a better grip on the various experiences that the trend highlights, and also clarifies the debated categories. The distinction between a complex but solvable (Bordwell's *complex*, and some of Buckland's *puzzle films*) and a confusingly insolvable (other examples of Buckland beyond the level of complexity that Bordwell allows for classical narratives) cinematic playfulness marks two distinct storytelling and filmmaking interests. Let me again call the products of these dissimilar attitudes *puzzle* and *riddle* narratives, respectively.[17] Although the recognition of this sub-categorisation's relevance is crucial to untangle the discrepancy of the debate

---

15 | Christopher Smith's DVD comment on his TRIANGLE clearly articulates the distinction between *puzzle* and *riddle* (films): "I didn't want this movie to be a movie that ends with one twist. I wanted to have a movie which ends with a riddle".

16 | For further reading on the same topic, see Jan Alber (2009) on reader strategies of finding "human substrate" (ibid., 94) in impossible storyworlds' transgressive experience, or Marie-Laure Ryan's *many-worlds theory* (2011, 176f.), in which readers narrativise storyworld paradoxes by employing interpretations based on quantum mechanics.

17 | The wording 'puzzle' is a misnomer for covering all the films that Buckland renders under it. Puzzles, like a picture cut up into pieces, usually offer a problem that only challenges the abilities of its trouble-shooter. Riddles may block the solution completely (by removing crucial pieces from, or adding contradictory ones to the puzzle).

between Bordwell and Buckland, one still has to answer our initial question of *what makes one film, by narrative-compositional means, a simple, complex, puzzle, or even a riddle experience?*

While *simple, complex* and (Bordwell)/or (Buckland) *puzzle* plots do not problematise the introduced overlap between real-life and plot-related orientation and navigation, *riddle films* offer—spatial—adventures seemingly beyond one's real-life physical experiences. Good examples are the cases of paradox character-decouplings, even multiplications, such as loop narratives' weird encounters, for example Fred Madison's Escher-like duplication in Lynch's LOST HIGHWAY.[18] What is interesting in these weird incidents is not the presence of multiplied characters, but the spatial (both film-diegetic and plot-structure) implications and consequences of this multiplication. The viewer's encounter with such an ontologically problematic spatio-temporal situation is not without narrative consequences either. *Riddle films*' diegetic paradoxes, through destabilising our vital, embodied, real-life experienced sense of the deictic centre (of inertia), make the viewer's narrative navigation, that is his/her cognitive plot-mapping, practically impossible. But at least the viewer faces great difficulties to uphold the narrative minimum of clear time-space relations ensuring causality and coherence, as *riddle films* deny our natural access, based on real-life skills of navigation and orientation, to their highly unnatural diegetic worlds and/or plot-structures. For Grodal this kind of disembodied narrative experientiality, connected to an impossible and deviant reality, merely excludes films from *classical* or *post-classical* categories. For him, films which block the embodied experientiality as a natural frame for comprehension, instead of forming a new category called *puzzle* or *riddle films*, simply fall under the division of *art-cinema narration*. With this Grodal's disembodied definition of art-film extends Bordwell's now-classic description in *Narration in the Fiction Film* (1985), providing an explanation based on embodiment (Grodal 2009, 208). All these seem to unravel the problem with Buckland's concept: On the one hand, films with simple or complex plots are, actually agreeing with Bordwell's argument, just differently intense variations of classical narratives. On the other hand, films with *entangled* plots, detaching from our physical embodied experiences, according to Grodal, leave the *classical* category, and receive the *art-cinema narrative* tag. Following this delineation, *riddle films* are beyond the classical category, certainly, since they are already within the class of *art-cinema narratives*.

However, the case that Buckland introduced, at least the way I have specified it, is probably not as simple as Bordwell or Grodal argues for. For Grodal certain movies that "presenting paradoxes and counterintuitive events [...] arrest the PECMA flow and overactivate the association areas, [...] will provide similar

---

18 | In the film Fred Madison calls from outside and answers from inside of his house via the door buzzer at the same time.

experiences of deep significance" (Grodal 2009, 149f.).[19] Nonetheless Grodal does not reveal more about this "deep significance," his description of art-experience, based on the blocked PECMA flow, covers indeed most of the films we, or Bordwell whilst using his own art-cinema definition, render to the art-narrative category. However there are film-examples, coming from my narrowed down category of *riddle films*, which with their narrative paradoxes and counterintuitive events do not encourage such viewer behaviour described by Grodal. Here I see a point beyond Grodal's argument: Lynch's cycle of (*riddle*-) films, such as LOST HIGHWAY, MULHOLLAND DR. (France/USA 2001) and INLAND EMPIRE (France/Poland/USA 2006), or the mentioned loop-films, do not let me escape from my natural, navigation-driven plot structuring struggle. Whilst watching LOST Highway or TRIANGLE, the viewer's narrative engagement, following the drive of a basic *source-path-goal embodied schemata*, means that they cannot escape their own curiosity towards the narrative's structure. In simple words: These films' complexity while stretching beyond a solvable puzzle, still lures viewers into continually trying to make rational sense of the otherwise obviously paradoxical and counterintuitive events, and do not encourage searching for some hidden, higher, abstract meanings instead. Throughout a sustained activity, upheld by a complex structure or/and an experiential ambiguity, viewers do not follow the cognitively logical trajectory that Grodal describes. Instead of relying on their natural 'defensive' reaction of categorising these films as *art-cinema narration* that offer some "deep significance," viewers of riddle films utilise their analytical toolkit trained on classical cinema, and approach these films through persistent attempts of rationalisation, *naturalisation* (Culler 1975, 134ff.), and *narrativisation* (Fludernik 1996). Here I support Fludernik's argument creating a nuanced view on Grodal's overly rational explanation: "Recuperation of narrativity from non-naturally coded texts [...] becomes possible through recourse to a variety of natural cognitive parameters [...]. Where narrativity can no longer be recuperated by any means at all, the narrative genre merges with poetry" (Fludernik 1996, 36).[20]

Riddle films' paradoxical diegetic worlds and perplexing narratives evoke ambiguity as they uphold and violate classical narrative ingredients, such as coherency, spatio-temporal unity, linearity, chronology, etc., *at the same time*. The sustained, sometimes frustrated, but still enjoyable efforts of construing a navigable narrative path do not direct the viewer automatically to search for

---

19 | Grodal's PECMA (short for perception, emotion, cognition, and motor action) flow chart is a sketch for explaining the full cognitive process of cinematic perception (Grodal 2009, 147).

20 | Readers' or viewers' shift in their evaluation from *classical* to *art-cinema narrativity* comes only in the moment, when paradoxes and counterintuitive events become completely unbearable rationally.

some higher meaning, as Grodal assumes. Planting the feeling of possibility of Fludernik's *narrative recuperation* in the viewer, the ambiguous narrative experience and its continuous re-evaluation provide duck/rabbit-like cognitive short-circuits in our challenged plot-mapping processes. Or, with a probably better example, the cognitive situation is somewhat similar to one's confrontation with the *Müller-Lyer illusion*: Even if we know (measure or learn) that the illusion's drawn lines are similar in their length, yet our eyes try continuously convincing us that one of the arrows is shorter.[21]

Similarly, even if the viewer knows precisely that *riddle films'* confronting narrative paths form a paradox, our embodied brain, searching for a rational plot-trajectory, repeatedly inspires us to create a coherent narrative. Quoting Christopher Smith, director of Triangle: "[T]he viewer always applies rational thought to the irrational".[22] The appeal of these films lies precisely in their maintained lure of imposing a clearly impossible yet still inviting challenge of solving their clearly unsolvable riddles. While *riddle films'* confusingly complex storyworlds and plot trajectories may be resolved by inventive interpretations, and hence they could be merely labelled as examples of *art-cinema narratives*, one gets better understanding of their evoked experience and trending attractiveness by analysing their playfulness related to, and actually with, embodied-cognitive skills of orientation and navigation.

Bibliography

Alber, Jan (2009): Impossible Storyworlds – and What to Do with Them. In: *StoryWorlds: A Journal of Narrative Studies* 1, 79–96.
Aristotle (1987): *Poetics*. Indianapolis: Hackett Publishing.
Bordwell, David (1985): *Narration in the Fiction Film*. Madison: The University of Wisconsin Press.

---

21 | At first guess, in Grodal's PECMA model this cognitive 'short-circuit' must happen somewhere between the *Association cortex* and the *Prefrontal cortex*, under the feedback-control of the *Somatosensory cortex*. Neurocinematic research on the experience of narrative ambiguity could support this assumption. The frustrated, still prevailing narrative drive, opposing Grodal's disembodied explanation, is based on deviant, but still real-life bodily statuses. Further empirical research on the connections between deviant bodily experiences (out-of-body experiences and other dysfunctional proprioceptions), and challenged efforts of laying down reasonable narrative trajectories is required.

22 | We may add that the viewer does this, especially if a classical narrative genre, here a horror, encourages him or her to do so.

Bordwell, David (2002a): Film Futures. In: *SubStance*, Issue 97, Vol. 31, No. 1, 88–104.
Bordwell, David (2002b): Intensified Continuity: Visual Style in Contemporary American Film. In: *Film Quarterly*, Vol. 55, No. 3, 16–28.
Bordwell, David (2006): *The Way Hollywood Tells It*. Berkeley/Los Angeles: University of California Press.
Bordwell, David (2008): *Poetics of Cinema*. London/New York: Routledge.
Bordwell, David (2011): *Common Sense + Film Theory = Common-Sense Film Theory?* Web. Retrieved from: [http://www.davidbordwell.net/essays/common sense.php]; posted: 2011/05; access: 2012/10/10.
Bordwell, David (2012): *TINKER TAILOR: A guide for the perplexed*. Web. Retrieved from: [http://www.davidbordwell.net/blog/2012/01/23/tinker-tailor-a-guide-for-the-perplexed/]; posted: 2012/01/23; access: 2012/10/10.
Bordwell, David/Thompson, Kristin (2008 [1979]): *Film Art. An Introduction*. 8th edition. New York: McGraw-Hill.
Bordwell, David/Staiger, Janet/Thompson, Kristin (1985): *The Classical Hollywood Cinema*. New York: Columbia University Press.
Branigan, Edward (2002): Nearly True: Forking Plots, Forking Interpretations: A Response to David Bordwell's "Film Futures". In: *SubStance*, Issue 97, Vol. 31, No. 1, 105–114.
Buckland, Warren (2003): Orientation in Film Space: A Cognitive Semiotic Approach. In: *Recherches en communication*, No. 19, 87–102.
Buckland, Warren (2009): *Puzzle Films: Complex Storytelling in Contemporary Cinema*. Oxford: Wiley-Blackwell.
Cameron, Allan (2008): *Modular Narratives in Contemporary Cinema*. Houndmills/ Basingstoke: Palgrave Macmillan.
Culler, Jonathan (1975): *Structuralist Poetics*. London/New York: Routledge.
Currie, Gregory (1995): *Image and Mind: Film, Philosophy, and Cognitive Science*. New York: Cambridge University Press.
Cutting, James E. (2007 [2005]): Perceiving Scenes in Film and in the World. In: Anderson, Joseph D./Fisher Anderson, Barbara (eds.): *Moving Image Theory. Ecological Considerations*. Carbondale: Southern Illinois University Press, 9–27.
Elliott, Paul (2010): The Eye, the Brain, the Screen: What Neuroscience Can Teach Film Theory. In: *Excursions*, Issue 1, Vol. 1, 1–16.
Elsaesser, Thomas (2009): The Mind-Game Film. In: Buckland, Warren 2009, 13–41.
Elsaesser, Thomas/Buckland, Warren (eds.) (2002): *Studying Contemporary American Film*. London: Arnold.
Eysenck, Michael W./Keane, Mark (2005): *Cognitive Psychology. A Student's Handbook*. 5th edition. Hove: Psychology Press Ltd.

Fauconnier, Gilles/Turner, Mark (2002): *The Way We Think: Conceptual Blending and the Mind's Hidden Complexities.* New York: Basic Books.
Fludernik, Monika (1996): *Towards a 'Natural' Narratology.* London/New York: Routledge.
Gallese, Vittorio/Lakoff, George (2005): The Brain's Concepts: The Role of the Sensory-Motor System in Conceptual Knowledge. In: *Cognitive Neuropsychology*, Vol. 21. Web. Retrieved from: [http://www2.unipr.it/~gallese/PCGNSIOBA9.pdf]; access: 2012/10/10.
Garbarini, Francesca/Adenzato, Mauro (2004): At the Root of Embodied Cognition: Cognitive Science Meets Neurophysiology. In: *Brain and Cognition*, No. 56, 100–106.
Grodal, Torben (2002 [1997]): *Moving Pictures. A New Theory of Film Genres, Feelings, and Cognition.* New York: Oxford University Press.
Grodal, Torben (2009): *Embodied Visions. Evolution, Emotion, Culture, and Film.* New York: Oxford University Press.
Heft, Harry (1996): The Ecological Approach to Navigation: A Gibsonian Perspective. In: Portugali 1996, 105–132.
Jacobs, Steven (2007): *The Wrong House: The Architecture of Alfred Hitchcock.* Rotterdam: 010 Publishers.
Johnson, Mark (1990 [1987]): *The Body in the Mind. The Bodily Basis of Meaning, Imagination, and Reason.* Chicago/London: University of Chicago Press.
Johnson, Steven (2006 [2005]): *Everything Bad is Good for You.* London: Penguin Books.
Lakoff, George (1987): *Women, Fire, and Dangerous Things.* Chicago/London: University of Chicago Press.
Menary, Richard (2008): Embodied Narratives. *Journal of Consciousness Studies*, Vol. 15, No. 6, 63–84.
Mittell, Jason (2009): Sites of Participation: Wiki Fandom and the Case of Lostpedia. In: *Transformative Works and Culture*, No. 3. Web. Retrieved from: [http://journal.transformativeworks.org/index.php/twc/article/view/118/117]; access: 2012/10/10.
Morrow, Daniel G./Bower, Gordon H./Greenspan, Steven L. (1989): Updating Situation Models During Narrative Comprehension. In: *Journal of Memory and Language*, No. 28, 292–312.
Panek, Elliot (2006): The Poet and the Detective: Defining the Psychological Puzzle Film. In: *Film Criticism*, Vol. 31, Nos. 1-2, 62–88.
Portugali, Juval (ed.) (1996): *The Construction of Cognitive Maps.* Dordrecht/Boston/London: Kluwer Academic Publishers.
Ramírez Berg, Charles (2006): A Taxonomy of Alternative Plots in Recent Films: Classifying the 'Tarantino Effect'. In: *Film Criticism*, Vol. 31, Nos. 1-2, 5–61.

Ryan, Marie-Laure (2011): Narrative/Science Entanglements: On the Thousand and One Literary Lives of Schrödinger's Cat. In: *Narrative*, Vol. 19, No. 2, 171–186.
Sholl, Jeanne M. (1996): From Visual Information to Cognitive Maps. In: Portugali 1996, 157–186.
Simons, Jan (2008): Complex Narratives. In: *New Review of Film and Television Studies*, Vol. 6, No. 2, 111–126.
Slors, Marc (1998): Two Concepts of Psychological Continuity. In: *Philosophical Explorations*, Vol. 1, No. 1, 61–80.
Staiger, Janet (2006): Complex Narratives, An Introduction. In: *Film Criticism* 31/1-2, 2-4.
Stockwell, Peter (2002): *Cognitive Poetics: An Introduction*. London: Routledge.
Thompson, Kristin (2001 [1999]): *Storytelling in the New Hollywood*. Cambridge (MA): Harvard University Press.
Tolman, Edward C. (1948): Cognitive Maps in Rats and Men. In: *The Psychological Review*, Vol. 55, No. 4, 189–208.
Tsur, Reuven (2008): *Toward a Theory of Cognitive Poetics*. Brighton and Portland: Sussex Academic Press.
Wyatt, Justin (1994): *High Concept: Movies and Marketing in Hollywood*. Austin: University of Texas Press.
Young, Kay (2002): "The Fabric of Times": A Response to David Bordwell's "Film Futures". In: *SubStance*, Issue 97, Vol. 31, No. 1, 115–118.

Films

CHASING SLEEP (Canada/USA/France 2000, Michael Walker)
DAIJIGA UMULE PAJINNAL (THE DAY A PIG FELL INTO A WELL, South Korea 1996, Sang-soo Hong)
DIE HARD (USA 1988, John McTiernan)
ETERNAL SUNSHINE OF THE SPOTLESS MIND (USA 2004, Michel Gondry)
FORBRYDELSENS ELEMENT (THE ELEMENT OF CRIME, Denmark 1984, Lars von Trier)
INCEPTION (USA/UK 2010, Christopher Nolan)
INLAND EMPIRE (France/Poland/USA 2006, David Lynch)
LOLA RENNT (RUN LOLA RUN, Germany 1998, Tom Tykwer)
LOS CRONOCRÍMENES (TIMECRIMES, Spain 2007, Nacho Vigalondo)
LOST HIGHWAY (France/USA 1997, David Lynch)
MEMENTO (USA 2000, Christopher Nolan)
MULHOLLAND DR. (France/USA 2001, David Lynch)
NORTH BY NORTHWEST (USA 1959, Alfred Hitchcock)
OLDEUBOI (OLDBOY, South Korea 2003, Chan-wook Park)
PULP FICTION (USA 1994, Quentin Tarantino)

Reservoir Dogs (USA 1992, Quentin Tarantino)
The Wizard of Oz (USA 1939, Victor Fleming et. al.)
Tinker Tailor Soldier Spy (France/UK/Germany 2011, Tomas Alfredson)
Triangle (UK/Australia 2009, Christopher Smith)
Suzhou he (Suzhou River, Germany/China 2000, Ye Lou)

Image Sources

Figure 1a: Heft 1996, 118.
Figure 1b: Bordwell/Thompson 2008 [1979], 69.

Leaving the Narrative Maze
The Plot Twist as a Device of Re-orientation

BERND LEIENDECKER

In the last two decades, an entire wave of a certain type of film has hit the cinemas. At first, those films appear to tell a rather straightforward story, only to pull out the rug from underneath the audience by introducing a surprising turn of events later on. As it turns out, the audience has been led into a narrative maze or in other words it has been intentionally disoriented, usually without even realising it. However, if there is a way into a narrative maze, there also is a way out most of the time. In the case of such films, which have been discussed under terms ranging from "puzzle films" (Buckland 2009b) and "twist films" (Lavik 2006) to "unreliable narration" (Laass 2008) and "mind-game films" (Elsaesser 2009), this way out is often called a plot twist.

Most research on plot twists has focused on the consequences of a twist rather than the actual twist. In contrast, the purpose of this article is to analyse the twist itself. After defining the term plot twist, the focus will be on two things: a historiography of some of the most common twists and an analysis of their aesthetics.

DEFINITION

Before any meaningful analysis of the plot twist can be conducted, an appropriate definition of the term is in order, including a brief survey of the preceding research on the topic. It seems logical to start any attempt of a definition with the distinction of story (or *fabula*) and plot (or *syuzhet*). According to David Bordwell (1985, 37ff./49f.), the story is an imaginary construct created by the viewer, who organises the events of a given film in a temporally ordered chain of cause and effect. However, this requires an effort by the viewer because the events usually are not presented that way. The actual arrangement and presentation of story events within the film is called plot and may differ very significantly from the story itself. The viewer has to actively piece together the story chain by generating hypotheses about it during the film. These hypotheses may, of course, turn out to be true or false. If one of them turns out to be false, it is discarded and eventually replaced by a new one. Bordwell goes on to put plot in relation to style, a film's systematic use of cinematic devices, but in order to define the term plot twist, the distinction between story and plot will suffice.

Bordwell also acknowledges that "a film may contain cues and structures that encourage the viewers to make errors of comprehension; in such cases the film 'wants' a short- or long term 'misunderstanding'" (ibid., 39). Erlend Lavik elaborates on the narrative structure behind this effect:

"Here we find [a] kind of 'doubling' of the syuzhet, where we are led to construct a fabula that initially seems quite straightforward until suddenly a new piece of information is introduced that subverts (or decenters) the fictional world we have created. We come to realize the presence of another fabula running parallel to the first one, but 'beneath' it, hidden from view. Once we become aware of it, though, everything in the syuzhet takes on new meaning." (Lavik 2006, 56)

In accordance with Lavik's terms, the plot twist[1] can be defined as the moment a new piece of plot information is introduced because of which the audience realises the presence of another story beneath the initially constructed one. This leads to the first story being discarded and replaced by the second, initially hidden one. While Lavik might exaggerate a little by claiming that everything in the plot takes on new meaning, it is safe to say that crucial plot information has to be re-evaluated and takes on a new meaning as a result of the plot twist.

A rather critical point seems to be the timing of a plot twist. Lavik as well as Wilson use a temporal qualification in their description of twists. Lavik (2006, 61) separates *microtwists* from *proper twists*.[2] A *proper twist* is placed at a mandatory point in the story[3], i.e. towards the end of a film, while a *microtwist* is not and can cover only a rather small misunderstanding that is cleared up shortly afterwards. Wilson (2006, 89) argues along similar lines by insisting that a twist

---

1 | Upon closer scrutiny, the term ‚plot twist' might be a little misleading. It is not the plot that is twisted by anything and the idea that the plot itself would be able to twist something implies a kind of agency on the part of the plot that is quite problematic. In reaction to this problem, some other terms are in use. Erlend Lavik simply uses the term ‚twist' while others have coined the term ‚epistemological twist' (Wilson 2006, 81; Hartmann 2007, 48ff.). However, one can also argue that the twist is caused by a careful selection and organisation of plot information, so that the twist is definitely related to the plot in some way and the term plot twist is justified.

2 | Lavik uses quotation marks for the terms *microtwist* and *proper twist*, probably in order to indicate the rather colloquial nature of his terms. In the context of this article, both terms will be used in italics to facilitate reading.

can only occur towards the end of a film. Neither Lavik nor Wilson elaborates on how far a twist can be removed from the ending of a film in order to qualify as a *proper twist*. However, it is doubtful that any precise indication would be really helpful and one might be tempted to stick to Wilsons assertion that a twist must clarify global aspects of the epistemic structure of the narration. Given that the time that the audience is misled is usually either really small or spanning almost the entire film, only few examples are really problematic. A BEAUTIFUL MIND (USA 2001, Ron Howard) is one of those examples. Here, the surprise revelation occurs around the halfway point of the film and while it does affect global aspects of what has been shown thus far, it is separated from the end credits by roughly another hour of screen time. The film is not mentioned in the articles by Lavik and Wilson, but it remains unclear if this is a coincidence or if both authors consider the twist too early to qualify as a *proper twist*. While A BEAUTIFUL MIND should be considered a *proper twist* in my opinion due to its impact on the global plot, the main merit of discussing the few problematic examples might just be to show the limitations of a binary categorisation of plot twists based on time.

Regardless of the uncertainty about how far a plot twist may be removed from the ending, it seems logical that a plot twist is most effective near the end of a film. On the one hand, this is because the feat of masking the actual story is more impressive the longer it is upheld and on the other hand, the last part of a film is very important for marketing purposes. Fritz Iversen gives out important advice to independent film-makers that is easily applicable on any kind of film:

"In general, the last fifteen minutes seem to be of great importance for building an effective network of word of mouth. The ending is the most important moment because it is the last impression one gets before leaving the cinema and because it is an especially important topic for the discussion of a film [...]. An emotional culmination, a punchline or a surprising resolution contributes decisively to the audience leaving the cinema with a feeling of satisfaction." (Iversen 2005, 190; transl. B.L.)[4]

---

3 | Lavik uses the Russian terms *fabula* and *syuzhet* instead of story and plot, so his use of the word 'story' at this particular point in his text does not necessarily imply Bordwell's concept of *fabula*/story.

4 | Original citation: "Generell scheint die letzte Viertelstunde von großer Bedeutung für das Zustandekommen eines leistungsfähigen Mundpropaganda-Netzwerks zu sein. Das Ende ist schon deshalb der wichtigste Moment, weil es der letzte Eindruck ist, den man vor dem Verlassen des Kinos bekommt, und weil es ein besonders wichtiges Thema beim Reden über einen Film darstellt [...]. Eine emotionale Zuspitzung, eine Pointe, eine überraschende Auflösung trägt entscheidend dazu bei, dass die Zuschauer mit einem Gefühl der Zufriedenheit das Kino verlassen" (Iversen 2005, 190).

In the age of DVDs and other media that enable the audience to watch a given film again whenever they want to, an effective plot twist might not only lead to members of the audience recommending the film to other people who have not seen it yet and who will thus spend money on seeing it. Those members of the audience might also feel the desire to spend more money on the film themselves, most often by buying the DVD. This is particularly true for complicated plot twists which encourage the audience to check if the 'new', definitive version of the story holds up during a second viewing or if the plot twist turns out to be a cheap trick.[5] Lavik (2006, 60) also sees the DVD as a factor in the new wave of twist films, but he rightfully points out that the starting point of this wave might be placed in a time where the videotape was still the dominating medium for re-watching a film.[6]

The emergence of storage and/or recording media is not the only reason that is cited for the recent prevalence of plot twist films. Wilson (2006, 93) is certain that copycatting of successful films has contributed to this trend as well and he also deems it possible that "some kind of postmodern skepticism about the duplicity of reality and the photographic image has drifted over Hollywood" (ibid.). Whatever the reasons behind a plot twist are, the fact that their amount has increased significantly within the last two decades does not mean that there have not been any predecessors throughout film history. Both Wilson (2006, 81) and Lavik (2006, 59) cite DAS CABINET DES DR. CALIGARI (THE CABINET OF DR. CALIGARI, Germany 1920, Robert Wiene) as an early example for a film with a plot twist and THE AVENGING CONSCIENCE: OR 'THOU SHALT NOT KILL' (USA 1914, D.W. Griffith) certainly is another one. A historical survey of some of the most common or most famous narrative mazes and the ensuing plot twists will reveal further examples. While it is acknowledged that there are others, the following analysis is limited to plot twists that are the result of sharing the subjectively distorted perspective of a character, as these kinds of plot twists have been particularly prevalent in the new wave of plot twist films.

---

5 | A similar encouragement of multiple viewings has also been noted with respect to TV's narrative complexity. Steven Johnson (2005, 88) notes that episodes of narratively complex TV series often become more entertaining during a second or third viewing, while Jason Mittell (2006, 31) points out that there is a trend towards maximising the "rewatchability" of contemporary programmes.

6 | Most texts on plot twists, unreliable narration, and other related phenomena see the 1990s as the vague starting point of the wave. However, there is no consensus on when exactly the starting point was and it is unlikely that a consensual starting point can be established as there is no single film that can be said to 'have started it all'.

Narrative Mazes: Categorisation and History

As it turns out, a given plot twist very often is not unique in its premise and execution, which means that many narrative mazes resemble one another. In accordance with Wilson's assumption of a certain amount of copycatting, one can find a relatively limited number of categories for those mazes. Films of a given category share certain characteristics and some of the categories have undergone distinct changes during the course of film history. Four of the most common narrative mazes will form the core of this historical survey: the *retroactive mode of dream representation*, the *lying flashback*, the *unconscious death*, and the *concealed split personality*.

Given its status as probably the earliest (and probably the most common) type of plot twist in film history, the *retroactive mode of dream representation* is the first plot twist to be looked into. Usually, there are certain indicators for the audience for the transition between the diegetic reality and a character's dream. These may include a shot of a character sleeping or falling asleep before the start of the dream, a cross-fade marking the transition from the diegetic reality to the dream, or effects like slow motion or a different colour scheme of the film image during the dream. Further dream markers can be the use of echo sound effects or a certain kind of accompanying music, for example harps or strings. Content can also be a factor if the action within a dream defies well-established laws of the diegetic reality like logic or physics. A more complete list of possible indicators for a dream can be found in the book *Traumbühne Kino* by Matthias Brütsch (2011, 130ff.), from which the aforementioned examples have been taken.

If a film lacks a sufficient amount of indicators for a dream[7] and thus the dream can only be identified retrospectively, this can be called the *retroactive mode of dream representation*—a term coined by Robert T. Eberwein (1985, 141) and also used by Brütsch (2011, 182). The first feature film to use this plot twist was the already mentioned THE AVENGING CONSCIENCE: OR 'THOU SHALT NOT KILL', but it can be found already in the short film LET ME DREAM AGAIN (UK 1900, George Albert Smith) as well. While the plot twist itself is not very spectacular, it does offer two rather interesting options. On the one hand, the usual laws of causality and even laws of nature don't have to apply as strictly in a dream as mentioned above. Whether the characters have to fight a giant octopus in the film SH! THE OCTOPUS (USA 1937, William C. McGann) or whether a young girl encounters a plethora of fairytale creatures in ALICE IN WONDERLAND (USA 1951, Clyde Geronimi/Wilfred Jackson/Hamilton Luske), once it has been revealed that parts of the film have just been a dream, every illogical, wondrous or far-fetched event can be explained.

---

7 | Note that some indicators may still be present, but if they are, they are not strong enough.

On the other hand, the *retroactive mode of dream representation* presents the opportunity to explore "what if"-scenarios. Sometimes, those scenarios remain on a rather general level, for example the dream in DANS LA NUIT (France 1929, Charles Varnel), which shows what would happen to a young couple if the husband suffered a disfiguring accident, or the dream in WENN D'FRAUE WÄHLE (Switzerland 1958, Umberto Bolzi/Ludy Kessler/Megge Lehmann), which explores the terrible—according to the film—consequences of giving Swiss women the right to vote. More often, however, those dreams offer the dreamer an opportunity to act out his desires or fantasies in a safe environment. He can start an affair with a beautiful and mysterious woman in THE WOMAN IN THE WINDOW (USA 1944, Fritz Lang) or he can decide not to join the American World War II effort in STRANGE HOLIDAY (USA 1945, Arch Oboler). He can even decide to murder his uncle, who is standing between him and the woman he loves, in THE AVENGING CONSCIENCE: OR 'THOU SHALT NOT KILL'. As the protagonist realises that his actions have terrible consequences, he wakes up. Relieved that it was all a dream, he can now take a different action in real life in order to avoid the negative outcome of his dream.

It is no coincidence that all the examples are rather old. In recent years the *retroactive mode of dream representation* has evolved from a global strategy to a *microtwist*. Most of the time dreams of a very short duration are used to provide jokes or shock effects. Nevertheless, there still are a few examples of dreams that are almost as long as the film or the episode of a TV series they are in. While rare cases still use the classic approach— e.g. NORTH (USA 1994, Rob Reiner), which explores what would happen if a young boy would actually go through with his plan to run away from home—most global occurrences of the *retroactive mode of dream representation* today are a parody of the trope. For example, an episode of the TV series DARKWING DUCK (USA 1991–1992, ABC) called DEAD DUCK (S1/E47) has the protagonist dreaming about his death. When he wakes up, he exclaims: "Wait. You're telling me I went through all that mental anguish over a dream? What a cheat!" A similar approach can be found in the film PSYCHO BEACH PARTY (Australia/USA 2000, Robert Lee King), which reveals that most of the action was a dream which in turn was shown in a film within the film. One of the cinema patrons voices his disappointment by saying "So it was all in her dream? What a jipp!" Both quotes mirror the possible audience reaction to the revelation that most of what they have seen is only a dream. Brütsch (2011, 202f.) quotes several articles that already criticise such a plot twist in the times of the classical Hollywood cinema and especially when compared to other more complex twists the *retroactive mode of dream representation* may seem like a cheap trick. Consequently, the 'safest' way to use the retroactive mode nowadays is by poking fun at it at the same time.

Another important plot twist that is deeply rooted in film history is the *lying flashback* as used for the first time in DAS CABINET DES DR. CALIGARI. This plot twist reveals that a flashback that has been triggered by the narration or the memories of a character within the film did not represent the truth. Instead, it was based on a conscious lie by the narrating character or his misperception of past events. In general the *lying flashback* is rather short, but the extent of the lie varies significantly from small details or omissions to completely fabricated statements without an ounce of truth. There are only three common reasons to cause a *lying flashback*, namely crime, madness, or love. Crime is probably the most obvious reason: Films that feature crime investigations can rely on flashbacks to visualise witness statements and of course there are reasons for a witness to lie—the most obvious one being that the witness is in fact the perpetrator of the crime. Unreliable flashbacks out of love work in a different way because the person whose memories are represented usually is not lying consciously. He is simply blinded by his feelings and suffers from a distorted perspective on the events surrounding his beloved one. Finally, madness seems to be quite similar to love in the sense that the source of the flashback is not lying consciously, but telling what he considers the truth. However, his madness alters his view of the action significantly, so that the flashback does not show what really happened at all.

The main similarity between the two plot twists that have been presented up to this point is that the twist itself is rather easy to process. The audience simply has to accept that parts of the plot information were not true in the sense that in contrast to the first impression, they did not present facts about the diegetic reality at all. However, there is another group of twists in which no part of the plot is discarded as entirely false. Instead, at least a part of the plot has been carefully constructed to present a subjectively distorted version of the truth. In hindsight, scenes appear in a new light, but what was shown before never was a complete fabrication.

One of the more famous plot twists that fits this category at least partly may be dubbed the *unconscious death*. In this variation, it turns out that at least one important character has already died without him or the audience actually realising this fact. This plot twist can be traced back to several examples in literature (Habibi 2002, 85) and, limited to the medium film, to the short film THE BRIDGE (USA 1929, Charles Vidor).

In these films, the character's death is caused by a trigger event—usually a car crash or a murder—early in the story while the plot twist that reveals this fact usually takes place near the end of the story. With few exceptions (e.g. SIESTA (USA 1987, Mary Lambert), THE ESCAPIST (UK/Ireland 2008, Rupert Wyatt)), there is no notable difference between story order and plot order, so the trigger event is also presented early in the plot. However, the event itself and/or its consequences are not represented truthfully. Instead, three variations are possible. Firstly, the character may imagine his survival in a "liminal, distended time flashforward" (ibid.). Secondly, the character may continue its existence in a realm between life and death that is somewhat linked to the diegetic reality and can at first not be told apart from it. And finally, the character may continue his existence in the diegetic reality as a ghost. While the first two variations of this plot twist have a lot in common with the earlier twists in the sense that most of what has been shown can be discarded as not real, a continued existence as a ghost means that the events that are shown before the plot twist are actually true at least to some extent. This means that the presentation of plot events has to be constructed very carefully: The ghost cannot interact with normal human beings, only with other ghosts or psychics, who have the ability to see ghosts. The lack of interaction with other characters can be difficult to conceal, which probably is the reason for the ghost variation of this plot twist being rather rare. Its most famous and most successful example is THE SIXTH SENSE (USA 1999, M. Night Shyamalan), in which child psychologist Malcolm Crowe lives on as a ghost. After the enormous box office success of the film, a lot of films tried to duplicate its success (and consequently its plot twist) with rather mixed results. Most of the ensuing films chose a car crash as the trigger event thereby throwing their characters in a realm between life and death. This enabled them to avoid the complexities of the ghost variation, but the lack of innovation probably led to the plot twist growing predictable and somewhat dull.

In contrast to the variations that have already been described, the last type of plot twist that will be introduced here may be called the *concealed split personality*, which has been made famous by FIGHT CLUB (USA/Germany 1999, David Fincher). In this film, it turns out that the narrator Jack[8] suffers from a split personality and that his friend Tyler Durden doesn't really exist. He is just the manifestation of Jack's split personality and consequently Jack is responsible for all the actions that have been attributed to Tyler. While there are earlier examples of plot twists that reveal a character's split personality (e.g. PSYCHO (USA 1960, Alfred Hitchcock)) as well as examples of 'imaginary friends' that seem to be as real as every other person at first (e.g. TRACK 29 (UK/USA 1988, Nicolas Roeg)), FIGHT CLUB is the first film to merge both devices into an imaginary friend serving as the representation of the "other" side of a split personality. After FIGHT CLUB, the plot twist has been used in other films like A BEAUTIFUL MIND—with the aforementioned caveat that the surprise revelation occurs rather early in the film—or SECRET WINDOW (USA 2004, David Koepp).

Once again, this narrative maze has to be constructed very carefully. For every scene in which the imaginary character interacts with other persons or objects, it has to be conceivable that the person suffering from a split personality was the one who did the interacting. Furthermore, the imaginary character can only exist in the vicinity of his real counterpart and can only be seen by him. Due

---

8 | The name of the narrator is not mentioned throughout the film. However, he is called Jack in the script and to facilitate understanding, this name will be used here as well.

to these limitation, the plot twist becomes harder and harder to conceal as soon as more films follow this pattern.

Of course, this short survey of narrative mazes is not complete. Nevertheless, the four types of narrative mazes offer enough diversity to analyse the plot twists that present a way out of them in a quite representative manner. As it turns out, the complexity of the plot twist often correlates with the complexity of the maze itself.

PLOT TWISTS: CONTENT AND AESTHETICS

Of all the narrative mazes, the *retroactive mode of dream representation* probably has the easiest way out. When the action of the dream reaches its climax, for example when the hero of STRANGE HOLIDAY has been captured by the Nazis or when the protagonists of SH! THE OCTOPUS apparently die in the collapse of a lighthouse, the plot twist is introduced. In order to compensate the lack of dream indicators at the beginning of the dream and throughout its course, the end of the dream has to be signalled most clearly (Brütsch 2011, 182). Early examples usually use a cross-fade—or in rare cases a fade-out followed by a fade-in—to the dreaming character tossing and turning in his sleep before waking up. In more recent examples, the revelation is more sudden. From the 1970s on, most films—especially those who just feature the retroactive mode as a *microtwist*—signal the end of the dream through a cut to the character awakening with a start—usually to the extent that the character is sitting upright in his bed, often screaming or covered in sweat (fig. 1).

All in all, this kind of plot twist is very easy to process. The content of the dream can be discarded as not real in reference to the diegetic world and the

Figure 1: Screenshot from KEEPING THE FAITH *(USA 2000, Edward Norton).*

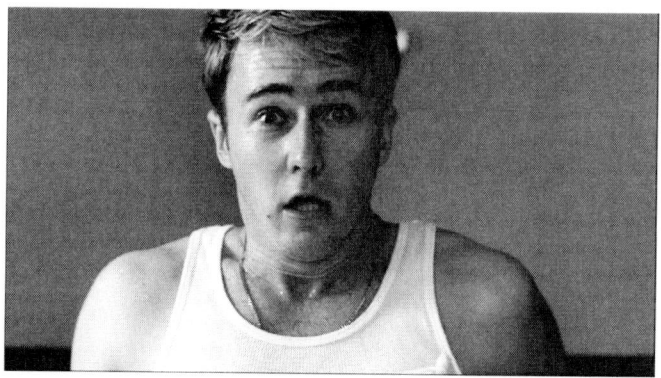

dream does not contain any ambivalent or "difficult" scenes that impede the construction of the new story. It is no problem to infer what has actually happened either. After all the character has been sleeping the whole time.

In the case of the *lying flashback*, it usually is rather easy to accommodate the new information offered by the plot twist as well. The first flashback or at least parts of it turn out to have been not true in the narrowest sense of the word. In order to correct the first flashback the plot twist usually offers a second flashback. Any contradiction between the two flashbacks is resolved by accepting the second version as true and identifying the first one as false. If there is any information in the first flashback that is not contradicted, it remains true in reference to the diegetic world. However, there are notable exceptions to this strategy of leaving the narrative maze, most importantly films whose *lying flashbacks* are almost as long as the film itself.

Evidently, there is no time for a correcting flashback of equal length in those cases. DAS CABINET DES DR. CALIGARI divulges that the flashback was just a lie by revealing that its narrator Frances is an inmate in an asylum for the insane. In short sequence, every important character from the flashback is shown to be related to the asylum as well. Most of them are other inmates who are clearly insane, but harmless, while Dr. Caligari himself is the director of the asylum. This is consistent to the flashback, but his character is not. Instead of being ruthless and insane like in the flashback, he seems calm and caring. All this leads to the conclusion that the flashback was a lie and in all likelihood, nothing Frances has narrated was true. The aesthetics of the plot twist are not really noteworthy as there aren't any particular cinematic devices used in the course of the twist. However, the expressionist set design in the flashbacks does contrast with the more realist setting of the framing narration.

A more recent version of *lying flashbacks* that almost cover the entire film can be found in THE USUAL SUSPECTS (USA 1995, Bryan Singer).[9] In the framing narration of the film, the seemingly harmless crook Verbal Kint tells the story of a failed drug deal with several casualties to Customs Inspector Kujan, who suspects that the legendary uber-criminal Keyser Soze was involved. The plot twist reveals that Kint has used names and other details that he picked up from around the room to flesh out his story. This and the fact that he has been identified by a witness as Keyser Soze himself as indicated by an identikit picture that arrives after Kint has left the police station mean that the audience has to doubt the entire content of the series of flashbacks that have been presented up to that point. However, this does not necessarily mean that everything was a lie. In other words: The audience is aware that it has been put in a narrative maze and

---

[9] | For a more thorough analysis of THE USUAL SUSPECTS and its plot twist, see Lahde 2002.

Figure 2: Screenshot from THE SIXTH SENSE.

is presented with a general idea of the way out of it. However, which route has to be taken exactly remains open for debate.

More important than the content are the aesthetics of the plot twist, which not only mark its importance, but also facilitate understanding. The plot twist is introduced by music that seems to announce that something important is going to happen. At the same time a close-up on the surprised face of Inspector Kujan, and several slow motion shots of his coffee mug falling to the ground and shattering prepare the audience for a revelation of major proportions before even the first piece of information that has been used in Verbal's story can be read. Every time another piece of information is revealed, it is accompanied either by a voice-over of its use by Verbal or by an image from the earlier flashbacks. This is important in order to make sure the audience understands what is going on because most of the details—the names of minor characters or places or persons from anecdotes Verbal tells—did not seem important for story construction when they were mentioned for the first time and the audience might have forgotten about them already. There is only one short flashback that offers new information: the flashback of Verbal firing a gun while wearing black clothes, which leads to the conclusion that he is Keyser Soze.

But what about films that do not discard most of the events preceding the plot twist as not real or at least put their veracity in serious doubt? A look at the ghost-variation of the *unconscious death* reveals that the three examples that fit this variation employ very different strategies. The film CAMPFIRE TALES (USA 1997, Matt Cooper/Martin Kunert/David Semel) places its ghostly protagonists in an empty field where they interact only with each other, so the plot twist can be processed without any problems. Alejandro Amenábar's THE OTHERS (USA/Spain/France/Italy 2001) also has few difficulties to solve. As it turns out the family whose house seems to be haunted by ghosts is in fact a family of ghosts itself unable to see or understand the presence of actual human beings in the house. On second thought, however, this doesn't change much of what has been seen up to that point—only the causal connections between the events have to be rethought. Consequently, most of the information triggering the plot twist can be delivered through character dialogue. Some shots from the perspective of the humans are added to underline that the ghosts are indeed invisible to them, but no flashbacks are necessary and neither is any other form of revisiting an earlier scene.

This is in direct contrast to THE SIXTH SENSE, which features some familiar devices also used in THE USUAL SUSPECTS. The start of the twist scene, in which the protagonist Malcolm Crowe learns that he is just a ghost, is marked by music to underline its importance. Once again, a character mimics the audience's reaction of surprise and dawning comprehension while his face is shown in close-up (fig. 2). Several key phrases from earlier dialogues are repeated in voice-over accompanied by very short flashbacks to earlier scenes that have to be reinterpreted. Lavik (2006, 56) states that these flashbacks help process the implications of the twist especially for scenes that precede it for more than an hour. However, as short as these flashbacks are, it seems rather doubtful that they are actually a big help in this respect. Instead, they might rather be interpreted as pointing out scenes that have to be revisited in detail during a second viewing rather than offering the definitive resolution of any doubts by themselves.

If two characters turn out to be manifestations of the split personality of a single person, the twist gets fairly difficult to process. After all, the imaginary character appeared to interact with his or her environment just like any other person. That's why the scene of the plot twist in FIGHT CLUB or SECRET WINDOW runs very much along the lines of THE USUAL SUSPECTS and THE SIXTH SENSE. While the portentous music, close-ups of the slowly comprehending character, and brief flashbacks which put earlier information in a new context, fill in gaps or just indicate critical scenes for a second viewing, are recurring elements, the twist is presented in a dialogue scene between the two personalities of the protagonist that clears up the most important questions. It is noteworthy that the flashbacks also provide new information: Several scenes are shown, in which the protagonist is seen doing things that were attributed to the imaginary character before—either because the imaginary character was actually shown doing these things in the first version of the events or because he was simply identified as responsible through the inferences of the audience. Once again A BEAUTIFUL MIND does not quite fit in with the other examples. Its plot twist shares some characteristics with FIGHT CLUB and SECRET WINDOW like expository dialogue or portentous music. The main difference, however, is that the plot twist occurs before the main character John Nash himself realises that he is mentally ill. Instead the film follows the comprehension process of Nash's wife and the expository dialogue does not take place between Nash and his other personalities, but between Nash's wife and a psychiatrist.

Conclusion

Although a plot twist emphasises narrative surprises, it is surprisingly easy to categorise. It appears that plot twists can be categorised by content without any serious difficulties. Most plot twists are subject to historical change, but some core elements usually remain intact throughout film history. However, in the last two decades, more complicated twists have been used, which did not really replace the older ones, but stole their spotlight in a way because they were more complex, more critically acclaimed, and more successful in generating ticket and DVD sales.

The aesthetics of a plot twist largely depend on the complexity of the twist as well, with the main question being: Does the plot twist negate most of what precedes it as not true in reference to the diegetic world or not? If the re-orientation process is simple because the events preceding the plot twist can simply be discarded as not true, the plot twist itself is short and simple as well. However, if re-orientation is more complicated, contemporary plot twists are conveyed through a longer scene which uses a rather standardised aesthetic. This may include the use of a surrogate character who goes through the same comprehension process as the audience as well as very brief flashbacks that fill in gaps or highlight key scenes that have to be reinterpreted. Further common devices are short dialogues from past scenes, which are now presented in voice-over, slow-motion effects, portentous non-diegetic music, and, of course, expository dialogue. Naturally, not every single film uses every single device on this list, but each device is prevalent enough to merit its inclusion. Although only a few examples have been analysed, a comparison with other examples reveals a remarkable consistency throughout the newest wave of plot twist films.

Apparently, these observations are even applicable to other audiovisual media like TV series to some extent. At the same time, contemporary TV seems to be a site for some innovative handling of plot twists by modifying the content, using somewhat different aesthetics, parodying established twists, or using them for different effects.[10] It remains to be seen if film can also find room for

---

10 | For example, the Fear Itself (USA 2008-2009, NBC) episode New Year's Day (S1/E06) turns the *unconscious death* into the unconscious living dead by having its main character realise that she has been a zombie all along. Scrubs (USA 2001-2010, NBC/ABC) pays its respects to The Sixth Sense in the episode My Screw Up (S3/E14), but it does not rely on the typical devices to introduce the twist, instead just showing the main characters attending the funeral of the deceased. The parody of the *retroactive mode of dream representation* in Darkwing Duck has already been mentioned and something similar can be observed in the Phineas and Ferb (USA 2007-, Disney Channel) episode Phineas and Ferb Get Busted (S1/E16), in which the characters uncover all the secrets that form the premise of the show. In the end, everything turns out to

the innovative handling of plot twists or if the wave of twists will subside because repetition of the same old tricks will turn them into stereotypes, thereby making what used to be unexpected pretty much expectable.

Bibliography

Bordwell, David (1985): *Narration in the Fiction Film*. Madison: The University of Wisconsin Press.

Brütsch, Matthias (2011): *Traumbühne Kino. Der Traum als filmtheoretische Metapher und narratives Motiv*. Marburg: Schüren.

Buckland, Warren (ed.) (2009a): *Puzzle Films: Complex Storytelling in Contemporary Cinema*. Chichester: Wiley-Blackwell.

Buckland, Warren (2009b): Introduction: Puzzle Plots. In: Buckland 2009a, 1–12.

Eberwein, Robert T. (1985): *Film & the Dream Screen. A Sleep and a Forgetting*. Princeton: Princeton University Press.

Elsaesser, Thomas (2009): The Mind-Game Film. In: Buckland 2009a, 13–41.

Habibi, Don A. (2002): The Experience of a Lifetime. Philosophical Reflections on a Narrative Device of Ambrose Bierce. In: *Studies in the Humanities*, Vol. 29, No. 2. Indiana: Indiana University of Pennsylvania, 83–108.

Hartmann, Britta (2007): Von roten Heringen und blinden Motiven: Spielarten Falscher Fährten im Film. In: Blaser, Patric et. al. (eds.): *Falsche Fährten in Film und Fernsehen*. Vienna/Cologne/Weimar: Böhlau, 33–52.

Iversen, Fritz (2005): Man sieht nur, wovon man gehört hat: Mundpropaganda und die Kinoauswertung von Independents und anderen Non-Blockbuster-Filmen. In: Hediger, Vinzenz/Vonderau, Patrick (eds.): *Demnächst in Ihrem Kino: Grundlagen der Filmwerbung und Filmvermarktung*. Marburg: Schüren, 176–192.

Johnson, Steven (2005): *Everything Bad is Good for You*. New York: Penguin Group.

Mittell, Jason (2006): Narrative complexity in Contemporary American Television. In: *The Velvet Light Trap*, No. 58, 29–40.

Laass, Eva (2008): *Broken Taboos, Subjective Truths: Forms and Functions of Unreliable Narration in Contemporary American Cinema*. Trier: Wissenschaftlicher Verlag Trier.

Lahde, Maurice (2002): Der Leibhaftige erzählt. Täuschungsmanöver in The Usual Suspects. In: *montage/av*, Vol. 11, No. 1, 149–179.

---

be a dream by the platypus Perry. Finally, How I Met Your Mother (USA 2005-, CBS) repeatedly uses plot twists for comedy purposes, especially *lying flashbacks* that are reserved for more sombre topics in film.

Lavik, Erlend (2006): Narrative Structure in The Sixth Sense: A New Twist in "Twist Movies"? In: *The Velvet Light Trap*, No. 58, 55–64.

Wilson George (2006): Transparency and Twist in Narrative Fiction Film. In: Smith, Murray/Wartenberg, Thomas E. (eds.): *Thinking Through Cinema: Film as Philosophy*. Malden/Oxford: Blackwell, 81–95.

FILMS

A BEAUTIFUL MIND (USA 2001, Ron Howard)
ALICE IN WONDERLAND (USA 1951, Clyde Geronimi/Wilfred Jackson/Hamilton Luske)
CAMPFIRE TALES (USA 1997, Matt Cooper/Martin Kunert/David Semel)
DANS LA NUIT (France 1929, Charles Varnel)
DAS CABINET DES DR. CALIGARI (THE CABINET OF DR. CALIGARI, Germany 1920, Robert Wiene)
FIGHT CLUB (USA/Germany 1999, David Fincher)
KEEPING THE FAITH (USA 2000, Edward Norton)
LET ME DREAM AGAIN (UK 1900, George Albert Smith)
NORTH (USA 1994, Rob Reiner)
PSYCHO (USA 1960, Alfred Hitchcock)
PSYCHO BEACH PARTY (Australia/USA 2000, Robert Lee King)
SECRET WINDOW (USA 2004, David Koepp)
SH! THE OCTOPUS (USA 1937, William C. McGann)
SIESTA (USA 1987, Mary Lambert)
STRANGE HOLIDAY (USA 1945, Arch Oboler)
THE AVENGING CONSCIENCE: OR 'THOU SHALT NOT KILL' (USA 1914, D.W. Griffith)
THE BRIDGE (USA 1929, Charles Vidor)
THE ESCAPIST (UK/Ireland 2008, Rupert Wyatt)
THE OTHERS (USA/Spain/France/Italy 2001, Alejandro Amenábar)
THE SIXTH SENSE (USA 1999, M. Night Shyamalan)
THE USUAL SUSPECTS (USA 1995, Bryan Singer)
THE WOMAN IN THE WINDOW (USA 1944, Fritz Lang)
TRACK 29 (UK/USA 1988, Nicolas Roeg)
WENN D'FRAUE WÄHLE (Switzerland 1958, Umberto Bolzi/Ludy Kessler/Megge Lehmann)

Television Series

Darkwing Duck (USA 1991–1992, ABC)
Fear Itself (USA 2008–2009, NBC)
How I Met Your Mother (USA 2005–, CBS)
Phineas and Ferb (USA 2007–, Disney Channel)
Scrubs (USA 2001–2010, NBC/ABC)

Image Sources

Figure 1: Screenshot from Keeping the Faith (USA 2000). DVD-Source: MAWA Film & Medien/Touchstone Pictures/VCL Communications.
Figure 2: Screenshot from The Sixth Sense (USA 1999). DVD-Source: Constantin Film AG.

Temporality

Twisted Times
Non-linearity and Temporal Disorientation in Contemporary Cinema

JULIA ECKEL

Orientation and disorientation are usually considered as spatial phenomena. Tracing the origins of the verb 'to orient', this attribution seems to be adequate because when the term was primarily used in 18th century France it described the alignment of maps towards the East (see e.g. Bogen 2010, 268f.)—an activity which is related to space in three respects: first by the factual, spatial movement of the map (on a table or in one's hands), second by its alignment towards a specific point in space (the Orient), and third by the map itself as a device of determining one's position in and movement through space. This close connection to the map and the spatial idea it embodies finally results in an expansion of the meaning of 'orientation': By and by the term signifies not only the movement *of* the map, but the movement *on* the map as well (ibid.). And even if 'orientation' nowadays can be used in a broader sense and as a synonym for nearly every type of navigation, localisation, direction, or alignment, for cognitive processes of way-finding, familiarisation, or even as its oppositional collocation 'disorientation', the spatial implications of the term normally prevail. 'Where am I?' therefore is the dominant question while dealing with the definition of (dis)orientation (Rüetschi 2010, 258).

But how can temporal forms of orientation and disorientation be described? What about the question 'When am I?'? Even if this phrase sounds strange or unfamiliar at first, it is this strangeness that makes phenomena of (dis)orientation in time particularly interesting for a closer examination.

TEMPORAL (DIS)ORIENTATION

One reason for the fact that the dimension of time only plays a minor or dispensable role in texts about (dis)orientation may be that the three-dimensionality of space requires a specific localisation via three coordinates. The manifold selectable values of X, Y, and Z thereby imply a certain risk to miss the right point or location in space—in other words: to become lost or disoriented. In contrast, our conception of the chronology of time does not offer such a plurality of options and therefore does not allow for detours, branches, or other movements, which exceed the exclusive one-dimensionality of time. Of course, temporality is imaginable as a time bar or arrow and therefore seems to offer a two-dimensionality of different points in time. But these theoretical constructs are only spatial metaphors that try to comprehend a phenomenon that is only perceptible via the unstoppable progression of the present 'now'. *Time*—so to say—leaves no *space* for a self-determined movement.

According to these assumptions, experiences of timelessness or time loss—and therefore the perception of temporal disorientation—are exceptions, which are normally ascribed to psycho-pathological symptoms and disorders (e.g. brain damages, dementia)[1], to mentally exceptional circumstances (e.g. torture (Kockot 2010, 128ff.)), or to scientific concepts of quantum physics and the theory of relativity.

As the loss, absence, or free accessibility of time therefore is no part of everyday life experience, it implies a fascination that makes it seemingly appealing for all kinds of fictional arts—especially for the genre of Science Fiction. Mostly common are stories about time travels (e.g. BACK TO THE FUTURE (USA 1985, Robert Zemeckis) or BILL & TED'S EXCELLENT ADVENTURE (USA 1989, Stephen Herek)), which generally demonstrate the problems that are provoked by disorientation in the temporal sphere: for example being sent to the wrong epoch by your time machine or meeting your past or future self.

Thus, narrations—be they Science Fiction or otherwise fictional—appear to be the only (imaginary) realms of experience that allow for a controlled and non-pathological observation of or exposure to temporal disorientation.

---

1 | Psychology normally differentiates between the pathological symptoms of temporal, spatial, and personal disorientation (Berrios 1983, 379f.), whereby these three types of mental confusions are organised in a hierarchy: Disorientations in time usually appear before disorientations in space, while confusions concerning the own personality are the last and worst condition (Scharfetter 2010, 117) (thanks to Andreas Weich for these hints). Temporal disorientation in these respects somehow seems to be less therapeutically relevant, perhaps because it is only noteworthy on a more abstract level: While a patient with spatial disorientations may concretely get lost in his environment or while he and his family may suffer extremely from the loss of his personality and history in the case of personal disorientation, temporal confusions only affect a mental judgement of an abstract dimension that does not allow for really and practically losing your way in it.

Time and Film

This article, however, will not focus on temporally disorienting narrations in general, but more specifically on their occurrence in film, because it seems that the flowing audiovisuality of moving images features a special connection to issues of temporality. The filmic experience is strongly bonded to the clocked progression of images in time, because without it film would only be a series of stills/photographs and thereby no film at all.

Of course, one could object that narration as such is basically dependent on creating ideas of action occurring over time and in space—and thus both are playing an important role in other narrative media, too (as for example in literature or comic strips). But film nevertheless appears to show a somehow closer connection to our everyday experience of temporality, because it consistently follows the same progression of time that we do and normally leaves no opportunity for us to stop, reverse, or repeat it without disturbing the filmic experience.[2] The time of literature or other non-moving narrative arts is subordinated to the reading speed and subjective temporal imagination of the reader, while with film the viewer and the medium itself seem to be subordinated to the progression of an external, objective clocking of time. In this respect, film can be defined as a *medium of time* par excellence—a thesis that is for example shared by authors like André Bazin, who strongly emphasises the ability of film to produce images of the duration of things by mummifying change (Bazin 1960)[3], or by Gilles Deleuze, who considers film to be a tool for philosophical thinking about time (Deleuze 1989).[4]

---

2 | This is of course one of the main aspects that is interesting about non-linear film narrations, because they create the impression of a skipped, twisted, repeated, reversed, or randomised time, while classical film narrations try to hide the fact that they manipulate temporality as well, e.g. by using techniques of continuity editing or established forms of orienting hints (for example caption insertions or the fast motion of the hands of a clock etc.).

3 | See Bazins text about *The Ontology of the Photographic Image*: "Now, for the first time, the image of things is likewise the image of their duration, change mummified as it were" (Bazin 1960, 8).

4 | See Gilles Deleuze's book *Cinema 2: The Time-Image* (1989, xii): "[...] the whole aim of this book is to release those [temporal structures] that the cinematographic image has been able to grasp and reveal, and which can echo the teachings of science, what the other arts uncover for us, or what philosophy makes understandable for us, each in their respective ways. [...] cinema is still at the beginning of its investigations: making visible these relationships of time which can only appear in a creation of the image".

But the fact that film is only thinkable and perceivable in time and that it can only extend and unfold across time is only one aspect that constitutes its special temporality. This formal feature is accompanied by the filmic ability to (re)produce time and thereby to include it as a theme and topic. That means that film firstly records past time by successively storing it via images and sounds, that it secondly creates time through the editing of the material, and that it thirdly reproduces this past or artificially created time in the new/present temporal context of the projection. Thus, in its technical, material, and ontological entity, film is inevitably subordinated to the linearity of time, but by choice of its contents it allows for temporal restructuring. This unique interplay (between the linearity of its manifestation and the possible timelessness of its content) enables film to provide instantaneous, audiovisually perceptible, temporal disorientation. But how are these cinematic confusions of time created in practice?

Temporal Non-linearity in Contemporary Cinema

The last two decades of independent as well as mainstream cinema in particular provide us with a full array of films that create temporal[5] disorientations or—as I would call it—temporal non-linearity. The term 'non-linearity' may of course include other types of narrative aberrations, too (for example disturbances in the spatial or causal composition of a film), because surely all three domains—time, space, and causality[6]—do contribute to every effect of narrative non-linearity. In fact, disruptions in the temporality of the narrated cosmos or plot, for example, can only be noticed by spatial changes or non-causalities of action. But because the main topic of the given considerations is the question of temporal disorientation, the focus and centre of attraction of the following shall explicitly be *temporal non-linearity*.[7] With this term, I comprehend narrations that are characterised by a discrepancy between the plot composition and order compared

---

5 | And not only temporal disorientations, of course: For other types of disorienting narrative effects, see the further contributions of the *Narrative Mazes* part of this volume (e.g. the articles by Kiss, Leiendecker, Rothemund, Uhl etc.)
6 | Bordwell and Thompson "consider a narrative to be *a chain of events in cause-effect-relationship occurring in time and space*" (Bordwell/Thompson 2004, 69; original emphasis).
7 | I think the terms 'non-linearity' and 'linearity' are especially suitable for the topic of time because they imply the metaphorical two-dimensionalty of the time bar that was mentioned before. With regard to spatial or causal irritations, I would rather speak of 'incoherences' or 'inconsistencies'.

to the underlying story chronology[8], thus making it more complex, variable, or sometimes nearly impossible to (re-)chronologise the chain of story events.[9]

Temporal or otherwise confusing narrations like these are momentarily widely discussed in a considerable number of publications and under keywords like "narrative complexity" (Mittell 2006)[10], "alternative plot" and "Tarantino effect" (Ramírez Berg 2006), "mind-bender" (Johnson 2006, Thon 2009), "mind-game film" (Elsaesser 2009), "complex storytelling" and "puzzle film" (Buckland 2009) etc.[11] But generally these approaches only embed exemplary cases of temporal non-linearity into a more extensive discussion about complex narratives, thereby being a little too imprecise to fully consider and analyse non-linearity as a singular theme and feature of film narratives.

Partial exceptions are the writings of Allan Cameron (2008) and Linda Aronson (2010), both of whom centre upon temporal non-linearity and describe it as a special quality of (contemporary) film narratives. But even in these cases the boundaries of the topic of temporality are—for my intentions—either a little too blurred or diffuse or the presented categories miss some aspects.

Aronson's screenwriting guide *The 21st Century Screenplay* for example focuses on "films that use several separate narratives running in parallel, often involving non-linearity, time jumps, large casts, or all of these" (Aronson 2010, 167). These *parallel narratives* (as Aronson terms them) can be divided into two groups depending on whether they include time jumps or not—the ones without time jumps being *ensemble films*, the ones with time jumps being *non-linear films* (ibid., 171ff.). Each category is further subdivided (into *tandem* and *multiple*

---

8 | With Gerard Genette (1980, 35ff.) this narrative phenomenon could be named "anachronism" as well, but as Genette uses the term in a very broad sense, including every minimal or established form of temporal reordering (also see footnote number 9), it seems to be too extensive for the present analysis.

9 | This—so to say—hindered *(re-)chronologisability* is an important aspect because it allows to differentiate these exceptional forms of non-linearity from other, general types of a-chronology in film, like for example flashbacks and flashforwards. The particular difference is that the latter are established forms of time leaps that are normally chronologically embedded in the cause-effect chain of story and plot. The change in time is, in these cases, either marked as an episode of remembrance (a well-known example for this can be found in CASABLANCA (USA 1942, Michael Curtiz)) or as a result of a vision of the future or a premonition (e.g. in FINAL DESTINATION (USA 2000, James Wong)). Non-linear narratives, on the contrary, normally do not indicate or explain their time confusions; they even seem to willingly complicate the process of putting the events together in their right order.

10 | For further reading on this topic, see Jason Mittell's and Christine Piepiorka's contributions in this volume as well.

11 | And, of course, the publication on 'narrative mazes' at hand joins the list.

protagonist narratives on the one hand, *flashback* and *consecutive story narrative* on the other, etc.), and additionally hybrids are possible (*fractured tandem*). The problem of this approach is that it (again) mixes different types of confusing narrative patterns, not focusing on time as the central and particular criteria. Although temporality plays an important role in distinguishing the different types of narrations, it is in fact the multitude of story arcs that is the main theme and focus of Aronson here. In contrast, it is the purpose of this paper to concentrate only on the temporality patterns that these films present (may they be dependent on a multi-protagonist cast or not). That means it is not so much about general forms of fractured or disorienting narratives in a wide range (however interesting and important these discussions may be), but about time and its transgression as a key element of specific film narrations.

Allan Cameron's book on *Modular Narratives in Contemporary Cinema* nearly concurs with this aim by offering another typology of temporal extraordinary, narrative forms. He distinguishes *anachronic, forking path, episodic,* and *split-screen narratives* (Cameron 2008, 6ff.), thereby putting explicitly more emphasis on the temporal aspects of disorienting narratives. But although his elaborate analyses and theoretical considerations about time, narrative, and culture offer inspiring insights and arguments, his classification of narrative patterns seems to disregard some important cases and internal differentiations—for example by summarising reversed, fractured, or repeated plots under one headline ("anachronic") or by ignoring circular or subjective time concepts, etc.

The following section therefore proposes an alternative (or adjusted) set of categories[12] that focuses on one specific question: Which types or ideas of temporality are presented in non-linear films?

As I mentioned before, these classifications will be developed along with film examples from the 1990s to 2000s that allow for an overview of possible patterns by which temporal non-linearity in film is created.[13] This typology is open for additions itself and the boundaries between the single categories are permeable so that one film may in some respects belong to one group or the other. But I think that this neither too-wide nor too-condensed view on the topic of disorienting time narratives may contribute to or even sharpen up the theoretical discussions offered by authors like Cameron, Aronson, and others.

---

12 | An elaborate and more detailed description of this systematisation (and the topic of non-linear narratives in general) can be found in Eckel 2012.

13 | By this I do not mean to say that non-linear narrative patterns are completely innovative or unprecedented. On the contrary, there have always been experiments with cinematographic time and chronology throughout film history. Why this seems to be a renewed topic of 1990s cinema, will be the topic of the last part of this article.

Categories of Non-linearity

Reversed Time

The category I want to start with summarises films that—in a way—follow the chronology of time—but in reversed order.[14] The main and much discussed example for this type of narrative is MEMENTO (USA 2000, Christopher Nolan), which presents a short time span (approximately one to two days) in the life of protagonist Leonard Shelby who suffers from anterograde amnesia. The chronological life/story of Leonard (which he himself can only access in its full extent via notes and photographs he makes for himself) is fragmented in the plot and then rearranged in the opposite order of the chronological cause-effect-chain. Additional black-and-white sequences, showing Leonard on the telephone in a hotel room, are placed in between the reversed parts conforming to their chronological succession, but because they are shorter and less action driven than the coloured reversed parts, the dominant impression the viewer gets from the film is that it mainly inverts the chronology.

Other examples for films with reversed time are IRRÉVERSIBLE (France 2002, Gaspar Noé) or 5x2 (France 2004, François Ozon). It is quite important to note that most of these films normally do not (or only in short sequences, e.g. in the beginning of MEMENTO) actually 'move' or 'run' backwards, that is to say most of the time the plot parts as such stay linear and chronological without reversing the actual progression of the film strip itself.[15]

Multi-linear Time

Narrations with multi-linear (or forking path[16]) plots transgress our common conception of time by not reversing but splitting the time-line. Films like LOLA RENNT (RUN LOLA RUN, Germany 1998, Tom Tykwer) or PRZYPADEK (BLIND CHANCE, Poland 1981, Krzysztof Kieślowski) present parallel temporal universes that allow for different outcomes of present events. The first film mentioned, for example, tells the story of Lola, who needs to come up with 10,000DM to save her boyfriend Manni. After a short introduction to this story arc, the film presents three possible endings in which either Lola is killed, Manni is killed, or both of them survive and win 10,000DM for themselves. The spatio-temporal continuum is seemingly divided into three incompatible branches, which are presented

---

14 | For a more detailed description of this narrative phenomenon, see the article of Matthias Brütsch in this volume. An additional analysis can be found in Runge 2008.
15 | For examples of films that actually run backwards, I again refer to the contribution of Brütsch in this volume.
16 | See e.g. Bordwell 2002 and Cameron 2008.

one after another. Alternatives to this sequential linear construction of a multi-linear plot are, for example, the continuous switch between the time branches (as in SLIDING DOORS (UK/USA 1998, Peter Howitt)) or their further splitting and subdivision (as in SMOKING/NO SMOKING (France 1993, Alain Resnais)). A kind of mixture between linear and multi-linear structures is thinkable, too, as can be seen in GROUNDHOG DAY (USA 1993, Harold Ramis) or THE BUTTERFLY EFFECT (USA 2004, Eric Bress/J. Mackye Gruber): These films basically follow the conception of partially or generally split timelines, but their protagonists do know about or even intentionally visit these parallel levels, thereby remaining a kind of linear and stable factor within the repeated or multiplied universes.

Multi-perspectival Time

The category of multi-perspectival time may at first sight be confusable with the concept of multi-linearity, because both repeat and return to already seen periods of time. But while the latter presents one protagonist in different temporal universes, the multi-perspectival pattern presents different protagonists in one temporal universe. The timeline therefore is not split in itself, but multifaceted by the repetition of events from different subjective perspectives. 11:14 (USA 2003, Greg Marcks), for example, is a film about two deadly accidents taking place during one night in a small US-town, thereby connecting the characters of five different story arcs. Both accidents (a dead body falls from a bridge onto a car driving by and a young girl named Cheri is killed by a van) happen at 11:14 p.m. This point in time occurs in every single one of the five episodes—sometimes in the beginning, sometimes in the middle, sometimes at the end. Additionally, the sequences are ordered inversely, so that every following episode starts a little earlier than the one before, entailing that the initial cause for the accidents is only revealed in the end.

Although the multi-perspectival plot thus generally depends on a multitude of characters appearing in it, not every multi-protagonist film must be non-linear. Important for the attribution of temporal non-linearity is the repetition of events and/or an a-chronological succession of the plot events. Other examples, therefore, are films like RESERVOIR DOGS (USA 1992, Quentin Tarantino), Go! (USA 1999, Doug Liman) or À LA FOLIE...PAS DU TOUT (HE LOVES ME...HE LOVES ME NOT, France 2002, Laetitia Colombani).

Encapsulated Time

The next category is based on the idea of multiplied universes again, though these are not conceived as parallel timelines (as in the multi-linear plot), but as nested time levels. Illustrative for this conception of encapsulated time are films like EXISTENZ (Canada/UK 1999, David Cronenberg) and INCEPTION (UK/

USA 2010, Christopher Nolan). The latter, for example, presents the story of the so called "extractor" Cobb and his team, who are entering and manipulating the subconscious of people with artificial, shared dreams to do some industrial espionage. To accomplish their current job, Cobb's team constructs a framework of different dreams that are built into one another. The story therefore unfolds across this encapsulated dream levels, which are characterised by a special temporal proportion: Five minutes on one level (be it reality or a dream) result in approximately one hour on the subordinated level, thereby allowing for years to pass at the lowest level. At its climax, the film even contrasts these different time zones and speeds by using extreme slow-motions and other special effects that create the impression of zero gravity. But it nevertheless stays challenging to imagine the parallelism of the different times and durations at once.

A final, interesting thing about these films is that they normally present certain causes or conditions which allow for a comprehensible and explicable encapsulation of time: The most famous motif besides dreams are media—for example computer games (as in eXistenZ), or literature (as in Reconstruction (Denmark 2004, Christoffer Boe)).

Subjective/Unreliable Time

Temporal non-linearity does not only imply the unusual or confusing order of otherwise chronological events. 'Linearity' as well means the regular, consistent, and steady progression of things (be it mathematical equations and graphs or be it time). Therefore, temporal non-linearity in film may also appear when the speed or pulse of time is modified.[17] Stay (USA 2005, Marc Forster) is an example for such a non-linear inconsistency. The film tells the story of psychologist Sam Foster, who tries to prevent his patient Henry Letham (an art student who has caused a deadly car accident) from committing suicide. Only in the last minutes of the film, the viewer finds out that the whole story is a phantasm and imagination of the wounded and dying Henry, who is lying on a bridge after a car accident that just killed his parents and girlfriend. The supposed story duration of the presented events is thereby shortened to a minimum: The three or four days during which Sam tries to rescue Henry are finally reduced to approximately two minutes during which Henry perishes. Other films, which use similar schemes of temporal unsteadiness[18], are Jacob's Ladder (USA 1990, Adrian Lyne), Lulu on the Bridge (USA 1998, Paul Auster), or (to some extent) The Escapist (UK/Ireland 2008, Rupert Wyatt).

---

17 | This is the reason why not only the plot order, but the plot composition and style as well are relevant for the definition of temporal non-linearity given before.
18 | In fact, it is a story pattern that traces back to the short story *An Occurrence at Owl Creek Bridge* by Ambrose Bierce from 1890.

Again, this category could probably be confused with the concept of encapsulated time. But the decisive difference is that the group of films described before represents somehow objective time universes within time universes (games, lucid dreams etc.), which can (despite their virtuality and simulativeness) be perceived as somehow externally existing and openly accessible to more than one protagonist. Instead, the films in this category present the subjectivity of time bounded to inner processes of temporal experience, thereby putting emphasis on its subjective unreliability[19] and relativity. Time and duration are conceived as dependent on mental activities which may deceive or mislead us.

Circular Time

Temporally circular films can—in short—be defined as films that end the same way they started and vice versa. The central example for this narrative pattern is BEFORE THE RAIN (Morocco/France/UK 1994, Milcho Manchevski), which consists of three at first seemingly separate but finally connected episodes that deal with the topic of violence caused by conflicts between ethnic and religious majorities and minorities in Macedonia. The film starts with an episode about a young orthodox monk who hides an Albanian girl (who is killed later on) in his monastery, while the last episode shows why and how the girl arrived there. The second episode in between these two is located in London and deals with a young woman who wants to leave the country to live with her boyfriend—a Macedonian war photographer. This photographer is the main protagonist of the third episode, in which he rescues the Albanian girl so that she can run away to the monastery.

At first sight, the last episode of the film thus precedes the first one while the second episode needs to remain after the first one (as there are photos of the dead Albanian girl appearing in it). But there are additional cues and hints that make it possible or even necessary to place the second episode before the third one, too. The film thereby presents an A-B-C-chain of events that may also be chronologised as C-A-B or B-C-A. The circular time scheme thus allows for entering or leaving the story at any point in time, thereby creating the impression of a never-ending story of reappearing events.

Another film that is sometimes mentioned in the context of circular narrations is PULP FICTION (USA 1994, Quentin Tarantino), because this film, too, returns to its beginning in the end. But since the plot circularity is not the only temporal confusion in this film and not embedded into the story, it does

---

19 | The unreliability of time mentioned here should not be completely confused with the concept of *unreliable narration* developed in other contexts (see for example Liptay/Wolf 2005 or Laass 2008), although many of the films with subjective or unreliable time schemes may fit into this category.

not feature the same strict circularity as BEFORE THE RAIN. The time jumps and repetitions may be more precisely defined by the metaphor of an astronomic *wormhole*, which allows the plot to switch quickly from one spatiotemporal point in the narrated universe to the next. Thus the film probably fits more into the next and final category.

Randomised/Chaotic Time

This category consists of films that probably are the most obvious examples of temporal non-linearity and disorientation because they confuse the chronological order of events to the fullest extent. Films like 21 GRAMS (USA 2003, Alejandro González Iñárritu) or (500) DAYS OF SUMMER (USA 2009, Marc Webb) fragment their story arcs into many different parts and realign them in a seemingly random[20] and accidental order. These narrations may also use time jumps because of multiple protagonists and perspectives (e.g. in BABEL (France/Mexico/USA 2006, Alejandro González Iñárritu), THE HOURS (USA 2002, Steven Daldry) or AMORES PERROS (Mexico 2000, Alejandro González Iñárritu)), but instead of presenting one episode and time span after another they continuously switch between them. This steady skipping is most of the time achieved only by the plot montage and its incongruity with the supposed chronology of events. But films may deal with this time chaos in its content, too—as for example in PREMONITION (USA 2007, Mennan Yapo), in which a housewife experiences a week of her life during which she wakes up the wrong day every morning, thereby losing her husband in a car accident on one day while meeting him alive and unhurt on the following.

THE CRISIS OF LINEARITY

What I wanted to show by means of these categories and examples is that the fictional cinema of the last 20 years especially offers a full array of mechanisms and patterns that experiment with the relation of story and plot chronology and that thereby raise and negotiate questions of temporal disorientation. Thus, film as such becomes a kind of *playground* for dis- and re-orientation that draws pleasure and interest from its unconventionality and complexity.

But, of course, this development is not all new or recent. Film made use of non-linear narrative patterns from the start (e.g. in INTOLERANCE (USA 1916, D. W. Griffith)) or experimented with temporal features, especially in the con-

---

20 | Of course there is always a (director's) intention behind the order of this 'unordered' segments. But, with regard to the concept of a split and jumbled time that these films present, the term 'random' seems to be suitable.

text of modernist cinema (e.g. in L'ANNÉE DERNIÈRE À MARIENBAD (LAST YEAR AT MARIENBAD, France/Italy 1961, Alain Resnais)). Furthermore, temporality and duration as well as their transgression and acceleration have been widely discussed topics in other contexts, too, for example in the field of literature around 1900, raised by modernist or academic writers like Proust or Simmel, who described the mental overload of the individual in the environment of growing cities and industries (Anz 1994, 111ff.). Thus, the current popularity of time as a topic of media and cinema seems to be just another revival.

Nevertheless, these thoughts suggest further questions concerning the reason for this renewed interest in the topic: Why do temporality and its exceeding seem to be relevant and interesting around the turn of the millennium? What other contexts or concepts can be taken into account to describe, explain, and analyse this development, besides narratology?

A short and concluding view on the writings of Vilém Flusser may be one exemplary way to approach these issues, because the films mentioned above somehow seem to be concrete realisations of thoughts about linearity, time, and media that Flusser repeatedly dealt with in his essays: In the year 1988, for example, Flusser read a paper at the art museum of Bern entitled *Die Krise der Linearität* (*The Crisis of Linearity*), which was later (in 1992) published as a book.[21] It may be just a coincidence that these explicit discussions about a change in linear thinking thereby appear at nearly the same time at which films like PRZYPADEK (1981), RESERVOIR DOGS (1992), GROUNDHOG DAY (1993), or PULP FICTION (1994) start to experiment more and more with non-linear narrative patterns. Is there thus a possibility to join Flusser's ideas of a linearity crisis with phenomena of non-linearity in 90s cinema and after?

Within his text, Flusser describes the transformation of contemporary discourses, which in his opinion are no longer dominantly coded and structured through linear writing, but within calculative processes and logics. His main thesis is that the initially linear alphabetical, then alphanumerical code, that was prevailing for centuries, hence is replaced by purely numerical code that converts and transforms the constitution of cultural artefacts and thereby our imagination of the world. Thus, the basic cultural structure of literal linearity finds itself in a crisis and is superseded by calculative processes which, in their enhanced precision and zero-dimensionality, do neither know space nor time anymore. Flusser describes this crisis as follows:

---

21 | For an English version of *The Crisis of Linearity*, see Flusser 2007a. Additionally it has to be mentioned that the talk and its publication summarised the arguments and ideas that Flusser had already presented in his book *Ins Universum der technischen Bilder (Into the Universe of Technical Images)*, which was first published in 1985. For an English translation, see Flusser 2011.

"The alphanumeric code is divided within itself, and this internal contradiction had to lead to its crisis, as we can discern from our current vantage point. From the perspective of the considerations undertaken here, this inner contradiction can be formulated as such: While letters unravel the surface of an image into lines, numbers grind this surface into points and intervals. While literal thinking spools scenes as processes, numerical thought computes scenes into grains. For a long time these modes of thought could walk jointly, with literal thinking keeping the upper hand because both modes were directed against surface thinking. But as images became increasingly enlightened, numerical thinking had to poise itself against literal thinking, to submit it to its grinding, analyzing critique. Linear, process-oriented, historical thinking sooner or later had to fall victim to analytical, structural, zero-dimensional, point-thinking." (Flusser 2007a, 20)

Flusser herein mentions two aspects that may be important for the considerations presented in this paper: on the one hand, it is the important role of technical images within the process of changing discursive frameworks, on the other hand, it is the aspect of temporality (historicity), which is affected by these changes. Media technologies and their outcomes—be they analogue or digital—thereby are the initial cause for this crisis of linearity, because they change the fundamental materiality of cultural products by dispersing them into small, zero-dimensional, and thus time- and spaceless points. This development is started with the emergence of photography, expedited by the audiovisual arts (film, video etc.), and (for the time being) crowned by the unifying digitality of today's mediascapes, which calculate images, sounds, and texts in the homogeneous code of 1 and 0.

Film, in this context, is often used by Flusser as an example to refer to the special temporality of this new kind of technical images: He describes cinema as a somehow ambivalent medium of change, because film seems to be the last truly linear and thereby textual/historical medium (as it consists of a linear strip of images), while the film image itself is truly calculated and thus ahistorical (as it consists of points and as its linear succession is only a pretext for the actual filmic experience) (Flusser 2007b, 192). Along with these assumptions, Flusser himself finally provides us with an explicit connection to the questions raised within the first part of this article—namely when he draws an analogy between the work of the film editor and the (comparably smaller) powers of God to explain the new dimensions offered by the ahistorical non-linearity of *techno-images*. He writes:

"[H]e [the operator, J.E.] is able to [...] intervene in the course of history in a way that the transcendent God is not entitled to: He can reorganise the progression of events. [...] He can shuffle single phases of history, decelerate or accelerate their succession, he can make them run backwards and he can repeat them at several points in history.

In short, he does not intent to re-establish the eternal recurrence of the same, but to split the historical time, in its linearity, into different dimensions—not to make a circle out of the line, but different extensive forms (triangles, spirals, labyrinths). [...] He is capable of doing something that the transcendent God of history was not capable of: to throw the historical time out of its linear joints and project it on a surface. That is an unprecedented gesture. The time is out of joint, not only because past and future lose every meaning through this gesture and the whole time becomes present. It is out of joint because one can handle it without participating in it." (ibid., 192f.; transl. J.E.)[22]

Within this citation Flusser almost explicitly names the non-linear narrative patterns worked out before and he also defines film as a medium that is able to transgress temporal borders—not only metaphorically by creating non-linear narratives, but concretely, too, by challenging our prevalent understanding of how time operates. Within the context of Flussers writings, the previously named films thus appear to be not just narrative 'gimmicks', but an expression of a development within which film—as a basically calculated, technical image—becomes more and more aware of its status and its inherent non-linearity. Content and aesthetics of these films thus reflect, scrutinise, question, and criticise not only narrative norms, but potential norms of temporality as well.

Flusser's essays on the one hand, and the non-linear narrations of contemporary cinema on the other hand, may thus both be symptoms of a rising cultural interest in questions of temporality and linearity—be they embedded in philosophical contemplations or cinematic productions. The questioning of temporal standards—appearing on a theoretical as well as practical level at the same time—may hence be representative for a specific discourse, which

---

22 | Original citation: "[E]r [der Operator, J.E.] kann [...] auf eine Weise in die Geschichte eingreifen, die dem transzendenten Gott nicht zusteht: er kann die Reihenfolge der Ereignisse umorganisieren. [...] Er kann einzelne Phasen der Geschichte umstellen, ihren Ablauf verlangsamen oder beschleunigen, er kann sie rückwärts laufen lassen und er kann sie an verschiedenen Stellen der Geschichte wiederholen. Kurz, er beabsichtigt nicht, die ewige Wiederkehr des Gleichen wiederherzustellen, sondern die historische Zeit in ihrer Linearität in verschiedene Dimensionen aufzufächern— aus der Linie nicht einen Kreis, sondern verschiedene Flächenformen zu machen (Dreiecke, Spiralen, Labyrinthe). [...] Er kann etwas, das der transzendente Gott der Geschichte nicht konnte: die historische Zeit aus ihren linearen Fugen geraten lassen und auf eine Fläche projizieren. Das ist eine vorher nie dagewesene Geste. Die Zeit gerät aus den Fugen, nicht nur weil Vergangenheit und Zukunft bei dieser Geste jeden Sinn verlieren und die ganze Zeit gegenwärtig wird. Sie ist aus den Fugen, weil man sie behandeln kann, ohne an ihr teilzuhaben" (Flusser 2007b, 192f.).

emerges and intensifies during the 1980s and 1990s and which accompanies the digitalisation not only of cinema, but of whole living environments as well.

As an element of popular culture the mentioned films and 'narrative mazes' allow us to question how far the mediatised experience of disorientation, which is enabled by them, mirrors general feelings of disorientation within media environments. These digitised mediascapes and their network structures seemingly elude conventional concepts and classifications, thus making it necessary to develop new or alternative descriptions. In this respect, the multitude of temporally confused or generally unconventional media texts of the recent years may be a reflection of the disorientations within these changing structures. The 'twisted times' and thought experiments of non-linear film thus appear to be especially fascinating and entertaining forms of a discursive consideration of disorienting media experiences.

Bibliography

Anz, Thomas (1994): Zeit und Beschleunigung in der literarischen Moderne. In: Sandbothe, Mike/Zimmerli, Walther Ch. (eds.): *Zeit – Medien – Wahrnehmung*. Darmstadt: Wissenschaftliche Buchgesellschaft.

Aronson, Linda (2010): *The 21st Century Screenplay. A Comprehensive Guide to Writing Tomorrow's Films*. Los Angeles: Silman-James Press.

Bazin, André (1960): The Ontology of the Photographic Image (transl. by Hugh Gray). In: *Film Quarterly*, Vol. 13, No. 4, 4–9.

Berrios, G. E. (1983): Orientation Failures in Medicine and Psychiatry: Discussion Paper. In: *Journal of the Royal Society of Medicine*, Vol. 76, May 1983, 379–385.

Bogen, Steffen (2010): Orienting Map. Two Historical Case Studies. In: Design2context 2010, 268–272.

Bordwell, David (2002): Film Futures. In: *Substance*, Issue 97, Vol. 31, No. 1, 88–104.

Bordwell, David/Thompson, Kristin (2004): *Film Art: An Introduction*. 7th edition. New York et al.: McGraw Hill.

Buckland, Warren (ed.) (2009): *Puzzle Films: Complex Storytelling in Contemporary Cinema*. Malden/Oxford/Chichester: Wiley-Blackwell.

Cameron, Allan (2008): *Modular Narratives in Contemporary Cinema*. Hampshire/New York: Palgrave Macmillan.

Deleuze, Gilles (1989): *Cinema 2: The Time-Image* (transl. by Hugh Tomlinson and Robert Galeta). Minneapolis: University of Minnesota Press.

Design2context (eds.): *Des-/Orientierung, Dis-/Orientation, Dés-/Orientation 2*. Baden: Lars Müller Publishers.

Eckel, Julia (2012): *Zeitenwende(n) des Films: Temporale Nonlinearität im zeitgenössischen Erzählkino*. Marburg: Schüren.

Elsaesser, Thomas (2009): The Mind-Game Film. In: Buckland 2009, 13–41.

Flusser, Vilém (1992): *Krise der Linearität*. Bern: Benteli Verlag.

Flusser, Vilém (2000): *Ins Universum der technischen Bilder*. 6th edition. Göttingen: European Photography.

Flusser, Vilém (2007a): The Crisis of Linearity (transl. by Adelheid Mers). In: *Boot Print*, Vol. 1, Issue 1, March 2007, 19–21.

Flusser, Vilém (2007b): *Kommunikologie*. 4th edition. Frankfurt a. M.: Fischer.

Flusser, Vilém (2011): *Into the Universe of Technical Images* (transl. by Nancy Ann Roth, introduction by Marc Poster). Minneapolis: University of Minnesota Press.

Genette, Gerard (1980): *Narrative Discourse. An Essay in Method* (transl. by Jane E. Lewin, foreword by Jonathan Culler). Ithaca (NY): Cornell University Press.

Johnson, Steven (2006 [2005]): *Everything Bad is Good for You*. London: Penguin Books.

Kockot, Stefanie-Vera (2010): The Freedom of Orientation. On Torture, Individual and Collective Mind Control, Propaganda, and the Danger of Legitimate Forms of Forced Disorientation. In: Design2context 2010, 128–140.

Laass, Eva (2008): *Broken Taboos, Subjective Truths: Forms and Functions of Unreliable Narration in Contemporary American Cinema – A Contribution to Film Narratology*. Trier: Wissenschaftlicher Verlag Trier.

Liptay, Fabienne/Wolf, Yvonne (eds.) (2005): *Was stimmt denn jetzt? Unzuverlässiges Erzählen in Literatur und Film*. München: Edition Text und Kritik.

Mittell, Jason (2006): Narrative Complexity in Contemporary American Television. In: *The Velvet Light Trap*, No. 58, 29–40.

Ramírez Berg, Charles (2006): A Taxonomy of Alternative Plots in Recent Films: Classifying the 'Tarantino Effect'. In: *Film Criticism*, Vol. 31, Nos. 1-2, 5–61.

Rüetschi, Urs-Jakob (2010): Scenic Orientation. On the Significance of Scenes for Wayfinding. In: Design2context 2010, 258–262.

Runge, Indra (2008): *Zeit im Rückwärtsschritt: Über das Stilmittel der chronologischen Inversion in Memento, Irréversible und 5x2*. Stuttgart: Ibidem.

Scharfetter, Christian (2010): *Allgemeine Psychopathologie – Eine Einführung*. 6th edition. Stuttgart: Thieme.

Thon, Jan-Noël (2009): Mind-Bender: Zur Popularisierung komplexer narrativer Strukturen im amerikanischen Kino der 1990er Jahre. In: Konnor, Sophia/Rohleder, Rebekka (eds.): *Post Coca-Colanization: Zurück zur Vielfalt?* Frankfurt a. M.: Peter Lang, 171–188.

Films

(500) Days of Summer (USA 2009, Marc Webb)
11:14 (USA 2003, Greg Marcks)
21 Grams (USA 2003, Alejandro González Iñárritu)
5x2 (France 2004, François Ozon)
À la folie...pas du tout (He Loves Me... He Loves Me Not, France 2002, Laetitia Colombani)
Amores Perros (Mexico 2000, Alejandro González Iñárritu)
Babel (France/Mexico/USA 2006, Alejandro González Iñárritu)
Back to the Future (USA 1985, Robert Zemeckis)
Before the Rain (Morocco/France/UK 1994, Milcho Manchevski)
Bill & Ted's Excellent Adventure (USA 1989, Stephen Herek)
Casablanca (USA 1942, Michael Curtiz)
eXistenZ (Canada/UK 1999, David Cronenberg)
Final Destination (USA 2000, James Wong)
Go! (USA 1999, Doug Liman)
Groundhog Day (USA 1993, Harold Ramis)
Inception (USA/UK 2010, Christopher Nolan)
Intolerance (USA 1916, D. W. Griffith)
Irréversible (France 2002, Gaspar Noé)
Jacob's Ladder (USA 1990, Adrian Lyne)
L'Année dernière à Marienbad (Last Year at Marienbad, France/Italy 1961, Alain Resnais)
Lola rennt (Run Lola Run, Germany 1998, Tom Tykwer)
Lulu on the Bridge (USA 1998, Paul Auster)
Memento (USA 2000, Christopher Nolan)
Premonition (USA 2007, Mennan Yapo)
Przypadek (Blind Chance, Poland 1981, Krzysztof Kie lowski)
Pulp Fiction (USA 1994, Quentin Tarantino)
Reconstruction (Denmark 2004, Christoffer Boe)
Reservoir Dogs (USA 1992, Quentin Tarantino)
Sliding Doors (GB/USA 1998, Peter Howitt)
Smoking/No Smoking (France 1993, Alain Resnais)
Stay (USA 2005, Marc Forster)
The Butterfly Effect (USA 2004, Eric Bress/J. Mackye Gruber)
The Escapist (UK/Ireland 2008, Rupert Wyatt)
The Hours (USA 2002, Steven Daldry)

When the Past Lies Ahead and the Future Lags Behind
Backward Narration in Film, Television, and Literature

Matthias Brütsch

Anyone who has ever taught film seminars when VHS tapes were still in use knows from experience that a sleepy classroom may suddenly awaken and become animated when a backwards image search is carried out in order to find a particular scene.[1] The sudden arousal and laughter this manoeuvre almost inevitably triggers is a first indication that the reversal of processes we are used to seeing unfold in a forward direction draws immediate attention and has the power to irritate or to amuse.

In dealing with backward narration, I will start with the premise that the chronological sequence and forward movement in time is not only the order followed by the vast majority of novels and films, but also a kind of default value automatically activated by readers and viewers in the absence of clear signs suggesting an alternative structure. The reversal of chronology or time's arrow is exceptional and defies our norms of perception and cognition. To what extent it also has a disorienting effect is one of the questions the following typology of backward narrations seeks to answer. After distinguishing the different types of storytelling in reverse, I will focus on issues of reception, narrative perspective, as well as dramatic structure and their orienting or disorienting effects. Themes and genres linked to reverse narratives are further topics that will be addressed. Finally, there will be some speculative remarks on the possible reasons for the increasing popularity of this extraordinary narrative form around the turn of the millennium in both television (with episodes from Seinfeld (USA 1989–1998, NBC, S9/E08), Star Trek: Voyager (USA 1995–2001, UPN, S3/E21), The X Files (USA/Canada 1993–2002, Fox, S8/E06), and ER (USA 1994–2009, NBC, S9/E10)) and film (Memento (USA 2000, Christopher Nolan), Bakha Satang (Pep-

---

[1] | I would like to thank Henry M. Taylor for helpful comments and the revision of the English text.

PERMINT CANDY, South Korea/Japan 2000, Lee Chang-dong), IRRÉVERSIBLE (France 2002, Gaspar Noé), 5x2 (France 2004, François Ozon), and ETERNAL SUNSHINE OF THE SPOTLESS MIND (USA 2004, Michel Gondry)).

DIFFERENT TYPES OF BACKWARD NARRATION

A good way to separate the different kinds of reverse narrative is to ask, what exactly is moving backwards in backward narrations? Is it the process of narration itself? Is it the plot, i.e. the order in which story events are presented? Or is it the events of the narrated story themselves? As to the first question, it would seem to be a fundamental rule that the actual act of narration cannot regress—unless the viewer reverses it, which is only possible in some cases.[2] This leaves us with only two viable options: either the events are reversed at the level of plot, or they really unfold backwards in the story.

The second question to ask is what pattern the reverse narratives follow. In a majority of cases the reversing only affects the order in which the episodes are presented and not the events within the episodes themselves, which unfold in a normal forward manner. In some cases, however, the reversing takes the form of a continuous backward movement involving each event of the story.[3] Following Chatman (2009, 33f.), I will call the former 'episodically reversed' and the latter 'sustained reversed narratives'.

Both oppositions with two alternatives each result in a total of four options (see fig. 1) with options 1a (the plot presents the scenes in reversed order) and 2b (the events in the story unfold continuously backwards) being more common than options 1b (the narration continuously reverses each story event) and

---

2 | To read a novel backwards is rather difficult, VHS and DVD players on the other hand offer the possibility of at least playing the image track in reverse mode. Special DVD editions of MEMENTO (Sony Pictures Home Entertainment, 2002) and SEINFELD: BETRAYAL (Sony Pictures Home Entertainment, 2009) contain a version of the narrative presented in chronological order, but I would argue that these cases are better understood as narratives of their own than as a reversal of the original (backward) narration.

3 | In order to remain comprehensible, dialogue is sometimes nevertheless "episodically reversed" (with sentences being spoken forwards but their order being regressive).

4 | In STASTNY KONEC and *Time's Arrow* the sustained reversal takes place at the level of both narrative discourse and story (at least as far as the experience of the homodiegetic character narrator is concerned).

Figure 1: Four Kinds of Reversals.

Reversal	1. Narrative discourse/plot	2. Events in the story
a) episodic	Films: • BETRAYAL (UK 1983, David Hugh Jones) • TWO FRIENDS (Australia 1986, Jane Campion) • MEMENTO • BAKHA SATANG • IRRÉVERSIBLE • 5X2 • KILLING THE CHICKENS TO SCARE THE MONKEYS (Sweden 2011, Jens Assur) TV Series: • SEINFELD (S9/E08: BETRAYAL, USA 1997) • ER (S9/E10: HINDSIGHT, USA 2002) Literature/Theatre: • *Goodbye to the Past* (1934) • *Christopher Homm* (1965) • *Betrayal* (1978)	Film: • ETERNAL SUNSHINE OF THE SPOTLESS MIND (partly) TV Series: • STAR TREK:VOYAGER (S3/E21: BEFORE AND AFTER, USA 1997) • THE X FILES (S8/E06: REDRUM, USA/Canada 2000) • SLIDERS (S2/E13: AS TIME GOES BY, USA 1996)
b) sustained	Films: • (STASTNY KONEC/HAPPY END, Czechoslovakia 1967, Oldrich Lipsky)[4] • .TIBBAR (Netherlands 2004, Leo Wentink) • REWIND (India 2007, Atul Taishete) Literature: • (*Time's Arrow*, 1991)	Films: • (STASTNY KONEC) • RÜCKWÄRTS (Germany 1980, René Perraudin) • NIE SOLO SEIN (Germany 2003, Jan Schomburg) • EVOL (UK 2006, Chris Vincze) • THE CURIOUS CASE OF BENJAMIN BUTTON (USA 2008, David Fincher) TV Series: • RED DWARF (S3/E01: BACKWARDS, UK 1989) Literature: • *Spiegelgeschichte* (1949) • *Counter-Clock World* (1967) • *The Curious Case of Benjamin Button* (1922) • (*Time's Arrow*)

2a (episodes in the story are experienced in regressing order by some of the characters).[5]

In order to illustrate this typology I will give an example for each variant: 1a) Elaine says good night to Jerry and leaves his hotel room. Intertitle: "One Hour Earlier". The two characters are seated in the hotel room, Jerry hands over a full glass of gin and says "Bless you!" Elaine says "Thank you!" and empties the glass. Intertitle: "Three Seconds Earlier". Jerry pours gin in a glass and Elaine sneezes.

In this scene from the SEINFELD-episode BETRAYAL, the events in the fictional world unfold in a straightforward manner, but for us as spectators they are episodically reversed—a pattern made fun of here by the brevity of the "episodes" and the play with ambiguities.

2a) REDRUM, an episode from the TV series THE X FILES, begins with the main character Martin waking up in a prison cell without remembering what has happened in the past few days. The next morning he is brought to court where the judge orders his imprisonment. Another day 'later', his attorney comes to see him to discuss the strategy for the impending court hearing. Martin is confused until he finds out that each morning after waking up he has moved one day into the past instead of the future. In other words: the order in which the days follow each other is reversed, but contrary to option 1a this reversal is experienced by the character in the fictional world and does not only relate to the plot.

1b) The short film REWIND begins as follows: The camera slowly moves downward until it faces a man who sits at a table in front of a small heap of diamonds and a scattered set of gambling cards. The man is smoking but the cigarette is getting longer instead of shorter and absorbing smoke instead of exuding it. He pushes half of the diamonds to the other side of the table, takes a gun and aims at a man lying on the floor who is suddenly lifted up with his chair and comes to life while the sound of a shot resonates through the room. Next, the man points his gun at his own head and a faint click can be heard.

REWIND is an example of sustained backward presentation of events. Within this category it represents a special case only possible in audiovisual narration since the backward representation (of a gang of robbers playing Russian roulette) on the image track is opposed to a normal forward account by the character narrator's voice-over on the sound track.

2b) The short film RÜCKWÄRTS presents an episode in the life of a somewhat peculiar man. After a lengthy morning workout, breakfast and bath, he leaves his house and realises with irritation that everybody he encounters is walking

---

5 | Chatman (2009, 33) only distinguishes between a and b ("episodic" versus "continuous reversal") and Marie-Laure Ryan (2009, 142f.) solely distinguishes between 1 and 2 ("narratives that tell stories in reverse chronological order" versus "reversed time narratives").

backwards and speaking an incomprehensible gibberish. Puzzled by what is going on around him, he bumps into several people, causes a commotion, and is finally arrested by the police.

In this example, processes in the fictional world are happening backwards, but this reversal (of a sustained kind) neither affects all the fictional characters (the protagonist acts in a normal 'forward mode') nor every aspect of time's arrow (although the movements and dialogue of the police officers are reversed, their actions follow a normal 'forward' logic and causality, or else they would not have arrested but released the main character and ought to have done so prior to and not after the tumult).

RÜCKWÄRTS therefore shows that films with reversals within the diegesis always raise the question what exactly and who is going backwards. In THE CURIOUS CASE OF BENJAMIN BUTTON, for instance, it is only the ageing process of the main character. In the short film NIE SOLO SEIN, dialogue, movements and ageing processes are reversed for all characters except the protagonist. And in the episode BACKWARDS from the science-fiction TV series RED DWARF, movements, historical time, causality and ageing are reversed, but only for the inhabitants of planet Earth. Rather than being all-embracing, reversals within the fictional world are usually quite selective as to which characters and which aspects of time's arrow are affected (see Ryan 2009, 145).[6]

If not only movement, dialogue or ageing processes but (historical) time is reversed (if, in other words, Monday follows Tuesday and the First World War follows the Second), the question arises whether the backward movement has to be understood as a re-experiencing or even undoing of events already lived through, which is explicitly the case in *Spiegelgeschichte*, *Counter-Clock World* (time reversal 1986) and THE X FILES: REDRUM, and implicitly in *Time's Arrow* and STASTNY KONEC.[7]

---

6 | Reversals on the level of narrative discourse can also be selective, as demonstrated by MEMENTO, THE RULES OF ATTRACTION (USA/Germany 2002, Roger Avery), or ETERNAL SUNSHINE OF THE SPOTLESS MIND in presenting only part of the story in reverse order.

7 | Although these examples differ from time travel narratives like THE TERMINATOR (USA 1984, James Cameron) or BACK TO THE FUTURE (USA 1985, Robert Zemeckis) in that their movement into the past is not a one-time leap but continuous, they share some features of what Catherine Gallagher (2002) has called the "undoing plot," including the "grandmother paradox" that goes with it.

Alignment and Dissociation

How time is structured in backward narration has direct implications as to narrative perspective.[8] Narrative reversals can lead to both alignment and dissociation between spectators/readers and characters. Analysing the examples listed in the bibliography and mediography, I found three different forms of alignment: first, examples with spatiotemporal attachment (and partly subjective access) to a character who moves, lives or ages backwards while all the other characters 'operate' in the usual forward manner (STAR TREK: VOYAGER: *BEFORE AND AFTER*, THE X FILES: *REDRUM*, THE CURIOUS CASE OF BENJAMIN BUTTON); or conversely, to a character who is forward-oriented while all the others move backwards (RÜCKWÄRTS, NIE SOLO SEIN). This kind of alignment presupposes that processes of reversal take place within the story and not just on the level of narrative discourse. Second, there are examples in which the episodic reversal results in an approximation of knowledge between spectators and characters. This is only exceptionally the case if the main character suffers from short-term memory loss (as in MEMENTO)[9] or has parts of his memory erased (as in ETERNAL SUNSHINE OF THE SPOTLESS MIND).[10] Third, we find episodic or sustained reversals supposedly imitating the way in which a character remembers past events (ER: *HINDSIGHT*, ETERNAL SUNSHINE OF THE SPOTLESS MIND and, according to some interpretations, *Spiegelgeschichte*). In all three cases the spectators or readers are aligned with the main characters as to their knowledge (and partly their perception) while at the same time distanced from all the other characters.[11]

Backward narration can also lead to a *dissociation* between spectator/reader and character. If the plot presents the scenes of the story in reverse order, at the beginning the characters know much more than the spectators, while at the end the spectators know much more than the characters. The difference in knowledge thus shifts and is eventually inverted, with the additional knowledge the spectators gain from the second episode onwards often being used for effects

---

8 | For an analysis of narrative perspective I prefer Smith's concept of alignment (1995, 142ff.) to Genette's concept of focalisation (1972, 206ff.). For a critique of the concept of focalisation, see Brütsch (2011a, 260ff.).

9 | For a detailed analysis of the complex structure of MEMENTO, involving aligning and distancing effects, see Hansen (2011, 172ff.) and Parker (2004).

10 | In both cases the special condition of the protagonist has a disturbing effect on what Ryan (2009, 144f.) calls the "cognitive arrow," an aspect of time's arrow involving the "accumulation of knowledge and memories at the expense of the unknown".

11 | The alignment is of course never complete but always an approximation, as MEMENTO illustrates well, since the shared lack of knowledge between spectator and protagonist about what happened in the immediate past stands in opposition to differences in knowledge about the future and the distant past.

of dramatic irony (see Hansen 2011, 174). The final episode of BAKHA SATANG (set at the beginning of the story) illustrates this quite well: The main character meets his future wife near a railway bridge and tells her that he has the feeling of already having been in this place. She replies that she hopes this is a good sign. For us as spectators, the place really is a *déjà vu*, but implying a bad rather than a good omen, since in the first scene (set at the end of the story) we witnessed the protagonist throwing himself in front of an approaching train on this same bridge. Similar effects of dramatic irony based on an asymmetrical distribution of knowledge can be found in BETRAYAL (both in play and film), MEMENTO, IRRÉVERSIBLE and 5X2.

A different form of distancing occurs if a character narrator relates the events of the story as if they unfold in normal forward chronology, while we interpret them as moving backwards. This is the case in the novel *Time's Arrow* and in the film STASTNY KONEC, as the following two excerpts illustrate:

"I can't tell—and I need to know—whether Tod is kind. Or how unkind. He takes toys from children, on the street. He does. The kid will be standing there, with flustered mother, with big dad. Tod'll come on up. The toy, the squeaky duck or whatever, will be offered to him by the smiling child. Tod takes it. And backs away, with what I believe is called a shiteating grin. The child's face turns bland, or closes. Both toy and smile are gone: he takes both toy and smile. Then he heads for the store, to cash it in. For what? A couple of bucks. Can you believe this guy? He'll take candy from a baby, if there's fifty cents in it for him." (Amis 1992, 22f.)

A fight is going on between Bedrich and his wife, accompanied by his voice-over: "And finally I've heard her first sweet words." On the street downstairs an ambulance approaches backwards. The paramedics unload a man and put him down on the street, from where he is suddenly lifted up and comes flying in through the window into the apartment of the quarrelling couple. The voice-over resumes: "Then I realised that life is full of tricky surprises. Instead of enjoying the first pleasant afternoon with Julia, something totally unexpected happened. That dandy showed up [...]. With symptomatic arrogance flown in through the window [...]." The intruder lands in the arms of Bedrich and then the two start moving swiftly around in the bedroom which as a result of their action changes from chaos to order, with the voice-over commenting: "I forced him to help me with the tidying up" (STASTNY KONEC, 19'–21').

In both instances, we reverse the backward narration drawing on our real-world knowledge (which includes forward movement and chronological progress as default values) and recognise, contrary to the character narrators, an act of donation in the first example and a fierce brawl between the two men with fatal consequences for the husband's rival (and the bedroom furnishings) in the second example. This form of narration can be called unreliable, with the explicit statement of the character narrator marking an ironic contrast to the implicit message of the text as a whole.[12]

Dis- and Re-orientation

After having sketched a typology of backward narrations and its implications on narrative perspective, I shall now examine more closely the process of reception. In doing so, I will focus on the disorienting potential of narrative reversals, while also pointing to elements of guidance and (re-)orientation.

Disorienting effects can above all be attributed to different kinds of discrepancies between:

- explicit backward and forward accounts or depictions;
- explicit backward accounts and the implicit forward norm;
- forward interpretations of character narrators and backward interpretations by the narratees;
- the character's and the narratee's levels of knowledge;
- the action on the film set and within the fictional world.[13]

Furthermore, as already noted, the reversal is selective in most cases, affecting only some of the characters and only some aspects of time's arrow. The spectators or readers are thus confronted with contrary developments or movements which complicate the understanding of what is going on in the story.

Despite the above mentioned effects of disorientation, I would argue that only few backward narrations try to confuse readers or spectators in a sustained manner, as is indicated by the establishment of various devices aiding orientation. First of all, the backwards pattern is often clearly emphasised through captions indicating time and date or other explicit clues in episodically reversed narratives, and through the staging of events which clearly show or symbolise the reversal at the very beginning of sustained reversed narratives (such as the

---

12 | In literary theory the term 'unreliable narration' is mainly used for ironic distancing, as mentioned above. In film theory, however, many authors rather use it for films giving false leads and ending in final plot twists (see Brütsch 2011b). That backward narration also qualifies for the latter dramatic structure can be illustrated by MEMENTO, which despite its partial reversal of chronology ends in a final plot twist unexpectedly forcing us to re-evaluate the main character and his behaviour.

13 | In watching NIE SOLO SEIN, RÜCKWÄRTS, or EVOL featuring protagonists who move forwards while all the other characters move backwards, one cannot help imagining the shooting of the film, during which the movements were staged in the opposite direction, of course.

smoke absorbing cigarette in REWIND and the watch hand moving counter-clockwise in THE X FILES: REDRUM). In both variants, hints as to the kind of reversal may also be provided by dialogue or a voice-over. Moreover, the title often alludes to the backwards structure, either semantically (*Spiegelgeschichte* (= Mirror Story), *Counter-Clock World*, *Time's Arrow*, BEFORE AND AFTER, RÜCKWÄRTS (= Backwards), REWIND) or, in the case of anagrams, formally (EVOL, REDRUM, .TIBBAR, NIE SOLO SEIN).

Orientation may further be facilitated if the narrative focus is on events evolving according to a predictable pattern, as for instance with the relationship of a couple and the typical stages of falling in love, getting married, having children, having affairs, followed by disaffection and separation (BETRAYAL, 5X2, STASTNY KONEC), or biographies with the usual steps of birth, childhood, school, entering professional life, starting a family, retirement, old age and death (*Goodbye to the Past*, *Christopher Homm*, STASTNY KONEC, *Spiegelgeschichte*, *Time's Arrow*, *Stuart—A Life Backwards*). A chain of events with strong causality—revenge following injustice (MEMENTO and IRRÉVERSIBLE) or escape and hideout following the commitment of a crime (*Time's Arrow*)—also helps reconstruct the forward logic of actions presented backwards. And despite the fact that backward narrations may vary as to their perspective and temporal structure, they usually focus on a clearly established main character whose actions, even if reversed, run through the story as a continuous thread.

Last but not least, the dramatic structure of backward narrations, which only rarely differ radically from the established patterns of conventional narratives, also proves to be more often orienting than disorienting: Questions raised in the setup are generally answered not until the resolution, and suspense may classically build towards a final climax (as in MEMENTO, *Time's Arrow* and REWIND).[14] And if events are reversed in the fictional world, classical plots with goal oriented protagonists having to overcome obstacles in order to achieve what they want are possible, the only difference being that their objective—e.g. adjustment to counter-clock logic (RÜCKWÄRTS, NIE SOLO SEIN) or the undoing of an

---

14 | See Bordwell's analysis of MEMENTO (2006, 79f.). Bildhauer's account (2007), on the other hand, appears to be problematic (at least her chart on page 85) insofar as her analysis is based on the story in chronological order whereas what is actually called for is a plot analysis. Thus she takes the strangling of Jimmy at the end of the film to be the midpoint (because it happens in the middle of the story) and the shooting of Teddy at the beginning of the film to be the climax (because it is the last action in the story chronology). If dramatic structure is meant to assess the dynamics and effects of narrative mediation, the latter action clearly functions as the climax and the former as a beginning in medias res or as a hook. The problem becomes even more visible in Matthias' analysis (2012, 182ff.) claiming that MEMENTO is conventionally divided into three parts but progressing from third to first act.

action having caused disaster (THE X FILES: REDRUM, STAR TREK: VOYAGER: *BEFORE AND AFTER*)—lies in the past instead of the future.

Furthermore, narrative beginnings and endings are often clearly signposted and staged conventionally, despite corresponding to the opposite ends of the story. In the first episode of the short film REWIND, as described above, the camera slowly discovers the scene and the characters involved who at the same time are explicitly introduced by the voice-over and with captions revealing their names. Although what is shown is the last action of the story, in many ways the scene functions as classical exposition. And the final shot of 5x2, depicting the two main characters swimming in the sea at sunset (which marks the beginning of their relationship) signals the end of the narration through a conventional long shot and hence spatial dissociation, aided by the dimming of the image, the sunset symbolising the end of the day, and the grand finale on the soundtrack—a romantic conclusion obviously (as in IRRÉVERSIBLE and BAKHA SATANG) in ironic contrast to the dreadful ending of the story shown at the beginning of the film.

RENEGOTIATING FAMILIAR TOPICS

What are the themes that backward narratives focus on? Traumatic events from the past often play a crucial role, causing retrospection or repression, raising questions of guilt and atonement or prompting the desire to cancel out what has happened. Free will versus determinism and chance versus fate are topics also privileged by the reversal of chronology.[15] In this context it is worth noting that the possibility of fiction to reverse chronology by contrast foregrounds the unrelenting progress of time in our own world. Accordingly, links between cause and effect, consequences of certain actions and the liability for one's behaviour gain particular significance. The option to go back and undo past events, more or less explicitly displayed in *Spiegelgeschichte*, *Time's Arrow*, STAR TREK: VOYAGER: *BEFORE AND AFTER* and THE X FILES: REDRUM, brings the idea of a second chance into play and thus adds a utopian aspect to these stories.

Besides foregrounding issues related to time and causality, narrative reversals may also subvert standard patterns of reception as triggered by certain motifs. Revenge is a good example for illustrating this. In fiction and especially film, we are quite ready to approve of acts of revenge, even of a highly violent kind, as long as they function as retribution for severe crimes such as the assault on defenceless wives and children. However, if the act of revenge is shown *before* we know what caused it (as in MEMENTO and IRRÉVERSIBLE), the necessary precondition for empathy and approval is missing and cannot easily be established after the fact, even if the cause is eventually clarified. Without emotional gratification,

---

15 | See the analysis of IRRÉVERSIBLE by Hansen (2011, 175ff.).

the concept of revenge is fundamentally put into question, even more so if it turns out that the wrong character has been the target, as is the case in the two films mentioned above (see Stiglegger 331ff.).[16]

Repetition is another interesting issue prone to reformulation by episodic reversals. MEMENTO seemingly obeys the classical pattern of a hero pursuing a clearly defined goal. At the end, however, it not only appears that Leonard's objective (vengeance for the murder of his wife) might not be justified after all, but also that—even according to his own logic—it has already long ago been achieved, every new attempt being a self-deception in which he takes advantage of his short-term memory loss. The twist at the end of the film thus reveals that the alleged "showdown" in the story presented at the beginning of the film (where, in retrospect, revenge finally seems achieved), in fact just represents one of countless acts of self-delusion, providing the pathological protagonist with only a brief moment of satisfaction. Leonard is caught in an endless loop always leading to the same point, regardless of whether the cycle runs forward or backward.

ETERNAL SUNSHINE OF THE SPOTLESS MIND has a similar structure—with one significant exception: Its narration also and surprisingly reveals after some time that the protagonists have already lived through what they are about to do at the beginning of the film (= at the end of the story), i.e. fall in love with each other and begin a relationship. They also have consciously chosen to erase every trace and memory of their previous love affair, however unlike Leonard not with the intention of doing the same thing again, but on the contrary out of the desire to start a new life without their former lovers. Contrary to MEMENTO, the self-deception fails and the two protagonists get together again. Giving love a second chance, repetition thus emerges as a positive force in ETERNAL SUNSHINE OF THE SPOTLESS MIND, while in MEMENTO it signifies endless recurrence and immobility, with all the concurrent negative connotations.

In general it can be said that backward narrations—at least the sophisticated ones—try to establish a link between structure and content, usually by connecting the formal with a content-related reversal concerning issues like moral judgement (*Time's Arrow*), society and its behavioural norms (RÜCKWÄRTS), the relation between offender and victim (*Time's Arrow*, BETRAYAL, MEMENTO), or disparities of knowledge and power between antagonistic characters (BETRAYAL).

BACKWARD NARRATION AND GENRE

Narrative reversals tend to favour new approaches not only to familiar topics but also to well-established genres. My list of examples includes the following

---

16 | A close analysis of both films is presented in Hansen (2011, 172ff.).

genres (which are not strictly exclusive categories, as the multiple entries indicate): science fiction (*Counter-Clock World*, STAR TREK: VOYAGER: *BEFORE AND AFTER*, RED DWARF: *BACKWARDS*, SLIDERS: *AS TIME GOES BY*), crime and psychological thrillers (THE X FILES: *REDRUM*, MEMENTO, REWIND), romantic comedies (STASTNY KONEC, NIE SOLO SEIN, SEINFELD: *BETRAYAL*, EVOL, ETERNAL SUNSHINE OF THE SPOTLESS MIND), romantic drama (*Spiegelgeschichte*, BETRAYAL, *Time's Arrow*, TWO FRIENDS, MEMENTO, IRRÉVERSIBLE, BAKHA SATANG, 5X2, ETERNAL SUNSHINE OF THE SPOTLESS MIND, THE CURIOUS CASE OF BENJAMIN BUTTON) and political allegory (*Time's Arrow*, STASTNY KONEC, RÜCKWÄRTS, .TIBBAR, BAKHA SATANG, KILLING THE CHICKENS TO SCARE THE MONKEYS).

Works of science fiction usually feature at least one supernatural element not (yet) known to our own world, but accounted for within the diegesis by pseudo-scientific explanations (see Spiegel 2007, 42ff.). Temporal reversal, whether affecting all the characters (*Counter-Clock World*), only the protagonist (STAR TREK: VOYAGER: *BEFORE AND AFTER*), or only the inhabitants of our planet (RED DWARF: *BACKWARDS*) is an instance of such a fantastic element which functions, especially in combination with a futuristic setting, as a typical marker of the genre. It is worthwhile noting in this context that the above mentioned examples ought to be called 'counter-clock worlds' (the title of Dick's novel) rather than backward narratives, since the narration simply adheres to the prevailing chronology within the diegesis, even if it moves in the 'wrong' direction.

Narrative reversals also suit crime fiction well. Many examples of this genre, featuring a detective trying to find out how or by whom the crime shown at the beginning was committed, are geared towards the past anyway. And they are often explicitly designed as a mystery, an aspect necessarily reinforced by the cognitively challenging episodic reversal. However, if the chronology is reversed, the questions raised differ from what we are used to. Thus, as to the punishment of the putative culprit at the beginning, MEMENTO prompts the spectators to ask: What was the crime? Has the right person been caught? And later on, as contradictions emerge: Did the crime really happen as the main character claims it did? The beginning of THE X FILES: *REDRUM* shows the main character in prison, unable to recall any crime and in addition moving back in time, which also raises a number of questions: What happened? Who other than the protagonist could be responsible for the crime? Will he succeed in altering the past in such a way that the criminal act can be prevented from happening?

The initially mentioned classroom laughter and amusement triggered by movies played in rewind mode indicates the opportunities that backward narrations also offer for comedies, especially if they feature sustained reversals taking place within the fictional world (variant 2b in table 1). The burlesque effect of reverse motion with its peculiar visual appearance[17] is often combined with content-related humour. In NIE SOLO SEIN and RÜCKWÄRTS, the comic effect derives from the difficulties of the main characters (who 'behave' in ordinary forward fashion) in adjusting to a counter-clock world. Thus the thirsty protagonist of the former movie faces the problem that full bottles can only be *returned* at the beverage stand, while in the places where people get them—from dustbins and garbage bags—they are empty. For this reason, he is able to quench his thirst only after finding a girl who fills him a glass by 'drinking' it backwards.

The episodic reversal can also be used for comic effect. SEINFELD: *BETRAYAL* (a parody of Pinter's play and its film adaptation) features several 'inverted' running gags of odd behaviour which are repeated throughout the episode (such as Jason refusing to go to the toilet) and explained only at the very end. Moreover, dialogue episodically reversed, even in narratives with otherwise sustained reversals, is bound to amuse through ambiguity, as the following exchange taken from STASTNY KONEC between the female protagonist and her cousin demonstrates: Julia (standing in the door of her apartment): "It's a little messy around."—Cousin: "It means you're alone."—Julia: "Pig."—Cousin: "Calf?"—Julia: "Hubby [her husband] went to relatives. To butcher."

Another source of comic effects are discrepancies between the comments of a character narrator who misinterprets the reversed action as ordinary forward movement and the knowledge of the spectator or reader. This results in irony typical of unreliable narration, as the above references to *Time's Arrow* and STASTNY KONEC have shown.

Backward narrated dramas often focus on the relationship between a couple of friends or lovers. In this context, the order of affection and disaffection is reversed—a constellation of particular interest regarding the emotional involvement of the spectators, who alternate between emphatic alignment and distanced observation. On the one hand, emotional engagement is possible because romantic dramas build, as already mentioned, on familiar evolutionary stages in the lovers' relationship which are easily recognised even if presented in reverse order. On the other hand, the audience's superior knowledge from the second episode on has a distancing effect, which is even stronger if the chronological reversal is accompanied by other 'rules' of staging which foreground the act of narration, such as the 'interdiction' to cut within episodes of IRRÉVERSIBLE

---

17 | Already the Lumière Brothers relied on this effect when they had their travelling cameraman stop the projector after screening DÉMOLITION D'UN MUR (DEMOLITION OF A WALL, France 1896, Louis Lumière) and rerun it backwards (as mentioned in the audio commentary on the DVD "Early Cinema: Primitives and Pioneers," British Film Institute, 2005). Other early examples are AVENUE DE L'OPÉRA (France 1900, Alice Guy) and PLONGEUR FANTASTIQUE (THE FANTASTIC DIVER, France 1905, Segundo de Chomón).

or the depiction of the couple's life in 5x2 through five key episodes of approximately equal length.¹⁸

Apart from establishing futuristic worlds, mysteries, comic entanglements and dramatic conflicts between lovers, the reversal of familiar procedures may also challenge our norms of perception and cognition, an effect which can be used to add a political dimension to the plot. Thus in .TIBBAR, the depiction of intensive live stock farming, familiar to everybody from TV documentaries, appears as a striking symbol of unnaturalness and perversity, but only due to the reversal of the image and sound track. In RÜCKWÄRTS, the clash of norms of opposing forward and backward movements, besides being highly entertaining, also serves as a critique of conformism ruling West German society in the early 1980s. STASTNY KONEC, produced during the Prague Spring, takes the liberty of a few side blows to the communist regime, for instance by permanently (rather than episodically) reversing the dialogue of official speeches and the reading of law orders, which are thereby transformed into incomprehensible gibberish. And *Time's Arrow*, in providing a striking new perspective on the perversity of Nazi ideology through its combined reversal of time and ethics, also calls for an allegorical and political reading.

Apart from these effects, backward narrations in all genres self-reflexively point towards films and novels being artefacts, with reversals on the level of plot (variants 1a and b) foregrounding narrativity and those within the diegesis (variants 2a and b) foregrounding fictionality.¹⁹

VERBAL VERSUS AUDIOVISUAL REVERSALS

So far I have dealt with films and novels as if there were no fundamental differences between filmic and literary backward narrations. As to episodic reversals, I would argue that in one sense, differences are indeed negligible, since the narrative structure (reversal of the order of episodes but chronological unfolding within each episode) works comparably and with similar effects. In sustained reversals however, there are considerable differences, since in addition to the narrative structure, the systems of representation (which function differently

---

18 | In addition to chronology, 5x2 also reverses expected patterns of behaviour, as illustrated by the sexual intercourse on the day of the couple's divorce instead of their wedding.

19 | In *My Cheatin' Heart* (S3/E07) from the TV series Home Movies (USA 1999-2004, UPN/Cartoon Network), featuring would-be film director Brendon trying to shoot a script telling its story backwards, self-reflexivity is highly explicit, since the comic effect of the episode owes much to the constant discussions between Brendon and his friends about the (im)possibility of chronological inversion.

in the two media) are directly affected by the backward movement. Due to their mechanical and iconic bases, audiovisual representations can automatically be reversed, an option not available to verbal representation.[20] For this reason, as Chatman (2009, 35ff.) has shown in detail, sustained reversals in literary narration depend heavily on the semantic reversal of verbs ("give" turns into "take from", "make a mess" into "tidy up"), prepositions ("out" → "in") and, in some cases, adjectives ("last" → "first") and nouns ("destroyer" → "healer"). Chatman calls this linguistic procedure "antonymising" and points to the fact that it only applies to process statements and not to stasis statements, since only the former are time-sensitive.[21]

Reversing audiovisual representations, on the other hand, raises the question of how to handle the sound track. Contrary to the objects represented in the image, dialogue, music and sounds, if played backwards, usually change in such a manner as to become unintelligible. Films can purposefully make use of this estrangement (.TIBBAR, REWIND, RED DWARF: *BACKWARDS*) or avoid it by adding synchronised "forward" sounds (STASTNY KONEC, REWIND).[22]

A CHALLENGE FOR NARRATOLOGY AND SCREENWRITING THEORY

Narrative theory has, especially in recent years and partly due to a movement called "unnatural narratology" (see Alber 2009), shifted attention from classical to experimental forms of narration that defy accepted norms and conventions. Regarding film analysis, dramatic theory and screenplay manuals in the last decade have also increasingly focused on alternative and complex structures of storytelling.[23] In this context, backward narrations have been treated or mentioned on occasion (Richardson 2002, 49f.; Alber 2011, 5; Hansen, 2011; Benke 2002,

---

20 | Phonetically reversing verbal utterances would be the literary equivalent to playing image and sound track in reverse mode. *Time's Arrow* uses this method ("dug" for "good" or "sthtib" for "bitch"), but for reasons of intelligibility only in some very short passages (see Chatman 2009, 36).

21 | By considering the possibility of antonymising actions such as laughing (2009, 43), Chatman disregards that time reversals are not always linked to semantic reversals: "to buy" backwards equals "to cash in," but "to laugh" backwards does not equal "crying".

22 | In RÜCKWÄRTS only the dialogue but not the sounds are reversed. All examples mentioned above with the exception of REWIND feature non-diegetic music played in standard forward fashion.

23 | Both trends were inspired by corresponding developments in literature and film, such as experiments in postmodern literature or the success of unconventional storytelling in independent film productions of the 1990s.

83f./266ff.; Bildhauer 2007, 82ff.; Krützen 2010, 267ff.)—for good reasons, since their deviant structure raises tricky questions in both fields. If it makes sense to call them "unnatural," this depends not only on the definition of this (ambiguous) term[24], but also on the kind of reversal in question. Brian Richardson, by claiming that "antonymic" temporality (as well as "circular," "contradictory," "differential," "conflated" and "multiple" temporality), generally leads to the construction of "impossible stories" (2002, 53), neglects (in his otherwise very useful study) that this only holds true for time reversals taking place within the story (variants 1a and b in my table 1) and not for those carried out on the level of narrative discourse (variants 2a and b). In these latter instances, the story told may very well entirely adhere to the norms of our world and may even appear realistic (as in the marital drama 5x2), even though the way it is told proves to be unconventional.

For screenwriting theory, backward narrations are also interesting, not least because they expose the shortcomings of concepts that not sufficiently distinguish between the dynamics of plot and story (demanding, for instance, that the inciting incident should not only set the narrative in motion, but also the protagonist, and that in the climax suspense should rise to a peak not only for the spectators, but also for the characters within the diegesis). Episodic reversals demonstrate on the one hand that other options are available, and on the other that classical dramatic patterns can be established without relying on this kind of correlation between plot and story.

Short Blossoming of an Extraordinary Narrative Form

Works like *Goodbye to the Past* (1934), *Spiegelgeschichte* (1949), STASTNY KONEC (1967) or BETRAYAL (1983) indicate that backward narrations have existed long before the 1990s. Nevertheless, the turn of the millennium saw in both film and television a noticeable increase of this form. What might be the reasons for this? First, a general trend in the 1990s towards more complex and demanding forms of narration not only in movies (see Buckland 2009), but also in quality TV series (see Mittell 2006 and Blanchet 2011). Second, the growing importance since then of secondary releases on DVD, which particularly offered interesting returns for demanding films which provided new insights on multiple viewings. Third, the internet as a new medium particularly apt for the promotion of

---

24 | Depending on the context, "unnatural" is used to qualify forms of narration judged as experimental, unconventional, antimimetic, antirealist, unusual or impossible. Apart from the fact that the variety of works thus embraced is quite large, qualifications of this kind, which are relative in nature, call for careful definitions of concepts such as realism or mimesis (see Hansen 2011, 163ff.).

innovative and enigmatic films and series through special sites and discussion forums. And fourth, the successes of SEINFELD: BETRAYAL and MEMENTO with both critics and spectators, which subsequently boosted similar projects.

Despite their short blossoming, backward narrations have remained marginal. On the one hand, they are too odd and experimental for mainstream adaptation, while on the other their structure is so constraining that even artistically ambitious writers and producers only rely on it in very special instances. If they do, it may well be worth their while, however, as *Time's Arrow* and MEMENTO, to name only two outstanding examples, convincingly demonstrate—not least because of their clever play with orienting and disorienting effects.

Bibliography

Primary Sources

Aichinger, Ilse (1979 [1949]): *Spiegelgeschichte*. Leipzig: Kiepenheurer.
Amis, Martin (1992 [1991]): *Time's Arrow or the Nature of the Offence*. London: QPD.
Burnett, William Riley (1934): *Goodbye to the Past: Scenes From the Life of William Meadows*. New York: Harper.
Dick, Philip K. (2008 [1967]): *Counter-Clock World*. London: HarperCollins.
Fitzgerald, F. Scott (2008 [1922]): *The Curious Case of Benjamin Button*. Claremont: Coyote Canyon Press.
Masters, Alexander (2007 [2006]): *Stuart: A Life Backwards*. New York: Delta Trade Paperbacks.
Pinter, Harold (1991 [1978]): *Betrayal*. London: Faber and Faber.
Sisson, Charles H. (1997 [1965]): *Christopher Homm*. Manchester: Carcanet.

Secondary Sources

Alber, Jan (2009): Unnatural Narratives. In: *The Literary Encyclopedia*. Web. Retrieved from: [http://www.litencyc.com/php/stopics.php?rec=true&UID=7202]; access: 2012/10/10.
Alber, Jan (2011): Introduction. In: Alber/Heinze 2011, 1–19.
Alber, Jan/Heinze, Rüdiger (eds.) (2011): *Unnatural Narratives—Unnatural Narratology*. Berlin: De Gruyter.
Benke, Dagmar (2002): *Freistil: Dramaturgie für Fortgeschrittene und Experimentierfreudige*. Bergisch Gladbach: Lübbe.
Bildhauer, Katharina (2007): *Drehbuch Reloaded: Erzählen im Kino des 21. Jahrhunderts*. Konstanz: UVK.

Blanchet, Robert (2011): Quality-TV: Eine kurze Einführung in die Geschichte und Ästhetik neuer amerkanischer TV-Serien. In: Blanchet, Robert et al. (eds.): *Serielle Formen: Von den frühen Film-Serials zu aktuellen Quality-TV- und Online-Serien*. Marburg: Schüren, 37–70.

Bordwell, David (2006): *The Way Hollywood Tells It: Story and Style in Modern Movies*. Berkeley: University of California Press.

Brütsch, Matthias (2011a): *Traumbühne Kino: Der Traum als filmtheoretische Metapher und narratives Motiv*. Marburg: Schüren.

Brütsch, Matthias (2011b): Von der ironischen Distanz zur überraschenden Wendung: Wie sich das unzuverlässige Erzählen von der Literatur- in die Filmwissenschaft verschob. In: *kunsttexte.de*, 1/2011. Retrieved from: [edoc.hu-berlin.de/kunsttexte/2011-1/bruetsch-matthias-8/PDF/bruetsch.pdf]; access: 2012/07/13.

Buckland, Warren (ed.) (2009). *Puzzle Films: Complex Storytelling in Contemporary Cinema*. Malden: Wiley-Blackwell.

Chatman, Seymour (2009): Backwards. In: *Narrative* 17/1, 31–55.

Gallagher, Catherine (2002): Undoing. In: Newman, Karen/Clayton, Jay/Hirsch, Marianne (eds.): *Time and the Literary*. New York: Routledge, 11–30.

Genette, Gérard (1972): *Figures III*. Paris: Editions du Seuil.

Hansen, Per Krogh (2011): Backmasked Messages: On the Fabula Construction in Episodically Reversed Narratives. In: Alber/Heinze 2011, 162–185.

Krützen, Michaela (2010): *Dramaturgien des Films: Das etwas andere Hollywood*. Frankfurt a. M.: Fischer.

Matthias, Lee A. (2012): *Lateral Screenwriting: Using the Power of Lateral Thinking to Write Great Movies*. Scotts Valley: CreateSpace.

Mittell, Jason (2006): Narrative Complexity in Contemporary American Television. In: *The Velvet Light Trap*, No. 58, 29–40.

Parker, Jo Alyson (2004): Remembering the Future: Memento, the Reverse of Time's Arrow, and the Defects of Memory. In: *KronoScope* 4/2, 239–257.

Richardson, Brian (2002): Beyond Story and Discourse: Narrative Time in Postmodern and Nonmimetic Fiction. In: Richardson, Brian (ed.) *Narrative Dynamics: Essays on Time, Plot, Closure, and Frames*. Columbus: Ohio State University Press, 47–63.

Richardson, Brian (2006): *Unnatural Voices: Extreme Narration in Modern and Contemporary Fiction*. Columbus: Ohio State University.

Ryan, Marie-Laure (2009): Temporal Paradoxes in Narrative. In: *Style* 43/2, 142–164.

Smith, Murray (1995). *Engaging Characters: Fiction, Emotion, and the Cinema*. Oxford: Clarendon Press.

Spiegel, Simon (2007): *Die Konstitution des Wunderbaren: Zu einer Poetik des Science-Fiction-Films*. Marburg: Schüren.

Stiglegger, Marcus (2005): Es könnte noch schlimmer kommen... Momente der Täuschung und chronologischen Inversion in den Filmen von Gaspar Noé. In: Liptay, Fabienne/Wolf, Yvonne (eds.): *Was stimmt denn jetzt? Unzuverlässiges Erzählen in Literatur und Film*. München: Edition Text und Kritik, 324–335.

Films

Feature Films

5x2 (France 2004, François Ozon)
Back to the Future (USA 1985, Robert Zemeckis)
Bakha Satang (Peppermint Candy, South Korea/Japan 2000, Lee Chang-dong)
Betrayal (UK 1983, David Hugh Jones)
Eternal Sunshine of the Spotless Mind (USA 2004, Michel Gondry)
Irréversible (France 2002, Gaspar Noé)
Memento (USA 2000, Christopher Nolan)
Stastny Konec (Happy End, Czechoslowakia 1967, Oldrich Lipsky)
The Curious Case of Benjamin Button (USA 2008, David Fincher)
The Rules of Attraction (USA/Germany 2002, Roger Avery)
The Terminator (USA 1984, James Cameron)
Two Friends (Australia 1986, Jane Campion)

Short Films

.nijnoK (.tibbaR, Netherlands 2004, Leo Wentink)
Avenue de l'Opéra (France 1900, Alice Guy)
Démolition d'un mur (Demolition of a Wall, France 1896, Louis Lumière)
EVOL (UK 2006, Chris Vincze)
Killing the Chickens to Scare the Monkeys (Sweden 2011, Jens Assur)
Nie solo seiN (Germany 2003, Jan Schomburg)
Plongeur fantastique (The Fantastic Diver, France 1905, Segundo de Chomón)
Rewind (India 2007, Atul Taishete)
Rückwärts (Germany 1980, René Perraudin)

Television Series

ER (USA 1994–2009, NBC; S9/E10: Hindsight, 2002)
Home Movies (USA 1999–2004, UPN/Cartoon Network; S3/E07: *My Cheatin' Heart*, 2002)

RED DWARF (UK 1988–1999, BBC; S3/E01: *BACKWARDS*, 1989)
SEINFELD (USA 1989–1998, NBC; S9/E08: *BETRAYAL*, 1997)
SLIDERS (USA 1995–2000, FOX/Sci Fi Channel; S2/E13: *AS TIME GOES BY*, 1996)
STAR TREK: VOYAGER (USA 1995–2001, UPN; S3/E21: *BEFORE AND AFTER*, 1997)
THE X FILES (USA/Canada 1993–2002, FOX; S8/E06: *REDRUM*, 2000)

IMAGE SOURCES

Figure 1: Table by Matthias Brütsch.

APPENDIX

About the Authors

Alina Bothe, Historian, M.A., born 1983 in Braunschweig. She studied History, Political Sciences, and Eastern and Southeastern European History at the Freie Universität Berlin. She has published articles on different aspects of digital history, cultural and literary history and translated the yiddish novel *Grenadierstraße* from Fischl Schneersohn into German. She is a PhD-candidate at the Freie Universität Berlin, where she writes her epistemological thesis on *The virtual in-between of memory: The Visual History Archive*.

Matthias Brütsch is senior lecturer (Oberassistent) in Film Studies at the University of Zurich. He is the author of *Traumbühne Kino: Der Traum als filmtheoretische Metapher und narratives Motiv (Screening the Dream: Cinematic Metaphors, Oneiric Narration and the Function of Dreams in Film*; Marburg: Schüren, 2011, PhD-thesis) and a number of articles on film narratology and aesthetics. He is currently preparing a book on concepts of focalisation in film and literary theory. He has co-directed the International Short Film Festival Winterthur from 1999–2003, worked as a script analyst for the Zurich Film Foundation from 2003–2007 and has been a member of both the board of trustees of the Swiss Arts Council and the promotion agency Swiss Films from 2007–2011.

Julia Eckel, M.A., studied Social Psychology and Anthropology (B.A.) and Media Studies (B.A./M.A.) at the Ruhr-University Bochum and at the University of Zurich. Since 2008, she is a PhD-student at the Media Studies Department of the Ruhr-University Bochum, where she worked as an Assistant Lecturer and Research Associate from 2008 to 2009, too. Since October 2009, she is holding a PhD-scholarship from the Faculty of Philology of the Ruhr-University Bochum. Her PhD-thesis focuses on anthropomorphic forms and motifs in audiovisual media and their relevance in the development of media theory. Other research interests are the temporality of film and narrative complexity in audiovisual media. Recent publication: *Zeitenwende(n) des Films – Temporale Nonlinearität im zeitgenössischen Erzählkino*. Marburg: Schüren 2012.

Benjamin Eugster is an M.A.-student of Popular Culture, Film Studies and Czech Literature at the University of Zürich. At the moment he is writing his M.A.-thesis on *YouTubePoop*, seeking to enquire the relation between a visual participatory culture and its stylistic diversification.

Katja Hettich, M.A., is a research assistant at the Department of Romance Languages and Literatures at the Ruhr-Universität Bochum where she is currently writing her PhD-thesis on the tension between narrative positivism and strategies of emotional reader engagement in the 19th century French novel. Since 2011, she is also a member of the editorial staff of the international film studies journal *Cinéma & Cie*. She studied Film and Television Studies, Journalism and Communication Studies, and Romance Philology at the Ruhr-Universität Bochum and the Université de Haute-Bretagne Rennes II. Her research interests include topics in both film and literary studies as well as interdisciplinary perspectives on genre theory, narratology, and the intersection of aesthetics, cognition, and emotion. Besides several articles, she has published a book in which she coined the term 'melancholy comedy' for a recent trend in Hollywood cinema, including films by directors such as Wes Anderson, Spike Jonze and Sofia Coppola (*Die Melancholische Komödie*. Marburg: Schüren 2008).

Miklós Kiss is Assistant Professor of Film Studies at the Department of Arts, Culture, and Media at the University of Groningen (The Netherlands). He has been an assistant and researcher at the University of Pécs (Hungary), and the University of Jyväskylä (Finland), where he received his PhD. His research interests include intersecting narrative and cognitive film theories, within which he analyses the relation between (folk) psychology and narrative compositions, and examines viewer navigation as embodied experience both in concrete filmdiegetic and abstract narrative spaces. He is the author of *Between Narrative and Cognitive Approaches. Film Theory of Non-linearity Applied to Hungarian Movies* (2008), and co-editor of *Narratívák 7* (2008).

Bernd Leiendecker, M.A., studied Media Studies and Romance Languages and Literatures at the Ruhr-University Bochum, the Karl-Franzens-University Graz, and the Université de Marne-la-Vallée. Since 2008, he is a PhD-student at the Media Studies Department of the Ruhr-University Bochum, where he has also taught undergraduate courses in 2011 and 2012. His PhD-thesis focuses on the history of unreliable narration in film. He has published several articles on unreliable narration and related phenomena.

Jason Mittell is Associate Professor of American Studies and Film & Media Culture at Middlebury College. He is the author of *Genre and Television: From Cop Shows to Cartoons in American Culture* (Routledge, 2004), *Television and American Culture* (Oxford University Press, 2009), *Complex Television: The Poetics of Contemporary Television Narrative* (New York University Press, forthcoming), and the blog Just TV, and the co-editor with Ethan Thompson of *How to Watch TV* (New York University Press, forthcoming). His essay was written while in residence as a Research Fellow at the Lichtenberg-Kolleg at Georg-August-Universität Göttingen.

Rolf F. Nohr is Professor for Media Aestethics/Media Culture in the Department of Media Studies at the University of Arts, Braunschweig, where he researches game culture, media theory, discourse analysis, and heavy metal. He is the editor of "Medien'Welten. Braunschweiger Schriften zur Medienkultur". For further Information and recent publications see: www.nuetzliche-bilder.de.

Daniela Olek, M.A., studied Comparative Literature (B.A.) and Media Studies (B.A./M.A.) at the Ruhr-University Bochum. She is a PhD-student and fellow of the Ruhr-University Research School. Her dissertation project deals with modified concepts of fictional characters in transmedia narrations based on contemporary television series. Besides the presentation of papers at several international conferences, she is working as a Support Specialist in an IT-company. Another main research interest is the spatiality of contemporary narrations in media. Recent Publication: *Lost und die Zukunft des Fernsehens. Die Veränderung des seriellen Erzählens im Zeitalter von Media Convergence*. Stuttgart: Ibidem 2011.

Julius Othmer, M.A., is scholar at the DFG graduate school "Automatismen" at the Paderborn University. He is working on his PhD-thesis on computer based profiles (German working title: *Spielen mit der Risikomaschine – Computerspiel als kulturelle Technik zum Umgang mit Risiko*). Since 2009, he holds seminars at the department of media studies at the Braunschweig University of Arts and until 2009 he was member of the research staff at the TU Braunschweig in two research projects on educational games. From 2003 to 2008 he studied media studies, communications engineering and sociology at the Braunschweig University of Arts and the TU Braunschweig. He is doing research in the field of computer based media, game studies, game design, social media and media literacy. Recent publication: WTF is my GearScore? Risiko und Sicherheit als datenbankgenerierte Elemente im Computerspiel. In: Böhme, Stefan/Nohr, Rolf F./Wiemer, Serjoscha (eds.) (2012): *Sortieren, Sammeln, Suchen, Spielen. Die Datenbank als mediale Praxis*, Münster: LIT-Verlag, (Medien'Welten Vol. 18), 183–208. Together with Andreas Weich and Stefanie Pulst.

Christine Piepiorka, Dipl. Media Economist/M.A., studied Media Management at the Business and Information Technology School Iserlohn and the University of Sydney (Australia) from 2001 to 2005. From 2005 to 2006 she worked for several film- and TV-productions. In 2009 she gained an M.A. in Media Studies at the Ruhr-University Bochum. Currently she is a PhD-student and a fellow of the Ruhr-University Research School. During her research she has participated in and presented papers at several international conferences. Furthermore she is a

Teaching Assistant for Television Studies. Her PhD-project focuses on complex narrations in television series as a symptom of a paradigm shift which includes a new kind of conception of TV formats in a transmedial environment and a new (self-)conception of the viewer. Another main research interest is the spatiality of contemporary narrations in media. Recent publication: *Lost in Narration – Narrativ komplexe Serienformate in einem transmedialen Umfeld*. Stuttgart: Ibidem 2011.

Kathrin Rothemund teaches and researches in media studies with an emphasis on film and television studies at the University of Bayreuth. Her research especially focuses on aesthetics of television series, German crime fiction and contemporary cinema. In her dissertation *Narrative complexity in contemporary US-American television series* she developed an analytic tool to interpret narrative complexity with a focus on diversity, interconnectedness, nonlinearity, openness and contingency with examples from the television series DEXTER (USA 2006-, Showtime), HEROES (2006–2010, NBC) and LOST (2004–2010, ABC). Her current research project centres on film focus and acuity. Some of her most recent publications are *Komplexe Welten. Narrative Strategien in US-amerikanischen Fernsehserien* (Berlin: Bertz + Fischer, 2012) and Facing complex crime – investigating contemporary German crime fiction on television. In: Gunhild Agger, Anne Marit Waade (eds.): *Northern Lights. Film and Media Studies Yearbook 2011* (Vol. 9), 127–142.

Martin Schlesinger is a scientific coworker and doctoral student at the Institute for Media Studies at the Ruhr-University Bochum since 2009. Research interests: aesthetics and theory of film and audiovisual media, Brazilian film. Most important publication: *Brasilien der Bilder (= Serie moderner Film*, Bd. 7), VDG Verlag, Weimar 2008. He is also director of music videos and documentaries. Most important film: ODYSSEE UND NAHVERKEHR/ODYSSEY AND SHORT-DISTANCE TRAVEL (together with Marius Böttcher, 2012)

Nele Uhl, M.A. studied at the Leuphana University Lüneburg from 2004 to 2012, where she earned a degree in Cultural Studies. She now works as a freelance journalist for the *Hamburger Abendblatt* and as an Academic Assistant at the Leuphana Graduate School. Nele Uhl has been working as a projectionist since 2001.

Nanna Verhoeff is Associate Professor of Comparative Media Studies at the Department for Media and Culture Studies, Utrecht University. Her books include *The West in Early Cinema: After the Beginning* (2006) and *Mobile Screens: The Visual Regime of Navigation* (2012). She has published articles on a wide range of topics, such as early cinema, painting and panorama's, moving-image installations, touch-screen technology, mobile screens, smartphones, game consoles, and urban screens. She is currently researcher in the project *Charting the Digital: Digital Mapping Practices as New Media Cultures*, funded by the European Research Council (ERC).

Andreas Weich, M.A. is scholar at the DFG graduate school "Automatismen" at the Paderborn University. He is working on the doctoral thesis on computer based profiles (German working title: *Selbstverdatungsmaschinen. Computerbasierte Profile als Wissenskomplex zur Subjektivierung und Automatisierung in der aktuellen Medienkultur*). Since 2010 he holds seminars at the department of media studies at the Braunschweig University of Arts and until September 2011 he was member of the research staff at the TU Braunschweig in a research project on educational games. From 2004 to 2010 he studied media studies, communications engineering and political science at the Braunschweig University of Arts and the TU Braunschweig. He is doing research in the field of computer based media, social media, discourse theory, game studies and media literacy. Recent publication: 'Plus Your World'. Profiling the Self between Analytics and Technologies of the Self. In: Noon, Derek/Giardina, Marco (eds.) (2013/forthcoming): 7th *Annual CGC Conference Proce.*